A COMPANION TO
ROMAN BRITAIN

A COMPANION TO
ROMAN BRITAIN

EDITED BY
PETER A. CLAYTON

Contributors

MICHAEL G. JARRETT
THOMAS F. C. BLAGG
JOAN P. ALCOCK
JOHN CASEY
RICHARD REECE

OMEGA BOOKS

First published 1980 by Phaidon Press

This edition published 1985 by Omega Books Ltd,
1 West Street, Ware, Hertfordshire, under license
from the proprietor.

ISBN 1-85007-086-5
(Formerly ISBN 0-7148-2031-8)

Printed in Yugoslavia

CONTENTS

PREFACE

When Britain became a province of the Roman Empire by conquest in AD 43 it was a fairly late acquisition with only a few more areas to be added before the Empire reached its greatest extent under Trajan in AD 117. Britain was also, in relation to the rest of the Empire, only a small part, yet for all that the books on Roman Britain are, literally, legion. Allowing for a certain element of prejudice in favour of this far-flung outpost on the part of British archaeologists, which is natural enough, it is still intriguing that there is so much interest, and has been since the eighteenth century. Before that time such monuments as remained above ground, or were accidentally found below ground, were viewed, depending on the period, with something ranging from superstitious fear to a polite interest in the antique. Many Romano-British sites served as convenient quarries for building materials, as so often can be seen from the red tile evidence in the walls and towers of numerous churches up and down the country. Bede tells us how cartloads of suitable building material were removed from the Roman site of Verulamium for use in the new cathedral that crowned the hill nearby to commemorate Britain's first martyr, Saint Alban. Roman Britain had little interest for its immediate successors who were more country than town orientated, and the ruins were generally shunned except when they could be a convenient source for some useful and free material.

In succeeding centuries, starting with John Leland, the self-styled King's Antiquary to Henry VIII, a few enlightened people took an interest in the past. In the eighteenth and nineteenth centuries, apart from a 'polite' interest in finds and 'curiosities' as exemplified by the drawings made of the Roman baths at Bath in 1755, the interest was largely from the standpoint of a classical education with a consequent emphasis on literary sources such as Tacitus. With the introduction of archaeological excavation techniques in the late nineteenth century at Cranborne Chase by General Pitt-Rivers, the 'father' of British archaeology, a different view began to emerge. The expansion and perfection of excavation techniques to obtain as much information and evidence as possible were carried into the twentieth century by the renowned archaeologist, Sir Mortimer Wheeler. His excavations in the 1920s and 1930s of important Roman sites like Caerleon, Lydney and Verulamium, and prehistoric sites such as Maiden Castle with its small late Romano-Celtic temple, opened new vistas of archaeological interpretation from the record 'written' in the soil. From such excavations, and the mass of information that lay dormant in collections merely awaiting recognition and interpretation, a framework was built up for Roman Britain. The literary sources tell us why the Romans came in AD 43, nearly a century after Julius Caesar's tentative forays in 55 and 54 BC. There were economic as well as political reasons for eventually taking the somewhat momentous step of crossing the tidal Channel, so unlike the *mare nostrum* of the Mediterranean. With the occasional short interludes of usurper British emperors (Clodius Albinus, Carausius, Allectus, Magnus Maximus, and Constantine III), Britain was to remain an outpost of the Roman Empire in the mists to the northwest until the early fifth century. All the material was therefore available for a historical framework to be built up and also a structure of statements based on the finds and their interpretation.

There are many different ways in which Roman Britain can be viewed: it can be seen in a military light, essentially as a nuisance that needed three legions stationed here (as against the single legion required for the whole of the North African coastline); it can be seen from an economic point of view as contributing to the wealth of the Empire, especially in terms of goods that leave no archaeological traces such as the slaves, furs and hunting dogs mentioned by Strabo; it can be viewed from a purely historical aspect, or simply as an area that presents numerous material remains of sites to be seen on the ground. Each approach, although perfectly valid and not necessarily excluding the others, inevitably has a certain point of focus.

The approach of this particular book is indicated by its title; it is not a guide in any way to lead the reader around the countryside of Roman Britain (although the aim of the Gazetteer is to act as a pointer for the reader who wishes for such guidance). It is essentially as the title states, a 'Companion' – 'one who accompanies another; associate *in*, sharer *of*', as the *Concise Oxford Dictionary* defines it. The contributors were selected with this end in mind; they have all been especially concerned with particular aspects of Roman Britain and have made contributions to our knowledge of it not only by virtue of their practical work in the field but also by their evaluation, synthesis and understanding of the problems. Archaeological interpretation nowadays relies more and more on scientific aids and reports, but there is a danger that the true subject – in this instance the people of Roman Britain – can be swamped and lost because of being dragooned into statistical or scientific compartments; the baby can so easily be thrown out with the bath water! Here the authors have taken their evidence, archaeological, literary, statistical, economic, and interpreted it in their own way in the light of their personal involvement and commitment to Roman Britain. Some of their views do not follow the 'party line' on certain aspects, but they are not at variance just for the sake of it, they are the result of personal conviction after long study of the evidence and a logical assessment of its implications. This is what brings the aspect of a 'companion' to the fore, here is the flesh and blood of Roman Britain. We can glean very personal details or inferences from even an abbreviated inscription on a tombstone; or ponder the circumstances of a find and its context, such as the recently discovered Water Newton silver. This has several interesting aspects: its importance as the earliest known Christian plate in the Roman Empire; its dedicatory inscriptions; and, not least, its richness in relation to its find spot in a very minor Romano-British town.

This book does not set out to answer every question possible on Roman Britain, no book can do that. It is intended to fulfill the function of its title, to be a 'companion' for the reader into the world of Roman Britain; to breathe life into some of the most interesting archaeological remains in the country. The vast and ever growing numbers of visitors each year to the sites of Roman Britain is proof enough of both popular and scholarly interest in the subject.

CHAPTER I
INTRODUCTION: SETTING THE SCENE

Pre-Roman Britain

Geography and Climate

In recent years the techniques of environmental archaeology have done much to increase our knowledge of the background against which our ancestors lived. We are learning more and more about their diet, the crops they cultivated, the animals they owned and the animals they hunted. Analysis of pollen and of snails is also producing evidence of less local significance; we are beginning to obtain a picture of changes in climate and of the natural forest cover which must have been an ever-present reality to a large percentage of the population. The evidence for Iron Age and Roman Britain is not as full as we could wish, and interpretations may well change as knowledge grows; but there are few areas of archaeology in which definitive statements can be made.

At the beginning of the Christian era the British climate was broadly similar to that of the twentieth century. From the third century onwards there may have been a deterioration to wetter conditions. Corn-drying kilns – if indeed they are for drying grain which had been harvested unripe – become common only in the later Roman period. Pollen samples from British and continental peat-bogs suggest the renewed formation of peat from *c*. 400, another indication of a damper climate. These are merely hints, and it must be confessed that more evidence would be most welcome.

Similarly, we can produce general pictures of land usage in late pre-Roman and Roman Britain, but may not be confident that the detail will bear inspection. Whatever general statements may be made there will certainly be many exceptions. The division of Britain into a southeastern Lowland Zone devoted to arable farming, and a northwestern, pastoral, Highland Zone is frequently put forward. As a geographic concept the division may be helpful, as long as we recognize that within the Highland Zone are many lowland areas. The separation between arable and pastoral areas is

less secure. It seems to be based partly on a theoretical model of land use and partly on the manifestly inadequate and second-hand report of Caesar, who tells us that 'most of the tribes of the interior do not grow corn but live on milk and meat, and wear skins'. At most the difference between the two zones is one of emphasis, and even that is difficult to detect in the archaeological record. Farms throughout Britain almost invariably produce the bones of domestic animals (though the balance between species may vary) and also querns for grinding corn. It is extremely improbable that at any period northern and western sites depended on the import of grain from the southeast, and the 'four-posters' which are usually interpreted as granaries are now being found on highland as well as lowland sites. Common sense suggests that we should envisage most Iron Age and Roman farms as engaged in mixed farming close to subsistence level. Doubtless the balance between arable and pastoral farming will have varied according to the suitability of land and climate. We may be tolerably sure that the surplus corn which Britain was exporting in the reign of Augustus was grown in the southeast, which not only offered the most suitable soils and weather for grain crops but also lay much nearer to the continental market. Unfortunately the scale of the export is not known. It need not have been great.

By present-day standards the crops grown were restricted in number. In particular, root crops played no large part in the economy, and the main field crops were various grains. Peas and beans were certainly cultivated in Roman Britain, and they may have been dried for winter consumption. If they were cultivated on a large scale they may have had a significant role in crop rotation, for their roots fix the nitrogen which is required by other crops. More usually fertility would have been restored by grazing animals on the stubble from grain crops, by leaving land fallow, and by dunging.

While agriculture certainly employed the vast majority of the population it would be wrong to suppose that the whole of Britain was under cultivation. Much land was exploited in the south, where chalk and river gravels give light and well-drained soils; the smaller Celtic 159 fields still survive in upland areas not subject to ploughing. On the clay soils of the Midlands and the higher land further north the picture is different: much of the area was still covered with natural forest in which hardwoods like oak and beech predominated. There was apparently no economic pressure sufficient to cause major clearances of this forest. The pressure would have been severe before Iron Age man attempted to cultivate these heavy clays with his relatively unsophisticated plough. Here settlement seems to be concentrated in the river valleys, though aerial photography is now producing evidence for field boundaries beyond them.

Forest probably covered most of the land with heavy clay soils, but its extent must have been considerable in all areas. It would provide pannage for domestic pigs, and would also be the principal source of fuel. Coal, known as early as the Bronze Age, was little worked before the second century AD. Even then it does not seem to have been economic to transport it to any great distance from the drifts where it was worked; clearly timber was readily available near most settlements. It remained an important building material throughout the Roman period.

People and Politics

The population of Britain at the time of the Roman invasions is usually termed Celtic. The word conceals much and reveals little. It is generally presumed that the whole population of Britain spoke Celtic languages ancestral to Welsh and Gaelic, and that pre-Celtic languages had died out. Celtic certainly was spoken, but in the absence of written evidence we cannot say that it was universal. We do not know when Celtic-speaking people arrived in Britain. Still less do we know their numbers or their relationship with earlier inhabitants of the island. Probably they had reached Britain by the early part of the first millennium BC. By the time of Claudius – and perhaps long before – they had dominated and absorbed the earlier inhabitants not only of Britain but also of Ireland. Probably we should envisage something like the Norman Conquest: relatively small numbers of people coming from the Continent to take control of the more accessible and attractive parts of Britain, retaining the native population in all but the most exalted roles and soon merging with them as a result of intermarriage.

This certainly seems the best interpretation of the Belgic immigration or invasion which began late in the second century BC and continued until after the Caesarian invasions.

Caesar tells us that 'Belgic immigrants occupy the coast. They came as raiders and warriors and later settled down to cultivate the land.' Like the Normans the new Belgic ruling classes seem to have retained contact with their continental homeland. Caesar tells of British assistance to the Gauls in the early 50s BC.

The career of Commius is particularly revealing. Caesar made him king of the Gaulish Atrebates in 57 BC, and in 55 sent him to Britain, where he was well-known and trusted, to persuade the British tribes to submit to Rome. His mission was unsuccessful, for he was arrested at once and only released after Caesar had successfully landed. He returned with Caesar in 54 and was prominent in the final negotiations between Caesar and Cassivellaunus. In 53 he was assisting the Romans as commander of a cavalry force in Gaul, but in the following year he joined the rebellion of Vercingetorix and was given command of the force entrusted with the relief of Alesia. He subsequently became a guerrilla leader in northern Gaul and survived Roman attempts at assassination. It was probably in 50 that he fled to Britain. It is generally assumed that he is the Commius who is known as king of the British Atrebates, but this cannot be proved. Atrebatic territory lay between the Sussex coast, the Thames and mid-Hampshire. This tribe may have been led by men who had arrived from Gaul a generation or two earlier, but the tribal name is not recorded before Commius became ruler, and the British Atrebates may represent a new unit created and named by Commius and his followers. Commius was well-known in Britain before 55, but not necessarily in the area he eventually ruled. He certainly did not aim for this area when sent as Caesar's envoy, nor is the area remarkable for the early appearance of the archaeological detritus of Belgic culture. For that we look rather to Kent and to the areas close to the Thames.

Archaeologically the Belgae are usually identified by the introduction of wheel-thrown pottery and of coins, and by a change from inhumation to cremation as the normal burial rite. (This last is not a very helpful indicator, for it can only be proved relevant for the aristocracy; we know virtually nothing of the burial practices of the man-in-the-field before or after the Belgic incursions, apart from a cemetery at St Albans which may or may not be typical.) These innovations are most common where we should expect them, in the southeast: even by the Claudian invasion they had not spread beyond the Humber or the Severn, and had not reached Devon or Cornwall, whose continental contacts had been closer with the non-Belgic tribes of Brittany. Many archaeologists believe that these changes imply substantial Belgic immigration into the areas north and south of the Thames; they suggest that the spread of Belgic innovations to other areas such as Lincolnshire or Gloucestershire and Somerset indicates the intrusion of a Belgic ruler or aristocracy.

An alternative interpretation should at least be considered. The Belgic immigrants certainly brought new ideas and techniques, but their arrival does not seem to have caused a complete revolution. The normal house type in Britain remained circular, whatever the local variations, in a tradition which can be traced back for several centuries. Moreover the Belgic groups in the southeast adopted the idea of chariot warfare which had long been abandoned on the Continent. The totality of the evidence may well lead us to believe that the Belgic invasions brought only a small number of warriors who managed to conquer and supplant the earlier Celtic rulers in the southeast. So much is implied by Caesar's account. North of Yarmouth and west of Southampton Water there is no need to suppose that Belgic-type artefacts or habits mean dominance by Belgic rulers. The evidence may just as easily – and more plausibly – be interpreted as an indication of the spread of Belgic ideas by trade and by political alliance.

This picture conforms more closely to the models we have made of Celtic society, based on the information supplied by classical authors and by Irish and Welsh legends which may relate to this period, though they were not committed to writing until several centuries later. This model is of a 'heroic' society, dominated by a small warrior caste devoted to personal valour and ostentatious display.

While the model owes its origins to literary sources, it seems to be supported by some archaeological evidence. Massive hill-forts may be seen as the 'castles' of a warrior aristocracy, engaged in fighting one another when not united against a more distant enemy. Hill-forts are not specifically a feature of the Iron Age; some at least have earlier origins. However, many were still in use at the time of the Roman Conquest, especially in Wessex and the Welsh Marches. What is characteristic of the Iron Age is the elaboration of their defences, with multiple ramparts and complex entrances; similar features recur in the stone castles of the thirteenth and fourteenth centuries AD.

Also associated with the warrior class, though not restricted to the Belgae, are the remarkable late La Tène metal (usually bronze) objects which for many people represent the whole of Celtic art. They are objects of great beauty, often decorated with enamel or with elaborate engraving. They imply a high standard of craftsmanship, and we may legitimately infer that they were used by a class with surplus wealth who could employ it to purchase display objects which (in terms of man-hours at

least) were extremely costly. There can be little doubt that we are right in deducing that the patrons were a wealthy and powerful aristocracy. Many of the objects are offensive or defensive weapons, personal ornaments like the gold or electrum torcs which seem particularly common in East Anglia, tankards and buckets which must surely have been used in great feasts, or pieces of decorated horse-harness. The only objects which look as though they might be intended for use by women are the bronze mirrors with intricate decoration on the reverse, like those from Birdlip and Desborough. Given the emphasis on male display implied by the other objects, one may wonder whether the mirrors also should not be assigned to the menfolk, though that from Birdlip was found in a woman's grave.

1 Aerial view of the Iron Age hill-fort at Hod Hill, Dorset. A Roman fort of the period of the Conquest lies in the northwest corner making use of the earlier fort's complex defences to form its own outer defence.

2 Maiden Castle in Dorset is the most famous hill-fort in Britain. Its multiple ditches and elaborate entrances are similar in design and purpose to the protected entrances of some medieval castles.

3 An electrum torc and bracelet from Snettisham, Norfolk. Torcs have been found far more frequently in East Anglia than in any other part of Britain. British Museum.

A heroic society implies a considerable number of people below warrior-status. We know very little about them in the British Iron Age. Many isolated farms have been recognized, but in some cases at least their owners may have been in the warrior class. Slavery was certainly known, but we have no evidence of its extent; slaves may have been more important as an export to the Roman world than as a part of British society.

Caesar's motives for invading Britain in 55 and 54 were complex. His alleged reason was that the Britons had been assisting his Gaulish enemies. More important was the effect which successful campaigns in the island would have at Rome: all Caesar's actions must be seen as part of the struggle for power there. The first campaign was evidently no more than a reconnaissance in force. Its chief effect was psychological: it proved that Rome could take an army across the ocean, which for many still represented the edge of the world. It also suggested that nothing could hold Caesar. The achievement was celebrated with an unprecedented twenty days of public holiday. The practical results were negligible; even Caesar's declared objective, to find suitable harbours, was not achieved. In 54, as in 55, his fleet was badly damaged by wind and tide. In both years he showed as little awareness of naval problems as a later conqueror-politician, Napoleon Buonaparte.

In 54 Caesar apparently intended to conquer at least a part of Britain. His army consisted of five legions and 2,000 cavalry, a force roughly comparable in numbers with that used by Claudius a century later, though the composition was not the same. In the event he was not wholly successful. His campaign started too late in the year, his scouting and reconnaissance were inadequate and reports from Gaul were sufficiently disturbing to prevent him from wintering in Britain or leaving any troops there. Although he was able to report the submission of several tribes, the installation of a Roman client as ruler of the Trinovantes, the capture of the main fortress of Cassivellaunus and a treaty by which Cassivellaunus agreed to give hostages and pay tribute, the campaign of 54 received no public notice at Rome. The terms used by Caesar in describing the treaty imply that it was the first step in the creation of a new province, but the situation in Gaul prevented Caesar from following up this success. A certain amount of evidence from Roman sources suggests that as late as *c.* 27 BC Britain was still regarded as a province of which possession might easily be taken; it is unlikely that similar ideas were prevalent in Britain.

Although Caesar's campaigns were inconclusive they exerted a profound influence on Romano-British relations for the next 100 years. The conquest of Gaul meant that Rome and Britain were separated only by the English Channel. Trading with the Continent now meant trading with a Roman province. The treaty of 54 gave Rome clients in Britain, and

4 Bronze and enamel shield found in the river Thames at Battersea. The elaborate curvilinear lines are typical of late pre-Roman metalwork. British Museum.

5 Bronze skillet from Canterbury with a naturalistically modelled dog's head at the end of the handle. It was probably imported from Italy or Gaul in the first or second century. Royal Museum, Canterbury.

therefore excuses for intervention whenever she wished. Those clients – or at least their aristocracies – developed an increasing taste for Roman luxuries, as is shown by the Italian wine amphorae, the silver and bronze vessels 5, 195 and the Arretine pottery which appear on pre-Claudian sites, and especially at Colchester, the Trinovantian capital. Moreover, the proximity of the Roman world meant that Roman aid was likely to be sought by one party or the other in British disputes. There is no evidence that military assistance was ever given, but we cannot be sure that its threat was not an important factor in British politics.

During the period between the invasions of Caesar and that of Claudius we begin to form a

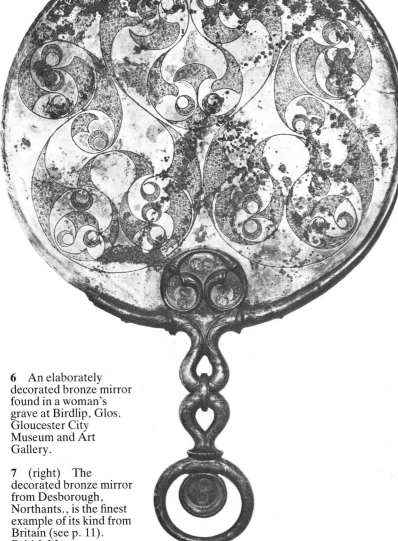

6 An elaborately decorated bronze mirror found in a woman's grave at Birdlip, Glos. Gloucester City Museum and Art Gallery.

7 (right) The decorated bronze mirror from Desborough, Northants., is the finest example of its kind from Britain (see p. 11). British Museum.

clearer picture of tribal groupings in Britain. The gradual spread of coinage, and the distribution of different types, can be used to indicate the approximate area belonging to one tribe; and the names of tribal leaders appear on coins and occasionally in Roman sources. After the Conquest the Romans used the tribes as the basic units of local government, and with due caution evidence for this may be used to throw light on the situation before the Claudian invasion.

Even though the documentary material is inadequate in both quantity and quality, its existence revolutionizes our approach to the past. Archaeology alone is at its best when answering technological questions: we may analyse a metal sword or brooch and determine its composition and its method of manufacture with confidence. Economic questions cannot be answered so satisfactorily. We may establish from finds of bones, shells and carbonized grain that a community ate beef, mutton, pork, shellfish and bread or porridge; we have no means of knowing the balance of these items in the diet, and we shall rarely have evidence of other items like fish, cheese or green vegetables. As we move further into questions which involve ideas rather than material facts archaeology becomes of less value and the answers based on it more speculative. Social

organization, religion and politics are aspects of man's past on which archaeology can at best throw only a faint and flickering light. We have already seen that two very different interpretations have been put on the appearance of coins and wheel-thrown pottery in Lincolnshire and Gloucestershire. Food, drink, weapons and ornaments buried with the dead are usually taken to imply a belief in life after death. If we accept that interpretation, we have no idea whether it means a reincarnation on earth or a different life in a remote paradise. Where they do not certainly include food and drink, grave goods may have nothing to do with an afterlife, but simply show that some possessions were so personal to the deceased that they could not be used by his surviving kin. Archaeology can offer no answer to the question posed.

Documentary evidence at once increases the number of questions which can validly be asked, though it rarely produces incontrovertible answers. We can now begin to think of individual rulers and their motives, and to see relatively precise and coherent political groups interacting one with another. We can also create a reasonably acceptable model of society, which will depend to a great extent on written evidence.

An eminent prehistorian spoke of the archaeology of historic periods as 'text-aided';

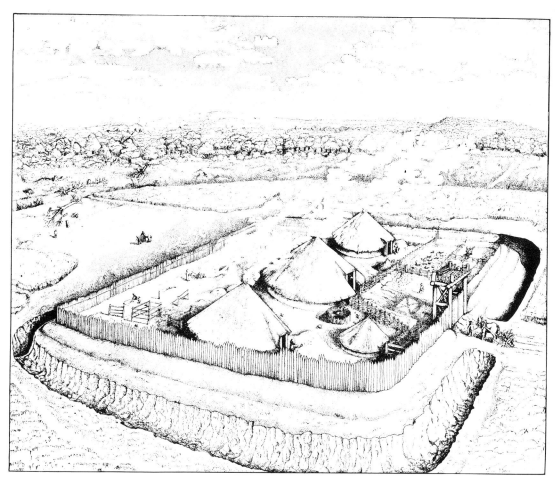

8 An Iron Age farmstead at Whitton, South Glamorgan. First occupied *c.* AD 25, this stage seen in the reconstruction of the site shows its development *c.* 40. The circular houses are typical Iron Age dwellings. (Reconstruction by Howard Mason.)

15

9 An Iron Age slave-chain from the great hoard of Celtic metalwork found at Llyn Cerrig Bach, Anglesey, in 1943. National Museum of Wales, Cardiff.

those who work in these periods would probably describe them as 'text-confused' or 'text-hindered'. For the Roman period in particular there is very little relationship between the documentary and the archaeological evidence. The documents are mainly concerned with military and political history, subjects on which archaeology can say little, and that with an infuriating lack of precision. This last statement may puzzle prehistorians, for whom Roman artefacts seem to have a very limited and firm dating which they would welcome. In the Bronze Age it is unusual to be able to date a specific object to a period of less than 150 years; some types of Roman pot may be firmly dated to a span of twenty or thirty years, and in the first two centuries AD the precise year in which a coin was minted can often be established. But coins are rarely lost when they are new, and a fort in Wales dated by a few pots of the period 50–70 and a coin of Claudius cannot be related with confidence to any one of the campaigns known to have taken place in those years. If there were a reasonable number of datable artefacts from many forts it might be possible to produce a tentative model showing relative dates of occupation and abandonment; but this is a dream which is unlikely to become reality in any predictable future. It becomes a nightmare when it is realized that a fort may have several periods of occupation and abandonment between AD 50 and 80. Archaeological evidence has often been used as the raw material for military and political history during the period of conquest, but rarely is it precise enough to justify its use.

There is in fact a good case to be made for treating the history and archaeology of Roman Britain separately, since there is little overlap between them. This is especially true of the period before 120, when the literary sources (down to 85) are reasonably full but inscriptions are few and unhelpful. Classical authors give us remarkably little information which can be related to specific sites. From them we learn of the establishment of a *colonia* at Colchester in 49, apparently on the site of a legionary fortress – which has since been discovered by excavation; of the destruction of Colchester, London and Verulamium by the Boudiccan rebels in 60; and of the building of walls by Hadrian and Antoninus Pius. The identification of those walls depends mainly on inscriptions found in association. It is impossible to make sense of the statements of later writers that Severus also built a wall; such epigraphic evidence as there is might suggest that this was a rebuild of Hadrian's Wall, but the length quoted (32 miles) is less even than that of the Antonine Wall. Beyond this we have nothing except a handful of place-names, like *villa Faustini*, which suggest the character of the site to which they refer. Even when inscriptions become plentiful their interpretation is often uncertain. Building or rebuilding may be described in the same terms, and it is rarely clear that an inscription provides evidence for a whole fort or town rather than a building within it.

In view of the apparently late establishment of Belgic control over Hampshire and Sussex, the territory of the Atrebates, it is surprising that they should be one of the two most important tribes in the period between the Roman invasions. The circumstances in which Commius came to Britain did not have a long-term effect on Atrebatic relations with Rome. Of the two British power blocs it was the Atrebates who consistently sought Roman support and advertised their Roman connection. Their rivals, the Catuvellauni of Hertfordshire and the surrounding area, did not ignore Rome, but clearly pursued a far more independent policy. They are likely to be the tribe of Cassivellaunus, and to have been bound by the treaty of 54 at least while he lived. One condition of that treaty was that tribute should be paid. It is often said that there is no evidence that this tribute was ever paid. The statement is misleading because the surviving Roman documents do not include the government accounts which would record payment; it is equally true, and probably more realistic, to say that we have no evidence that the tribute was not paid. The only evidence we have is a hoard of perhaps 2,000 gold coins from Whaddon Chase, which Stevens has plausibly interpreted as evidence for both intended payment – since it is difficult otherwise to explain the collection of such a vast sum – and actual non-payment, since the money had presumably been stolen and not recovered either by the authorities or the thieves.

Apart from paying tribute Cassivellaunus was also bound by treaty not to attack the Trinovantes, who had been Caesar's allies in

54. The Trinovantes maintained a precarious independence – apart from a brief takeover by the Catuvellauni in *c*. 16 BC, which was probably ended by Roman diplomacy – down to *c*. AD 5–15 when they were finally absorbed by their western neighbours. From this time Camulodunum (Colchester) became the capital of the Catuvellauni.

The conquest of the Trinovantes was but one aspect of Catuvellaunian expansion. The distribution of successive issues of their coins shows them taking over Kent, part of the southeast Midlands, and areas in Berkshire and Hampshire where coins of the house of Commius had formerly circulated. The shrinking area of Atrebatic territory is similarly reflected in the distribution maps of find spots of their coins. On the eve of the Claudian invasion they seem to have retained no more than west Sussex and southeast Hampshire.

Though Rome had problems nearer home which prevented her from exploiting the conquests of Caesar, her interest in Britain remained. Down to about 27 BC she may still have regarded Britain as a province, to be occupied in the fullness of time. After that it is clear that Augustus had no thought of occupying Britain, though he still regarded it as an area in which Rome had legitimate interests. Strabo tells us that the island paid no tribute; he was probably writing soon after the death of Augustus in AD 14. He also describes a considerable and profitable trade with Britain. By *c*. 15 BC it seems that a treaty relationship with Britain had been established. At much this date Tincommius of the Atrebates started to produce coins with Roman types; this is the first sign of Roman concern with the tribe. This, and the ending of Catuvellaunian rule at Camulodunum after only a year or two, probably indicate Augustan intervention. It is generally assumed that Augustus was seeking a British power to counterbalance the Catuvellauni. (This need not mean that the Catuvellauni were regarded as enemies; there are hints that they too may have come to terms with the emperor.) There are clear indications that from this date the Atrebates had close ties with Rome. The new romanized coins indicate the presence of Roman moneyers – a technical mission, in Boon's felicitous phrase. When Tincommius was driven out, his brothers Eppillus and Verica successively bore the Roman title *rex*, presumably by imperial grant.

Patronage of the Atrebates was important, for it seems clear that under Cunobelinus (*c*. AD 5–40) the Catuvellauni were pursuing an expansionist policy with considerable success. The *Res Gestae* of Augustus, probably not revised after AD 7, speak of two British kings who sought refuge with him. One was Tincommius, the other Dubnovellaunus, who had a brief reign over the Trinovantes *c*. AD 1–6. His expulsion was probably caused by Catuvellaunian conquest, for no later ruler is recorded on the coins before Cunobelinus.

In his last years Augustus seems to have achieved another success, for Strabo tells us that certain British rulers sent embassies to Rome and set up offerings on the Capitol, making the island virtually a Roman possession. Clearly these are not the refugees of the *Res Gestae*. Frere suggests that they might be Verica, who must have supplanted Eppillus at about this time, and Cunobelinus, whose coins for a brief period bore the title *rex*. Certainty is impossible, and we must remember that there were many kings in Britain whose names have not come down to us.

Under Tiberius (14–37) Roman policy in Britain, as elsewhere, was unadventurous. Roman sources tell us nothing of the island at this period. Coins indicate that Cunobelinus and Verica retained their thrones throughout the reign; they further indicate the gradual expansion of the Catuvellauni at the expense of their neighbours. If Verica asked Tiberius to intervene his request was not granted; if Cunobelinus was also a client the situation may not have seemed serious.

Under Caligula (37–41) that situation changed. One of Cunobelinus' many sons, Adminius, was expelled by his father and persuaded Caligula that Britain could easily be conquered. An expedition was prepared but never sailed, the troops being ordered by their crazy emperor to pick up sea-shells to prove that Ocean had been conquered. Roy Davies has suggested that the story as we have it is distorted by malice, and that Caligula may not have been intending invasion at this juncture; perhaps this was really a military exercise in which an opposed landing was simulated. This may well be a better interpretation, but if the story was current that a planned invasion of Britain had been a fiasco its truth or falsehood is of little importance: crossing the Channel, such a rumour can only have given confidence to the anti-Roman party. They certainly did not lack confidence. About the year 40 Cunobelinus died. Togodumnus and Caratacus, his successors, lacked their father's political skill. He had been careful not to push his conquests to the point where Roman intervention was provoked. Soon after his death his rival Verica was ejected from the last remnant of free Atrebatic territory and went to Rome to plead with the new emperor Claudius (41–54) for Roman intervention.

The case was a strong one. The Augustan plan for Britain had finally collapsed. To add insult to injury the sons of Cunobelinus demanded the extradition of Verica, and British raids harassed the coast of Gaul. If Rome was to retain any interest in Britain the challenge could not be ignored, even if the cross-Channel raids were not a serious threat to the peace of the Empire. There was another political reason for invasion which must have weighed heavily with Claudius. Roman policy had led to the creation of a number of client kingdoms on her frontiers. They served as an extra protection to the Empire, and if in due course it seemed advisable to absorb them they would already be partly Romanized. Such clients were particularly numerous and important on the eastern frontier, where the Parthian Empire constituted the most serious rival that Rome faced. If Claudius had rejected Verica's appeals the morale of all client rulers would have suffered; it would have appeared that Rome was only concerned with clients as long as they did not need support, whereas the patron–client relationship laid obligations on both parties. It is clear that the Parthians were just as interested in these kingdoms as the Romans. If Roman prestige suffered many of them might have changed their allegiance. Claudius, in fact, had no real alternative to invasion.

The Conquest

From the time of Tacitus, who wrote with optimism of the wealth of Britain, historians have sought other and less likely reasons for the invasion. No doubt many people at Rome hoped to profit from the conquest of Britain, but this does not prove that Claudius' motive was economic. Others have suggested that 'this most unmilitary of emperors' (what about Pius?) needed military prestige: but it was only two years since the army had put him on the throne. At all periods the dynastic loyalty of the army was one of the unresolved constitutional problems of the Empire, producing inadequate rulers like Elagabalus or Gordian III. Revolts were not the result of dissatisfaction amongst the rank and file of the army, but of political ambition in powerful army commanders. Some think that Claudius preferred to have troops in Britain, which would help pay for them, rather than on the Channel coast of Gaul; but there is no evidence that British raids were serious enough to necessitate a substantial army in Gaul. Nor do arguments about power balances between the Rhine and Danube armies carry conviction. If this were a problem there would have been no difficulty in moving troops in order to restore the necessary equilibrium.

The aims of Claudius are as important as his motives. For long modern scholars have been unduly influenced by the persuasive writing of Tacitus, whose accounts (especially in the *Agricola*) suggest that at all times it was imperial policy to conquer the whole of Britain. We shall do well to consider his merits and faults as a historian of Roman Britain before we proceed further with our story of the invasion.

Three of Tacitus' works concern us. The earliest is the *Agricola*, written in 97–8; it is a laudatory biography of Tacitus' father-in-law, who is portrayed as an ideal governor in an idealized province. The account of British history from 43 to 78 is primarily designed to show Agricola as the greatest of first-century governors, since he virtually completed the conquest of the island. Individual predecessors are judged solely on their contribution to the Conquest, and no allowance is made for other factors such as the need for consolidation, or changes in imperial policy. The work is manifestly biased and infuriatingly vague. There are so few place-names that opinions about the area covered by a campaign can legitimately differ. Nevertheless, even before Agricola's governorship it includes some valuable information not found in other sources. It would be as foolish to ignore Tacitus' information as it would be to accept uncritically his interpretations. In the *Agricola*, written at the age of forty when he had just vacated the consulship, as in his more mature works, Tacitus reveals himself as master of his facts; our problem is that he did not understand history as we do. For him it was a branch of literature, with certain conventions, and it was also a medium for political expression. There may be no deliberate falsification but his writing is coloured by his own preconceptions. Nonetheless, he is fair to us, in that he often incorporates material which does not support his thesis, and we are therefore able to suggest different interpretations of his facts.

The *Histories* was a major history of the Roman Empire between 68 and 96. It was published about the year 107. Only the early books survive, so that we have no account of Agricola's governorship in its imperial perspective, and have virtually no written evidence for the thirty years which followed it. What we have deals mainly with the civil wars of 68–9 and with the subsequent rebellion of Civilis.

The last and greatest of Tacitus' works was the *Annales*, published early in the reign of Hadrian and covering the years 14 to 68. Substantial sections are missing, one of which certainly covered the invasion of Britain: presumably it also gave a brief account (but no more) of the governorship of Plautius (43–7). The account will have been brief because it is clear that within the very complex structure of the *Annales* Britain was treated as a drama in three acts: The Great Invasion, The Last Stand of the Noble Savage, and The Great Rebellion. Incidents outside this framework received at best scant notice, and time and again the *Agricola*, with all its faults, provides a fuller and more balanced account.

Apart from Tacitus there are only two

Roman writers who give any substantial information about Britain in the first century. Suetonius was a younger contemporary of Tacitus. As Secretary of State (*ab epistulis*) under Hadrian he had access to official documents, but he used little which is of value to us. His imperial biographies, from Julius Caesar to Domitian, are concerned with court gossip and scandal rather than with the wider affairs of empire. Britain is mentioned only because of the visit of Claudius and because Vespasian commanded a legion there during and after the invasion: there is no attempt to give a full account of the conquest, and even the Boudiccan rising failed to attract attention.

A century later than Tacitus and Suetonius, Cassius Dio wrote a history of Rome from its foundation to his own time. Dio was a conscientious but uninspired writer, and is a valuable source for events during his lifetime. The portions of his work which concern us survive only in a Byzantine epitome by Xiphilinus. The most important section is the account of the Claudian invasion, for which the Tacitean account is lost. Presumably here, as elsewhere, Tacitus was one of Dio's principal sources, though other histories now lost were available to him. His brief account of Agricola is a poor summary of what Tacitus had written and inspires little confidence in the value of his other references to Britain.

In recent years we have developed a more critical approach to the Roman authors, and the archaeological evidence has improved both in quantity and in quality. While he remains the prime source for the period of conquest, we can no longer use Tacitus alone nor can we accept his judgements at face value. It is now thought that imperial policy in and towards Britain underwent several important changes in the period from 43 to 85, and we now appreciate that a governor might be chosen for non-military qualities. We can go further, and say that to the emperor Britain consisted of a number of autonomous political units who might pursue divergent policies and require different treatment. This had been an important factor in determining imperial policy since Augustus gave his support to Tincommius, and remained important at least into the third century.

In 43 many British rulers faced a choice; but it was not between Roman rule and liberty. It was a choice between the Romans and the Catuvellauni. Small wonder, therefore, that Claudius was able to claim the submission of eleven kings in 43. Probably negotiations had been opened even before his army landed, for it is abundantly clear that Claudius had more and better information about Britain than was available to Caesar. Unfortunately we can only guess at a handful of these kings who are subsequently recorded as clients of the emperor. Their tribes include the Iceni of Norfolk, the Brigantes of what is now northern England – the most populous tribe in the island according to Tacitus – and the Atrebates. We can only guess at the others, with very little evidence to support us.

It is virtually certain that in 43 the plans of Claudius did not involve the conquest of more than the Lowland Zone, if they were even so ambitious. The first objective was clearly the conquest of the Catuvellauni and their allies. It may be that Claudius envisaged no more than a province based on the Catuvellaunian kingdom, surrounded and protected by client states. Subsequent changes of policy were dictated in part by the changing situation in Britain, and in part by pressures on other frontiers of the Empire.

For the invasion our chief source is Dio; the account of Suetonius is too sketchy to be of value. As commander, Claudius appointed A. Plautius, and gave him four legions – II Augusta, XIV Gemina, and XX Valeria from the Rhine and IX Hispana from the Danube. The legions were heavy infantry; light infantry and cavalry were provided by auxiliary units. The total number in the expeditionary force is unknown, for we have no list of auxiliaries; we may guess at about 40,000, of whom rather more than half were legionaries.

After delays caused by the reluctance of the soldiers to campaign 'beyond the limits of the known world', the army sailed 'late in the season'. It cannot, in view of subsequent events, have been very late. The delay was useful, for the Britons no longer expected the invasion and were not ready to oppose a landing: but Plautius had expected opposition, and his army sailed in three divisions as a countermeasure. Presumably, therefore, they landed at three separate points, rather than in three waves at the same place. One landing-point was certainly Richborough, which was to become a principal cross-Channel port. It provided the sheltered harbour which Caesar had failed to find. The ditches of the bridgehead fortification have been excavated. The other landing sites are uncertain, but they cannot have been distant from Richborough. Dio never suggests that there was more than one army operating in Britain in 43, and reunion must have been rapid. Later we find roads from Richborough, Dover, and Lympne converging on Canterbury, and elsewhere the road system seems to reflect campaigning routes; but there is no corroborative evidence from Dover, Lympne, or Canterbury, and we should possibly think of landings nearer Richborough.

The landing was unopposed, and for some days Plautius was unable to bring the enemy to battle; but the presence of Togodumnus and Caratacus in Kent indicates that they were not entirely unprepared. They were defeated sev-

10

19

10 Aerial view of the fort at Richborough. The ditches of the Claudian base can be seen running across the site of the later Saxon Shore stone fort.

erally and retired to the line of a river which must be the Medway. Meanwhile Dio records the submission of 'a part of the Bodunni who were ruled by the Catuvellauni'. The tribe is otherwise unknown, and it is usually assumed that the reference is to the Dobunni of Gloucestershire and Somerset. By this stage they were divided, and coins of one of their rulers, Bodvoc, suggest a pro-Roman policy. Pottery from sites like Bagendon indicates links with the Catuvellauni, though it cannot prove political subordination. But Dio implies that the Bodunni lived in Kent and says that Plautius left a garrison in their territory before advancing further. Unless he is more than usually muddled the reference can scarcely be to the western Dobunni.

The crossing of the Medway was disputed by the Catuvellauni and was not secured without a two-day battle in which Vespasian distinguished himself. The Britons retreated across the Thames, probably downstream from London, and the Romans followed: some forded the river and others found or built a bridge. Skirmishing ensued, and Togodumnus was killed, but this did not weaken the British

resistance and there was a halt in the Roman advance.

Before the expedition had sailed Claudius had made provision for reinforcements and had arranged to command them himself. Modern scholars believe that the use of these reinforcements was predetermined, Plautius being ordered to ask for help when he reached the Thames. The suggestion is that the real purpose was to give Claudius the prestige of leading his victorious troops into Camulodunum. The brevity of the campaign would support such an interpretation – Claudius was only in Britain for sixteen days – and so would the sneering attitude of Suetonius, who says that 'he rapidly reduced a large part of the land to submission without battle or casualties'. This may derive from the triumphal arch of Claudius, erected in 51–2, which tells of the submission of eleven British kings achieved without any Roman casualties (*sine ulla iactura*). Dio gives a fuller account. He speaks of heavy Roman losses in the marshes beyond the Thames and strong resistance as the reasons why Plautius called for support. After his arrival Claudius defeated the enemy in a battle

54

north of the Thames and captured Camulodunum. 'He won over numerous tribes, some by submission, some by force.' He then left Plautius 'to conquer the remaining areas' – surely an indication that Roman objectives at this stage were limited.

Doubtless Claudius wished to be present at the surrender of Colchester which was the highlight of this campaign. Even if no major battle was fought during his stay in Britain, his presence (along with many distinguished senators who could not safely be left at Rome) was doubtless important in confirming Roman interest in the new province. It was a clear guarantee to Roman clients that Roman rule was to be permanent. The crushing of the Catuvellauni and their replacement by Rome changed the face of British politics. It is not therefore surprising that so many rulers submitted. Some of them may have been in communication with Claudius' agents before the invasion, and others will have opened negotiations with Plautius while he awaited the emperor. We may guess at formal ceremonies of submission to Claudius in person arranged beforehand (in view of his short stay in Britain) and designed to impress the kings with Rome's power and wealth. Like the British in nineteenth-century India, Claudius sought to control much of his new territory through native rulers; there is no evidence that this policy was intended to be of short duration.

After the imperial visit and the defeat of the Catuvellauni the army seems to have been divided. Probably this division was effected in 44. The best evidence for it comes from the life of Vespasian, commander of the second legion and subsequently emperor. Suetonius tells us that 'he fought thirty battles, conquered two powerful tribes and brought more than twenty *oppida* and the Isle of Wight under Roman rule'. *Oppida* would normally be translated 'towns', but in this context must be hill-forts. Vespasian must have been cooperating with a fleet, and possible store-bases are known at 11 Fishbourne – with military occupation at nearby Chichester – and at Hamworthy on Poole Harbour. One of the tribes he conquered must be the Durotriges, but the other cannot be certainly identified. The massive and complex defences of the hill-forts had not been designed against Roman artillery fire. After a barrage the forts were stormed: sieges do not seem to have been necessary. Maiden Castle, with its war cemetery, gives clear and dramatic evidence of the Roman success; so does Hod Hill, where the 'chieftain's hut' was the focus for 1, 13 *ballista* attack, and where a Roman fort for legionaries and auxiliary cavalry was built in one corner of the hill-fort. Storming native hill-forts was a routine activity even as late as the end of the first century according to Juvenal (*Satires*, XIV.196).

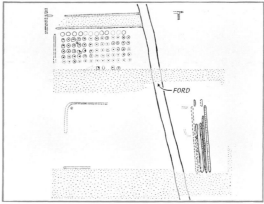

FORD

11 Foundation trenches and postholes of timber store-buildings at Fishbourne which are possibly associated with Vespasian's campaigns of 43 or 44. (*After* B. W. Cunliffe.)

The activities of the rest of the army are known only from archaeological evidence. Recent excavation has confirmed that one legion – probably the Twentieth – was installed at Colchester. Subsequently we find the Ninth operating in the east, with its base at Lincoln from the late 50s or early 60s and at York from *c.* 72. Probably it was always on the right flank of the Roman advance, with the Fourteenth in the centre. The earliest certain fortress of this legion was at Wroxeter, again from the mid-50s. The activities of the legions under Plautius are matters for speculation rather than certainty; our guesses will depend on what we believe to have been imperial policy and what we deduce about tribal attitudes to Rome.

Plautius seems to have left in 47, to be succeeded by P. Ostorius Scapula. Tacitus tells us that under these two governors 'the nearest part of Britain was gradually formed into a province, and a colony of veterans was established. Certain *civitates* were given to King Cogidumnus (who remained most loyal right down to our own times) according to the old and accepted Roman custom by which even kings are the means of enslaving others.' (*Agricola* XIV.1). A fragmentary inscription from

12 In the attack on Maiden Castle under Vespasian the Iron Age defenders were outclassed by the superior Roman arms. The iron bolt from a Roman *ballista* (heavy crossbow) lodged in the spine shows how one defender died. Dorset County Museum, Dorchester.

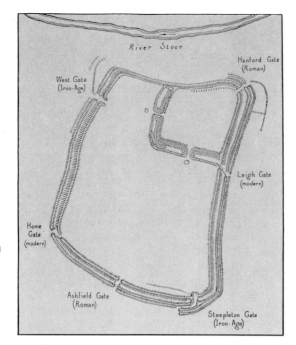

13 Plan of Hod Hill, one of the several Iron Age hill-forts in the southwest captured by Vespasian. The Roman fort built in the northwest corner is clearly marked, and should be compared with the aerial view in illus. 1. (*After* I. A. Richmond.)

Chichester, assignable on stylistic grounds to the first century, was set up *[ex] auctoritat[e Ti.] Claud. [Co]gidubni r[egis] lega[ti] Aug. in Brit.* . . . ('on the authority of Tiberius Claudius Cogidubnus, king and imperial legate in Britain').

14, 47

Cogidumnus presents many problems of interpretation: at best we can only choose what we consider to be the most likely of several possible solutions. We assume that Tacitus and the inscription refer to the same man. If they do, even his name is uncertain: the manuscript evidence is balanced between Cogidumnus and Togidumnus, and the inscription offers no help. Cogidumnus has become traditional, and has the merit of avoiding confusion with the son of Cunobelinus. His names indicate that he received Roman citizenship from Claudius or Nero, that is in the period 41 to 68, and the words of Tacitus (*is ad nostram usque memoriam fidissimus mansit* – who remained most loyal right down to our own times) must mean that he lived at least into the 70s. The title king must imply a client status. The record at Chichester suggests that he may have been in some sense a successor of Verica. (Of Verica himself nothing is recorded after his appeal to Claudius; he was by then an old man, if he was really the son of Commius.) *Legatus Augusti* is more difficult to assess. It is the formal title of imperial governors, and implies senatorial rank with at least the status of an ex-praetor. No other client ruler in the Roman Empire is attested with such a title. It has been suggested that it was honorary, granted by Vespasian to an old friend of campaigning days who may also have been an important supporter in 69 – the Year of the Four Emperors. There is no parallel for the honorary title of *legatus Augusti*, and it is easier to suppose that it reflects

14 The inscription from Chichester, set up on the authority of Tiberius Claudius Cogidubnus, king and imperial legate. It cannot be precisely dated, but must be earlier than *c.*80. Chichester. (See also illus. 47.)

some real responsibility. It may be significant that Claudius gave senatorial rank as ex-consul and ex-praetor to Herod Agrippa and Herod of Chalcis in 41 (Dio LX.8.3). Claudius is known to have made considerable use of client rulers, and was responsible for the admission of Gauls to the Senate. The title should perhaps be taken with the grant of certain *civitates*, not later than 52, to a reigning king. It would imply that as a client Cogidumnus ruled his own lands and as imperial legate had administrative responsibilities (under the governor) for the territories given to him. What those territories were is a field for speculation rather than confident assertion. There are the following pointers. They were presumably areas which did not require a military garrison; they were probably adjacent to the kingdom of Cogidumnus, though the extent of that kingdom is unknown; and they are unlikely to have been involved in the Boudiccan rising. On this rather shaky foundation we may tentatively suggest a *regnum* in mid- and west Sussex (on the assumption that he was successor to Verica and so favoured) and other territory covering something like the tribal area of the Atrebates at its widest extent. His presence may well have been important to successive governors, who spent much of their time on campaign, and would welcome a loyal deputy handling at least some administrative and legal matters.

Local Resistance and the Aftermath

Ostorius Scapula arrived in Britain late in the summer of 47. We have a fairly full account of his governorship in the *Annales*. There is general agreement that by this date the Romans must have controlled the whole of Britain south and east of the line of the Fosse Way, the Roman road from Lincoln to Exeter. There is not agreement that this road, or any other line, constituted a planned and defended frontier. Such a concept of a frontier was probably not current as early as the reign of Claudius, and the number of military sites of the period which are certainly known is too few to prove it. Nonetheless Plautius had probably carried Roman rule as far as Claudius had intended when he launched the invasion. If such a province was to survive it required the goodwill of the

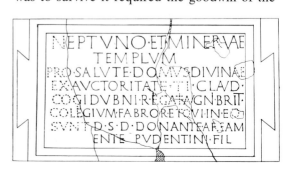

tribes beyond it. Brigantia had probably been a client since 43, and the Romans devoted considerable effort to maintaining the pro-Roman party in power. The tribes of Wales were, however, hostile. Before Scapula arrived one or more of them had invaded Roman territory. Scapula at once dealt with the threat. He then prepared to disarm suspects within the province and to consolidate all lands as far as the rivers Trent and Severn. (We should note that this statement depends on the inspired guess which gave us *cunctaque cis Trisantonam et Sabrinam* for the meaningless *cuncta castris Antonam et Sabrinam* of the manuscripts; *Annales*, XII. 31.) This presumably involved the annexation of territory belonging to the Dobunni, the Cornovii and the Coritani. If the Fosse Way is regarded as an earlier provincial boundary then some of their territory had been incorporated in the province under Plautius.

The immediate reaction was not from these tribes, or from their unconquered neighbours, but from the Iceni and adjacent tribes. The revolt does not seem to have involved the whole of the Iceni, for they retained their client status – though perhaps under a new ruler, Prasutagus. The only battle recorded was in a fortification with access too restricted for cavalry: the site was taken by auxiliary infantry and dismounted troopers. This again suggests only small-scale activity.

It is not clear whether these events took place in the winter of 47–8 or whether they occupied the campaigning season of 48. In 48 or 49 a clear policy emerged. Scapula invaded the territory of the Decangi, who are presumably the same as the Deceangli of Clwyd. We may suppose that he attacked from the Chester area along the Dee estuary, for 'he almost reached the sea facing Ireland'. However, he halted in mid-campaign in order to suppress an anti-Roman rising in Brigantia. This was the first of several interventions in support of Cartimandua, and is clear evidence of the importance attached to maintaining a friendly power in the north. Doubtless the rebels had seen that if Scapula could establish control of the Cheshire gap he would divide them from the anti-Roman forces in Wales.

The campaign against the Decangi was the last in which Scapula had the initiative. Before the next season important changes were made. The fortress at Colchester was given up and a colony of veterans established there. Apart from providing time-expired legionaries with a land-gratuity it had two functions according to Tacitus: to provide a reserve force in the event of rebellion, and to set an example of Roman respect for law. In the Boudiccan rising of 60, Colchester failed on both counts. (A colony was established by a single act, and its population was not increased by later settlements, so its military value was in any case short-lived.)

The reason for this change was to enable the Twentieth Legion to be moved westward against the Silures of South Wales. This tribe was now the most serious threat to the province. It was led by Caratacus, who had presumably fled to the west after the loss of his kingdom in 43.

We have no clear evidence for the base of Legio XX Valeria. The most likely site is at Kingsholm, in the suburbs of Gloucester. The fortress which underlay the later *colonia* and the modern city centre was apparently not established before the mid-60s. We do not know whether the whole legion was at Kingsholm but probably it was split up into smaller detachments, as other legions seem to have been at this period; they may sometimes have been brigaded with auxiliaries. There are now a considerable number of forts in the Midlands and the Welsh Marches whose size is too small for a legion but far too large for any one auxiliary unit; their areas differ one from another. They are sometimes called 'half-legion fortresses', though none has been sufficiently excavated to provide evidence for its garrison. The variations in size suggest that the

15 Clyro, Powys, a large fort beside the river Wye dating to the middle years of the first century.

garrisons will also have varied. In the mid-first century the Roman army had not yet realized the full potential of its auxiliaries. The idea of controlling a conquered area by a network of permanent forts, each containing a cohort or *ala*, had not been fully developed: forts were still, to some extent, winter quarters for an army which would spend the summer fighting. At the end of a campaign it was not certain that a unit would return to a base which it had previously held. The very number of forts, many with several rebuilds, indicates that the situation changed from season to season. Some of the large forts we are considering may have housed legionaries, or a mixture of legionaries and auxiliaries; others again probably held several auxiliary units without any legionaries.

Whatever the base for Legio XX, the significance of its move westwards was not lost on Caratacus. Immediately after Scapula's invasion of South Wales – probably in 50 – he shifted the centre of the war to the territory of the Ordovices. It is customary but erroneous to place this tribe in the northwest of Wales; this area may or may not have belonged to them, but it is certain that they occupied much of mid-Wales, and many of the hill-forts of the central Marches may also have been theirs. Somewhere in Ordovician territory Caratacus made a stand on a hill, with stone ramparts blocking the easier routes to the summit; before his position lay a river which was sufficiently impressive to cause the Romans to hesitate. It was his last battle. Despite the success of guerrilla warfare in earlier years, Caratacus chose to face the Romans in full-scale battle. The result, inevitably, was a disaster. The British were crushed, and although Caratacus made good his escape to Brigantia he was promptly surrendered by Cartimandua. His wife, children and brothers had already been captured.

Tacitus says that it was a notable victory, and so it doubtless seemed to both Scapula and Claudius. The last of the house of Cunobelinus had been captured and displayed at Rome as a sign of success. But in Britain the war continued. For the moment we hear nothing further of the Ordovices – nothing in fact until they attack an *ala* operating in their territory in 77 or 78. Once more the Silures fill the stage, and until after the death of Scapula they play the tune to which the Romans dance.

The Silures made no attempt to fight a pitched battle. Tacitus gives a vivid picture of guerrilla warfare in which the Romans were constantly harassed by men with nothing to lose, for they had heard that Scapula spoke of a 'final solution' – extermination or transportation to Gaul. Some Roman losses were serious: in one battle a *praefectus castrorum*, eight legionary centurions and the pick of their men were killed in an attack on a fort-building party. On another occasion two auxiliary cohorts were defeated. A battle which began with the routing of a foraging party ended only when Scapula threw in his legions: even then the Silures escaped without serious loss. In 52 Scapula died, 'worn out with the burden of his responsibilities, killed by warfare if not in battle'. Before the arrival of his successor, A. Didius Gallus, the Silures had defeated a legion under Manlius Valens – otherwise noteworthy only as the oldest consul on record, holding office in 96 at the age of 90 – and were raiding far and wide in Roman territory.

We have no full account of the governorship of Gallus, which lasted from 52 to 57, covering the last two years of the reign of Claudius and the first three years of Nero's. In the *Agricola* we are told that 'he held firmly what his predecessors had conquered and even moved a few forts forward, so that he would be reputed to have extended his province'. The *Annales* add a little to this. The arrival of Gallus ended the Silurian incursions. There is an account of successful intervention in Brigantia, but no mention of the forts moved forward to extend the province. Tacitus ends with the devastating judgement that 'laden with his years and with manifold distinctions he thought it sufficient to act through his juniors and to contain the enemy'.

It has been suggested that Claudius remained wedded to his original idea of a province restricted to the Lowland Zone, and that Gallus would therefore have received instructions to avoid new conquests. But Scapula had already been attempting to build forts in Silurian territory, and conquest certainly seems to have been his aim. There is no evidence for the military dispositions which would have been necessary if the Silures were to be contained rather than conquered. More likely Claudius had recognized that his policies had to be changed to meet a new situation. We may suppose that, at least until the death of Claudius in October 54, Gallus was concerned with the problem of the Silures. Here is one area where new forts may be expected, and recent excavations at Usk, Abergavenny, and Cardiff show military occupation of at least some Silurian territory from about the mid-50s. Usk is of particular interest. The finds from extensive excavations suggest that it was first occupied *c.* 55–60, and its size (19.4 hectares, about 49 acres) is sufficient for a whole legion. Presumably Legio XX was now united and moved forward from Kingsholm. Similar activity further north is indicated by the establishment of a new fortress for Legio XIV at Wroxeter, certainly before 60. Both fortresses may of course have been built by Q. Veranius or Suetonius Paulinus, rather than by Gallus: archaeological evidence alone cannot give us the precise year in which construction took

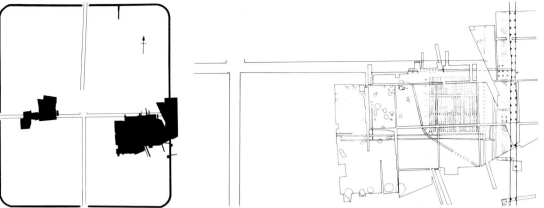

16 Plan (left, with detail, right) of the legionary fortress at Usk, Gwent, built in the mid-50s and occupied for ten to twelve years. Archaeology cannot give a sufficiently precise date to associate it with a specific governor. (*After* W. H. Manning.)

17 Tombstone of Marcus Petronius from Wroxeter. He was a standard bearer in the XIV Gemina who died aged 38 after serving for 18 years. He died before 60 when the legion was awarded the battle honours *Martia Victrix*, won in the campaign against Boudicca. They would certainly have been recorded on his tombstone had he died after that date. Rowley's House Museum, Shrewsbury.

place. Sites between these two fortresses, such as Clifford, Clyro, and Jay Lane (Leintwardine) may well be as early, though Clifford and Clyro are unlikely to be contemporary with one another. All probably represent garrisons in or close to Ordovician territory.

The accession of Nero in 54 may have halted any plans for conquest. Nero is said to have considered the abandonment of Britain, and Eric Birley has argued convincingly that this must precede the appointment of Q. Veranius in 57, since he was clearly given instructions to conquer the recalcitrant tribes of Wales. If Nero – or rather his ministers and his mother – contemplated withdrawal from Britain, conquest would have been forbidden. Small wonder therefore that Gallus failed to measure up to the Tacitean standard for governors of Britain, or that the one event of his term of office to attract attention was a second Roman intervention in Brigantia.

Tacitus is far from lucid in his accounts of the internal problems of Brigantia. In 48 or 49 Scapula helped to crush a rebellion against Cartimandua. At some time during the governorship of Gallus her ex-husband Venutius appears as leader of the opposition. With external support – presumably from tribes further north – he invaded the kingdom. Gallus had already prepared for this by sending auxiliaries, and later despatched a legion (presumably the Ninth) to support the queen. As a result Cartimandua retained her throne until 69 or 70. Apparently she did not require extra support even in 60–1, though Roman troops may have been stationed in her territory from the time of Gallus.

The recall of Gallus in 57 marks the end of any period of indecision by Nero's advisers. The new governor, Q. Veranius, had gained a military reputation in Cilicia. He died only a year after his appointment, and in his will claimed that if he had lived for another two years – presumably to complete his expected term of office – he would have conquered the whole province. Tacitus, and modern scholars who have followed him, have regarded this as outrageous boasting; but if we believe that at this date there was no plan to occupy Brigan-

tia, the claim was reasonable enough. Veranius achieved only 'minor raids against the Silures'; but after two successful years, conquering tribes and establishing forts, his successor, Suetonius Paulinus, was in a position to occupy Anglesey in 60. Enough damage was done to the tribes of Wales to keep them quiet during the Boudiccan rising. Some new forts which may belong to these years have already been mentioned; to them we may perhaps add the unexcavated fort known as Caersws I. Caersws II was occupied from the Flavian period onwards, so this is presumably earlier. It suggests an advance up the Severn Valley after the establishment of Wroxeter, and like Leintwardine was presumably directed against the Ordovices.

Any gains made by Veranius or Paulinus were probably held for only a short period. In 60 the rising of the Iceni under Boudicca, soon joined by the Trinovantes and others, jeopardized not only recent conquests but the whole province. Prasutagus, client-ruler of the Iceni, had died and the treaty with Rome was thereby ended. It was not renewed; instead it was decided to incorporate Icenian territory into the province, as well as securing for the Emperor the half-share in his property which had been bequeathed by Prasutagus. We do not know whether the Iceni would have accepted this decision if the situation had been handled delicately, but it is clear that Roman mismanagement provided ample excuse for Icenian protest. The kingdom was treated as though it had been conquered, and fearing worse the people rose under the widowed Boudicca. The Trinovantes joined them. Much of their land had been expropriated for the *colonia* at Colchester; their chiefs bore much of the burden of maintaining the Temple of Claudius there, and all had suffered from the arrogant behaviour of the veterans. As Caesar's allies they must have had great hopes of the Roman Conquest, but they had gained little from the invaders.

Colchester was the first target of the rebels. Despite its alleged function it had no defences, and no attempt was made to provide them now. The small garrison, the veterans, and the

200 men sent by the procurator, Decianus Catus, were unable to withstand the rebels. A relief expedition under Petillius Cerealis suffered a crushing defeat. Catus fled to Gaul.

Meanwhile news of the disaster had reached Paulinus in Anglesey. The speed of his reaction is shown by the fact that he reached London with his cavalry before the rebels from East Anglia; but he had too few troops to hold it. The Ninth Legion had already been crushed, and the acting commander of the Second had failed to obey the order to join Paulinus. The governor had only one possible course of action. He fell back through the Midlands until he joined his main force – the Fourteenth Legion, part of the Twentieth, and some auxiliaries. He was able to select an advantageous site for battle, and as usual the Roman army proved more than a match for the larger but undisciplined native force. The victory was complete and final, and for practical purposes the rebellion was over. Its cost was tremendous. Tacitus estimates the British casualties at 80,000, the Roman at 400 in the final battle: we have no means of correcting the incredible figure of 80,000. More important were the earlier losses. Colchester had been sacked, and Paulinus had been compelled to leave London and Verulamium to a similar fate. The rebels had shown no mercy. Thick layers of burnt material are an indication of the fate of these towns; for the brutal treatment of those found there we have to turn to the writings of Tacitus, and for more lurid detail to Dio.

Recovery was inevitably slow. The rebels had failed to sow corn in 60, so that the province was further impoverished. Paulinus made things worse by his harsh treatment of rebellious or suspect tribes, ravaging their lands with fire and sword. He provoked the enemy to the resistance of those who have nothing to hope for. New troops were sent to Britain: 2,000 trained legionaries brought the Ninth up to strength, and 5,000 auxiliaries (1,000 of them cavalry) came with them from Germany.

At Rome someone in authority had understood the message of the rebellion, that Britain could only be held if Roman rule was made acceptable. In the winter of 60–1 a new procurator was appointed. We know nothing of the earlier career of Iulius Alpinus Classicianus; but we know that his career ended in Britain, for portions of his tombstone have been found in London. He was married to Iulia Pacata, the daughter of the pro-Roman Treviran chief Indus, and there is good reason to suppose that Classicianus also came from the Moselle Valley. In an age when virtually all members of the imperial administration were Italian his appointment to Britain indicates a clear determination to make a new start. He was clearly the right man for the job. He saw that Paulinus would never bring a lasting peace to the province. His reports to the Emperor led first to a commission of inquiry and then, in the summer of 61, to the recall of Paulinus.

The new governor, Petronius Turpilianus, had obviously been given instructions to restore peace and order. There can have been no question of new conquests, and those made by Veranius and Paulinus in Wales do not appear to have been retained. For the time being troops were more urgently needed in the east. Tacitus in the *Agricola* dismisses this governorship in the phrase *compositis prioribus nihil ultra ausus* – having settled the existing troubles he risked nothing more – and is no more complimentary in the *Annales*. But Turpilianus was only in Britain for two years: if he settled the problems rising from the rebellion in that time his achievement was considerable. It evidently satisfied Nero, for Turpilianus was given *ornamenta triumphalia* in 65. Tacitus suggests that this was for loyalty to Nero, but it may be that the reason was success in Britain.

18 Tombstone from Colchester of Longinus, a Thracian auxiliary cavalryman serving in the *ala I Thracum*. It was found thrown down and mutilated by the Boudiccan rebels. Colchester Museum.

Amongst his activities must have been the reorganization of the army, but as usual archaeology cannot give us certain evidence of what was done. The fortress at Lincoln for Legio IX Hispana cannot be much later than this, and might be a few years earlier. Cerealis does not seem to have had the whole legion available for his relief force, suggesting that it was still split into several vexillations in 60. It may be significant that the large fort at Long-thorpe was abandoned at about this time. A new fort at The Lunt, Baginton (near Coventry), may be a response to the rebellion. Other forts have yet to be discovered, though they must surely exist. Doubtless changes were made elsewhere, some forts being abandoned or given smaller garrisons, while others were strengthened or enlarged.

M. Trebellius Maximus, governor from 63 to 69, is castigated by Tacitus for military inactivity which led to mutinies in the army. Elsewhere Tacitus describes mutinies during the civil wars which followed the death of Nero in 68, and there is no need to suppose any earlier disaffection amongst the troops. By 67 the situation in Britain was sufficiently stable for Nero to withdraw one of the four legions, XIV Gemina, for a projected eastern campaign. This suggests that wars of conquest in Britain were neither in progress nor in prospect. Yet there may have been advances in the 60s. We have little information on the area west of Exeter, but the small fort at Nanstallon, Cornwall, was perhaps not erected before c. 65; it can hardly have stood alone. It may be during this period that Cornwall was first occupied, though some of the changes may be the result of the departure of XIV Gemina.

This involved the move northwards of II Augusta to Gloucester, where a new fortress replaced that at Kingsholm after 64. XX Valeria Victrix is likely to have moved to Wroxeter, leaving the fortress at Usk empty. Doubtless these changes involved many movements of auxiliary units, but these cannot now be identified with any certainty. There was little civilian development in this period; most towns do not seem to emerge before the Flavian period, and there is little evidence of immediate rebuilding in the three towns destroyed by the following of Boudicca.

Britain was little affected by the civil wars of 69, and there is no evidence for fighting in the province. Trebellius Maximus was apparently already unpopular with the army, and especially inimical to Roscius Coelius, legate of Legio XX: Coelius now exploited the conflict for the imperial throne between Otho and Vitellius to make Maximus' position untenable. Presumably Maximus supported Otho, for without him the legions of Britain gave their allegiance to Vitellius, who was able to use 8,000 men from the province in his march

on Italy. Maximus was driven out, but by the time he reached the Continent Otho was dead and perforce he had to report the British situation to Vitellius. Vitellius replaced him with a new governor, Vettius Bolanus.

If the three legions in Britain supported Vitellius, XIV Gemina was persistent in its opposition even after the defeat of Otho. To avoid embarrassment Vitellius ordered it to return to Britain. Bolanus may well have welcomed the arrival of more troops, even if they were of dubious loyalty. His other legions were below strength and reluctant to accept discipline, and military intervention in Brigantia had become essential.

Once again Venutius had secured external help for an internal rebellion; this time he was successful. Bolanus sent auxiliary troops who were able to rescue Cartimandua but not to save her kingdom. Legionaries were not sent north, presumably because they were not thought sufficiently reliable. Despite their early adherence to Vitellius they seem to have been ready to acknowledge Vespasian, and Vettius Bolanus was evidently not strongly partisan. The attitude of the legions is easily understood. Vespasian had been legate of Legio II Augusta during the Claudian invasion and his son Titus had been tribune of one of the British legions, probably in the early 60s. Legio XIV Gemina had been a staunch supporter of Otho, and like other Othonians will have welcomed Vespasian. Only the Twentieth, over which Roscius Coelius had inadequate control, was slow to change its allegiance.

The situation in Britain was now serious. A client ruler had been expelled and the northern border of the province was no longer protected. Action was clearly necessary, but it was not yet possible. Vespasian had serious financial problems, and faced a major revolt on the lower Rhine. To assist in restoring Roman control there XIV Gemina was finally withdrawn from Britain in 70. The most that could be done for Britain was to send Iulius Agricola to replace Roscius Coelius (whose loyalty was probably suspect) as commander of XX Valeria Victrix. Clearly his first task would have been to restore discipline in the legion and make it once more an effective and reliable unit.

By 70 or 71 Bolanus may have been able to take positive action against the Brigantes or their allies. Tacitus says nothing of campaigning during his governorship, but Vespasian retained him until 71, and the poet Statius speaks of Bolanus establishing forts and capturing trophies from a British king. Doubtless Bolanus' achievements were restricted by a shortage of troops: his successor, Petillius Cerealis, fresh from the defeat of Civilis, brought with him Legio II Adiutrix and probably a number of auxiliary units.

19 Tombstone of Gaius Saufeius from Lincoln. He was a soldier of IX Hispana who died aged 40 after 22 years' service. An early date is suggested for the tombstone by the absence of a cognomen. British Museum.

These extra resources were used to resume the advance, and a forward policy continued for the next fifteen years. The success of Venutius meant that Brigantia had to be conquered before Wales. IX Hispana was moved forward to a new fortress at York, its place at Lincoln being taken by II Adiutrix; the other legions probably remained at Gloucester and Wroxeter, though Agricola (and presumably his legion) was involved in the campaigns.

Little can be said about those campaigns. The earlier career of Cerealis suggests that he was a rash and impetuous commander. One may suspect that he would never have reached the governorship of Britain but for the prompt and enthusiastic support which he gave to his relative Vespasian in 69: Lower Germany,

20 Tombstone from York of L. Duccius Rufinus, a standard-bearer of IX Hispana. The Yorkshire Museum, York.

21 Tombstone from Lincoln of T. Valerius Pudens, a soldier of II Adiutrix. He died aged 30 after six years' service, and the inscription also records that 'his heir set this up at his own expense'. British Museum.

Britain and a second consulship were his rewards. His achievement in Britain is hard to assess. The enormous fortifications at Stanwick, near Scotch Corner, enclosed 295 hectares (about 850 acres) in their final form; they were destroyed before completion and are plausibly interpreted as a major fortress of Venutius, since they cannot be earlier than the mid-first century. Imagination rather than evidence makes Stanwick the site of Venutius' last stand.

We have Tacitus' authority for the defeat of the Brigantes, but there is little archaeological evidence that Cerealis took serious steps to hold their territory. The first forts at Brough-on-Humber, Hayton and Malton may well be earlier than his governorship, though they continued to be held. The only new fortification known is the legionary fortress at York. It is difficult to escape the conclusion that Cerealis regarded his task as finished when the enemy was beaten, and had little notion of securing the territory of the defeated. His immediate successors were to prove very different in outlook, and between them evolved patterns of control which remained substantially unchanged as long as Rome maintained an army in Britain. It is significant that the defences of York were rebuilt on a far more substantial scale within a decade; though the site itself could scarcely have been better chosen, as its continued importance through the centuries demonstrates.

In 74 Cerealis left Britain, to be succeeded by Sextus Iulius Frontinus. Presumably the reports from Cerealis suggested that no further action was required in Brigantia, for Frontinus turned his attention to the long-deferred conquest of Wales. 'He subdued by force the Silures, a powerful and aggressive tribe, conquering a valorous enemy and a difficult terrain.' For once, archaeology can put a little flesh on the documentary skeleton. A number of temporary camps are known in South Wales and the largest of these must certainly represent the campaigns of Frontinus. The siting of forts like Neath and Loughor at the head of tidal estuaries suggests that Frontinus may have used a fleet to support his army, and perhaps to land troops ahead of his main advance. We have noted a handful of earlier forts in Silurian territory; Frontinus now instituted a carefully planned military occupation of the whole area. The fortress at Usk was not reoccupied, though an auxiliary fort was built there. A new site at Caerleon became the depot of Legio II Augusta. Usk was liable to flooding, and the river was too shallow to allow it to be supplied by water. By contrast the river was still tidal at Caerleon, and Roman quays have been excavated there. The rest of the territory was to be controlled from a series of forts each designed to hold one auxiliary

281

286

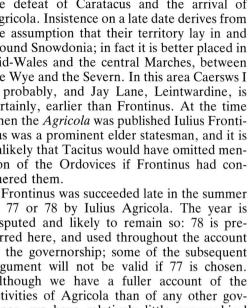

22 Map of Wales in the Flavian period. Garrisons do not seem to have been necessary in the territory of the Deceangli (northeast) or the Demetae (southwest).

cohort or *ala*. These forts were set at intervals of about fifteen to twenty kilometres, allowing easy support in case of attack. A similar system was to be applied with striking success by Agricola in northern Britain. An important feature is the recognition that auxiliary units could stand alone and could undertake routine police and patrol duties.

It is sometimes suggested that Frontinus was also responsible for conquering the Ordovices. There is no evidence for this. They may have been conquered much earlier, for we do not

hear of them opposing the Romans between the defeat of Caratacus and the arrival of Agricola. Insistence on a late date derives from the assumption that their territory lay in and around Snowdonia; in fact it is better placed in mid-Wales and the central Marches, between the Wye and the Severn. In this area Caersws I is probably, and Jay Lane, Leintwardine, is certainly, earlier than Frontinus. At the time when the *Agricola* was published Iulius Frontinus was a prominent elder statesman, and it is unlikely that Tacitus would have omitted mention of the Ordovices if Frontinus had conquered them.

Frontinus was succeeded late in the summer of 77 or 78 by Iulius Agricola. The year is disputed and likely to remain so: 78 is preferred here, and used throughout the account of the governorship; some of the subsequent argument will not be valid if 77 is chosen. Although we have a fuller account of the activities of Agricola than of any other governor, we have relatively little geographical information; there may well be reasonable disagreement about the scene of various campaigns.

Agricola's previous knowledge of the province enabled him to start a brief campaign as soon as he arrived. The Ordovices had almost destroyed an *ala* which was operating in their territory. Agricola inflicted a crushing defeat on them and then moved on to occupy

23 Two successive 'marching camps' at Y Pigwn. On campaign the Roman army would defend its overnight camp with a bank and ditch. The size of the camp was obviously related to the size of the force occupying it.

24 Lead water pipe from the legionary fortress at Chester. It mentions Agricola, and can be dated to AD 79 by the imperial titles mentioned. Grosvenor Museum, Chester.

25 In County Durham and Northumberland the modern A68 still follows the line of Agricola's eastern road into Scotland for long stretches. In the aerial view it is easy to see how the road has been laid out in straight lengths, often changing direction on hill-tops which the Roman surveyors used as sighting points.

26 (opposite) Map of northern Britain under Agricola. Not merely were all the sites marked occupied under Agricola, most of them must have been built in his governorship.

Anglesey; since he had no fleet at hand his auxiliaries had to cross the Menai Strait partly by ford and partly by swimming. This completed the conquest of Wales, and though Tacitus does not tell us so we may be certain that those areas which had been hostile now received an auxiliary garrison. The absence of forts from the southwest and northeast of Wales suggests that the Demetae had welcomed the Romans, and that the Deceangli had caused no trouble after their defeat by Scapula. Over the rest of Wales the pattern of occupation was modelled on that established by Frontinus in Siluria. Forts were established to control the main routes, often close to the junction of two valleys. Apart from those forts already named none has produced certain evidence of occupation before the 70s; archaeology cannot, of course, provide a dating so precise that we can distinguish the forts of Agricola from those of Frontinus. Almost equally startling is that so far only two Roman forts in Wales seem likely to have been founded later than Agricola's time. Here is clear evidence of the strategic genius of these two governors. The military control of the area was completed by the establishment at Chester of a new fortress for the II Adiutrix. It may have been founded by Frontinus, for the lead water pipes were being installed in 79.

According to Tacitus, Agricola spent his first winter in Britain in improving its administration. In particular he sought to impose his own high standards on his subordinates, ending abuses which made Roman taxation more of a burden than was necessary and a source of profit to the collector. Tacitus is describing the behaviour of the ideal governor. Agricola may well have come close to that ideal, but we can be tolerably certain that corruption was not eradicated during his first year of office; it was too much a part of Roman administration.

In 79 Agricola was again leading his army on campaign. We assume that he was operating in northern England and southern Scotland, though Tacitus gives us no precise information: a reference to woods and estuaries is unhelpful, and none of the 'many tribes' whose lands were garrisoned is named. Probably much of the newly occupied territory belonged to the Brigantes or their allies, and had been fought over by Cerealis some six years earlier. The routes of Agricola's advance may be marked by the two principal Roman roads into Scotland. On the west the road corresponds to the line of the A6 and the main railway to Glasgow, running through Warrington, Preston, Lancaster and Carlisle; from there it ran up Annandale towards the Clyde Valley. In the east, Dere Street ran from York to Catterick

and crossed the Tees at Piercebridge, near the Brigantian fortress of Stanwick. Its line through County Durham and Northumberland is close to that of the A68, crossing the Tyne at Corbridge. From here the motorist can still follow the Roman road for long stretches and appreciate the Roman method of surveying from hill-top to hill-top. Roads linking these two routes cover the major Pennine passes.

Himself a provincial, one of the recurrent themes of Tacitus is the relationship between Rome and her provinces. If Roman rule was to last it must be made acceptable – in effect the provincials must become Romans. Agricola therefore had important new tasks in his second winter. In 78–9 Agricola had dealt with the negative aspect: maladministration; now his actions were positive. Encouragement and subsidy were given to religious, public, and private buildings in the Roman style; and excavation has shown major progress in town building during the Flavian period. One inscription survives, from the forum at Verulamium, dated precisely to the second half of 79. It looks almost too good to be true: and so it is. The inscription would be set up when work was completed, and building of the forum must certainly have started some time before Agricola's governorship; but Agricola's recollection of the 'opening ceremony' may lie behind the ascription of schemes of romanization to this winter. For all his provincial sympathies, Tacitus had no doubt about the aims of this policy – 'to accustom scattered, uncultured, and belligerent men to the luxuries of peace and idleness'. 'The ignorant talk of "civilization", which is really a part of their servitude'.

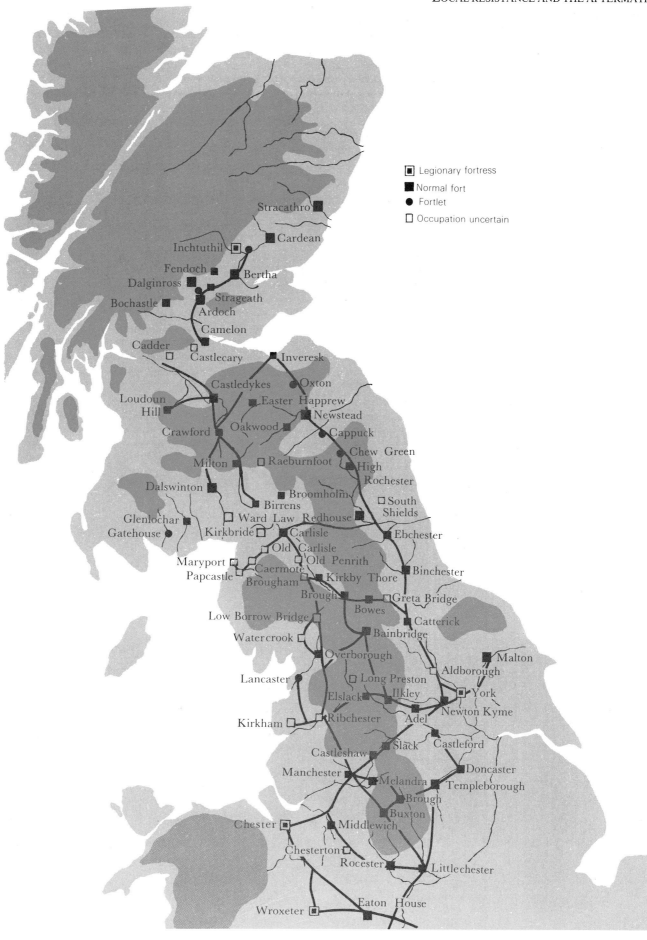

Legionary fortress
Normal fort
Fortlet
Occupation uncertain

Stracathro
Cardean
Inchtuthil
Fendoch
Bertha
Dalginross
Strageath
Bochastle
Ardoch
Camelon
Cadder
Castlecary
Inveresk
Castledykes
Oxton
Loudoun Hill
Easter Happrew
Newstead
Crawford
Oakwood
Cappuck
Chew Green
Milton
Raeburnfoot
High Rochester
Dalswinton
Broomholm
Glenlochar
Birrens
South Shields
Gatehouse
Ward Law
Redhouse
Kirkbride
Carlisle
Ebchester
Old Carlisle
Maryport
Old Penrith
Binchester
Papcastle
Caermote
Kirkby Thore
Brougham
Brough
Greta Bridge
Low Borrow Bridge
Bowes
Catterick
Watercrook
Bainbridge
Overborough
Malton
Lancaster
Aldborough
Long Preston
Elslack
Ilkley
York
Kirkham
Ribchester
Adel
Newton Kyme
Castleshaw
Slack
Castleford
Manchester
Doncaster
Melandra
Templeborough
Brough
Buxton
Chester
Middlewich
Chesterton
Rocester
Littlechester
Eaton House
Wroxeter

In 80 Agricola faced new tribes, campaigning as far north as an estuary called Tanaus and also building forts in conquered territory. This is the first occasion on which Tacitus mentions new tribes, and would make sense if activity in 79 had been confined to the lands of the Brigantes and their allies. The river Tanaus is unknown: it is generally and reasonably supposed to be a copyist's error for Taus, the Tay. Fort building did not necessarily extend so far north – perhaps no further than the Tyne–Solway line: a glance at the map shows that even the forts and roads south of this line represent an enormous building programme. To this must be added the new forts in Wales which may not yet have been completed. The use of timber rather than stone for building doubtless saved time and labour, but it is clear that the army must have been hard worked.

The year 81 was spent in consolidation, and Agricola apparently decided that it would be possible to make a frontier on the Forth–Clyde line. Forts were established there and in the hinterland. The forts on the isthmus have proved elusive; the one thing that is now tolerably certain is that they do not occupy the same sites as those of the Antonine Wall. Agricola did not construct a frontier; he merely pointed out a suitable line if one were deemed necessary. It may be that the emperor Titus, who had succeeded his father Vespasian in 79, had determined to halt the advance at this point. However, Titus died in September 81, to be succeeded by his brother Domitian who had so far played little part in government. It was to be expected that he would at least make a review of policy to see whether changes were required. Agricola had now been in Britain for four years, and might well have hoped for transfer to another province; but all his military experience had been in Britain, and it was by no means sure that he would be as successful in another province with different conditions.

Domitian's solution was to retain Agricola in Britain for a further three years, presumably on the basis of a report that he expected to finish the conquest of the island in that period. While awaiting instructions from Rome Agricola was presumably forbidden to advance further north. 'In his fifth campaigning season [82] Agricola crossed in the leading ship and in sharp and successful fighting conquered tribes hitherto unknown. He spread out his troops in that part of Britain which faces Ireland, in hope rather than fear . . .' The area involved was almost certainly Galloway and Ayrshire, and the army was transported across the Solway to avoid the long and arduous land route. Agricola's dream of an invasion of Ireland with only one legion was probably unrealistic, but the Romans never made the experiment.

By 83 Domitian had evidently accepted Agricola's recommendation to push ahead with

27 Bennachie in Aberdeenshire has been suggested as a possible site for Agricola's victory at Mons Graupius. The large temporary camp of Durno lies in the foreground.

26

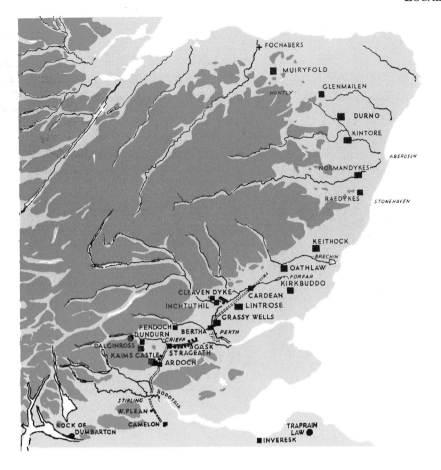

the total conquest of Britain, and he retained Agricola to implement the policy. It is not clear that he allowed Agricola the necessary resources, for in that same year vexillations from each of the four legions were serving on the Rhine. Agricola now advanced north of the Forth. The route lay fairly close to the coast, enabling him to make constant use of the fleet for reconnaissance, to harass the enemy, and to supply his army. Tacitus tells us nothing of the site of this campaign except that it lay beyond the Forth. While it appears to have been successful it did not give Agricola the overwhelming victory needed to bring peace in Britain and prestige at Rome.

In 84 Agricola once again led his forces against the Caledonii and their allies. As in northern England his route was dictated by geography. In Scotland this meant that his advance had to lie east of the Highlands. Once again he used his command of the sea to great advantage. The climax of the campaign, and indeed of his governorship, was an overwhelming victory in a pitched battle at a site called Mons Graupius for which a plausible site has at last been found at Bennachie. Tacitus records 360 Roman casualties and 10,000 British – one-third of their force. The figures are un-

likely to be accurate, but we have no means of correcting them. After the battle the victor marched into the lands of the Boresti; philologists connect the name with Forres on the south side of the Moray Firth. He then returned slowly to his winter quarters, apparently by a route not previously used, since his object was 'to terrify new tribes'. Perhaps he marched through the Highlands instead of through the gentler country to the east. In the winter of 84–5 Agricola was recalled to Rome and given *ornamenta triumphalia* but no further command. His long term in Britain was probably regarded as the equivalent of two normal governorships.

In reaction against Tacitus it has become fashionable to see Agricola as a great organizer rather than a brilliant soldier. This begs the question whether military greatness is not usually dependent on organization. Of Agricola's administrative ability there can be no doubt. Frere estimates that he was responsible for upwards of 70 new forts and 2,100 kilometres of roads. If that stood alone it would be an outstanding achievement. It was in fact an important part of Agricola's military success, for it was by these forts and roads that control was established over the areas con-

28 Map showing Flavian dispositions in Strathmore. These may be the work of Agricola or his successor. The legionary fortress at Inchtuthil, which was the focus of the area, was never finished.

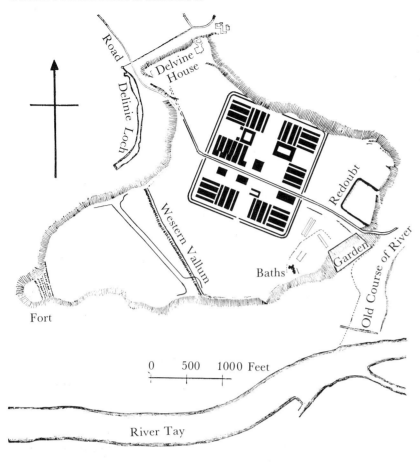

29 Plan of the legionary fortress at Inchtuthil. The small timber headquarters building was probably a temporary measure, intended to be replaced by a larger stone building, and the large house for the legionary legate was never started. The fortress was abandoned shortly before 90, and the whole carefully demolished or rendered useless. (*After* I. Richmond and J. K. St. Joseph.)

quered by Cerealis, Frontinus and himself. Frontinus may have invented the system, but Agricola grasped its importance and extended it over a vastly greater area. In his concept of combined operations with the fleet he was far ahead of most of his contemporaries, and though his reliance on auxiliaries in defence, and in battle at Mons Graupius, was not a complete innovation it was by no means standard military practice. Agricola completed the conquest of Wales, consolidated the work of Cerealis in Brigantia, and not merely fought over much of Scotland but also brought under control the area as far north as Strathmore; this gave the possibility of dominating the Highlands without the expense of occupation. His real genius lay in seeing beyond a battle to the imposition of permanent control over conquered territory; this implies a strategic insight and a vision which are in marked contrast to the attitudes of most Roman generals who sought little more than glorious victories in battle.

Agricola handed over to his successor a province which was 'peaceful and secure'. Unfortunately we cannot determine whether the military dispositions north of the Forth represent Agricola's plan for control of the Highlands, or whether they were the work of an unknown successor with less confidence in what had been achieved or in what could be

held. The best evidence comes from Inchtuthil, a new legionary fortress at the mouth of the Great Glen, presumably intended for XX Valeria Victrix. This was abandoned before it had been completed and the timber buildings were carefully demolished. The iron nails were buried to prevent them from falling into enemy hands, for they would provide a supply of iron which could easily be re-forged into weapons or tools. The demolition layers contained coins of 86 and possibly 87 in mint condition, and abandonment must have come by 90 at the latest. It was the focus for a whole series of forts in Strathmore which effectively controlled access to and egress from the Highlands by all practical southward routes. Agricola or his successor evidently decided that occupation of the Highlands was impossible or unnecessary and devised an alternative strategy (though it is possible that Agricola saw Inchtuthil as the starting point for further advance northwards).

We have no means of knowing whether this strategy would have proved adequate, for before 92, and probably in 86 or 87, Roman reverses on the Danube compelled Domitian to withdraw Legio II Adiutrix from Britain. Legio XX had to be moved to Chester to take its place, both Wroxeter and Inchtuthil being abandoned. With the abandonment of Inchtuthil came the evacuation of Strathmore and most of the forts north of the Forth–Clyde line. Many of the forts in southern Scotland were rebuilt with stronger defences and in some cases for larger garrisons; but no attempt was made to create a formal frontier, a concept which the Romans were only just developing as the period of expansion drew towards its close. In Britain that period really ended with the recall of Agricola.

From then until the reign of Hadrian we have very little information from either documents or inscriptions. The withdrawal from Strathmore in the late 80s was followed by the violent destruction of forts as far south as the Tyne–Solway line. Coins from Corbridge, the most southerly fort involved, suggest that destruction was later than 98 and rebuilding after 103. The very slight evidence from other sites is usually taken to imply a date *c.* 100–5. This poses problems. The first books of the *Histories* of Tacitus were probably written before 105. Introducing the themes which would occupy him in that work Tacitus says 'Britain was conquered and at once abandoned'. This judgement on the Flavian period implies a very sophisticated interpretation of the dispositions in Strathmore, if that was all that had been given up before the death of Domitian in 96: with the abandonment of the defensive positions in Strathmore went all hope of controlling the areas beyond it. If we could date the second withdrawal from Scotland to the last years of Domitian – which is possible if we regard the destruction at Corbridge as a later, isolated, incident – the Tacitean epigram would have more force. Moreover, if we do not do this, we must surely put this withdrawal after the composition and publication of Book I of the *Histories*: even Tacitus would scarcely have commented adversely on Domitian's abandonment of British territory a year or two after Trajan had given up a far more extensive area. There is evidence to suggest a British war in the mid- or late 90s, and if this occurred before 96 (or even before the accession of Trajan in 97) it might be the occasion on which the forts of southern Scotland were abandoned.

Little need, or indeed can, be said about the sole reign of Trajan (98–117). Elsewhere it was a period of dramatic expansion. Dacia was conquered, Arabia annexed, and in his last years the Emperor was attempting to extend his rule far beyond the Euphrates: this over-ambitious policy ended abruptly with Trajan's death. Britain appears to have been almost a backwater. Southern Scotland may have been lost early in the reign, and at some date between 103 and 117 Cohors I Cugernorum acquired the battle-honours *Ulpia Traiana*. The only other activity known is the rebuilding in stone of the defences of all three legionary fortresses; this should be seen as an indication that the period of conquest was ended.

30, 31

31 Inscription from York, dating the rebuilding of a gate to the reign of Trajan, about 107–8. The Yorkshire Museum, York.

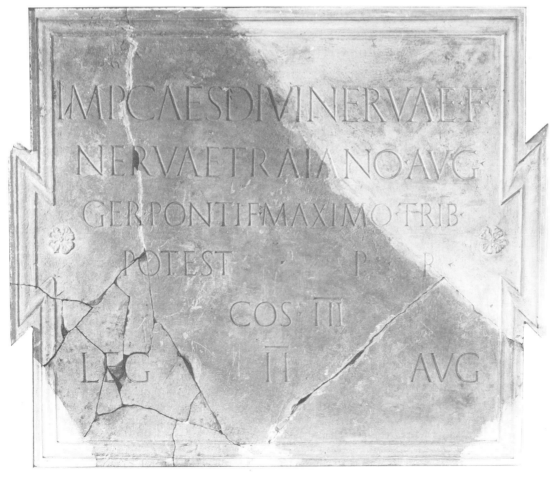

30 Inscription from the legionary fortress at Caerleon, Gwent, dating the rebuilding of the west gate to AD 100. Caerleon Museum.

CHAPTER II
SOCIAL ORGANIZATION

Military

The Roman army was not merely an instrument of military conquest. It provided the first contact for a majority of Britons with a number of basic Roman institutions: the concept of a systematic and hierarchical organization which reached beyond local and tribal boundaries; the equally systematic levying of taxation to support that organization and others; the use of large quantities of coin, which the army received and spent and the tax-collector then recovered; the Latin language; various techniques of building and construction; road and water engineering; and, perhaps the greatest change of all, the public enforcement of law and of peace.

It is misleading to think of the Roman army simply as Romans. There were three main branches of the service: the legions, the auxiliaries and the fleet. Of these, only the legions were exclusively composed of men with the status of Roman citizens, and even this did not mean that they were actually born in Rome, or even in Italy. The auxiliaries, who constituted a good half of the whole army, were mostly provincial subjects. In some cases they were recruited from outside the limits of the Empire. Being in that way not far different from the native regiments of the British army in India, the Roman military units which most Britons encountered were formed of men with a very similar background to their own. The pp. 38–9 popular picture of Hadrian's Wall as the last outpost of shivering Italians is one very far from the truth.

Organization and Equipment of the Army – the Legions

The legion was the basic formation of the Roman army. Three, or on occasion four, were stationed in Britain, of which Legions II Augusta and XX served there continuously from the time of the Conquest in AD 43. By the end of the first century their permanent bases were fixed at York, Chester and Caerleon-on-Usk, forming the three main points on the base line which divided the civilian lowland zone from Wales and northern Britain, where some form of military occupation continued for most of the Roman period.

Each legion had an establishment of 5,000–5,300 men. It was divided into ten cohorts, of which the first numbered 800 and the remainder 480 men each, theoretically. The nine ordinary cohorts were further subdivided into six units of command, the centuries, so-called, though their actual strength was about eighty men. The first cohort had five centuries of double that size. There were also 120 mounted men attached to each legion, too few in number to have been of much use tactically as cavalry, though they did supplement the auxiliary cavalry in battle occasionally. Their main use was for reconnaissance and as escorts and despatch riders.

The legionaries were infantry soldiers, heavily armed with standard equipment and highly trained and disciplined. The training included arms drill, route marches, assault courses and practice in building camps and forts, such as those at Cawthorn in Yorkshire, constructed as training exercises by Legio IX from York.

A legionary's personal weapons included a short broad-bladed sword, the *gladius*, a dagger (*pugio*) and a throwing-spear seven feet long, the *pilum*. There were also two main types of artillery weapon, the *ballista*, which fired an iron-headed bolt, and the *onager*, which launched a large rock. These catapults had an effective range of 300–400 metres. 32 33 34

For protection, a legionary wore a helmet and body armour of various types. The most common was the *lorica segmentata*, composed of iron plates held together by a strapwork of leather underneath, hinges and buckles at the shoulder and chest, and laces down front and back. It combined the advantages of durability, flexibility and the easy replacement of damaged parts. It was worn over a woollen tunic. Other types of body armour consisted of scales wired to the tunic, and shirts of chain-mail. The legionary's dress was completed by a stud-

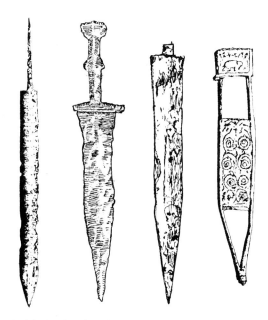

ded belt, leather knee-breeches, a thick cloak and heavy hob-nailed sandals. He carried a rectangular metal-bound shield of laminated wood or hardened leather.

The permanent career officers in a legion were the centurions. These men might have worked their way up through junior ranks in the century, among which was the *optio*, so-called because he had originally been *chosen* by the centurion as his second-in-command. It was also not uncommon for a man who had served in the Emperor's Praetorian Guard to move directly to a post as legionary centurion, and there were other instances of direct entry or accelerated promotion to the centurionate for a man with appropriate qualifications. His pay as well as his position made the centurion a man of importance. He had enough money to own slaves, for example: the tombstone of M. Favonius Facilis was erected at Colchester by his freed slaves Verecundus and Novicius.

Favonius is shown holding in his right hand the vine stick which was both the emblem of a centurion's office and the instrument by which he enforced discipline with corporal punishment. His position had its perquisites. Bribery of the centurion to avoid routine duties was not uncommon.

The senior centurions in a legion were those of the first cohort, of whom the *primus pilus* ranked highest and had considerable additional responsibilities. Promotion did not confine a centurion to the legion he had first joined or to the same province: he was quite likely to have served in two or three legions on his way up. The highest post that a centurion might reach after being *primus pilus* was that of camp prefect, whose main responsibilities were those of quartermaster.

The other officers in the legion, superior to the centurions, held their positions as part of the separate career structures of the upper two ranks of Roman society, the senatorial and equestrian orders, whose public service included both military and civilian posts. The career of an *eques*, or knight, which may have begun with a municipal magistracy, normally involved three military appointments, of which the second was service as a tribune, usually in a legion. A legion had six tribunes, who acted mainly as staff officers. Five of these were equestrian, called the *tribuni angusticlavi*, denoting the narrow purple stripe on the border of their toga in civilian life. After their military service they would hope to become procurators in the imperial civil service. The sixth tribunate was a first post for a young man of senatorial family, whose status entitled him to a broad stripe on his toga, the *tribunus laticlavius*. Previous service as tribune was the only military experience a senator would normally have had before returning to command a legion as its *legate*, after holding posts in the financial

34 (above) Model of an *onager* (siege engine). Museum of Roman Civilization, Rome.

32 (above left) The legionary soldier's weapons: *spatha* (two-edged sword); *pugio* (dagger); and *gladius* (broad-bladed sword), with decorated sheath, from Fulham. (Not to scale.) See illus. 35 for the *pilum* (throwing spear).

33 Reconstruction of a *ballista* at Chesterholm (Vindolanda) fort.

HADRIAN'S WALL

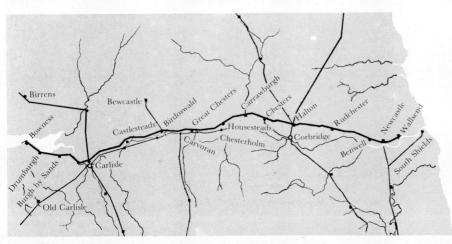

Two similar turrets (below) were built into the Wall between each milecastle. Milecastles and turrets on the turf wall were built of stone. Their line was continued for 26 miles or more down along the Cumberland coast.

The emperor Hadrian visited Britain in AD 122. As a result, the wall named after him was built from the Tyne to the Solway Firth, serving as a fortified base line for the northern garrison. In the central sector it rises along basalt ridges to command magnificent views of the country to the north. Further west, in closer country, it was less advantageously placed, and forts north of the line of the wall at Birrens, Bewcastle, and Netherby helped to control the territory. Active operations north of the wall were part of the concept. It was an obstacle to aggressive enemy movement rather than a shelter for a timid defender.

The original design, modified in the course of construction, consisted of a wall with a ditch in front of it. Its first 45 miles, up to the River Irthing, consisted of a stone wall ten feet wide. From there westwards, since limestone for the mortar was not locally available, the wall was built of turf.

Spaced at intervals of about one Roman mile along the Wall were small forts or milecastles (above), built behind a gateway which permitted controlled access through it. The milecastles contained barrack-rooms for between eight and thirty-two men, and the gate had a watchtower above it.

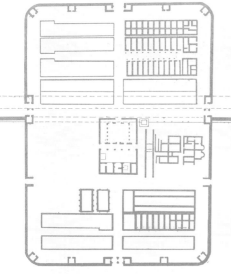

The Wall was constructed by the Legions II Augusta, VI and XX, each being allotted various sectors. The stages of the work proceeded at different rates: laying the foundations, building milecastles and turrets, and completing the wall. The first modification was the addition of new forts to the line of the Wall. The cavalry fort at Chesters (left), for example, was built across the ditch and Wall foundations and a demolished turret. The Wall was also reduced in thickness to between six and eight feet.

A continuous earthwork was added behind the Wall and its forts, a flat-bottomed ditch with a bank on each side, known as the Vallum. It demarcated the military zone and protected it against approach from the rear. In due course, forts like Chesters received such amenities as bath-houses (below), and attracted the usual external settlements. Allowing for all the changes in design, apart from the rebuilding of the turf wall in stone, which was done later, the whole enterprise took about four years to complete, with a work-force of 10,000–15,000 men. By any standards, it was a splendid achievement of organization and engineering.

The forts were placed at an average distance of 7⅓ miles apart. The names of several are given on a bronze bowl, the Rudge Cup, which is decorated with a representation of the Wall, apparently showing it with crenellations, our only evidence for its superstructure (Museum of Antiquities, Newcastle upon Tyne).

The bulk of the garrison of auxiliary cavalry and infantry was initially stationed at forts a mile or two to the rear of the Wall along the earlier Stanegate road between Carlisle and Corbridge. The fort at Chesterholm (Vindolanda) was tactically placed to control the point where the Stanegate crossed the steep defile of a small burn. Its line is followed by a modern track, and Hadrian's Wall runs along the ridges about a mile to the north.

One of the old Stanegate forts remained as a key site in the Roman occupation of the north. Corbridge (above), two miles south of the Wall, where Dere Street, the main Roman road to Scotland, crossed the River Tyne, was reoccupied when, twenty years after Hadrian's Wall was built, his successor Antoninus Pius moved the frontier north. The granaries at Corbridge were built to hold supplies for the associated campaign. Subsequently, it was retained as an important stores base and legionary workshop servicing the northern garrison.

The move north resulted in the building of a new wall from the Forth to the Clyde, this time completely of turf, though with forts partially built of stone. This, the Antonine Wall, was also built by the legions. An inscription from the east end at Bridgeness, records the completion of four miles of it. The scene on the right depicts a commemorative sacrifice by the commander of the IInd Legion. After the Antonine Wall was abandoned, probably in the 160s AD, Hadrian's Wall and its outpost forts remained the basis for Roman occupation in the north. (National Museum of Antiquities, Edinburgh.)

and legal administration. He would then be in his late thirties and his next appointment would be a provincial governorship. Julius Agricola, for example, had three spells of duty in Britain: as legionary tribune at the time of Boudicca's rebellion; as commander of Legio XX; and finally between AD 78 and 84 as Governor of the province.

This remained the basic structure up to the third century. In the late third and fourth centuries the military and civilian administration was radically reorganized by the emperors Diocletian and Constantine, at a time of considerable social change.

A legion had to be self-sufficient in almost all the functions which in a modern army are provided by specialist branches of the service. It needed carpenters, wheelwrights, blacksmiths, armourers, stonemasons, potters, tilemakers, architects, surveyors, water engineers, clerks, priests and doctors. The legionaries who were trained to do many of these things might be rewarded by being excused routines, such as guard duty and cleaning the latrines, or by higher rates of pay. Every legionary was equipped to build as well as to fight, with a

saw, a carrying-basket, a hook, a rope and a hand pick-axe.

The ability to undertake such diverse activities made the Roman legions more than just a military instrument. The roads which they pioneered for strategic purposes also opened new lines of communication for all who cared to use them. Experience in the engineering of aqueducts could be made available to provide water for newly founded civilian towns. The legions worked in the mines – inscriptions record that Legio II Augusta controlled early lead-workings in the Mendips. Others mention some of the legionaries who formed the administrative staff of the provincial governor in London. Many of these skills were also valuable in later civilian life.

Organization and Equipment of the Army – the Auxiliaries

The auxiliary troops of the Roman army differed from the legions in that they did not have to be Roman citizens to join. Indeed, that status was the reward that they received on discharge, and therefore a great incentive to recruitment. On occasion, a whole unit which distinguished itself was given citizenship en bloc. As time went on, more and more inhabitants of the provinces inherited that status, so that the distinction had come to mean much less by the time that the emperor Caracalla in AD 212 or 214 extended the citizenship to all free-born inhabitants of the Empire.

Many auxiliary regiments were first raised from newly conquered provincials. It was a convenient way of harnessing their warlike traditions. Several regiments of Britons were formed in the years after AD 43 and transferred to the Rhine and Danube garrisons.

The auxiliaries provided for the Roman army a number of special fighting abilities. Most important among these was the cavalry, recruited principally from such areas famous for their horsemanship as Gaul, Spain and Thrace, as was Longinus, a Thracian cavalryman commemorated on his tombstone at Colchester. Syrian archers and sling-shot men from the Balearics, for example, increased the range of battle skills at the disposal of Roman commanders.

The auxiliary regiments formed much smaller units than the legions, with nominal strengths which the Romans expressed in round figures of 500 and 1,000, quingenary and milliary units, though their actual numbers were usually rather less. The size was appropriate for their main peace-time function, the garrisoning of a chain of small forts strung out over the area of military occupation. There were three types of regiment: of cavalry, named *ala* (wing); cohorts of infantry; and part-mounted cohorts. Milliary cohorts were less common than quingenary, and the milliary

18,
262

37 Third-century AD bronze cavalry parade helmet found in the river Wensum, Worthing, Norfolk. Norwich Castle Museum.

ala rarer still: Britain had only one, the *Ala Petriana* stationed for much of its time at Stanwix, near Carlisle.

The regiments were commanded by men of equestrian status. Often they were members of the landowning class, but the senior centurions of a legion would, on retirement, usually be rich enough to qualify. Commanders of a quingenary unit had the title Prefect, those of a milliary unit, Tribune. The sequence was normally: prefect of a cohort; tribune in a legion or of a milliary cohort; prefect of an *ala*. For men of exceptional ability, a fourth command as tribune of a milliary *ala* might follow. The rank structure of an auxiliary cohort was similar to that of its legionary counterpart. An *ala* was divided into *turmae* or squadrons, of which there were apparently sixteen in a quingenary and twenty-four in a milliary *ala*. The *turmae* were commanded by decurions.

In addition, irregular units of infantry and cavalry were raised from the more barbarous peoples in the frontier regions, for use against their own kind. They were known as *numeri* and *cunei* (wedges) respectively, and since their members were mostly illiterate, we know little about them, for they produced few of the inscriptions which have told us so much about the rest of the Roman army. At least ten

35 (opposite left) Model of a fully equipped Roman legionary soldier. Caerleon Museum.

36 (opposite right) Tombstone of Marcus Favonius Facilis, a legionary centurion, from Colchester. Colchester Museum.

numeri of Britons are recorded on the Upper German frontier in the first half of the second century. Presumably they were recruited following one of the northern campaigns of Agricola, Hadrian or Antoninus Pius. In the third century the fort at Housesteads on Hadrian's Wall contained a *cuneus* of Frisians and a *numerus* named after its German commander Hnaudifrid.

The equipment of the auxiliaries was varied, and to a large extent derived from the weapons and dress of their native lands. The long sword, or *spatha*, was used instead of the *gladius*, and the shield was usually oval. Cavalry were armed with spears, swords or in some cases bows. Chain-mail was the most usual form of armour. The Thracian cavalryman Longinus is shown on his tombstone wearing a tunic with scale armour, and his horse has a saddle-cloth and harness with decorative roundels at the junctions of the straps.

18

The Fleet

Since the Romans did not have to encounter any great sea power, the function of the fleet was to transport and supply the army rather than to fight, and its status was correspondingly inferior. The *Classis Britannica*, as the fleet attached to the Roman army in Britain was entitled, was based in part at Dover, where its fort has been excavated; at Lympne, where an inscription set up by the prefect who commanded it has been found; and at Boulogne. Apart from regular transport between Britain and the Continent, its chief periods of activity were in conjunction with large-scale campaigns in the north, bringing supplies up the coast to such stores bases as South Shields. Transport of bulk goods was considerably easier and quicker, and consequently cheaper, by water than

280

38 Large building tile stamped with the mark of the *Classis Britannica*. From Beauport Park, Sussex.

overland. It is no accident that legionary fortresses were sited on easily navigable rivers, and some of the harbour installations have been excavated at Chester and Caerleon.

During the second century sailors were employed in the iron industry of the Weald, to judge from the discovery at iron-working sites there of tiles stamped with the fleet's abbreviated designation CL.BR. The *Classis Britannica* came more into its own late in the third century in dealing with attacks by Germanic sea-raiders. The construction of a chain of coastal forts from Brancaster in Norfolk to Portchester in Hampshire had begun earlier in the century, although the series was not completed until about AD 286, the year in which Carausius was given a special command to deal with the raiders. He appears to have been successful in the combined operations which included the use of ships with camouflaged sails to intercept the pirates. The forts are known as those of the Saxon Shore, which was the name of the coastal defence command in the late fourth century. Unfortunately, nothing is known about any British fleet that the Count of the Saxon Shore then had under him in addition to his field army.

38

39

279

228

Forts and Fortresses

Although no two legionary fortresses or auxiliary forts are exactly alike, all have a number of features in common, for they represent an orderly system devised for the efficient performance of a number of military functions. Their defences, a rampart, wall and ditch, are oblong in plan with rounded corners except in some late Roman forts. In earlier forts, ramparts were of turf and buildings of timber, but from the beginning of the second century it was more usual to build in stone, particularly where permanence was expected. There are gates in the middle of each short side from one of which a street leads to a T-junction with the main street across the fort, which connects gates placed about a third of the way along the two long sides. At this junction is the headquarters building, the focal point of the fort, with a courtyard, a large hall and offices at the back. To one side of this a large courtyard-house provided the commanding officer with accommodation of the kind to which one of his social rank was accustomed. Other main buildings are the buttressed granaries, with raised floors to protect the stores from damp and vermin; workshops; and in a legionary fortress, baths, a hospital and tribunes' houses. Auxiliary forts usually had baths outside the walls, and only rarely a hospital. Barrack blocks, one per century, contained pairs of rooms shared by about eight men, a verandah in front and larger quarters for the centurion and *optio*.

40

41

256

42

pp.
58–9

250

43

39 Aerial view of the Saxon Shore fort at Portchester, at the head of Portsmouth Harbour, Hampshire.

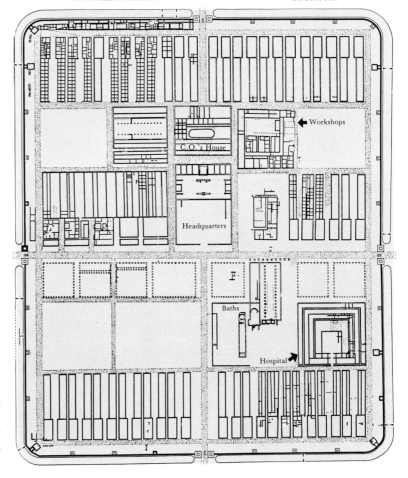

40 Plan of the legionary fortress at Caerleon.

Conditions of Service

By the second century the term of service for both legionaries and auxiliaries was 25 years. Whereas in the early Empire the legions were still mainly recruited in Italy, the pattern altered in favour of the provinces in which the legions were stationed. From Hadrian's reign onwards, Italy contributed barely 1% of the soldiers whose origins are known. Several factors favoured local recruitment: service on the frontiers was decreasingly attractive to men in Italy and the remoter provinces; extension of Roman citizenship increased the number of provincials eligible to serve; sons followed their fathers' profession. The same seems to have applied to the auxiliaries, for whom we have the additional evidence of the engraved bronze diplomas which they received on discharge as copies of the decree which gave them citizenship. Although some specialists, like Syrian archers, continued to be drawn from the provinces in which their units were first raised, in most cases local recruitment meant that an *ala* of Thracians or a cohort of Spaniards, for example, might have few of those nations serving in it. We lack much direct evidence for Britain, but there is no reason to suppose that it was any different from other provinces. By the end of the second century, many soldiers serving in Britain had probably been born

43

41 Reconstructed gateway and defences of the Roman fort at The Lunt, Baginton, near Coventry, Warwickshire.

42 Reconstruction of the timber granary at The Lunt, Baginton. It now houses the site museum.

diplomas as receiving citizenship at the same time as the soldiers. Such male children would then, as citizens, be eligible to join the legions.

A military career was attractive; there was little problem in recruiting volunteers, at least during the first two centuries AD. A soldier had both status and money; the two were not unconnected. Legionaries, in addition to their regular pay, received substantial bounties from most emperors on their accession and some-times on other occasions. They also received a cash sum on discharge, the equivalent to the grants of land on retirement which had been the earlier practice. Auxiliaries received only their pay; even so, this was often a much better income than that enjoyed by most ordinary provincials, one which did not depend on the success or failure of crops or on the fluctuations of trade.

Out of his pay a soldier had to provide for many necessities. Staple rations of wheat, cooking oil or fat, table wine, and perhaps other basic foodstuffs like salt and vegetables, were provided. Deductions were made from pay, however, towards the cost of issued ra-tions. An important source of meat was the animals sacrificed at the religious ceremonies which were a regular feature of camp life. Otherwise, and particularly in peacetime, it was up to the individual soldier to supplement his diet as he chose. The evidence of bones excavated at military sites shows that a wide variety of domesticated and hunted animals were eaten, as well as fish, oysters, mussels and other shellfish, and snails. He also had to prepare and cook meals for himself. The army had no catering corps, and the Roman fort no mess hall. Bread-ovens were built into the earth ramparts of fortress defences, but sol-diers did their own baking. The centuries were divided into *contubernia*, groups of about eight men who shared a tent in camp, a pair of barrack-rooms in the fort, and a quernstone for grinding flour. Generally, they cooked and ate together.

Deductions were also made from a soldier's pay for clothing and the replacement of equip-ment. Much standard equipment was made and repaired in the legion's workshops, but a specially decorated sword or a fine set of harness decorations could be had if a man paid for his choice. He also contributed to camp feasts, and to the fund for funeral expenses which was kept by the standard-bearer.

Some of the soldier's recreation was pro-vided within the fort. As in Roman civilian life, the baths were not only somewhere to get clean, but also a place for games, conversation with friends and relaxation. Legionary fortres-ses and some forts had amphitheatres for mili-tary displays and for gladiators and wild-beast shows. The many religious feasts and festivals observed by the army provided variations from

there, whatever the name of their regiments.

In order to have sons to follow their profes-sion, legionaries had to get round the obstacle that during their service they were prohibited from marriage. That did not, of course, mean that they were expected to be celibate; apart from having girl-friends or more transitory relationships, some soldiers, particularly when long-stationed in one place, contracted what we would call common-law marriages and pro-duced children. If the women were not Roman citizens themselves, nor would be the children, but recruiting officers might well have turned a blind eye to such irregularities. It is not clear how these matters were rectified after the legionary had been discharged and could legally marry.

Auxiliaries, though probably under the same prohibition, could at least make marriages valid by native law. Certainly, the existence of their families was officially recognized to the extent that wives and children were named on the calendar's routine and, as numerous altars erected by all ranks bear witness, a deeper spiritual satisfaction. The veneration of the unit's emblems, the standards enshrined in the chapel in the headquarters building, reinforced the soldier's ties with his legion, *ala* or cohort. Sacrifice on the birthdays of living and deified emperors renewed the bonds of loyalty to his supreme commander. The worship of the gods to whom he was particularly devoted assured him of their favour towards him.

45, 46

Outside the fort, there were other attractions. The market provided by a large number of men settled in one place with money to spend led to the growth of substantial civilian settlements beyond the fort gates. There, the soldier could buy food, good wine and clothes. There were inns where he could gamble and drink, and presumably there were brothels. If he had a wife, she would have had to live there, in the civilian lines, for only equestrian or senatorial officers had accommodation for their families within the fort walls. There too, if the soldier owned slaves or had freed them, they might well run a little business for him on the side. Beyond, in the country, he could hunt for sport and for the pot. And when his discharge came, it was quite often in the town, next to the fort where he had spent most of his adult life, that the veteran made his home.

Civil Administration and Law

The Emperor and his Deputies

When Julius Caesar invaded Britain in 55 and 54 BC, he did so in his capacity as Roman proconsul, or governor, of Gaul. At that time, the Senate and People of Rome administered the territory which they controlled outside peninsular Italy by allotting the government of areas to senators who had held office as elected magistrates in Rome, the consuls and praetors. As pro-consuls and pro-praetors, they served as the equivalent of the magistrates in Rome, and administered the charters which had been enacted by the assembly of the Roman people when the provinces were formed.

The civil wars between Caesar's and Pompey's factions, and later between Caesar's great-nephew and heir Octavian and Mark Antony, culminated in the exhausted acceptance of the monarchy of Octavian, the ultimate victor. Rome's long anti-monarchist tradition, however, required that the reality of power be concealed behind a facade of established Republican institutions.

In 27 BC the Senate voted Octavian the honour of an additional surname, Augustus, by which thenceforth he was known. The names Caesar and Augustus became the titles by which the Romans referred to the emperors who succeeded him. The 'emperor' initially owed his position to the fact that he was voted, for life or recurrently, a number of republican offices which had formerly been held separately and annually. Among these was the proconsular governorship of most of the Roman provinces in which the legions were stationed. He administered both the legions and these provinces through deputies, called legates. Thus, the commander of a legion was the *Legatus Legionis*, and the governor of an imperial province like Britain the *Legatus Augusti Pro Praetore*, the Deputy of the Emperor with the authority of a Praetor, who was directly responsible to the emperor for his appointment and his conduct.

Other chief officials in the province's administration owed their position equally to the delegated authority of the emperor as nominal proconsul. The procurator, or imperial agent, of the province of Britain was responsible, again, directly to the emperor and so independently of the governor, for the collection of taxes and other aspects of provincial finance. Others with the title of procurator superintended the exploitation of mines and minerals, which were State property, and the emperor's personal estates in the province. We have records of procurators in Britain in charge of the taxation census, of a State weaving factory, and of the gladiators here and in other north-western provinces.

By the time Britain was made a province of

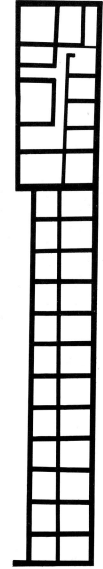

43 Plan of a typical legionary barrack block at Caerleon.

44 Legionary Eagle and standards inlaid in bronze on a sword blade from South Shields. Museum of Antiquities, Newcastle upon Tyne.

45 Gilded bronze eagle found in excavations of the forum at Silchester, thought likely to have come from an imperial statue. Collection of His Grace the Duke of Wellington, Stratfield Saye House, Hampshire.

46 Bronze decoration showing the vexillations of Legio II Augusta and Legio XX Valeria Victrix. Bibliothèque Nationale, Paris.

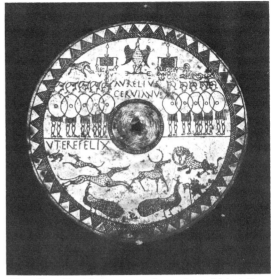

Claudius Cogidubnus, native ruler of his tribe. It, too, is a symbol; the gods protected the dynasty; they sanctified the emperor's power and justified the obedience of his deputies and those whom they governed on his behalf.

Central Administration: the First and Second Centuries

A governor of Britain already had a distinguished career behind him. He was a Roman senator. He had been quaestor, or financial administrator, in Rome or one of the provinces; as praetor, he had presided over Roman law-courts; he had commanded a legion, and had usually governed one or two other provinces, often on the Rhine or Danube frontiers, and had been consul, presiding over meetings of the legislature in Rome. We are used to more specialized career structures; but the Roman system provided indispensable experience for a post which combined the roles of civilian administrator, chief justice and commander-in-chief.

Rome by Claudius in AD 43, the monarchy was an accepted reality. In describing the revolt led by Boudicca in AD 60, the historian Tacitus referred to the great temple of Claudius at Colchester, dedicated after his death to his deified spirit, as a symbol of Britain's subjection, 'the citadel of Rome's eternal domination'. The emperor and Rome were seen as one, which indeed was the policy behind the establishment of the joint worship of Rome and Augustus in the provinces. At Chichester a

14, 47 temple to Neptune and Minerva was erected 'for the well-being of the divine household', that is, the imperial family, by a guild of metalworkers under the authority of Tiberius

47 Inscription from the temple of Neptune and Minerva at Chichester, erected under the authority of Ti. Claudius Cogidubnus, King of the Regni. Chichester. (See also illus. 14.)

The military function was important. It was often for his capacity in that role that he was selected, and by his performance in it that he was judged. Suetonius Paulinus, for example, appointed in AD 58 to conquer the hill tribes of Wales, had previously campaigned against the Mauretanians, when he became the first Roman to cross the Atlas Mountains. Iulius Agricola's previous experience in Britain as military tribune under Paulinus in Wales and as legionary legate campaigning in northern England made him a natural choice for a governor whose task was to complete the conquest of Wales and the north.

Agricola's biography by his son-in-law Tacitus makes it clear that even for a governor who was active and successful in war there were other equally important duties. He checked the maladministration of his subordinates. He toured the province to judge lawsuits. He encouraged urban development and the education of the provincials. He was responsible, too, for the system of trunk roads and posting stations which served the *cursus publicus*, the imperial despatch service, and those moving about the province on official business.

The staff of the governor's headquarters, the *praetorium*, consisted in the first place of men detached from service with the legions, with a centurion at their head as *princeps praetorii*. Among them were thirty *speculatores*, who assisted the governor in his judicial functions by guarding criminals awaiting trial or execution, and who acted as official messengers. The tombstone of one of them, Celsus of Legio II Augusta, has been found in London. There were also *beneficiarii* whose work seems to have been away from headquarters as intelligence officers, as organizers of supplies and in the maintenance of roads and posting stations. In addition, the governor needed a large secretarial and clerical staff, normally composed of slaves and freedmen, and he usually had with him a number of friends and unofficial advisers.

It seems clear that by the second century the governor's headquarters were in London. In addition to Celsus' tombstone there are those of a centurion and soldiers of Legions II, VI and XX, for whose presence service in the *praetorium* would be the likeliest explanation. There is the early second-century fort at Cripplegate, which also seems best explained as the accommodation of the legate's infantry and cavalry escort. In addition, the remains of a palatial building of the late first century under Cannon Street Station, with a huge audience hall and an ornamental garden, seem likely to have been the governor's official residence.

Originally, Camulodunum (Colchester) was an obvious site for the centre of Roman provincial government. It had been the chief place of

48 An artist's reconstruction of a palatial building, possibly the governor's residence, at London. (*Drawn by* Alan Sorrell.)

49 Tomb of Iulius Classicianus, procurator of the province of Britain, from London. Reconstructed in the British Museum.

51 (right) Inscription from Nomentum (in Central Italy) in honour of Cn. Munatius Bassus, *censitor* of Camulodunum. Vatican Museum, Rome.

50 Stamp of the procurator of the province of Britain on a wooden writing tablet from London. British Museum.

have been older than the average. Procurators were graded according to their annual salary, at 60, 100, 200 and 300 thousand sesterces.

The career in Britain of M. Maenius Agrippa provides a good illustration. His auxiliary commands included a cohort of Britons in Moesia, on the Danube, and a cohort of Spaniards in Britain under Hadrian. Subsequently, he returned to Britain as prefect of the *Classis Britannica*, a procuratorial appointment worth 100,000 sesterces, and finally served as procurator of the province at 200,000, the climax of his career, as it was for most of those known to have held the post.

The provincial procurator's position, independent of the governor, sometimes brought them into conflict, as is shown by the dispute between Classicianus and the governor Suetonius Paulinus over the latter's repressive policy after Boudicca's rebellion. Classicianus foresaw that this would prevent the province's economic recovery, and complained to Rome. Suetonius was eventually recalled.

The main responsibility of the provincial procurator was the collection of taxes: the *annona*, the levy of grain which fed the army, and tribute. The *tributum soli* was a tax on land, the *tributum capitis* a tax on other forms of property, against which immunity might be granted to favoured communities. The basis of taxation was the census of property, for which special procurators were periodically appointed. Cn. Munatius Bassus, for example, died in Italy having in his time served as *censitor* of the Roman citizens in Camulodunum. Indirect taxes included duties of 2–5% on goods which crossed certain provincial boundaries, and on the sale or liberation of slaves. Roman citizens also paid a 5% inheritance tax.

51

the most powerful tribal rulers in southern Britain, the Catuvellauni. In AD 49 the former fortress there of Legio XX was given urban status as a *colonia*, and Camulodunum became the first town in Britain to be laid out on the Roman model. But the point at which the new Roman road from the Kentish coast crossed the Thames was a much more convenient centre for the network of communications going northwards and westwards, and a settlement of merchants and traders, Londinium, grew rapidly. Its geographical advantages over Camulodunum soon became clear. The provincial procurator's office had almost certainly been transferred to Londinium by the time of Boudicca's rebellion, since the then procurator, Catus Decianus, was evidently not based at Camulodunum. His successor, Iulius Classicianus, died and was buried in Londinium. A wooden writing tablet with the official stamp of the provincial procurator has also been found in the City.

Some procurators were imperial freedmen, but most were of the equestrian order, whose earlier career had involved three periods of service as army officers. Their qualification for equestrian rank depended on the possession of property worth 400,000 sesterces. This may be compared with the property qualification of a million sesterces for senators, or with the annual pay of a legionary soldier in the second century, which was 1,200 sesterces. Many procurators were fairly well-off native Italian or provincial landowners. Senior centurions of the legions would also at their discharge have been rich enough to qualify, and the recorded careers of several have shown that they went on to become procurators, though they would

GN·MVNATIVS·M·F·PAL
AVRELIVS·BASSVS
PROCAVC
PRAEF·FABR·PRAEF·COH·III
SAGITTARIORVMPRAEFCOHITERVMII
ASTVRVMCENSITORCIVIVM
ROMANORVMCOLONIAEVICTRI
CENSISQVAE·EST·IN·BRITTANNIA
CAMALODVNI·CVRATOR
VIAE·NOMENTANAE·PATRONVS·EIVSDEM
MVNICIRI·FLAMEN·PERPETVS
DVVMVIR·ALIP·OTESTATE
AEDILIS·DICTATOR·IIII

Local Administration

When Britain was made a Roman province, it remained for some years under the direct rule of the governor, with the exception of certain tribes which were left under their native princes. The Iceni in East Anglia retained that status until the death of their king Prasutagus in AD 60, when the inept Roman handling of the takeover provoked the rebellion led by his widow Boudicca. There is little evidence for Romanizing influence in the kingdom before that date, and the consequences of the rebellion retarded it still further. In the south, another native kingdom based round Chichester presents a much more Romanized picture. The ruler was Tiberius Claudius Cogidubnus. The form of his name tells us that he had been made a Roman citizen. Possibly he had been a political exile in Rome before the Conquest; clearly, he was an enthusiastic ally of the Romans during and after it. His territory formed part of the pre-Roman kingdom of the Atrebates, but in the Roman period that name was confined to the people governed from Silchester, and those ruled from Chichester were called the Regni. It is not agreed how much further Cogidubnus' dominions extended. They may well have included Silchester and the northern Atrebates. Tacitus tells us that other unidentified tribes were placed under his rule.

In the north, a treaty relationship was established with a third native kingdom, the confederation of the Brigantes under its queen Cartimandua. Her overthrow in AD 68 substituted a hostile for a friendly neighbour, and led to eventual Roman annexation.

The campaigns of the 70s in Wales and north Britain required the removal of troops from most of lowland Britain, and provided the occasion for the establishment there of self-governing communities. These communities consisted of towns of certain status and of tribal areas. One such town has already been mentioned: the *colonia* at Camulodunum (Colchester).

The *colonia* was a community of Roman citizens with a constitution based on that of Rome. Equivalent to the Roman Senate was the *ordo*, a council composed of 100 men who possessed the required property qualification and were called decurions, such as Aurelius Senecio, for example, a decurion of Lincoln who erected the tombstone of his wife Volusia Faustina, citizen of the same place. Originally the decurions were elected by an assembly of the citizens, but in practice they became a self-perpetuating body. The *ordo* was headed by two magistrates whom it elected annually, the *duoviri iuridicundo*, who judged local lawsuits, presided over the *ordo* and were also responsible for the administration of public ceremonies. Every five years the *duoviri* had

52 Tombstone of Volusia Faustina, erected by her husband Aurelius Senecio, a decurion of Lindum Colonia (Lincoln). British Museum.

special powers to appoint new members of the *ordo*, to make public contracts and revise tax assessments, and were entitled *duoviri quinquennales*. Public buildings, streets and amenities were superintended by elected junior magistrates, the *aediles*.

Most of the early colonies in the provinces were founded as settlements for veteran legionaries, and had allocations of territory to be divided among the colonists. Their constitution and administration were regulated by the terms of laws passed in Rome to authorize the foundation of some, if not all, of them. They provided something of a model of Roman urban institutions for other inhabitants of the provinces.

In addition to Colchester, colonies of veterans were founded at Gloucester and Lincoln before the end of the first century, also sited in former legionary fortresses. An existing town might also be upgraded to the rank of a *colonia*. The *cannabae*, the civilian settlement outside the fortress at York, had been made a *colonia* by AD 237, when it is mentioned on an inscription. It is very likely that London, as the capital and largest town of the province, also had that status.

The *municipium* was a self-governing town ranking below the colony, but with a similar constitution. *Municipia* might be communities of Roman citizens, or those with what were called Latin rights, which permitted their citizens to make contracts and marriages with

49

53 Pedestal of a statue erected in honour of Tiberius Claudius Paulinus at Caerwent by the *ordo* of the *civitas* of the Silures. Caerwent church.

Roman citizens that were valid by Roman law, and which gave its *duoviri* Roman citizenship by virtue of their holding office. Verulamium is referred to by Tacitus as a *municipium*, and important towns like Cirencester and Leicester may also have been so.

These were towns on the Italian model, and they represent the fundamental concept of the classical Mediterranean, that civilized life and the fulfilment of human potential depended on the institutions of the city and on membership of its community. Even quite small places represented this to some degree. The *vicus* was the name given, both to a subdivision of a larger town, and also to a township less important than a *municipium* but which had its own administration. The small town of Durobrivae, near Peterborough, for example, and the civilian settlements outside a number of the northern auxiliary forts, are recorded on inscriptions 170 as being *vici*, and their inhabitants as collectively owning property, making decrees and appointing magistrates.

Probably the major feature in local self-government in Britain was the institution of the 174 *civitates peregrinae*, the communities of non-Roman provincials which were based on the pre-Roman tribal system, following the model successfully adopted in another Celtic province, Gaul. The chief towns from which they were administered were physically no different from the colonies and *municipia*, and the *civitas* had a similar constitutional structure with an *ordo* and *duoviri*. Nevertheless, a *civitas* is better seen as an area of territory with a town in the middle rather than as a town with a territory round it.

An inscription on a statue pedestal from 53 Caerwent (Venta Silurum) records the honour given by the *Respublica Civitatis Silurum* by decree of the *ordo* to a former commander of Legio II Augusta at nearby Caerleon. It was an act of the tribal *civitas*, not of the town near whose forum the pedestal stood.

These towns were often very close to, if not built on top of, the pre-Roman tribal centres. If they did not have individual status as a *municipium*, as Verulamium did, they ranked only as *vici*, and were properly known by their own name coupled with that of the *civitas*; thus, Venta Silurum, Caerwent of the Silures. The colonies retained their independence from this tribally-based structure; hence Lincoln and its territory formed an enclave within the *civitas* of the Coritani, which was administered from Leicester.

The institution of many of these *civitates* seems to have been the policy of the emperor Vespasian, a consequence of the removal of troops from lowland Britain required for the conquest of Wales under the governor Julius Frontinus. The inscription recording the dedication of the forum at Verulamium early in the

54 Gold *aureus* of the emperor Vespasian issued in 73, some thirty years after his military campaigns in Britain (×2). British Museum.

second year of the governorship of his successor Agricola implies that the building must 168 have started some years earlier. At about the same time, towns such as Cirencester and Silchester began to acquire the public buildings and street plans appropriate to their new function. Wroxeter, however, was still at that time a legionary fortress, and the forum built when it became the *civitas* capital of the Cornovii was not dedicated until the reign of Hadrian, fifty years after that at Verulamium. The development clearly took some time. Later on, some *civitates* seem to have been divided and some new ones created. There were also large areas, particularly in the hill country of Wales and north Britain, which remained under military occupation and never received this form of self-government.

Law

Roman citizens, in the provinces as much as in Rome, had the advantage that their affairs, whether they involved business contracts, the sale or use of land, marriage, inheritance or claims for injury to person or property, were regulated by what is perhaps the most lasting contribution of Ancient Rome to posterity, the great institution of the Civil Law.

In Britain, the governor had jurisdiction in all cases involving Roman citizens, and his previous tenure of the post of praetor in Rome had given him the necessary legal experience. Going on circuit to colonies, *municipia* and

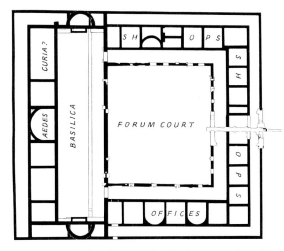

cases which were of sufficient general interest to be included later in Justinian's Law Codes.

Those who were not Roman citizens continued to be subject to native law. In the *civitates*, this was administered by the *duoviri iuridicundo*. Complications and inconsistencies were bound to arise in reconciling Roman and native law, and from Vespasian's reign a *legatus iuridicus* was appointed to assist the governor in legal matters. The first two recorded holders of the post in Britain, Salvius Liberalis and Iavolenus Priscus, both distinguished lawyers, were there very shortly after the establishment of the first *civitates*, a reorganization which would have produced many legal problems. One of Iavolenus' British cases, is recorded in Justinian's Digest.

The provincial Council of Britain, an assembly of delegates from the *civitates*, had little to do except superintend the ceremonies of the provincial cult of Rome and Augustus. It was the body, however, which could effectively bring proceedings in Rome against maladministration by the governor or the provincial procurator. It did so in other provinces, but we have no record of such an occasion in Britain. Had it been necessary, the Council would have enlisted the aid of the patron of the province, whom it elected as a man of power and influence in Rome sufficient to represent the interests of the province with authority. He was usually one who had held senior office in the province or who owned substantial estates there. We know of only two Patrons of the Province of Britain, one being M. Vettius Valens who had been *legatus iuridicus* there in the mid-second century.

civitas capitals, he sat in judgement in the tribunal of the basilica of the town's forum, in the presence of the statues of the gods and emperors, the divine and human authorities of the State of which the governor was representative. He dealt also with cases for which capital punishment – death or condemnation to the mines – was the penalty, cases involving more than a certain sum, and appeals from decisions under native law. So Pontius Pilate, governor of Judaea, is shown (anachronistically dressed in the trappings of a late Roman magistrate), seated in judgement over Christ in the presence of the imperial portraits, though one hopes that Roman governors of Britain enjoyed a better subsequent reputation.

As in another Judaean case, a Roman citizen could appeal to Rome, as Paul of Tarsus did, from a governor's decision. The governor could also refer difficult cases to the emperor for a ruling. We know of a few such British

56 A Roman governor as judge: Pontius Pilate shown seated in judgement over Christ in the sixth-century Rossano Gospels.

58 Routes II and V of the Antonine Itinerary, an official route-list compiled in the early third century. An invaluable source for major routes and original town names, it helps us to reconstruct the network on which the provincial administration was based.

57 Gold medallion (five-*aureus* piece) of the joint emperors Diocletian and Maximian, struck in 287. From the Aboukir find (× 2). Staatliche Museen zu Berlin.

Administration in the Third and Fourth Centuries

Under the emperor Septimius Severus, probably in AD 197, Britain was divided into two provinces. Britannia Superior included the legions at Chester and Caerleon, and thus the bulk of lowland Britain, with a consular governor based presumably on London. Britannia Inferior (Lower Britain) included Lincoln, York and the Hadrian's Wall garrison. Its governor, of praetorian rank, also commanded Legio VI at York.

A far more radical change took place at the end of the third century as part of a wholesale reorganization of the Empire after fifty years of political and military chaos. The Empire came under the rule of two Augusti, Diocletian and Maximian, each having a deputy and heir presumptive with the title of Caesar; Maximian and his Caesar Constantius ruled in the western half of the Empire. Britain now formed a diocese in the praetorian prefecture of Gaul, with a governor entitled *vicarius*. It was divided into a total of four provinces. Britannia Prima in the southwest had its capital at Cirencester where the governor rebuilt a column dedicated to Jupiter, describing himself on one side of its pedestal with his official title *praeses*, and on another, more vaguely, as *rector* (ruler). Maxima Caesariensis was based on London, which was also the headquarters of the *vicarius*. The other two provinces, Britannia Secunda and Flavia Caesariensis, had their capitals at York and Lincoln. Later in the fourth century a fifth British province, Valentia, was created, probably as a subdivision of that based at York.

57

59

60

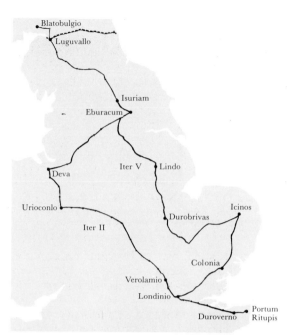

An important feature of the reorganization was that military and civil responsibilities were divided, though this change was not put fully into effect immediately. New military commanders with the titles *Dux* and *Comes* (Duke and Count) succeeded to the military functions of the former imperial legates, leaving the *praesides* – the new governors – with purely civilian duties.

In local administration, additional responsibilities had made the role of decurions a miserable task. They had to arrange military recruitment, keep the state roads in repair, and were made personally liable for any deficit in the revenue from taxation, which they also had to collect on behalf of the government. It became necessary to make the increasingly unpopular duties of decurions compulsory and hereditary for those who were qualified. Many were ruined. Those who could do so escaped into the higher grades of the bureaucracy which carried a social rank exempting its holders from the decurion's burdensome service.

Public Buildings

We are told by Tacitus that Agricola, during the second winter of his governorship, in AD 79, encouraged individual Britons and assisted communities to build temples, forums and houses. Compulsion was unnecessary: the competition for public honour provided a sufficient incentive. The passage provokes many questions. How readily were these ideas adopted? By what mechanism were they officially encouraged? Which Britons were involved? How long did it take, and how long did it last?

It is an apt coincidence that the year of this activity is that in which the forum at Verula-

168 mium was dedicated, part of the urban building programme which followed Vespasian's decision to transfer much of lowland Britain to self-governing *civitates*. For the *ordo* of a *civitas*, a *colonia* or a *municipium*, there was a property qualification; those who were given the honour of membership paid a substantial entrance fee, one of the main sources of communal revenue. Additionally, it was a long-standing tradition elsewhere in the Roman world that decurions and others of equal or greater wealth were expected to use the resources to which they owed their position for the benefit of the community. The benefactor received public honour, and the community received at his expense new baths, a temple, repairs to the streets, a charitable foundation or some such amenity. Special levies, rents or local indirect taxation such as market tolls were additional sources of revenue.

In the absence of explicit information, it is a fair assumption that this applied in Britain too, and that most public buildings and, equally importantly, their maintenance, were paid for by the decurions of the *civitates*, either collectively or individually, by rich merchants or by magnates of greater standing. This is what Agricola was encouraging the Britons to do, and this was the honour for which they competed.

What then of official assistance? In some cases, this might come from the emperor himself, in others through the initiative of a governor or a local military commander. The first-century four-way arch at Richborough,

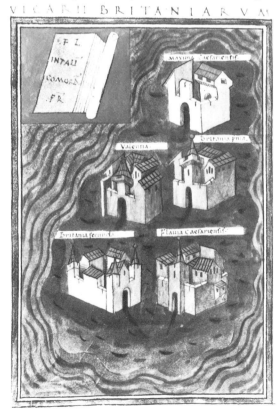

the port of Claudius' first landing, may well have been an imperial building project. It was veneered in imported marble, which would have required imported marble-workers too. Standing as it did as a symbolic gateway to Britain, it was clearly an expensive official monument.

It is often assumed that the army played a big part in the layout and construction of Romano-British towns. The implications of the assumption have not always been considered very carefully. It is one thing to supply an architect or a surveyor; quite another, to lay on a few hundred legionaries as builders' labourers. At the time when towns like Silchester, Cirencester and Verulamium were being laid out, the army was heavily involved in fighting in Wales and north Britain. In addition to the commitment of its manpower, its architects and surveyors were required to lay out miles of new roads and supervise the construction of new forts. It is also questionable whether at this date the British legions could have provided experienced builders in stone. Except for legionary baths at Exeter and Usk(?), built about AD 60, the earliest military stone buildings appear to belong to the 80s, when development in the early towns was already well under way.

It is perhaps more likely that architects, surveyors and skilled builders came from other provinces initially. The governor's official assistance in securing their services would have been invaluable. They may have come from the legions of the Rhine or Danube provinces, or from the towns of Gaul. The Corinthian column capitals of such buildings as the Temple of Sulis Minerva at Bath and of the basilicas at Silchester, Cirencester and Caerwent are of a type which evolved in northeastern Gaul, and the master stonemasons who carved them must have come from that region. Possibly architects and other skilled builders did so too, and are likely to have trained local craftsmen here.

The construction of roads and aqueducts, also an important factor in urban development, might be thought more likely to have required the legions' manpower. The situation may also have been different in the relatively quiet years between Agricola's Scottish campaigns and the building of Hadrian's Wall, when the army was less committed elsewhere, and was also involved in construction work on its own

60 Fourth-century inscription from Cirencester erected by L. Septimius, *praeses* (governor) of the province of Britannia Prima. Corinium Museum, Cirencester.

59 Page from the *Notitia Dignitatum* showing the five provinces of the diocese of Britain. Bodleian Library, Oxford.

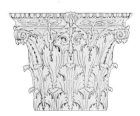

61 Corinthian column capital from the Temple of Sulis Minerva at Bath. Roman Baths Museum, Bath.

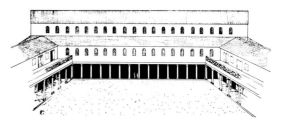

63 Reconstruction drawing of the forum basilica at Silchester. (*After* G. Boon.)

account. The argument advanced here, however, that British legionary manpower may not have played much part in subsidizing the earlier town developments, would imply that the cost fell mainly on those British benefactors who competed for the approval of the governor and of their colleagues.

The Forum and Basilica

As the centre of the town's public life, the forum and basilica occupied an appropriate position at the intersection of the main streets through the town. The forum was a rectangular open market-place, paved or gravelled. Behind a covered colonnade around three sides were ranges of rooms for various commercial purposes: shops, workshops, eating-places. Outside, there was usually a similar colonnade along the street frontage. On the fourth side of the forum, opposite its main entrance, was the basilica. This was a large hall for meetings and ceremonies. It ran the full width of the forum. Its roof was carried on columns up to ten metres (thirty feet) in height, and at the ends were semi-circular or rectangular chambers, one providing the tribunal in which the governor or the decurions might sit as judges. Along the side away from the forum was a range of rooms which accommodated the offices and records of the local administration and probably a shrine.

This is a generalized description. In practice, most Romano-British forums are similar, but no two are identical in plan, and the size varies considerably. The forum at Cirencester, for example, measured 107 × 84 metres, whereas that at Caerwent was only 33 × 31 metres.

The type of plan is very like that of the headquarters of a Roman fort. It has been deduced that the former derived from the latter. The origin of this plan, however, seems to lie in a type of forum developed in north and central Italy late in the first century BC and found also in Gaul, so it must remain an open question whether the immediate antecedents of the British forum lie in civilian or military architecture.

The forum at Verulamium was of a different type from the rest. It had a building on the opposite side from the basilica which may have been the *curia* where the *ordo* met; a temple was added on each side of it in the second century. The forum entrances were in the centre of its two other sides.

The internal decoration of a basilica was usually of some magnificence. At Silchester, for example, it included walls with marble veneers and painted plaster, and contained the remains of bronze and stone statues, one of the Tutela or city goddess, the others probably of emperors.

Temples

Public temples, apart that is from the meeting places of such exclusive religious minorities as Mithraists and Christians, were of two main types: classical, and that called Romano-Celtic. Both types were normally set apart in a walled precinct, occasionally surrounded by a colonnade, giving it the appearance of a cloistered courtyard.

The classical temple was a rectangular room, or *cella*, standing on a high platform, the podium, with a row of columns providing a porch in front and a flight of steps leading up to it. At the bottom of the steps there was an altar for public sacrifice. The temple was not itself used for congregational worship, but for housing the cult statue of the god and for private devotions. Little is known of the original appearance of the temple dedicated to the deified Claudius at Camulodunum. Its enormous podium now forms the substructure of the Norman castle at Colchester. It was set in a large precinct with a screen wall sumptuously decorated with imported coloured marble. The Temple of Sulis Minerva at Bath was built in the 60s or 70s AD adjoining the hot springs sacred to the goddess which gave the town its Roman name Aquae Sulis. Part of the fluted

62 Inscription from the forum at Wroxeter dedicated in the reign of Hadrian by the *civitas* of the Cornovii. Rowley's House Museum, Shrewsbury.

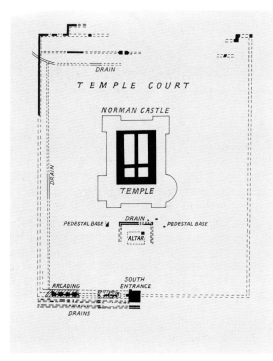

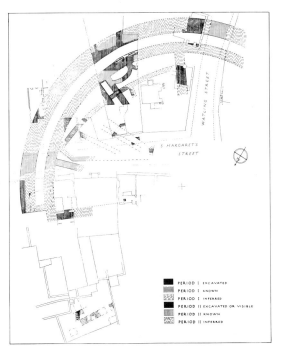

tower above the lean-to roof of the ambulatory. The latter has commonly been restored as a verandah with Tuscan columns, but it has recently been argued that it was more usual for it to be enclosed. This type of temple is found in the northwestern, Celtic, provinces. Its design may originate from pre-Roman ritual enclosures; certainly, it must have a functional origin in Celtic religious practice. The building techniques, however, are Roman – the use of stone and brick, painted plaster walls, tesselated floors, columns and statuary. The temples thus provide an interesting example of cultural fusion. They tend to be smaller than classical temples, but more numerous. Colchester, for example, had five, in addition to that which continued the cult at the pre-Roman sanctuary at Gosbecks, two miles away, and Silchester had four.

Theatres and Amphitheatres

The theatre does not seem to have been widely popular in Britain. Only five are known, and of these the one built near the temple at Gosbecks, outside Colchester, clearly had little to do with urban entertainment. That at Verulamium was also immediately adjacent to a Romano-Celtic temple. The association between theatre and temple is not uncommon in the Greco-Roman world. Even so, the link in Britain between theatres and temples of Romano-Celtic type suggests that their use was mainly connected with local cults of native origin. With estimated seating capacities of between four and seven thousand, they must also have attracted many people from the surrounding countryside. The Canterbury and Verulamium theatres were sufficiently popular to require enlargement. That at Gosbecks,

Corinthian columns and much of the pediment
125 survive. The bronze head from a statue of the goddess was found near the temple. Second-century classical temples are known at Verulamium and Wroxeter, and architectural fragments suggest their presence at Canterbury and Cirencester.

The Romano-Celtic temple consisted of a square *cella* (shrine) with an ambulatory round
273 it, producing a characteristic plan of a square within a square. Less commonly, the temple
131 was polygonal. The *cella* was raised up as a

65 (left) Front elevation of the temple of Sulis Minerva at Bath. (*After* B. W. Cunliffe.)

66 (right) Plan of the theatre at Canterbury. (*After* S. S. Frere.)

55

67 The theatre at Verulamium (St Albans), when excavated; the buttressed wall is that of the earlier, smaller, building.

68 The amphitheatre outside the legionary fortress at Caerleon.

however, was demolished about AD 200. A fourth theatre, at Brough-on-Humber, is known only from an inscription recording the erection of a stage building by M. Ulpius Januarius, aedile of the *vicus*: a rare case in Britain where we know who was actually responsible for a civilian building.

At Gosbecks and in the rebuilt theatre at Canterbury the seating takes the form of the semicircular *cavea* of the classical Roman theatre, supported at Canterbury on radial stone walls. Gosbecks lacked a proper stage building, and little is known about that at Canterbury. The theatre at Verulamium, built in the middle of the second century, is of a type common in northern Gaul, where the seating surrounds an orchestra that is circular, not semi-circular. It had a stage building with a proscaenium of Corinthian columns. None of the theatres or amphitheatres in Roman Britain was large enough to require the vaulted substructures that are so impressive a feature of these buildings near the Mediterranean. Seating was supported on earth banks within retaining walls.

The amphitheatre had seating all round an elliptical arena, in which gladiatorial combats and wild beast shows were presented. Representations of gladiators on mosaics and pottery indicate a fairly general interest in Britain in such entertainment. The arrangement of these expensive displays was one of the functions of the aediles.

At Carmarthen, Chichester, Cirencester, Dorchester and Silchester, amphitheatres were built on the outskirts of the town, to spare it from the congestion and excitement which the displays often involved, and so were left outside the city walls when these came to be built. They date from the end of the first century to the middle of the second. Caerwent had what was probably an amphitheatre, apparently never completed, inside the town walls. It would be surprising if London and the colonies did not also have amphitheatres, but none has been discovered. In this context it is relevant also to mention the amphitheatres outside the legionary fortresses at Caerleon and Chester, and that associated with the civilian settlement outside the fort at Richborough.

Mosaics such as that from Horkstow in Lincolnshire and representations on pottery and glass reveal a degree of interest in chariot-racing, but no circus building is known in Britain.

180, 181
69, 105
68, 182
70

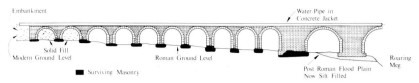

Aqueducts, Walls, Gates and Arches

The presence of public baths, of water supply pipes or large drains in most towns shows that they must have had aqueducts, even though few have been found. Open channels contoured round hillsides and capable of delivering several million gallons a day are known at Dorchester, Leicester and Wroxeter. At Lincoln, water had to be brought across the course of a stream from a more distant source and then raised seventy feet to the height of the town. This was done in terracotta pipes encased in waterproof cement to withstand the pressure. Household water, where not supplied from wells, might be obtained at public 72 fountains, such as have been found at Catterick and Lincoln.

Town defences were a major item of public expenditure. Silchester, Verulamium and Winchester exceptionally had earth ramparts in the first century, and the colonies at Gloucester and Lincoln were built within the already standing legionary defences. Most other major towns did not acquire defences until late in the second century, when the building of earth ramparts appears to have been the response to a central directive. The more expensive and time-consuming addition of stone walls, in front of the ramparts where they already existed, took place at an uneven rate mainly during the third century, and was evidently more dependent on local initiative. Some towns, like Caerwent, had external bastions 73 added to the walls in the fourth century. The scale of these works may be judged from the estimate that the walls of Silchester would have required 45,000 waggon loads of bonding stone and 105,000 loads of flint, together with 10,000 cubic metres of mortar. The history of the defensive works of individual sites is often much more complicated than the outline just given.

Town gates were impressive structures, with one or two major carriageways, often footways at the sides, and guard-chambers with towers. The Newport Arch at Lincoln is the only 74 example in Britain where the archways still survive. Some gateways, at Silchester and Verulamium, for example, were built before the stone walls of the town were constructed, but most were part of the same operation.

Free-standing monumental arches, adorn-

71 The Lincoln aqueduct, at the crossing of a stream at Nettleham. (*After* J. Wacher.)

69 Scene on a jar from Colchester of two gladiators fighting. On the left is a heavily armed 'Samnite', on the right a lightly armed *retiarius*. The latter signals that he has been beaten, and his trident lies on the ground. Colchester Museum.

70 Chariot racing on a mosaic from a villa at Horkstow, Lincolnshire. Transport and Archaeology Museum, Hull.

BATHS

The Roman baths provided not only somewhere to wash, but also a place for leisurely conversation, meeting friends, relaxation, refreshment, taking exercise and playing games. Many had a magnificence of decoration which offered a welcome contrast to the conditions in which most ordinary people lived. They were visited by all classes, from emperor to slave. In a province like Britain, the introduction of the baths was not only that of a particular sort of building: it was the embracing of a way of life.

The artist's reconstruction of the Wroxeter baths shows the hall, the main bath range and the open-air swimming pool. Although the concrete vaulting is shown as exposed, it is more likely that it was protected from rain and frost by a tiled roof. (*Drawn by* Alan Sorrell)

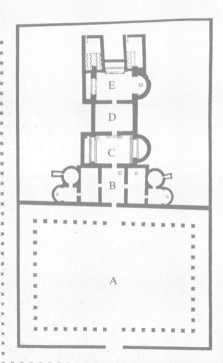

sweat scraped off with a curved bronze instrument, the *strigil*, and he could soak in the immersion bath of hot water. He then retraced his steps, closing the pores with a dip in the cold immersion bath of the *frigidarium*, was rubbed down and anointed with oil. The process could be short-circuited by going straight into the *laconicum* or spartan room, one of intense dry heat. (*Strigil* and oil flask above, Museum of London.)

The water and the rooms were heated by furnaces next to the *caldarium*. The floors of the *caldarium* and *tepidarium* were hypocausts, that is, they were supported on short pillars of stone or tile around which the hot air circulated. The illustration shows the hypocaust of the legionary baths at Chester under the scrutiny of a Victorian antiquary. The air was drawn up flues of hollow box-shaped tiles set into the walls, with outlets at the top. These provided the necessary draught and inhibited condensation of the steam by warming the whole structure of the building. The cooler temperature of the *tepidarium* resulted from its being further away from the furnace.

The Roman bath, of which the Turkish bath is the lineal descendant, consisted of a series of rooms of graduated heat. The legionary baths at Wroxeter (seen in ground plan above) illustrate the sequence of events. First, the visitor might take exercise in the open courtyard, the *palaestra* (A). He (or she) then went into the anteroom, the *apodyterium* (B), where he left his clothes. He then went into the cold room (*frigidarium*, C) which had a bath in which he could wash off the worst of the dirt, into a warm room (*tepidarium*, D) and finally a hot room (*caldarium*, E).

There, with pores opened, perspiring freely in the steamy atmosphere, he had the dirt and

The warm rooms were usually vaulted in concrete, since the steam was likely to rot a roof supported by timbers. Public baths had a large hall, like the basilica of the forum opposite which they were built, in place of the open *palaestra*, a concession to the climate also found in the Jewry Wall baths at Leicester (right).

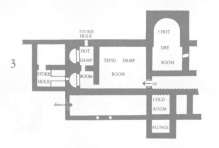

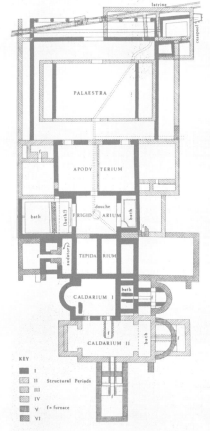

Many public baths had a complicated structural history. Those at Silchester, for example, were in use from the first to the fourth century, and underwent various additions and subtractions of hot, warm and cold rooms. Some baths had a double sequence of rooms, so that men and women could bathe separately at the same time. Mixed bathing was not approved, but the repetition of imperial edicts against it shows that it persisted in less respectable establishments. (*After* W. H. St. John Hope)

The baths at Bath are exceptional in that the two main pools were filled by the mineral waters from the hot springs, while baths of normal type were added at the east and the west ends. An illustration drawn when they were first discovered in about 1755 shows, on the left, one of the pools filled from the spring, and on the right part of the east baths with their hypocaust. (The British Library)

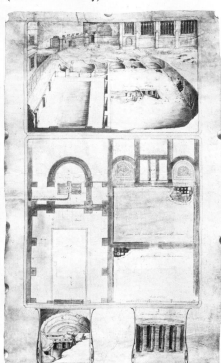

The richer villas, however, sometimes had two or even three sets of baths. The second set at the Chedworth villa (above) possibly incorporated a *laconicum* in addition to the regular sequence in one of its stages. (*Drawn by* Roger Goodburn)

The *frigidarium* of the west baths at Bath with its circular pool. (*Drawn by* Alan Sorrell)

72 A water fountain excavated at Catterick.

ments to a town rather than of any practical use, are rare. Apart from Richborough, only Verulamium and London have produced physical evidence for them. Verulamium was grand enough to have had three. Little more survives than their foundations. Two were constructed in the first half of the third century, and it has been suggested that they commemorated the points at which Watling Street had crossed the earlier line of the town boundaries, recently extended by the late second-century fortifications. The third was built next to the theatre in the fourth century. The London Arch, in contrast, has been reconstructed from the richly sculptured stones which had been incorporated in the city's riverside defences, but its original location is unknown. It may have been free-standing, or have formed a splendid entrance into some precinct.

Town Development

The building of the forum and basilica seems to have been the first main object of expenditure in most towns. The work, particularly in the case of such large sites as Cirencester and Verulamium, is likely to have taken several years. Accumulation of capital beforehand may have taken even longer. The forums at Leicester and Wroxeter were not complete until the reign of Hadrian, half a century after that at Verulamium was dedicated. That at Caistor-by-Norwich is even later, a reflection

73 The south wall of Caerwent, with its later bastions added to act as bases for mounting artillery.

presumably of the impoverishment of the area after Boudicca's rebellion. Next to these in order of importance were the baths. Those at Silchester must have been started at about the same time as the forum; work on the public baths at Leicester and Wroxeter seems to have begun as the forums in those towns were nearing completion. Some temples also belong to the earliest stage of a town's development, and several theatres and amphitheatres followed soon afterwards.

In general, most towns had acquired their main public buildings within less than a century of their constitution as self-governing communities or *civitas* capitals. Public benefaction clearly took priority over private luxury. Neither in the towns nor in the country are first-century houses to be found with more than half-a-dozen rooms, with a few notable excep-

tions in the southeast, nor in the first half of the second century are they at all common. Thereafter, public expenditure was concentrated on alterations and additions to baths, theatres and amphitheatres, on maintenance and repair, particularly after fire. Private houses became much more elaborate.

At the end of the second century and in the third, however, the construction of town defences represented a demand on resources comparable with that on public buildings in the towns' early stages. Some could take this in their stride. Silchester was able to rebuild its basilica after a fire in the third century or later, and to continue modifying its baths in the fourth. Verulamium, in the fourth century, enlarged its theatre, altered its market building and the theatre temple yet again, and indulged itself in the luxury of a third monumental arch; and individuals had money to spare for large courtyard houses. Wroxeter, it appears, may have exhausted its treasury, since it failed to rebuild the forum after a second fire about the end of the third century, and the baths were in such disrepair that most of them had been converted to slipshod tenements or commercial use. If in general, however, investment in public building declines noticeably after the early years of the fourth century, Britain is little different from most parts of the Roman Empire at the time, and better off than many.

The public buildings described above were the physical expression of the distinctive nature of Roman urban civilization. By what standards should those in Roman Britain be judged? They did not, as a whole, rival the fine temples, theatres and amphitheatres of the Roman cities of Provence. Further north in Gaul towns such as Autun and Sens, or Trier before its elevation to being an imperial capital, would not have put Cirencester and Verulamium to shame. As a more modern standard,

75 Reconstruction drawing of the recently discovered London Arch. (*Drawn by* Sheila Gibson.)

FISHBOURNE

Ornate Corinthian column capital used in the 'proto-palace.'

Fishbourne stands at the head of a tidal creek a mile and a half west of Chichester. Shortly after the Roman Conquest, the granaries of a military store base were constructed on the site. One of these was later replaced by two timber-framed buildings, one of which had clay and mortar floors and painted plaster walls; it was probably a dwelling-house of some comfort by contemporary standards. These buildings were demolished in the 60s, and a substantial stone-walled house was built a little way to the south. This is incompletely known, but it included a courtyard garden with colonnades and a bath suite.

Little of the residential rooms of this 'proto-palace' could be excavated. Corinthian column capitals used in it, probably carved by south Gaulish masons, were broken up when the new palace was built. The capitals, marble inlay and wall paintings used here all indicate skills of craftsmen from outside Britain, who may also have worked at one or two of the other early villas in Sussex.

Shortly after AD 73 work was started on the Palace itself, a building of quite outstanding luxury. In its southeast corner it incorporated much of the 'proto-palace'. It consisted of four wings with colonnaded fronts arranged around a rectangular formal garden. The north and east wings had suites of rooms grouped around courtyards, with a large aisled assembly hall in the northeast corner and a monumental entrance in the middle of the east wing. The west wing contained what

were probably state rooms on both sides of an audience chamber, with a gallery along the back. A ceremonial reception room of this nature, the size of the Palace and the Mediterranean quality of its decoration all indicate an owner of considerable social and political importance and great wealth. The excavator of Fishbourne, Professor Barry Cunliffe, has made a strong case for his being none other than Tiberius Claudius Cogidubnus, the native king of the Regni. The site is close to the pre-Roman tribal centre, probably at Selsey, and to Chichester, later the *civitas* capital of the Regni. Tacitus refers to his position and unswerving loyalty and the Palace at Fishbourne would be most appropriate to his philo-Roman character and favoured position.

The artist's reconstruction reveals the scale and splendour of the Flavian-period Palace. The grand approach through the entrance hall led across the formal garden directly to the audience chamber. The vaulted roofs of the old baths of the 'proto-palace' can be seen in the bottom left-hand corner.

The Palace stood for over two centuries, and in the course of time there were several modifications. If indeed it had been built for Cogidubnus, its status as a royal mansion would have ended when he died, which cannot have been much after the end of the first century.

During the second century the north wing was substantially replanned from

Plan of the Palace.

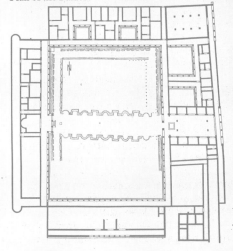

Bedding trenches for hedges in the centre of the formal garden.

being a suite of rooms, possibly for guests, grouped round two courtyards. The east end of the wing, which had already been converted to a bath suite, was demolished. The west courtyard was retained as the central feature of a new grouping of rooms, and several of the larger rooms were divided by wooden partitions. The effect was to convert the north wing into a villa in its own right. New baths were built in the

Geometric Flavian mosaic in the north wing.

The cupid and dolphin mosaic with sea-beasts in the lunettes.

Marble head of a youth.

east wing, which was also partly demolished.

One remarkable discovery was that of the bedding trenches for the hedges which bordered the pathways; those on the main path were laid out with recesses alternatively square and semi-circular. Pits for the planting of trees were also found. Remains of the plants were not preserved, but fruit trees and small shrubs like box were regular features of the formal gardens described by Roman writers. Lines of terracotta pipes carried water to basins and fountains along the sides of the paths.

The skill and the materials with which the Palace was decorated were of the highest quality. A black and white mosaic from the north wing was composed of geometric figures arranged in a perspective box design, reflecting contemporary fashions of floor decoration in Rome and Italy. Though plain in comparison with the later coloured mosaics such as the cupid

and dolphin, it should be seen as a fitting part of a scheme of interior decoration, a contrast to the highly coloured wall plaster.

On one fragment there was a very impressionistically painted seaside villa on a deep blue background, remarkably like the wall paintings of Pompeii and Stabiae that were buried by the eruption of Vesuvius in 79, within a year or two of the time that Fishbourne was being decorated.

The broken head of a late first-century marble statue of a young man gives some idea of what there may have been amongst the internal decorations.

Several new mosaics were laid as part of the mid-second century alterations. One of the best-preserved was in the main room which opened on to the courtyard. In the central roundel a cupid rides on a dolphin while sea-horses and sea-panthers occupy the semicircular lunettes around him.

Further changes were in progress in the north wing in the late third century. A

channelled hypocaust was being inserted in the northwesternmost room and the room next to it had been converted into a workshop: its original black and white mosaics had largely been worn away. In the former state rooms the mosaics had been ripped up, perhaps so that the tesserae could be used again. The floor of the grand east entrance had become overgrown on one side and was a rutted cart track on the other; its portico had been demolished.

Amid this decaying grandeur life evidently continued on a modest scale, and there was some money available for renovation, but the work was never completed. The hypocaust was still unfinished, and had not been covered with a floor, when a disastrous fire swept through the north wing. The damage was too extensive to repair and the shell of the building stood for some years, and was then systematically dismantled.

perhaps the county and market towns of Georgian England, with their town halls, corn exchanges and colonnaded market places, convey an impression of unpretentious solidity similar to that which the rurally based Romano-British gentry evolved as the version of Mediterranean civilization best suited to their inclinations.

76 Tombstone of Flavia Augustina, from York. The Yorkshire Museum, York.

The Structure of Society

In the early Roman Empire there was a basic distinction between those who were Roman citizens and the rest, the *peregrini*. The distinction was one both of law and of social treatment. Originally citizens were people born in Rome or its immediate territory who had the right to vote in public elections there, and to marry, make contracts and be judged by the law of the city. As Rome's power extended, these rights were given to other Italians. Colonies of legionary veterans, Roman citizens by definition, were established in the provinces. Other individuals or communities were given the same status as had earlier been conceded to the Italians. Thus, many people acquired Roman citizenship irrespective of their place of birth; indeed, there were many who had never set foot even in Italy.

The institution gives us some indication of the social changes that happened in Britain after the Conquest. There were, of course, Romans who settled here, chiefly merchants and legionaries. Veterans were established in the first-century colonies, and others will have bought themselves farms or set themselves up in trade with their capital pensions. If we accept that in due course most legions were recruited in Britain, the effect on the pattern of society of intrusive settlements of veterans will have diminished. Local recruitment for service with the auxiliaries, however, will have produced a different side-effect, for it provided one of the main ways in which a man of peasant or labouring family might rise in the social scale. He could use his capital to buy land or set up a business just like the legionary veterans.

A Roman citizen was distinguished by his three names: his *praenomen*, one of a small number of Latin personal names, e.g. Caius, Marcus, Titus, conventionally abbreviated on inscriptions to their initial letters; his family name, the *nomen*; and his *cognomen*, originally an optional extra, denoting a personal distinction such as a trade, an achievement or a physical peculiarity, but almost universal by the end of the first century AD. When an auxiliary soldier received citizenship, it was customary for him to take as his *praenomen* and *nomen* the names of the reigning emperor. To this he usually added his own given name as *cognomen*. Thus, M. Ulpius Novantico, born at Leicester, was discharged in AD 106, having already, in his case, received his citizenship under the emperor Trajan (M. Ulpius Trajanus). This convention gives us an indication of when the first member of a family received citizenship. M. Ulpius Ianuarius, aedile at Brough-on-Humber in the reign of Antoninus Pius, is likely to have belonged to a family which also acquired its citizen status under Trajan half a century earlier. As was usual in later generations, his rather ordinary Roman *cognomen* says nothing of his family's national origins. Similarly, the family of Flavia Augustina, who died at York, probably owed its citizenship to one of the Flavian emperors in the late first century.

Another factor behind the increased chances of social mobility in Britain's early years as a Roman province was trade, stimulated by improved communications, greater contact with an imperial market, and a monetary economy. Since in general the most secure form of investment in the Roman world was land, the profits from trade and industry affected not only individual families and their fortunes, but also the overall pattern of landownership in the province and the political power which largely depended on it.

Slavery was also an element in social change. It existed in pre-Roman Britain, but was a much more deeply rooted institution of Roman society and is likely to have been extended considerably, not only by enslavement of Britons after the Conquest and subsequent wars, but also by the importation of slaves from elsewhere. Many worked in the mines and as labourers on agricultural estates with little prospect of relief from their toil, but the condition was by no means always one of misery and oppression. The domestic slave or one with skill and intelligence was potentially in a much more favoured position. Such a slave might well buy or be given freedom, though the master might expect continued service afterwards, or a share in the profits of a trade in which the slave had been established. The Moorish freedman Victor must have been a young man of promise, for he had been freed by his owner, the cavalryman Numerianus, before his early death at the age of twenty. His elaborate tombstone bears witness to his former master's deep affection.

If a freed slave's master was a Roman citizen, the freedman acquired the same status and normally took his master's family name. The tombstone of C. Calpurnius Receptus, priest of the goddess Sulis at Bath, was erected by his wife Calpurnia Trifosa, whom he had freed and then married, a quite common practice. The inscription is explicit, but her name Calpurnia would have implied it, since Roman women did not change their name on marriage.

A slave who was freed and became a Roman citizen continued to be somewhat stigmatized for his former condition. He was ineligible, for example, for municipal office, though it was open to him to become an official of the imperial cult as *sevir augustalis*. The freedmen of the emperor, however, enjoyed a more influential position. Usually, they continued employment in the imperial service, often with a wealth and power which to some extent compensated for their social disadvantage. An inscription from Combe Down, near Bath, records one such imperial freedman, Naevius, who served as procurator's assistant at what may have been an imperial estate there. Educated slaves and freedmen, often of eastern Mediterranean origin, were commonly employed as secretaries and clerks.

One British slave who eventually enjoyed better fortune was Regina, a woman of the Catuvellauni who, like Calpurnia Trifosa, was freed and married by her former master, in this case Barates from Palmyra in Syria, who was rich enough to erect a fine tombstone in her memory. As this shows, native-born inhabitants of the western provinces continued to be identified by their tribal as well as their personal names; also, the Roman Empire was a cosmopolitan society; people travelled widely and mixed freely. Another example is provided by Philus, portrayed on his tombstone at Gloucester wearing his native Gaulish hooded cloak. His tribe, the Sequani, lived in Burgundy. Where the tribe or nation is mentioned specifically, we can still identify the ethnic origins. The increasing use of Roman names, however, tended greatly to obscure these origins. This did not only apply to those who became Roman citizens; others followed the fashion. On an altar at Chichester, dedicated by Lucullus, son of Amminius, the father's name is Celtic, the son's Roman.

This picture of assimilation must of necessity be biased, since it is provided by those who were literate and Latin-speaking, almost invariably from the towns and the army. In the country, it is generally held that Latin was little spoken by the peasantry. Roman names and Roman manners will have been correspondingly uncommon among them. That much of their native culture survived is indicated by the continued loyalty to native gods, with many rural temples still in active use in the fourth century, at a time when the Roman Empire was officially Christian. This rural conservatism is particularly important to remember

77 Inscription from the tombstone of C. Calpurnius Receptus, a priest (*sacerdos*) of the goddess Sulis at Bath. Roman Baths Museum, Bath.

78 Inscription put up by Naevius, a freedman of the emperor (*libertus Augusti*) on a building at Combe Down, near Bath. Roman Baths Museum, Bath.

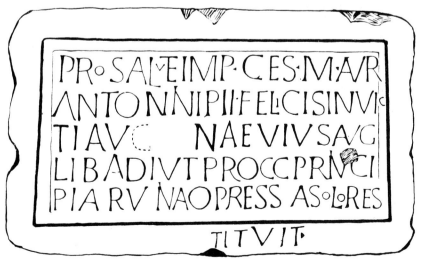

79 Tombstone of Philus of the Sequani (see p. 65). Gloucester City Museum and Art Gallery.

when we consider the relationship between peasant and landowner, and the way in which land was managed and inherited. By far the greatest proportion of Roman wealth derived from agriculture. Only documentary evidence could tell us about the landholdings of any one person or area, and there is none in Britain. We can, however, form some broad ideas about the nature of rural society.

The Roman Conquest was followed by a certain amount of confiscation and redistribution of land. Some of the Trinovantes were evicted to provide territory for the colony at Camulodunum; Icenian nobles were dispossessed after the death of king Prasutagus. Several tribes made peaceful accommodation with the Romans at the time of the Conquest, and one might expect that the policy of the Vicar of Bray would have had its usual advantages. Many Romano-British landowners were probably descended from those of the pre-Roman period, and their tenants and peasants also. Some at least of the small number of rich first-century villas in the southeast are likely to have belonged to native nobles. The increased social mobility of the post-Conquest years, however, will have introduced into the pattern

the merchants and veteran soldiers who invested in land.

John T. Smith has suggested that the plans of many villas appear to be divisible into two or more separate establishments, indicating joint occupancy by as many families. They have this feature in common with villas in other Celtic provinces, and it might imply the survival of a native system of land tenure, and presumably inheritance. In the less Romanized parts of Britain, notably the uplands which remained under military occupation, the pattern of settlement alters little, with a similar implication of continued native traditions. It is also becoming increasingly clear that in lowland Britain too there were many rural settlements of native type, interspersed among the villas and probably dependent on their owners. It may be that many of the long-established customs of rural society continued to a greater extent than the Romanized architecture of the villas has led us to suppose, not to be eradicated until the Saxon settlement.

In one respect the impact of the Romans on rural life was unmistakable. The imposition of peace, the *pax Romana*, removed the field of battle from being one of the favourite means a

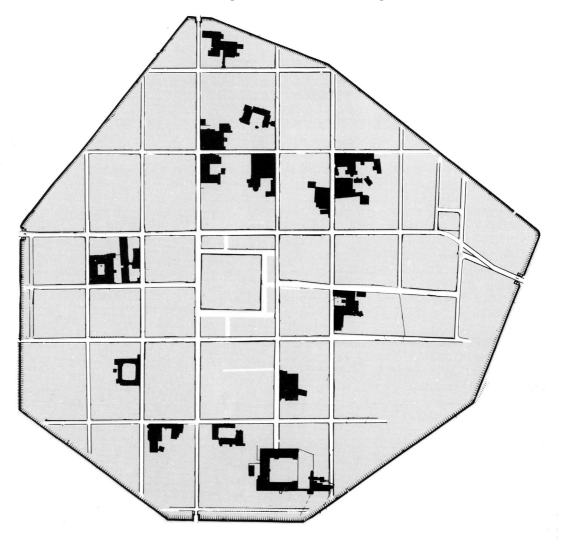

80 The principal houses of Roman Silchester. (*After* G. Boon.)

landed aristocracy has of ruining itself and others in the process. The quiet enjoyment and peaceful inheritance of landed property resulted, indeed, in the accumulation of the wealth that was spent on public buildings in 114, towns and on the comfortable, in some cases 115, luxurious, villas of the third and fourth centur- 164 ies. It will also have broadened rural society by permitting the rise in fortune of independent peasant proprietors.

How does the Romano-British governing class, the decurions, fit into this picture? One may start with the proposition that most decurions derived their wealth from land; secondly, that they lived in larger houses than those who lacked their wealth; thirdly, that of the larger houses in a town, most will have belonged to decurions. A possible example of one such family is that of the Tammonii at Silchester, of whom T. Tammonius Victor erected a tombstone there to his wife Flavia Victorina, and T. Tammonius Vitalis, the son of Saenius Tammonius, put up an inscription in the forum. The basis of the argument receives some support from the observation that there are often relatively few villas in the immediate vicinity – say, a ten-mile radius – of a town, whereas 81 many larger town houses have outbuildings, evidence for corn-drying or other activities usually found at rural villas; i.e. they were farm centres from which the land surrounding the town was worked.

80 Only at Silchester and Caerwent have all or most of the houses of this type been excavated. Each site has only about sixteen of them. The *ordo*, however, normally contained 100 decurions. There are several possible explanations of the discrepancy, not necessarily mutually exclusive. The *ordo* may have been below strength; some families may have produced more than one decurion (fathers, sons, brothers); some decurions may have lived in smaller houses; some may not have lived in the town at all.

It would follow from the last explanation that some of the villas were the country seats of decurions. The area covered by a *civitas* makes it likely that the estates of many of sufficient wealth to qualify as decurions will have been distant from the *civitas* capital. Some landowners may have maintained town houses as well as or instead of villas; others may have stayed with their colleagues on the occasions when they emerged from the backwoods to attend to public duties. Others may have avoided office.

There is little evidence that many in Britain achieved the highest ranks of Roman society, or that other members of those ranks acquired significant interests in Britain. The province seems to have seen few senators and *equites*, or dignitaries of the later Empire, the *clarissimi* and *perfectissimi*, other than those who came here as imperial administrators. An *Eques*

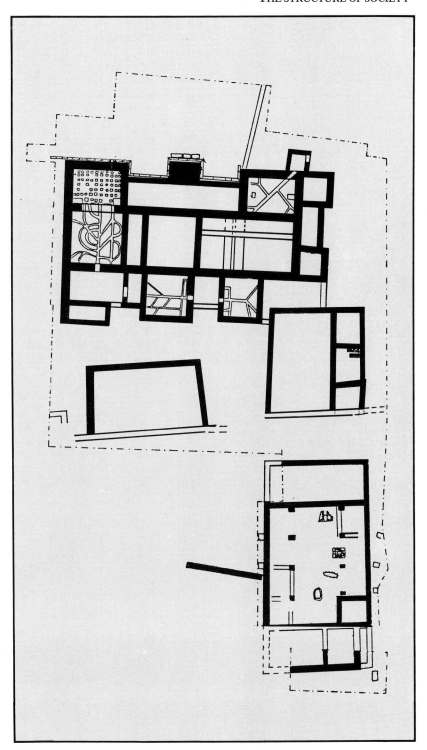

81 Plan of a town house with agricultural outbuildings, Cirencester. (*After* A. D. McWhirr.)

82 Inscription of a Roman knight (*eques romanus*), erected by his wife Valeria Frontina together with Florius Cogitatus and Florius Fidelis at Colchester. Colchester Museum.

83 Marble bust, possibly of an ancestor of the owner, from the villa at Lullingstone, Kent. British Museum.

Romanus who died at Colchester at the age of twenty, too young to have been an official, may thus have been the only knight born in Britain of whom we have record. The luxury of some of the third- and fourth-century villas, particularly in the southwest, has been thought to imply owners whose wealth would have raised them above the status of decurion, and is a reflection of an increase in social stratification in the later years of the Empire. If, as is thought likely, the marble busts from the villa at Lullingstone, carved in the Mediterranean, are the ancestors of its late second-century owner, they suggest that he was a man of distinguished family elsewhere in the Empire who came to live here. We also have record of a Roman noblewoman who had estates scattered through several provinces, of which Britain was one. The evidence, as one would expect, for such immigrant or absentee landowners of the senatorial order is sparse. The impression remains that the roots of Romano-British rural society were as distinctively British as they were Roman.

82

117

83

CHAPTER III
THE PEOPLE

Romano-British Society

In the Victorian era the predominance of classical thought amongst an educated élite gave emphasis to the Romanness of Roman Britain. The island was regarded as a barbarous Celtic country, civilized by a superior culture, an attitude which owed much to an expanding British Empire and little to known fact. Gradually, increasing knowledge of the Celtic world led to an appreciation of a civilization different but equally worthy of consideration. Celtic society has been revealed as alert and vigorous, having its own values and beliefs. The imposition of Roman culture may have checked the native growth but the alliance of Celtic and Roman beliefs and activities produced, in certain areas at least, not an uneasy marriage of Roman and Briton but a Romano-British civilization which was but one facet of a multi-cultural Empire.

There is some contemporary evidence for Celtic society. Caesar's account of Gallic society in the first century BC may be applied to the Belgic areas of southern Britain – with one major difference. By his time kingship in Gaul had been replaced by the rule of tribal chieftains who acted as political leaders and chief magistrates. In Britain kings still ruled tribes in both the Belgic areas and in the northern parts where the people were descended from Bronze Age stock. Not only kings ruled. The queens Cartimandua and Boudicca were accepted as leaders; and the career of the latter suggests that a woman could lead her tribe into battle. Client kingship, as established elsewhere in the Empire, suited the Roman political hierarchy and proved its worth. Cogidubnus's loyalty ensured that the Romans secured their position in the southeast; his title 'Legatus' indicates Roman approval. Cartimandua's handling of the Brigantes was important enough to guarantee strong Roman support. Caesar noted that there were two main classes; the knights (*equites*) and the Druids (*Druides*). He also speaks of *nobiles* who were obviously the more important of the knights. Below these came the common people whom he dismisses as slaves (*servi*); if they were not enslaved in battle they sold themselves into slavery in order to avoid heavy taxes. Slavery was a feature of Celtic society and Strabo records slaves amongst his list of exports from pre-Roman Britain. Caesar also speaks of *obaerati* who may have been akin to the medieval villeins owing services rather than earning money, and *ambacti* who were free in one sense of the word but whose status was that of a serf. However, not all the people were enslaved, although certainly there was some degree of dependency implied by Caesar's use of the term *clientes*. In Ireland there were certain groups who gained respect and independence by their profession – metalworkers, craftsmen and charioteers. The latter especially held an honourable place. In the Ulster cycle of stories the charioteer, Loeg, has a very close bond with his master, Cu Chulainn.

Archaeological evidence for the distinction between the king or chieftain and his followers is found in graves. Death was not the great leveller; a man's goods went with him to the Otherworld, often broken to kill their life-spirit. By the first century BC the Trinovantes, indulging a Roman taste, placed amphorae containing wine, silver cups and glass and bronze vessels alongside a great man. In the Welwyn Garden City burial gaming pieces were included to provide further entertainment. A Belgic cemetery near to Verulamium contained 436 burials of which at least six richly equipped graves were set in rectangular enclosures surrounded by a bank and ditch; burials close by were placed in such a way as to emphasize the richer graves' position. In the territory of the Parisii on the Yorkshire Wolds the graves of chieftains contained their chariots.

It was from the ranks of the Celtic aristocracy that the Romans would seek recruits for the provincial administration. These included delegates to the native provincial council, where the duties involved the upkeep of the imperial cult, and to the local council (*ordo*) in

14, 47

84 A smith depicted on a tombstone from York. The Yorkshire Museum, York

86 (right) The tombstone of Julia Velva from York shows her reclining on a couch; her heir stands at one end. The Yorkshire Museum, York.

the cities. For this the *ordo* of a *colonia* might provide a model because it would be filled with army veterans used to a Romanized way of life. Normally, members of the *ordo* were not necessarily Roman citizens unless the town had the status of *municipium* with the 'greater Latin rights'. Verulamium, the only certain *municipium* in Roman Britain, did not possess this privilege, although its magistrates, after their term of office, were eligible to become Roman citizens. It is likely, however, that some of the capitals of the tribal areas such as Cirencester, Leicester or Dorchester (Dorset) later received the status of one or the other type of *municipium*. Members of the *ordo* would be expected to pay for the trappings of office and the provision of amenities and entertainment out of their own pocket; if they could not there were always Romans such as Seneca ready to lend money, possibly without too much emphasis on means of repayment. In the first two centuries there was no shortage of candidates eager to seek election.

A Romanized way of life would spread. Tacitus remarks that 'Agricola trained the sons of the chieftains in a liberal education'; probably this had happened before the 80s AD, for the Boudiccan rebellion must have convinced the Government that they had neglected this aspect of Romanization. The sons may have been hostages for the good faith of their fathers, a practice familiar to the Romans. The training produced results at least amongst the upper classes. Spoken Latin replaced Celtic, the toga became fashionable and appreciation of Roman comforts grew. Tacitus may sneer at the aping of Roman customs and call the habits

85 A tombstone from the Roman cemetery at Murrell Hill, Cumbria, shows the elaborate folds of the draped garment and gives particular emphasis to the fan. The lady holds a pet bird. Above her a sphinx, flanked by lions each devouring a human head, crouches over a similar head. Carlisle Museum.

of idle conversation, hot baths and the convivial dinner table 'alluring vices', but men have sold their souls for less. In some areas, the frontier zones, the wilder parts of the Pennines, the country farms, such comforts did not penetrate. There, Romanization might consist of no more than some pottery and a few trinkets possibly obtained as booty. In the towns, however, in the *vici* outside them and the villas, the benefits and consequent obligations of a Romanized way of life were accepted.

Some idea of the way of life can be deduced from a study of funerary reliefs, although it is possible that the representations on them are stereotyped. Nevertheless the smith, on a relief 84 from York, dressed in tunic and apron, hammering out an ingot held in a pair of tongs, suggests a living model. At Murrell Hill, Car- 85 lisle, a relief of a woman sitting in a high-backed chair shows her elegantly dressed in mantle and tunic. Great prominence is given to her fan as if the sculptor had been given particular instructions about this. The tombstone of Julia Velva at York is one example of 86 the funerary banquet relief. Julia lies on a couch. At its head is her heir, Mercurialis, bearded and warmly wrapped in tunic and cloak. Equally warmly dressed in tunic and mantle is a female relative. Several reliefs reinforce an impression that thick warm clothing was an absolute necessity in Roman Britain. The warm cloak worn by the *optio*,

mantle emphasizes the shape of the body. He carries a purse, she a weaving comb, to indicate the division of occupations. In the quietness of the Grosvenor Museum, in Chester, prolonged study evokes speculation as to whether these solemn, dignified figures were really to be found on the streets of Roman Chester, or whether these are portrayals of those qualities which the Romans admired most – *pietas et gravitas* (piety and gravity).

If they do depict reality then the change from pre-Roman Britain was striking. Classical writers noted particularly the appearance of the Celts. Diodorus Siculus mentions that 'the nobles shave the cheeks, but let the moustache grow freely, so that it covers the mouth', a contrast to the Romans who until the second century AD preferred men to be clean-shaven. Strabo noted that the Celts were naturally blond but to increase the colour they washed their hair in lime water; then they drew it back from the forehead over the crown to the nape of the neck. Ammianus Marcellinus in the fourth century commented that the 'Gauls were of lofty stature, fair and of ruddy comple-

87 Tombstone of the *optio* Caecilius Avitus. He wears a thick cloak and carries a staff and a wax writing tablet. Grosvenor Museum, Chester.

87 Caecilius Avitus, on a relief at Chester, may have been army issue, but the mason has pockmarked it heavily as if to represent thick rough wool; and Diocletian's price edict of AD 310 was to show the value attached to British cloaks.

On a funerary banquet relief from Chester 88 Curatia Di(o)nysia lolls elegantly in what can only be described as an inviting manner, which is enhanced by the loose fall of her garments; on another stone the reclining female is more decidedly clothed. The women of Chester were lucky in having sculptors who could portray their elegant style of dress, usually a long tunic with a mantle or wrap thrown over the shoulders. One stone reveals a lady with draped sleeves. Her maidservant, less fashionably dressed, carries a jewellery or vanity box. Men wear the tunic and the toga, the latter loosely thrown over one arm. Sometimes they wear only a loose, thick tunic. One rather portly gentleman, warmly clad in a tunic with trailing sleeves, stands by his wife, whose tight-fitting

88 The tombstone of Curatia Di(o)nysia is in the traditional style of depicting a funerary banquet. Grosvenor Museum, Chester.

90 A sculptured head found at York reveals an elaborately dressed hair style. The Yorkshire Museum, York.

xion, terrible from the sternness of their eyes.' Strabo noticed their height, 'in Rome very young boys tower over the Romans', and commented on their fitness, 'their arms compare in size to their physique . . . they try not to become stout or pot-bellied and any young man who exceeds the standard length of a girdle is fined.' There were some dark-skinned Celts because the Irish hero, Cu Chulainn, is called a 'dark, melancholy man'. He certainly dyed his hair for it is described as being dark at the roots and blond at the ends. Reliefs in Britain show male heads with the short hair style favoured by the Romans in the first century. No doubt the wearing of the toga with long flowing locks was frowned upon and those eager to embrace Romanized life soon trimmed them.

Classical writers were not so enthusiastic about Celtic women. Dio remarked that Boudicca was 'huge of frame, terrifying of aspect and with a harsh voice; a great mass of bright, red hair fell to her knees'. Ammianus Marcellinus commented that 'a whole host of foreigners would not be able to withstand a single Gaul if he called to his aid his wife, who is usually very strong and has blue eyes; especially when swelling her neck, gnashing her teeth and brandishing her sallow arms of enormous size, she begins to strike blows mingled with kicks as if they were so many missiles from a string of catapults.' The Roman matron was expected to behave with decorum; she achieved her ends by subtlety not aggression. The Irish tales praise the beauty of Celtic

89 A detail from the tombstone of Flavinus, standard bearer of the *ala Petriana*, shows the defiant features, and the hair style, of his Celtic enemy. Hexham Abbey, Northumberland.

women, in particular the length and thickness of the hair. Fedelm, the prophetess, had long golden hair, 'three tresses of it wound round her head, another tress fell behind which touched the calves of her legs'. Sculpture reveals that hair continued to be elaborately dressed in Roman Britain. It could be drawn back from the forehead and coiled in a bun at the nape of the neck. Julia Velva's hair seems 86 to fall loosely behind her. A head from York reveals a most elaborate style. The centre piece 90 is plaited, drawn back from the forehead and wrapped round the head, above the forehead the front hair is pulled back in loose waves. Ved(r)ic, at Ilkley, a woman of the Cornovii, 91 has a more homely style – a long plait hangs over the front of each shoulder; if her hair was loose it would hang to the waist. Some women would be sure to copy Roman styles similar to that seen on a head dating to the Flavian 92 period, found at Bath, where an arrangement of tight curls forms a ridge outlining the forehead while the rest of the hair is drawn into a bun.

The distinction between a fair-haired Celtic and a dark-skinned Mediterranean race no doubt remained. However, many people who settled in Britain would be provincials from every corner of the Empire. These would in-

93 clude officials sent from Rome attached to the governor's or the procurator's staff and legionaries and auxiliaries discharged from the army. Many wives of veterans would be of British origin and before Severus' army reforms allowed soldiers to marry there would be unofficial liaisons. Merchants would make their home here. Barates of Palmyra married a Catuvellaunian wife whose Roman name, Regina, may imply that at least one of her parents had been Roman. On her tombstone she is described as a freedwoman; she had probably been freed by Barates himself, certainly she had risen in status. Her tombstone at South Shields emphasizes her elegant gown and her womanly tools of distaff, spindle and workbox with balls of wool. She holds her jewel box; jewellery displayed on a wife is one of the ways in which a man may reveal his wealth to the world. Regina was aged thirty at death. At Corbridge is a tombstone which may commemorate Barates himself. He is described as a *vexillarius* – either a standard-bearer or a dealer in or maker of standards. He died aged sixty-eight, time enough for him to have taken a second wife and had children of mixed blood. Another example of a mixed marriage is recorded at York. Julia Fortunata married Marcus Verecundus, who is recorded as a *sevir augustalis* of the *colonia* and a tribesman of the Bituriges Cubi. She came from Sardinia; he

was an Aquitanian. There would be numerous examples of such marriages, for under the tolerance of the Empire intermarriage was accepted as normal practice.

To these people can be added persons of other races. Greek teachers and medical men came to Britain. Demetrius, a Greek teacher, visited York; Aulus Alfidius Olussa, born at Athens, was buried in London, aged seventy. His tombstone dates from the first century AD. Aurelia Aia died at Carvoran, the daughter of Titus from the *colonia* of Salonae in Dalmatia. Victor, a Moorish tribesman, died at South Shields and his somewhat effeminate figure is pictured on his relief. The auxiliaries who lived and died in Britain included Gauls, Batavians, Thracians, Spaniards and Syrians. After AD 367, German mercenaries, brought by Theodosius to stiffen the defences, began to settle round the Saxon Shore forts and along the eastern coast. A cemetery at Dorchester-on-Thames provided evidence of their presence inland. The later Roman Empire employed German and Saxon mercenaries as part of its last line of defence and, although their employment was as soldiers, it is highly probable that they arrived with their families or contracted marriages and liaisons. Evidence from Orton Hall in the Peterborough region suggests that by the end of the fourth century at least one

94

91 The tombstone of Ved(r)ic, a woman of the Cornovii tribe, has her hair drawn into two long plaits. Ilkley Museum.

92 A sculptured head of a lady dating from the late first century AD shows the elaborate hair style favoured in the Flavian period. Roman Baths Museum, Bath.

Daily Life: Work and Leisure

Life in some areas of Britain, particularly the remoter parts, altered very little during the Roman period. For some people life consisted of intensive use of daylight hours with long wearisome periods spent in industrial or agricultural tasks undertaken to survive hostile environmental conditions, and the burden of life could be intensified by the sudden and additional demands of a military power. For others, and particularly those who lived in the towns and the villas, life became infinitely more pleasant. Most persons are gregarious by nature, enjoying the company of their fellow men, especially if meetings take place in comfortable surroundings. Evidence from other parts of the Roman world indicates that the pleasures of town life were eagerly sought and there is no reason to believe that this was not the case in Britain. Indeed, Tacitus' remarks on the changes during Agricola's governorship confirm this.

In the Roman world work continued for seven days a week although the hours of each day varied according to the seasons of the year, being longer in summer and shorter in winter. Work started as soon as the sun rose and came to an end as the light faded. Two things, however, need to be borne in mind: no one can

93 The tombstone of Regina of the Catuvellauni of Hertfordshire, Roman Fort Museum, South Shields.

94 Victor, a Moorish tribesman from Mauretania, was only twenty when he died. Roman Fort Museum, South Shields.

landowner, either voluntarily or under compulsion, yielded land to such a group. The penetration of the Saxons had begun long before the traditional arrival of Hengist and Horsa, and the acceptance of these groups was merely one more strand in the society of Britain to which the term multi-cultural may be considered truly applicable.

It is difficult to estimate the total population of Roman Britain. Collingwood and Wheeler suggested 1,000,000. Frere gave a figure of 2,000,000 for the population at the end of the second century AD. Of this the army would account for 63,000 (18,000 legionaries, 45,000 auxiliaries). If 2,000,000 seems a small number it has to be set against a population of just over 3,000,000 in the early Tudor period. Even by 1801 the population of Britain had reached only 8,000,000.

95 A diorama of a carpenter's shop reconstructs a scene that could have been found in the town at Silchester. Reading Museum.

96 (below) A fan-tailed brooch found at Greatchesters (Aesica) on Hadrian's Wall. The relief design of trumpet scrolls shows that Celtic art forms were still prominent in Roman Britain in the late first century. Museum of Antiquities, Newcastle upon Tyne.

work all the time and the Roman economy was a slave one which enabled many citizens to have an employing or overseeing role. Once the set tasks had been done, then, in the towns at least, citizens were able to attend places of entertainment and to use what leisure they had in enjoying themselves.

The most varied work and entertainment would be found in the towns. These would be noisy places; cart wheels rattled over cobbled streets, shopkeepers shouted out their wares, craftsmen of every kind banged, hammered and clanked as they turned out a wide variety of goods. Towns would also smell not only of undeodorized humans but also of the variety of industrial processes, sharp sulphur of the cloth processes, hot iron of the blacksmith, leather-soaking, urine pools of the tanners and the smells of kitchen, byre and stable. The majority of trades relied on individual craft skills. Carpenters and joiners would be much in demand. So would cart-makers who provided all the wooden parts but relied on the blacksmith to provide iron tyres, lynch pins, and hub caps. Blacksmiths would provide a more general service than the specialized one of shoeing horses with which they later became associated, making tools of every description, agricultural gear and individual items for a household – locks, chains, keys and kitchenware. Tanners provided vast quantities of leather and cloth workers often saw the wool through the whole process from bale to finished garment.

Metalworkers, who had been highly valued in a pre-Roman society, retained their status. Smiths working in gold, silver and bronze produced articles for personal and household use. A working jeweller's shop was discovered at Verulamium; and an inscription from Malton wishes good luck to the slave who seems to be taking over a goldsmith's shop. Silver-smithing establishments were discovered at Silchester, Wroxeter and Verulamium. Bronze-smith's workshops, as found at Silchester, Catterick, Colchester and Verulamium, produced jewellery, bronze figurines, fittings for household chests, and the more practical kitchenware. Some of the jewellery, like the Aesica brooch and the dragonesque brooches, reproduces the abstract patterns of Celtic art. One localized industry, that of jet, was situated in the York and Malton areas, and was enterprising enough to export its wares to the Rhineland, producing glossy black jewellery: Gorgon's heads, particularly necessary for averting the evil eye, necklaces, bangles and tiny figurines like the attractive small bears designed so as to capture the essential characteristics of that animal.

The hardest work of all would be done by labourers in mines and quarries. Many of these would be slaves, for slavery was part of the established social system of the Empire, including within its ranks those who had been enslaved by war and those who had sold themselves into slavery because they could not

97 A delightful small carved jet bear found at Colchester (see p. 75). Colchester Museum.

support themselves. Slaves were employed in imperial, provincial and local administrations and formed part of households in town and country. The large number of infant burials in the courtyard of the Hambledon villa suggests one way in which a slave establishment got rid of unwanted children. Well-educated slaves, many of them of Greek descent, were welcomed in private households as tutors, bookkeepers or estate agents. Slaves could marry; Anencletus, a provincial slave, set up a tombstone in London to his wife. An imperial slave, Ateius Cocceianus, is recorded on a tombstone at Carlisle; another slave has already been noted in a goldsmith's shop at Malton and a guild of slaves is recorded on an inscription at Halton Chesters. Membership of a guild was essential to a slave because guilds provided some form of social club and mutual assistance. A master was compelled by law to bury a slave but if he could not, or would not, the guild saw that this was done and the correct rites were performed both on that occasion and on the anniversaries of death.

Many slaves lived and died in captivity. Their poignant condition is personified by the bronze *balsamarium* (incense container), 98 found at Aldborough (Yorks.) depicting a tired, crouching slave. Some did manage to earn or buy their freedom and rise to important positions. Emperors relied on them because they were loyal and well-educated; it was a freedman whom Nero sent to inquire into conditions in Britain after the Boudiccan revolt. Sometimes slaves were manumitted on the death of a master, which may have been the good fortune of Verecundus and Novicius mentioned as freedmen and heirs to the will of the centurion, Marcus Favonius Facilis, on his tombstone set up at Colchester soon after the 36 Conquest.

Little is known of the role of women in Britain. In pre-Roman Britain a few had been accepted as leaders of a tribe; in Roman Britain their place in society was dictated by their social class. Women of the lower classes shared the lives of their husbands working in shops, in the fields or on farms. Inscriptions can bear testimonials: Anencletus set up the tombstone to his most devoted wife. The well-to-do had a more pleasant life. Many loved jewellery even to the extent of having it buried with them in their coffins, as revealed in the burials discovered at York during the nineteenth century.

98 (left) The weariness and pathos attached to the condition of slavery is well observed in the figure of the sleeping slave boy, designed as a *balsamarium*, from Aldborough. British Museum.

99 (right) A small bronze toilet set, a strigil and a razor.

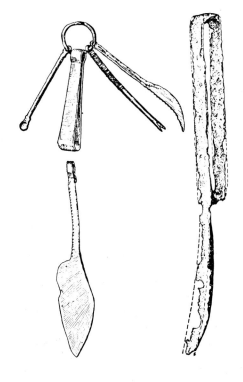

One coffin contained jet bracelets, pins and two small glass bottles. Roman matrons were expected to devote a great deal of time to daily adornment so that bottles for unguents, chalk and rouge were common household articles. Some of their contents were lethal; white lead for the cheeks, powdered antimony for eyebrows and red ochre for lips contributed more to the destruction than to the enhancement of beauty. Sets of toilet articles consisting of earpick and scoop, nail scrapers and tweezers were essential equipment. Slaves dressed hair into elaborate styles which were held in place by goats' fat and hair combs. Rescued from one grave at York, and now in the Yorkshire Museum, is a thick twisted length of hair, held in place by jet pins and once coiled round the head of a matron of Eburacum. Trinket boxes, personal possessions, fans, elegant clothes are all part of what has been termed 'conspicuous wealth'. A rich woman expected to have these and a sensible husband realized that they reflected his status in society. On inscriptions status is consciously emphasized. Two at York record Aelia Severa, who is described as an *honesta femina* or wife of a local dignitary, and Sosia Juncina, who describes herself, in an inscription dedicated to the goddess Fortuna, as the wife of the legionary legate. At High Rochester, Julia Lucilla takes care in recording her husband's death to state that she is of senatorial rank.

Yet what status these women had resulted from their husband's or father's rank, for women had few rights in law. A wife's main duty was to produce children and manage the affairs of the household. Accompanied by slaves she would make a daily journey to the market to buy produce for the household and presumably to give herself an outing. She had the choice of buying grain, which her household slaves would grind into flour, or bread from a baker's shop – flat unleavened loaves, which lasted only a day before going as hard as pumice stone. Archaeological evidence from Silchester shows shops could provide a varied diet. Meat included deer, hare and wild boar; freshwater fish included pike and perch. The most frequent seafish was herring, probably

eaten either smoked or dried. Salt and brine were also used for preserving foods. Mussels, oysters and cockles, in fact all shellfish, were very popular. Several new foods were introduced into Britain by the Romans, black plums, cherries, walnuts and herbs, dill, coriander and thyme. Vineyards were laid out for the cultivation of grapes. The range of vegetables was greatly extended, including cabbage, peas, turnips, carrots, parsnips and celery. The main sweetener was honey. If the handbooks of Columella and Palladius were available Britons could gain instructions on how to trap swarms of wild bees and keep them in wicker or wooden hives. These perishable materials have not been found, but at the Rockbourne villa a large jar pierced with holes was believed to be a pottery hive, although readers of Columella would know that bees would become bad-tempered in a hive of this material where there could be little control over temperature.

Imports included olive oil, wine and garum or liquamen, the strongly flavoured fish sauce so popular to Roman taste that it was added to almost every dish. These liquids were imported in long or globular-shaped amphorae which, judging by the frequency of the remains found, went to almost every part of Britain. Some had pitch on the interior which acted as a seal but also imparted a taste to the contents. The overwhelming impression of any study of Ro-

99
100
101

103, 195

100 Human hair, carefully dressed, that was preserved in a stone coffin found in a cemetery at York. The Yorkshire Museum, York.

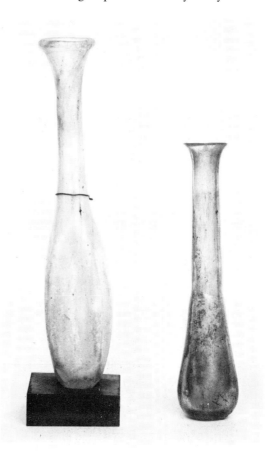

101 Small glass unguent bottles were used to hold perfume or incense. British Museum.

77

102 A Roman table laid with the various kinds of pottery and fruit. Verulamium Museum, St Albans.

103 Pottery amphorae of different shapes and sizes could contain all manner of things such as wine, oil, or *liquamen* (a salty fish sauce). Museum of London.

man food is that it was highly flavoured, possibly to disguise a tainted taste, for it was difficult to prevent food going bad, and even a daily visit to the market could not stop shopkeepers from trying to get rid of poor quality produce. Poor people must have always eaten it. Wine was imported in wooden barrels, which the citizens of Silchester put to a secondary use to line wells. Mead and beer were also drunk and probably most Roman Britons took seriously the invocation on pottery cups, BIBE, 'drink up', or DA MERUM, 'unmixed [neat] wine, please'.

In the towns, public amenities for relaxation were provided either from a local taxation system or by individuals who were expected to be generous because of the office which they held. Large bathing establishments were considered essential both for cleanliness and because they provided a means of social contact where business deals could be made. Wroxeter, Silchester and Leicester had large establishments; Bath and Wroxeter provided public swimming baths. These would be free but the owner of the Gadebridge (Herts.) villa seems to have decided that he might make some money by providing a swimming bath on his estate. pp. 58–9

Public entertainment was provided at the theatre, the amphitheatre and the circus. There were few theatres in Britain. An inscription from Brough-on-Humber records that the aedile, Marcus Ulpius Januarius, presented a new stage at his own expense during his term of office. Two theatres, at Gosbecks (Colchester) and at Verulamium, had a temple close by; there are indications of a theatre near the temple at Bath, but it is uncertain whether a temple was associated with the theatre at Canterbury. In the classical world the arrangement of theatre and temple was not uncommon, for festivals were held on days dedicated to certain deities and often scenes would be enacted illustrating parts of divine legends. These festivals would always attract fringe groups who would entertain, feed or sell to the crowds so that the result would be a mixture of a fair, pilgrimage and market. The theatres would also provide mimes, plays, recitations and 179 66

fighting and bear and bull baiting; fights between more exotic animals might include the 'Caledonian bear' mentioned by the poet Martial. Amphitheatres were also used for public spectacles of a more sinister kind, including public executions; the martyrdom of the Christians Julius and Aaron, recorded at Caerleon (by Geoffrey of Monmouth), and of others at Chester (by Bede) and Carlisle (by Gildas), probably happened in the amphitheatre.

104 A miniature ivory carving in the form of a tragic mask as worn by actors. Caerleon Museum.

Gladiators wore special armour. A gladiator's helmet was found at Hawkesdon (Suffolk) and the contest of a heavily-armed *mirmillo* and a *retiarius*, armed only with a net and trident, was embossed on a pot found at Colchester. A more playful representation of their contest is on a mosaic at the Bignor villa where Cupids enact gladiatorial roles, and on a terracotta plaque found at Colchester where a *mirmillo* lunges at a monster fish. The seriousness of these contests is underlined by the altar found in the *nemeseum* (shrine) in the Chester amphitheatre and dedicated to Nemesis, a goddess popular with those to whom death and the malevolence of fate were constant companions. An otherwise unnoticed love story comes from Leicester where scratched on a sherd are the words 'Verecunda, actress, Lucius, gladiator'.

69

105

other performances, often by actors who wore theatrical masks similar to the miniature ivory one found at Caerleon. The Romans preferred knockabout farce to more serious dramas and the business of keeping 5,000 people entertained would be a constant headache to the public authorities. This was one reason why the entertainments became increasingly cruel and degraded as taste became debased and the public demanded increasingly sensational experiences.

104

Amphitheatres on the military sites at Caerleon and Chester provided space for drill and military exercises in between performances. Those at Dorchester, Cirencester, Silchester, Chichester and Caerwent provided for purely civilian needs. In these structures gladiatorial contests, brutal but popular, took place where the combatants accepted their lot with resignation. Other entertainments included cock

68,
182

There is no physical evidence of a circus in Britain, although it has been suggested that at Wroxeter a long, walled enclosure close by the temple would have been suitable for horse races, particularly as a relief to Epona, goddess of horses, was discovered near to the site. Horse races can be run anywhere; in the seventeenth and eighteenth centuries they took place on coastal sands around Britain. In Roman times Lincolnshire may have had races because the Horkstow mosaic pavement depicts an exciting race in which a wheel is coming off one chariot, and at Lincoln was found a most delicately carved relief of a boy charioteer. In Rome betting took place on red, green, white and blue companies who raced for

105 A detail from a mosaic in the villa at Bignor shows cupids acting out the role of gladiators. Two on the left are of the same types as those shown on the pottery jar from Colchester (illus. 69), while to their right stands the trainer holding a long wand.

106 A sensitively carved relief of a young boy, probably from a funerary monument. He stands in a chariot and stretches out his left arm to grasp the reins. Private collection.

pp. 154–5

107

victory. A similar system might have been used in Britain, for someone at Chedworth scratched on a well his liking for a green company.

People do not always have to be entertained publicly. They can provide their own amusements and what better way than to indulge in a convivial banquet at the traditional time of the ninth hour? How pleasant to come into a room adorned with silver such as that discovered at Mildenhall (Suffolk) and be entertained by jugglers, reciters and singers. A group of terracotta figures found in a grave at Colchester satirizes the scene. If people did not aspire to such pleasantries or could not afford them, there was always a snack with friends and a

game of dice. Loaded dice found in the pre-Hadrianic fort at Vindolanda showed that it was as well not to let one's wits become too fuddled. Pottery and stone counters are frequently found, chequered boards came from Richborough and Cirencester, and at Lullingstone one was placed in the mausoleum to provide entertainment for its owner in the other world. Those who sought entertainment elsewhere could resort to the alehouse or the brothel.

This picture of daily life must necessarily be very general and incomplete. Generations could live and die without seeing any change in their relatively primitive way of life. Country

dwellers could go all their lives without visiting a town, or enjoying the amenities of a theatre or a brothel. Town dwellers would be dependent as much on their own resources as on those provided by the public authorities, and they could find time for entertainment only when the day's work was done. In several aspects, life in Roman Britain could be said to be better than life in Celtic Britain but it was still a struggle. At Vindolanda the average age of death has been suggested as being thirty-six for men and twenty-eight for women; this is confirmed by the evidence from the Trentholme Drive cemetery at York and the tombstones at Caerleon. The tombstone of Titus Flaminius at Wroxeter laments that 'the Gods prohibit you from the winegrape and water when you enter Tartarus'. Many Roman Britons might indulge in that thought and take every opportunity of seeking what entertainment they could to relieve a somewhat precarious existence, while they still had the chance.

Romano-British Houses

There was no typical Romano-British house. Rather there were a number of different types of houses which, as is the case today, reflected the life-style of their owners. In the towns, the streets were laid out in a grid pattern which, in certain places like Caerwent and Brough-on-Humber, can still be traced in the modern street plans. Buildings were not constructed in terraced houses along the streets but were placed in isolated settings within the *insulae* ('islands', i.e. pieces of land divided by

107 Terracotta figurines from a group found in a child's grave at Colchester. They humorously represent reclining diners and reciters at a banquet. Colchester Museum.

108 A sad note is struck by the tombstone of Titus Flaminius at Wroxeter; it records the prohibition of not only wine but also water in the netherworld. Viroconium Museum, Wroxeter.

109 An artist's impression of a courtyard house in the town at Silchester. (*After* G. Boon.)

110 A model of a row of shops, based on the evidence of the foundations discovered during excavations at St Albans near the theatre in the 1950s. Verulamium Museum, St Albans.

streets). Silchester, with about 180 known houses in its forty hectares, has been called a 'garden city', but much of its so-called unoccupied land could have been covered with wooden buildings which the excavations of 1890–1909 did not discover. Town houses could take several forms. The simplest house consisted of a long, oblong block, divided into rooms, entered from a corridor, which ran along one, or more unusually, both sides. Two blocks could be placed at right angles to each other or a single block might have projecting wings. More elaborate houses had the blocks placed round a courtyard, usually a garden or a cobbled area, or completed a courtyard by building one or two walls to form up the blocks.

Attached to many houses were shops, with a counter opening onto the street and closed at night with wooden shutters. At Verulamium a pent roof, supported on a colonnade, ran the length of ten or eleven shops which fronted onto a wide pavement. Shops at Caerwent, though oblong in shape with their shorter axis facing the street, still had a continuous pent roof shading the frontage. In the second century the buildings were extended to the rear to provide more working space.

Houses built round a courtyard would have few or no windows in the outer walls, thus lessening the street noises. In Italy the intention in building such a house would also be to exclude the sun's heat; in Britain an enclosed courtyard could allow a build-up of heat during the day and reduce the draughts. Many houses known from the Verulamium excavations have their protruding wings facing in an easterly direction, thus presenting the back of the long range to the prevailing westerly wind.

Narrow oblong areas at Caerwent and Silchester have been interpreted as staircase wells. Houses with stone foundations and lower walls could have supported an upper storey of wattle and daub, but there was ample space available on the lower floors for the extension of bedroom and storage accommodation.

In country areas many people would still inhabit the same type of house which had been built in the pre-Roman period, a round house with mud or wattle walls, supporting a thatched or turf roof. Such a house is typified by that excavated at Little Woodbury and attempts at a reconstruction based on the position of the postholes have envisaged several different roof styles. The experimental Iron Age house constructed at Little Butser has a waterproof, spacious interior which could be divided into compartments round its circumference. This type of house is also familiar from

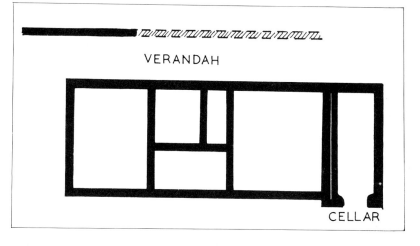

VERANDAH

CELLAR

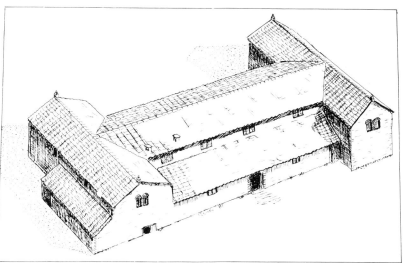

the Irish texts. In the northern regions stone-built round houses, with outbuildings, grouped within enclosures, were a common feature in a wild landscape; sometimes several would cluster together to form nucleated settlements, and at Riding Wood four oblong houses were situated within a cobbled enclosure. Stone houses of all shapes and sizes were also a feature in the southwest and have occasionally, as at Chysauster in Cornwall, their own gardens or arable spaces forming nucleated villages. These were essentially Bronze Age type houses that continued to be inhabited during the Roman period.

More sophisticated were the villas. This term, in the original Latin sense, implied the whole estate and not just the building. Indeed, some of the smaller buildings are better called farmsteads and the greatest one of all, that at Fishbourne, has been given the title of a palace. Whatever term is applied to the buildings, they were far more comfortable than the round and oblong houses already mentioned. Some of the buildings developed on a site previously occupied in the Iron Age, as at Park Street, St Albans, where the Iron Age hut thought to have been destroyed during the Boudiccan rebellion was replaced, not necessarily by the same family, by an oblong block of several rooms. In the next century two projecting wings were added which doubled the accommodation. At Lullingstone and Latimer the original buildings were enlarged, altered and rebuilt until a comfortable residence resulted. Some buildings always re-

pp. 62–3

112

113

83

mained small. Ditchley, built in the second century as an oblong block with two wings, always remained compact.

The golden age of the villa was in the fourth century. The modest houses of the first and second centuries were then remodelled on a vast scale as at Woodchester, North Leigh, Chedworth and Bignor to mention only four examples. At Bignor an extra court was added to accommodate those who where working outside. Aisled buildings were added, as at Lullingstone, either as a barn or to house labourers. In the Nene and Welland valleys were separate aisled buildings serving a dual purpose of housing men and workshops under one roof. Some of the villas are so large that they cannot be explained as just housing large families or extended families. J. T. Smith has suggested that such buildings were occupied by two or more families who lived in separate ranges, an idea which would account for the irregularity of many of the villa plans. A villa would comprise 'two or more houses and sometimes a large work-hall as well and they can be sited either without regard to each other or strung out in a long line'. If this was the case, then the social implications need to be reconsidered.

Even in a large house only the principal rooms had mosaics, but many of these can be splendid, in particular the Orpheus designs in southwest Britain and the Dido and Aeneas design from the Low Ham villa. At Lullingstone a semi-circular band of red tesserae set opposite the design of Europa may indicate where diners reclined; their view would be of both a classical design and a classical tag. A Romano-British room might be regarded as colourful or overpowering depending on taste. Wall paintings were often in dark colours, red,

olive green and brown; a reconstructed frieze from Verulamium reveals 'marbled' panels divided by columns. A ceiling painting had an octagonal pattern representing a coved ceiling with yellow doves on a purplish background.

There would be little furniture. Silchester and Dorchester have provided examples of table legs, chairs and tables made of Kimmeridge shale, a dark bituminous material, which could be highly polished. The table leg found at Colliton Park, Dorchester, was animal-shaped, with a head jaunty and alert, a chest gracefully bowed. Couches and three-legged tables would be similar to those seen on the funerary banqueting reliefs: Julia Velva's couch has a high back; Victor's couch has no back but he reclines on a well-padded mattress. Julia's female companion sits in a basket chair; so does the lady on the Murrell Hill relief, and figurines of the Dea Nutrix reveal her sitting in a well-woven basket chair.

Folding stools, footstools and small tables, chests, caskets and cupboards would be dotted round the room; only the locks and fittings of the latter objects have been discovered in excavations. A welcome addition would be a portable brazier in which smokeless charcoal was burned. Lighting was provided by candelabra or small terracotta lamps which, filled with oil and with a small wick coming out of the nozzle, would give a reasonable light for between two and three hours.

One of the most important rooms would be the kitchen. Cooking was done in pots and pans placed on a gridiron set over a charcoal fire kindled on a raised platform. Sometimes, as at Silchester, there was evidence of an oven which worked on the heat-retaining principle. After fuel had been burned inside the oven and the ashes raked out, the food was placed there

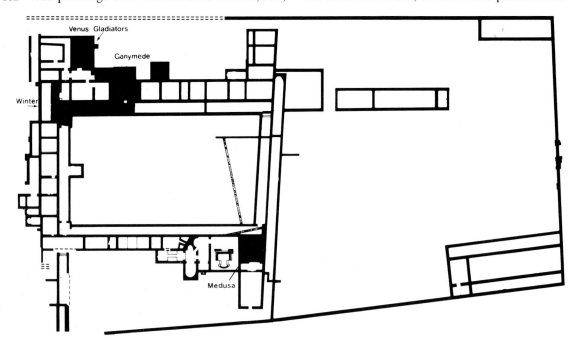

114 Plan of the large courtyard villa at Bignor, Sussex.

115 An artist's reconstruction of the villa at Lullingstone in its final phase. (*Drawn by* Alan Sorrell.)

116 (below) The mosaic in the apse of the dining room at the Lullingstone villa, with a scene showing the abduction of Europa by Zeus in the guise of a bull, is one of the few from Roman Britain with an inscription. It is an allusion to a couplet from Virgil. In the background, beyond the geometric decoration, another mosaic has a scene of Bellerophon riding the winged horse Pegasus and killing the Chimaera. In the roundels at the corners are represented the Four Seasons.

117 One of the finest mosaics from southwest Britain was found in the bath suite of the villa at Low Ham, where it covered the floor of the cold room (*frigidarium*). Its series of scenes are based on the story of Dido, Queen of Carthage, and Aeneas, as told in Virgil. Somerset County Museum, Taunton Castle.

118 (left) One of the houses excavated at Verulamium had wall plaster painted with columns set between 'marbled' panels. Verulamium Museum, St Albans.

119 (right) A fragment of ceiling panelling from a Verulamium house. The octagons imitate coffering; in the centre of each panel is a yellow dove. Verulamium Museum, St Albans.

120 A reconstructed room from Roman London. The folding stool is of the type found in the Roman barrow excavated at Holborough, Kent. Museum of London.

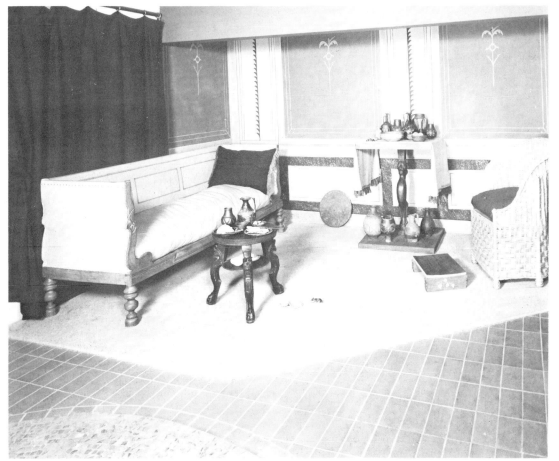

121 Another reconstruction of a typical room in a house in Roman London. Items such as the basket chair are known from their representation on grave reliefs; the three-legged table is of a type common throughout the Roman Empire, and examples have been found at Pompeii. Museum of London.

122 A diorama of a kitchen based on objects found at London sites. Museum of London.

to cook, a method which is still used in some parts of Europe today. Kitchen implements included steelyard beams and weights, knives, choppers, pastry cutters and a variety of pots and pans. Some of the most useful tools were the pestle and mortar, used extensively in the preparation of ingredients for sauces, and the mortarium, where the gritty interior surface helped pulp vegetables and fruit.

Often pots were sunk into the floor of the kitchen. George Boon has suggested these might hold valuables and be disguised by a rough covering of earth. Another suggestion is that they served as urinals, but there is no soakaway. Normally the latrine was an earth closet placed in a corner of the yard. An

enterprising shopkeeper at Verulamium provided a public latrine but usually these would be found at the baths, which were frequented by both men and women. Very few town houses had their own bath system; the public baths provided opportunities for social contact as well as for cleanliness, but houses at Lincoln, Verulamium, Cirencester, Colchester and even Caistor-by-Norwich were connected to a sewer system. Many villas had a bath system sited either within the house or as a separate building, and some villas, like Chedworth, provided both moist and dry baths. In some aspects, Roman Britain provided a standard of comfort which was not achieved again until the twentieth century.

pp. 58–9

196

Religion

The most important section of Celtic society was the Druids. Caesar noted that they were a priestly caste held in high honour and having many privileges which included religious and legal powers, making decisions in disputes and allotting rewards and punishments. Druids did not pay taxes or take part in warfare. They kept control by banning from religious rites and sacrifices anyone who disobeyed their commands; persons who helped an offender became contaminated with his guilt so that effectively they became outlawed. Education was under Druidic control. It was restricted to an élite few who underwent twenty years of oral instruction – a form of rigorous memory training which ensured the survival of texts, laws and facts.

Inevitably Druidic power was to be challenged. The Romans were extremely tolerant in religious belief except in two areas where they persecuted rigorously not on religious but on political grounds. Christianity supported the will of the individual against the State, rejected the worship of the emperor and claimed to worship the one true God. Druidism demanded loyalty from the Celtic aristocracy, claimed political obedience and practised human sacrifice. Both Pliny and Suetonius comment on the suppression of Druidism in Gaul, which seems to have been eliminated as a political force during the reign of Claudius. Caesar's remarks, that Druidism was believed to have originated in Britain and that those who wanted to study the subject went there, imply that British Druidism had great prestige. Hence its ruthless suppression culminating in AD 60 in Suetonius Paulinus' attack on Anglesey. Graham Webster has suggested that Druidic power was greater than has been suspected in that it kept alive anti-Roman propaganda and exploited grievances such as those which inflamed the Boudiccan revolt. The shattering defeat of the Iceni and the attack on the sacred groves appear to have smashed Druidic power, although there are some references in later British history to individuals who may have been Druids, and Druidism certainly continued in Ireland. The connection of Druidism with religion in Britain has long been analysed and debated. In the word 'Druid' lies the fascination; if the word 'priest' is substituted half the interest would vanish and, to quote T. D. Kendrick, 'a whole library of books discussing their origin would never have been written'. No firm conclusions can be drawn regarding their influence but more substantial evidence has been discovered to provide a picture of religious life in Roman Britain.

There were four main areas of religious belief – cults of the official Roman religion, Celtic cults already present in Britain or brought over by traders and soldiers, oriental beliefs, of which the most popular was Mithraism, and Christianity, which eventually was to emerge as the dominant religion of the Empire after Constantine's conversion about AD 314. Besides these, there were, no doubt, various superstitious practices which lingered on beyond the Roman era.

Official Roman religion was promoted as part of the policy of Romanization and one of its main promoters was the army. The chief deities were the Capitoline Triad composed of Jupiter, Juno and Minerva. Frere suggests that temples to the Triad would be erected in the four *coloniae* and in the *municipia* of the province. No direct evidence has been found although one of the three temples in the Verulamium forum approximates in size to a Capitolium and at Caerwent one side of the forum was altered to provide a large square podium suitable for such a temple. Numerous inscribed altars dedicated by members of the army to the chief deity, Jupiter Optimus Maximus, have been found in the forts. At Maryport, Castlesteads and Housesteads, altars were ceremoniously replaced each year on 3 January; and the old ones were buried by the side of the parade ground.

Under the Empire the worship of the Capitoline Triad was second only to worship of the Divine House. In the eastern regions there was a long tradition of deifying a ruler. Augustus, while allowing his divinity to be worshipped in that area, refused this in the western Empire although he did permit an altar to be dedicated to Rome and Augustus at Lyons. After his death he was deified and it soon became customary to worship the genius or *numen* of the living emperor, a practice strongly opposed by Christians. Altars dedicated to the *Numen Augusti* are found in Britain, mainly in the northern areas, but the main centre of the cult was at Colchester. Duncan Fishwick has suggested that an altar to Rome and Augustus was established here after the Conquest and that this was followed, soon after Claudius' death in AD 54, by the erection of a temple dedicated to his divinity. The building had progressed far enough by AD 60 to allow the inhabitants to shelter within its walls. Damage in the Boudiccan revolt was so extensive that the remains were cleared to the foundations to allow a complete rebuilding. The final complex provided a classical temple set on a podium with a 64, 123 large *cella* and octostyle portico situated at one end of a courtyard entered by a monumental gateway. In the centre of the courtyard was an altar surrounded by a drainage area, presumably to help to cleanse the area after sacrifices. Colchester was the centre of emperor worship in the province and was the seat of the provincial priest of the cult. Elsewhere the imperial cult was attended by *seviri augustales*, a group

123 Model of the imposing temple built at Colchester for the worship of the emperor Claudius. Colchester Museum.

restricted to freedmen. Marcus Verecundus Diogenes had that title put on his coffin at York and Marcus Aurelius Lunaris described himself as a *sevir augustalis* of York and Lincoln on an altar which he dedicated at Bordeaux.

Although classical temples may have been a feature of most important towns, actual remains are scarce. Five classical temples existed in the Corbridge fort and one at Richborough. It is likely that the temple dedicated by the guild of ironworkers on the authority of Cogidubnus to Neptune and Minerva at Chichester

was a classical-type temple, and the same is probably true of at least one of the three buildings in the Verulamium forum. At Wroxeter a temple may have been constructed in association with an enclosure for religious rites or theatrical performances. A curved piece of walling at Bath may be the remains of a theatre situated close by a huge temple with a tetrastyle portico, an altar decorated with figures of classical deities and a colonnaded enclosure. These linked with the baths complex to provide a well-organized religious centre, functioning by the end of the first century

14, 47

65, 124

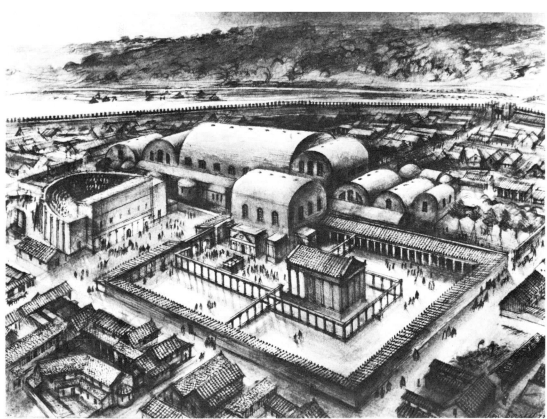

124 Artist's impression of the classical temple complex and the baths at Bath. (*Drawn by Alan Sorrell.*)

AD, staffed by priests and sacrificial attendants and dedicated to the healing deity, Sulis Minerva. Another temple at Lydney, not built on classical lines, was part of a healing complex dedicated to Nodens, a Celtic deity.

144

Temples were not intended for congregational worship. They housed the cult statue of the deity, and a gilt-bronze head of a female, presumed to be Minerva, found at Bath in 1774, may have been part of such a statue. As well as being a healing goddess, Minerva was worshipped as a patron of warriors and craftsmen. Evidence in the form of inscriptions, statues, reliefs and bronze figurines reveals that other gods of the Roman pantheon had their share of devotion. Apollo was a healing deity; Jupiter, Minerva and Mars were particularly worshipped by soldiers; Vulcan was the protector of smiths; Mercury as guardian of roads and travellers was invoked by merchants, and the large number of small bronze figurines depicting this deity are of a size that could be packed easily into their baggage. The fine bronze statue of Mars found at the Gosbecks temple site may have been presented by a grateful merchant. Hercules as a mortal translated to immortality was popular with traders on account of his constant travelling, and with soldiers because of his bravery. In Lincoln two inscriptions mentioning Mercury and Apollo are associated with guilds; these could indicate that the *colonia* was divided into wards, each placed under the protection of a deity, as at Ostia, the port of Rome.

125

126–9

The most frequent type of temple in Britain are those known as Romano-Celtic, so called because they are to be found in the parts of the Empire that were originally occupied by the Celts. In Britain they lie to the south of a line drawn between the Severn and the Wash. The

125 Roughly life-sized bronze head of the goddess Minerva which may have been part of the cult statue set up within the temple of Sulis Minerva at Bath. Roman Baths Museum, Bath.

126 (left) Bronze figurine of Jupiter found at Ranksborough Hill, Rutland. Figures such as this stood on the *lararium*, the shrine of the household deities. British Museum.

127 (centre) Bronze figurine of Venus from Colchester. British Museum.

128 (right) Bronze figure of Mercury found in the Thames at London Bridge. It may have been tossed from the bridge as a votive offering for a journey about to commence, or one safely completed. British Museum.

129 (opposite) A large bronze figure of Mars found at the Foss Dyke in Lincolnshire. The inscription records a dedication to Mars and to the Emperor's divine power by the Colasuni, Bruccius and Caratius, and that the figure was made by the bronze-worker Celatus. British Museum.

majority are revealed on the ground by a square within a square. They had a tall inner *cella*, illuminated by small windows in the upper parts and surrounded by a portico or verandah. The temple excavated at Harlow in Essex shows a typical sequence of events. The site had been a major religious centre in the Iron Age. In Vespasian's reign a small temple, on the lines described above, was erected and later the *temenos* or sacred precinct was enclosed. At the end of the second century two rooms were added to flank the entrance to the temple and an altar was placed at the front. Two narrow rooms were erected, one on either side of the enclosure, which was entered by a massive gateway. The complex fell into ruins in the reign of Constantine, probably because of Christian opposition. Other Romano-Celtic

temples were octagonal, round or sixteen-sided in shape. Some of these had a design similar to that of the square temples; others may have been enclosed by solid outer walls with the *cella* supported on open arches. Romano-Celtic temples were built in town and country. At Silchester and at Caistor-by-Norwich two were placed side by side within a precinct; at Springhead four lay within one *temenos*. In the country the original reason for their siting may have been that they occupied a dominant position in the landscape or that they continued a pre-Roman religious site.

The Celtic world had already evolved a comprehensive mythology based partly on the worship of natural phenomena, partly on the worship of those aspects of life which the Celts considered vital – fertility, prosperity, war,

131

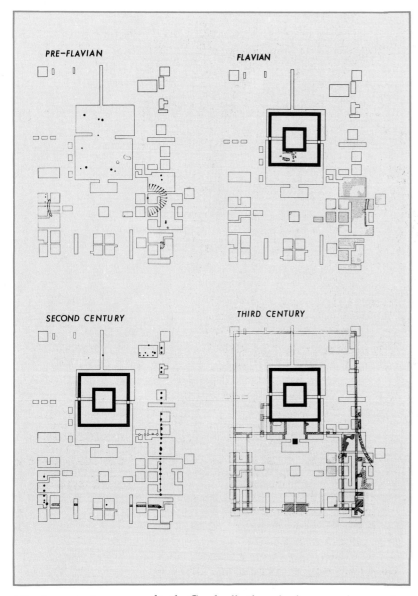

PRE-FLAVIAN

FLAVIAN

SECOND CENTURY

THIRD CENTURY

130 Stages in the development of the Romano-Celtic temple and its temenos at Harlow.

131 Plan of a typical multi-angular Romano-Celtic temple at Weycock. The type is better known from larger examples on the Continent.

death. Gradually there had emerged a complex pantheon of divinities which included Taranis, a warrior deity; Cernunnos, a horned god linked with fertility; Epona, goddess of horses; and the Mother Goddesses, depicted as three seated women holding objects representing the fruits of the earth. The triple nature of some deities indicated intensity of power. There were the Genii Cucullati, represented artistically as three mysterious, hooded figures, and the three-horned bull. The Celts had practised head-hunting and from this grew the cult of the human head. In sculptured form individual heads displayed powerful features, and statues were often three-headed or three-faced. Many individual deities remained local to a given area. Coventina presided over a well at Carrawburgh; Antenociticus is found only at Benwell, where an apse-shaped, oblong building served as his temple. The name of the goddess Verbeia is recorded only at Ilkley; she was the goddess of the River Wharfe. Other cults were more widespread, but although Roman artistic

132

133, 244

traditions portrayed Celtic deities in human form, and Roman masons inscribed Latin names for Celtic gods, no Roman writer lifted the veil that shrouds Celtic mythology.

The toleration of the Romans, however, did allow fusion between Celtic and Roman religion. Roman religion had adopted wholesale the classical pantheon of the Greeks and had grafted onto this Italic or Etruscan beliefs often associated with fertility and vegetation. Classical deities therefore often covered a wide range of functions which easily enabled Celtic deities to be linked to them by means of a process of identification known as the *interpretatio Romana*. Apollo was a healing god; he became associated with Celtic deities thought to inhabit healing waters. Mars became linked with Celtic warrior deities such as Cocidius and Bellatucadrus, found along Hadrian's Wall, but he had originally been an Italic god associated with fertility and untamed woodlands. As such he has the name Mars Braciaca on an altar found near Bakewell, a god whose name implies malt and the brewing of beer. This practice of linking Celtic and Roman deities, or syncretism, is the main method of identifying the character of Celtic deities. Even so, identification can range widely. Brigantia, tribal goddess of the Brigantes, was associated with Minerva to become by implication warrior goddess and patron of craftsmen. The inscription *Dea Nympha Brigantia* at Castlesteads suggests a connection with healing waters. She is also called Victoria Brigantia and a relief at Birrens shows her with the attributes of Minerva Victrix. Silvanus, the woodland deity, was identified with Vinotonus, a deity local to the wild places of Scargill Moor, but at Housesteads he is also syncretized with Cocidius whose association with Mars implies a warlike aspect. The temple of Sulis Minerva not only linked Celtic and Roman deities but also presented, in the great Gorgon's head, the centre-

129

134

135

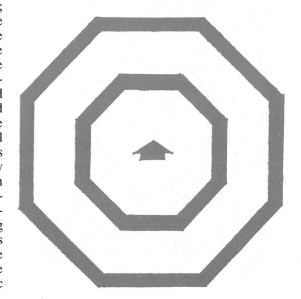

132 Relief from the *vicus* of the fort at Housesteads showing the three cloaked and hooded figures known as the Genii Cucullati. Housesteads Museum.

piece of the pediment, a complex mystery of male Gorgon's head, wings and water serpents. 65 It is obvious that Celtic deities had a flexible and wide-ranging character which could be loosely interpreted by a particular worshipper.

Under the Roman tolerance the choice of deity was a matter for the individual. Medical men in the army might choose to worship the Greek god of medicine, Aesculapius, and his companion, Salus, goddess of healing. Soldiers might invoke Mithras, Mars or Setlocenia, pp. 98–9 goddess of long life. Owners of villas could erect *nymphaea* in honour of the nymphs or *lararia* on which to place small, bronze statuettes representing classical deities. All natural phenomena could have their godlings, and inscriptions to the *Genius loci*, the spirit of the place, are common. Native gods were adopted by soldiers and traders who also brought into Britain the worship of gods from further afield – Olludius from Southern Gaul, Garmangabis, Harimella and the Urseni Fersomari from the Rhineland. Few men, however, went as far as did Marcus Cocceius Firmus, centurion of Legio II Augusta, stationed at Auchendavy, who dedicated at least four altars to ten, possibly eleven, deities to protect himself in the hostile territory where he was stationed.

Roman tolerance extended to oriental cults, some of which provide examples of syncretism.

133 A relief found in a well outside the fort at Carrawburgh dedicated to the water-goddess Coventina. She is shown reclining on a water-lily leaf in a posture commonly taken by water deities. It was dedicated to her by Titus Domitius Cosconianus, prefect of the First Cohort of Batavians stationed in the fort. Chesters Museum.

134 A relief of the goddess Brigantia from Birrens. On her breast-plate is the *aegis* of the goddess Minerva with whom she associates herself. The battlemented wall around the base of her conical helmet indicates a Tyche (city goddess), which in this instance would be of the chief Brigantian city, York (Eburacum). National Museum of Antiquities, Edinburgh.

134

135 The centre-piece of the pediment of the classical-style temple at Bath took the form of a Gorgon's head, a most powerful piece of sculpture combining classical and Celtic features. Roman Baths Museum, Bath.

the cult of Astarte and Heracles of Tyre, and of Panthea, who was linked with the Phrygian Magna Mater cult. The Great Mother appeared in many guises, and her most popular oriental manifestation in Britain was as Cybele, whose rites included purification by ram's blood and whose consort, Attis, was often depicted on funerary monuments. He appears at Corbridge, in Phrygian cap, on the side of an altar dedicated to Dea Panthea; on an altar from Gloucester, where he is playing pan pipes; as a statue from Bevis Marks in London, and on sepulchral monuments from York, Chester and Caerleon. Cybele is represented as a small bronze head on the ritual forceps found in the Thames. It is suggested that this instrument was used for castration purposes because one of the more unpleasant aspects of her cult, which the Roman authorities viewed with distaste, was the rite of self-mutilation performed by her priests while in a state of frenzy. An altar from Carrawburgh was dedicated to the Magna Mater, and a triangular temple established near the London Gate at Verulamium has been associated with her worship mainly on the grounds that pine cones, symbolic of death and immortality, found on that site could have been used in her ritual. In connection with the worship of Heracles of Tyre, mentioned above, a large gilded-bronze statuette found at Birdoswald showed the god dressed in a short tunic, with a lionskin over his shoulder and its mask resting on his head. Heracles had become associated with the Phoenician god, Melquart, and the worship of the god under this guise in Britain almost certainly was introduced by traders.

The cult of Dolichenus came from Syria, and as lord of the firmament the deity was associated with Jupiter. In Britain, his worship is confined to the military areas. It is particularly marked at Corbridge, where an elaborately decorated temple was erected; the remains found include a fragment of a statue showing the god standing, in traditional fashion, on a bull. His consort was often referred to in the Roman world as Juno Regina. A headless statue may represent Juno in this capacity or in her other role as consort of Jupiter Optimus Maximus. A centurion of Legio II Augusta dedicated an altar to Jupiter Dolichenus, Caelestis Brigantia and Salus. As Juno was consort of Jupiter so Caelestis Brigantia was associated with Juno; the Birrens relief, mentioned above, links Brigantia with Minerva – a complex association which was accepted with equanimity in Britain. Salus, as goddess of good health, was someone to whom every soldier could pray. Caelestis was the daughter of Astarte, mythical foundress of Carthage but here identified with Dea Syria, in compliment to the empress Julia Domna who had connections with that area.

Corbridge has also produced evidence of

The evidence for the worship of Egyptian deities includes small bronze figurines of Osiris and Harpocrates. A particularly fine one of Harpocrates was found in the river Thames at London. Made of silver, it depicts the godling with his dog, tortoise and bird companions and a delicate gold chain looped round his body. A temple of Isis probably existed in Southwark, on the evidence of an inscription scratched on a jug, and a bronze steelyard weight depicting the goddess was found in the City. More recently, during work on the riverside wall, an altar was found recording that one Marcus Martiannius Pulcher, a senator and pro-praetorian legate, had ordered the temple of Isis to be restored since it had collapsed through old age. Serapis was worshipped at York where a legate of Legio VI erected a temple to him. Finely carved heads of the god have been found at Silchester and London. The latter, showing him with the traditional *modius* or corn measure on his head, quite obviously imported and a gift of an admirer, was found in the Walbrook mithraeum.

The most prominent of the oriental cults was that of Mithras. He was a Persian god whose cult became especially important to soldiers because he was a youthful, invincible deity who represented the victory of the soul after death, and to merchants because he was a god of sworn obligation and fair dealing. His temples were quite small oblong buildings, often built partly underground, with benches along each side of the interior on which worshippers could recline. As little light as possible was provided, partly to enhance the mystery effect. Dominating one end of the building would be a portrayal, either in stone or in paint, of Mithras' greatest task, the slaying of the wild bull which represented Untamed Creation. At least four mithraea have been excavated in Britain – at London, Housesteads, Carrawburgh and Caernarvon – and one has been discovered recently at Leicester. Evidence for the worship of Mithras also exists at Caerleon, York, Chester and Rudchester.

The cult was open only to men, one reason why it was to disappear, for a religion which aspires to universal truths cannot deny these to one half of the human race. (Women were encouraged to worship the Magna Mater or Isis, and this may account for the founding of a temple to Isis in London.) The cult was also practised in secrecy and many details of its rituals remain obscure. Part of these was certainly a ritual meal which initiates believed strengthened them and was indicative of a better life beyond this world. It was this, together with other symbolism, the celebration of the birth of Mithras on 25 December and the ritual use of bread and water or wine, which aroused the wrath of the Christians against the cult. Mithraism was especially popular in the Danube regions and the Rhineland in the second century AD. It reached its height of popularity in Britain a century later but the rise of Christianity resulted in violent attacks being made on mithraea.

Christianity in its origins also began as an oriental cult. The persecution in the early days of the Empire drove it underground, but after Constantine its triumph was assured. The evidence for Christianity in Britain is scattered and varied but Professor Toynbee argues that it is 'far from unimpressive'. The best evidence for a Christian chapel is the suite of rooms at the Lullingstone villa; there is the mosaic from Hinton St Mary featuring the head of Christ in a central roundel; and a wordsquare was found at Cirencester, and another more recently at Manchester, where the doggerel reading can be rearranged into 'Pater Noster'. Added to these are the ever-growing numbers of objects which have the *Chi-Rho* monogram inscribed on them. But Christianity did not go unchallenged, for both Mithraism and the Celtic gods fought to keep their adherents. There was a pagan reaction in the late fourth century and many of the Romano-Celtic temples are known to have been in use at that date. Despite three British Bishops attending the Council of Arles in AD 314 the Christian faith still had competition and the struggle of Christianity for the hearts and minds of men was to continue in Britain long after the Roman era.

136 Silver statuette of Harpocrates, the infant son of the Egyptian deities Isis and Serapis-Osiris. He has his right hand to his lips cautioning silence and there is a fine gold chain around his body. At his feet stand a dog, a tortoise and a bird. The statuette was found in the river Thames near London Bridge. British Museum.

137 A recently discovered altar from the Thameside river wall at London dedicated by M. Martiannius Pulcher and recording the restoration of the temple to the goddess Isis. Museum of London.

MITHRAISM

Mithras was said to have sprung fully grown, either from a tree or a rock, but from Housesteads (right) there is a rare representation of the god emerging from an egg, holding a torch in one hand and a dagger in the other. The egg represents Universal Time and this is an attempt to link him with Kronos. Round him is an oval frame complementing the shape of the egg; on it are the signs of the zodiac. A lamp, placed behind the sculpture, would shine through the part cut out of the background and make the god appear to be encircled by a halo of light. The effect in a darkened mithraeum was one intended to inspire awe.

A mithraeum was an oblong building, often built partly underground, with benches along each side of the interior on which worshippers could recline, as can be seen in these reconstructions by Alan Sorrell. As little light as possible was provided, partly to enhance the mystery effect. Dominating one end of the building would be a portrayal, either in stone or in paint, of Mithras' greatest task, the slaying of the wild bull which represented Untamed Creation. This took place in a cave – hence the darkened mithraeum. From the bull's body sprang plants useful to man, from his blood sprang the vine of life, and from the spinal cord and tail came wheat. A scorpion, a serpent, a dog and an ant, all beneficent companions, were depicted, together with the raven, who guided Mithras to the cave.

At least four mithraea have been excavated in Britain – at London, Housesteads, Carrawburgh and Caernarfon, and one has been discovered recently at Leicester. Evidence for the worship of Mithras also exists at Caerleon, York, Chester and Rudchester. Mithras was a Persian god whose cult became especially important to soldiers because he represented the victory of the soul over death, and to merchants because he was a god of sworn obligation and fair dealings. He appears in a Persian collection of theological doctrine called the *Avesta*. The Romans elevated him to the position of a supreme deity, making him the centre of a complex mythology. This included a monstrous being, Kronos (or Aeon), portrayed as a lion-headed winged figure, encircled by a serpent and holding a sceptre and a thunderbolt; on his body are signs of the zodiac (above, from Ostia).

A small relief of Mithras slaying the bull (above, Museum of London), dedicated by a veteran of Legio II Augusta, was found on the Walbrook site, but this was not the main portrayal. A lifesize head of the god (right, Museum of London), wearing the characteristic Phrygian cap – an integral part of him for he was born wearing it – was found within the mithraeum and this is most likely to have been part of a large-scale scene. Other figures associated with his worship include Cautes, who held an upturned torch indicating light and life, and Cautopates, whose downturned torch indicated darkness and death. Figures of these were found at Housesteads and remains of statues came from the Carrawburgh mithraeum.

The cult was open only to men, one reason why it was to disappear, for a religion which aspires to universal truths cannot deny these to half of the human race. (Women were encouraged to worship the Magna Mater or Isis and this may account for the founding of a temple of Isis in London.) The cult was also practised in secrecy and many details of its ritual remain obscure. According to Saint Jerome, devotees had to pass through seven grades – Raven, Bridegroom, Soldier, Lion, Persian, Courier of the Sun and Father. For some of these grades special dress was worn; heads of birds and lions, worn as masks, are seen on reliefs and a fourth-century source comments: 'Some flap their wings like birds, imitating the cry of crows; others growl like lions.'

Progression to each grade was by initiation tests which included ordeals of fire and water. Some tests were symbolic; hands were covered with honey because honey washed away evil and cured wounds. Others could be more unpleasant. To the left of the entrance to the Carrawburgh mithraeum (plan and view below) the excavators found a pit, nineteen inches (48cm.) wide and seven feet (2.13 metres) long, large enough for a man to have lain down in it. The pit would have been covered by stones. Anyone who suffered from claustrophobia would undergo a terrifying experience and other persons might wonder how long their ordeal would last. Some of these developments belonged solely to the West. In the worship of Mithras in the East, there is no trace of

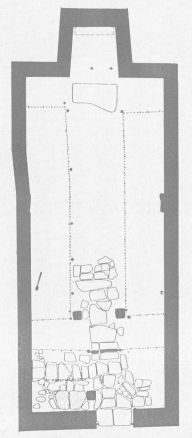

mysteries or of grades. These seem to have been invented by western Roman mithraism.

After the tests had been passed, the initiate could take part in the sacred banquet which also represented the culmination of Mithras' work on earth. Initiates believed that the ritual meal strengthened them and was indicative of a better life beyond this world. It was this, together with other symbolism, the celebration of the birth of Mithras on 25 December and the ritual use of bread and water or wine, which roused the wrath of the Christians against the cult.

Mithraism was popular in the Danube regions and the Rhineland in the second century AD. It reached its height of popularity in Britain a century later but the rise of Christianity resulted in violent attacks being made on mithraea. Carrawburgh and Housesteads are thought to have been desecrated by Christians; Caernarfon was dismantled when the garrison left; but, long after, the remains were deliberately smashed as if to profane the site for ever.

CHAPTER IV
CHRISTIANITY IN ROMAN BRITAIN

The origins and growth of Christianity in Britain present the scholar with peculiar difficulties. On the one hand, the literary evidence from the Roman period is quantitatively minimal and of doubtful reliability while architectural remains largely elude detection. On the other hand, the impression created by the literature of the early post-Roman era suggests an overwhelming Christian presence in Britain in the Roman period. A study of the evidence naturally falls into two broad time divisions: after the Edict of Milan, promulgated by Constantine and Licinius in 313, and before this event, when the Church was either tolerated by virtue of official indifference, or persecuted with greater or lesser vigour.

That Britain had its share of clandestine worshippers is attested by both archaeological discoveries and epigraphic evidence, even if we discount the claim by the third-century writers Tertullian and Origen that, in *c.* 200, 'the word of Christ had been preached in areas of Britain beyond Rome's control', or that, in *c.* 240, 'the Christian religion acted as a unifying force even in the land of Britain'. Neither Tertullian nor Origen had direct contact with Britain, but the former was perhaps writing in the context of Septimius Severus' campaigns in Scotland: it is not impossible that some rumour of a Christian presence could have reached him in distant Carthage. There is evidence to suggest at least a certain Christian element in military circles in Britain at this period.

The earliest recorded Christian martyr in Britain is Saint Alban, whose name now graces the site of the Roman city of Verulamium. Dispute exists as to the date of his martyrdom but opinion favours a date in the reign of Septimius Severus (193–211) during the period when he was campaigning in Britain (209–11). A Severan context would well suit the circumstances of the martyrdom, especially since Alban was a convert, and Severus had prescribed the death penalty for converts in an attempt to stifle proselytization. Alban, a soldier, was martyred when he sheltered a Christian priest, who converted him, during the persecution. The presence of a priest is evidence itself of a Christian community at Verulamium by the early third century, and its continuity is proved by the preservation of the details of the circumstances of the martyr's death and the place of his burial. Two other possible military martyrs may be in evidence at either this time or several decades later. The scene of the martyrdom of Aaron and Julius was the legionary fortress of Caerleon in South Wales, and it seems quite likely that they were soldiers serving in Legio II Augusta. The martyrdoms must have occurred before the dismantling and abandonment of the fortress during the reign of Carausius (286–93), and may have occurred at any time from the reign of Severus to that of Valerian (253–8), though the fierce persecution initiated by Trajan Decius (249–51) would provide a good context for the event.

The possibility that Christianity spread to Britain through military as well as mercantile channels would be consonant with the movement of troops who had served in the East to Britain in the Severan period. A further military context is provided by the recent discovery, at Manchester, of a pottery vessel, datable to the later second century, bearing a wordsquare of Christian significance. The wordsquare is similar to one scratched on the painted wall plaster in a Roman house at Cirencester, reading:

```
R O T A S
O P E R A
T E N E T
A R E P O
S A T O R
```

A translation would read, 'Arepo the sower carefully holds the wheels'. This seemingly innocent acrostic can be reassembled so that the letters form an equal-armed cross composed of the opening words of the Lord's Prayer ('Pater noster'), prefaced and termin-

138 The wordsquare found scratched on a piece of wall plaster at Cirencester can be arranged to provide the opening words of the Lord's Prayer. Corinium Museum, Cirencester.

ated by A and O (Alpha and Omega), the first and last letters of the Greek alphabet, used symbolically to represent Christ's words, 'I am the beginning and the end'.

A

P

A

T

E

R

A/PATERNOSTER/O

O

S

T

E

R

O

Other such acrostics have been found in Christian contexts at Dura Europos, the city on the Euphrates which fell to the Persians in 256, and in a first-century context at Pompeii. These cryptograms must have been understood by covert Christians in an intolerant age, perhaps bringing them the comfort of companionship, and perhaps advertising to them the availability on the premises of the sacraments. The Cirencester example may well be as early in date as the newly discovered specimen, and date to the persecution of Marcus Aurelius.

While the literary and archaeological evidence for pre-Constantinian Christianity is very scarce, evidence for its structure and organization can be extrapolated backwards from early in the age of toleration. The edict which finally relieved Christians from the weight of persecution was issued in 313. Within a year, bishops from London, York and, probably, Lincoln were participating in the Church Council which assembled at Arles in Gaul. It is extremely unlikely that these bishoprics were new creations, and they may be seen as evidence for a pre-existing hierarchy based upon the major population and administrative centres of Britain, which participated fully in the life of the Church. Such participation took place at the Council of Ariminium (Rimini) in 359 where controversial amendments to the Creed were formulated by the Emperor, Constantius II. The British bishops appear to have been reluctant to attend what promised to be an endorsement of Arian practices under imperial compulsion. Three bishops pleaded poverty, perhaps the equivalent of a diplomatic cold, but, if so, they were tactically outflanked when Constantius offered them the free use of the imperial transport system and a subsistence allowance. This incident cannot be used to demonstrate the poverty of the British church, or to conclude that at this period Christianity was still the faith exclusively of the poor and the humble. The reluctant bishops, while accepting imperial assistance, refused 'the collections made for them' by their congregations. A community which could afford to finance episcopal journeys to Italy was not necessarily poverty-stricken.

Nevertheless, physical evidence for urban worship is all but impossible to define archaeologically. This absence of churches is in marked contrast to pagan structures which have been recognized in, or adjacent to, many Romano-British towns. Literary evidence, however, suggests that urban churches did exist in the Roman period. Bede records the presence of an identifiable Roman church at Canterbury which was re-dedicated by Saint Augustine by permission of King Ethelbert. Further, the same Ethelbert after his own conversion permitted Augustine to '. . . preach openly and build or repair churches in all places'.

At present the only generally accepted evidence of an urban church of the Roman period in Britain is that at Silchester (Calleva Atrebatum). The Silchester 'church', dating to the fourth century, lies within a few yards of the administrative centre of the town, a position of considerable prominence, and one which is thought to be an unlikely location for a newly built temple in a period when imperial policy strongly favoured Christianity and deprecated paganism. Nonetheless, the Silchester building presents a number of problems which belie its superficial resemblance to a church. The building had two aisles and a nave terminating in an apse, flanking the apse were two rooms or transepts. A narthex gave admittance to the interior of the building, the nave of which was floored with red tesserae. In the chord of the apse, a black and white mosaic panel served as the base for a structure which may have been an altar. Liturgical problems arise from the

139

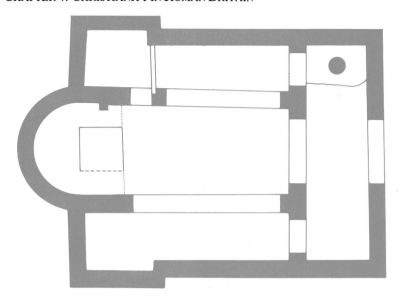

139 Plan of the Silchester 'church'. The worn floors of the apse indicates activity around what may have been an altar (*After* J. Wacher.)

countryside where the rural dwellings of aristocratic townsmen bear witness to the strength of post-Constantinian Christianity, not so much among the meek and humble as among the rich and powerful. It is, perhaps, not too unkind to see a swing to Christian observance as sometimes proceeding from social needs rather than personal fervour, especially in a society in which the new faith was vigorously propagated by the emperor and his agents.

However, at Lullingstone, in Kent, the evidence suggests a genuine concern not merely for the spiritual welfare of the inhabitants of the villa, but also for worshippers from the surrounding countryside. The Lullingstone villa was founded in the first century, reconstructed as a substantial country dwelling in the 115 second, and again radically remodelled in the first quarter of the fourth century. The new decorative scheme included the provision of a splendid new dining-room decorated with a mosaic floor depicting Europa and the Bull, 116 and Bellerophon killing the Chimaera, stock motifs from the repertoire of pagan mythology. The scene of Europa being abducted by the disguised Zeus is accompanied by a couplet based on Virgil's *Aeneid* which may have not only proclaimed the literary cultivation of the villa owner but also protected him from 'the evil eye'. The whole ambience is one of cultivated paganism. Within a few years of the completion of the dining suite an adjacent set of rooms was set aside for Christian worship, the evidence for which consists of painted wall plaster that survived the decay of the villa by

position of the 'altar' and the wear of the panel in a position which makes any celebration of the Mass with the celebrant standing behind the altar to face the congregation, as was the custom of the time, quite impossible. Further, although the building possessed what has been seen as an external font, its alignment puts the altar at the west end, and thus reverses the normal east–west orientation of churches of the period. The demise of this building in the later fourth century and its use for secular activity may further argue against its having been a consecrated Christian structure.

The absence of urban Christian structures is compensated for by direct evidence from the

140 The impact of Christianity on the upper classes of late Roman Britain is reflected in the richness of the costume of the praying figures in the frieze of 'orantes' in the chapel of the Lullingstone villa. British Museum.

141 The Christian *Chi-Rho* monogram, based on the first two letters of Christ's name in Greek, occupied a central position in the decorative scheme of the Lullingstone villa chapel. The cross as a Christian symbol did not come into prominence until late in the fourth century. British Museum.

142 (below) The mosaic from the villa at Hinton St Mary, laid down in the fourth century, has as its central motif the bust of a young man identified as Christ by the *Chi-Rho* monogram behind his head. British Museum.

falling into a cellar which lay immediately below the decorated rooms. Reconstruction of the plaster fragments revealed a decorative 140 scheme of human figures standing in a roofed colonnade; the richness of their costume suggests that these figures represent the villa owner and his kin. Each member of the family is represented with his arms raised to shoulder height with the palms outstretched in the fourth-century attitude of prayer. The Christianity of these praying figures is made clear by 141 the depiction of the sacred *Chi-Rho* (Christos) monogram in a prominent position in the overall decorative scheme. Evidently this range of rooms was sealed off from the dining-room and could be entered directly by its own external door, so that it was accessible to others than members of the immediate family and household. The conversion of houses, or parts of houses, to ecclesiastical use is not uncommon elsewhere in the Roman world in the fourth century.

The direct association of Christian worship with pagan symbolism can be found in other rural settings. At Hinton St Mary this syncretism is at its most explicit. Here, in what appears to be the dining-room of a very large villa, a depiction of Christ is associated with pagan motifs. The room is divided into two parts by lateral cross walls with the larger division occupied by a mosaic whose focal point is a roundel containing the representa-142 tion of a young beardless man, behind whose head appears the *Chi-Rho* monogram. There seems little doubt that this is a representation of Christ himself, perhaps accompanied, in the corners of the mosaic carpet, by the four Evangelists. Here is the clearest demonstration of Christianity, though it may be disconcerting to find the symbols of faith placed underfoot. The adjacent portion of the room, however, contains nothing overtly Christian, rather a representation of Bellerophon killing the many-headed Chimaera. The comparison with Lullingstone, where the same motif is displayed, is compelling, and suggests that at a very early date selected pagan motifs had been fully assimilated into Christian iconography. This conclusion is reinforced by the appearance of a *Chi-Rho* monogram on an otherwise pagan pavement in the villa at Frampton in

143 While essentially pagan in inspiration and design, the Frampton villa mosaic betrays its Christian intention by the inclusion of the *Chi-Rho* symbol.

Dorset. Once again the figure of Bellerophon is prominent as representative of good overcoming evil. By an extention of reasoning, it may be conjectured that when such mosaics appear in other villas, albeit bereft of associated Christian symbolism, they may be indicative of a widespread Christianity among villa owners in the later part of the fourth century. Or, if not Christianity, at least a Gnosticism heavily permeated by Christianity.

Villa owners, however, were essentially townsmen, and the influence of such pockets of Christian belief may have been very small on the rural population in general. Something of the impact of Christianity at a personal and an official level can be deduced from the fate of pagan temples in the period of Christian expansion. If the fourth century was a period of Christian spirituality, it was equally so for paganism, and there is abundant literary evidence for a revivification of pagan thought and doctrines as a reaction to the imperial encouragement of Christianity by law and benefaction. Paganism had no access to imperial funds, except briefly in the reign of Julian (359–63), and any evidence for an architectural revival of pagan structures must be seen as funded by donations from devotees. The scale of such benefactions could be impressive. Few Christian structures could match the temple of Nodens which overlooked the estuary of the 144 Severn at Lydney, Gloucestershire. This temple complex occupied, as did other temples of this late period, the site of an Iron Age hill fort. The earliest development took place in the late third century when a large bath-house and residential quarters were constructed. The nature of the temple structure in this period is not known, though it may have been nothing more than a natural fissure in the bedrock of the site used to communicate with a chthonic deity. In the late fourth century a temple of great architectural pretension was constructed, apparently with the assistance of a naval officer who dedicated a mosaic adjacent to the temple's inner shrine.

The shrine of Nodens was not merely a place for worship but, as votive objects attest, one where healing took place. It was also, if the scale of the residential quarters is any guide, a place of contemplation and retreat. It is perhaps to the new spirituality of paganism that is owed the creation of temples in locations withdrawn from the bustle of towns. Such a temple is that built upon the Maiden Castle 273 hill fort, in the fourth century, a few miles outside Dorchester (Durnovaria). Others would see such creations as being necessitated by the Christianization of the towns with a consequent withdrawal of paganism to the countryside. Although imperial edicts were, from time to time, levelled against the continuity of temple worship, the repetitive nature

144, 145 The temple of Nodens in Lydney Park is surrounded by a complex of residential buildings and a bath house which suggest that the site was one of retreat as well as worship. (*After* R. E. M. Wheeler.)

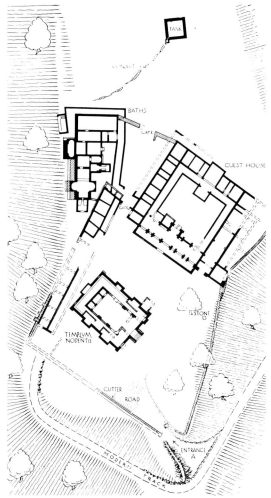

underwent considerable reconstruction at the period of the height of institutional Christianity, while the temples of Silchester, with or without the presence of a church in the centre of the town, continued to be visited throughout the fourth century.

One class of pagan temple can be excluded from the general indifference with which most were treated by the administration of late Roman Britain, itself not necessarily Christian at the level of individuals. The cult of Mithras, which had its origins in the Persian empire, spread through the agency of the Roman army and merchants, reaching Britain by the second century (pp. 98–9 above). The essence of the cult lay in its exclusive and mystical nature and entry to the grades of the cult was by a series of spiritual and physical ordeals. Worship was communal and took place in small temples intended to represent the cave in which the redeemer god, Mithras, had been born. The moral precepts of Mithraism would not have discomforted any Christian. What did create a Christian reaction to Mithraism was the ritual of the Mithraic service itself which included a communal meal similar to the form of the Eucharist in the early Christian Church. Christian writers inveighed against Mithraism, seeing in its rituals a blasphemous parody of their own. Five mithraea are known from actual remains in Britain, others are attested by inscriptions or sculptures. Three were attached to forts on Hadrian's Wall, and one was outside the fort at Caernarfon. The only mithraeum in a civilian context is that discovered beside the river Walbrook in the City of London. None of the military mithraea survived the reign of Constantine and his sons, and the London temple which survived in some attenuated form into the second half of the fourth century, shows signs of the panic burial of its temple sculptures some decades before its 146–8 final closure, perhaps under threat from Christian reaction.

The closure of mithraea associated with forts

of the laws indicates the degree to which they were ineffective. The evidence from temples in the towns of Britain hardly suggests that the imperial writ ran more effectively in this area of the Empire than in, say, Gaul. Whilst it is difficult to define changing function in a structure from non-specific finds, it is possible to show that most urban temples continued in use to the end of the fourth century. At St Albans (Verulamium) the largest temple in the city

146 The fine marble head of the Graeco-Egyptian deity Serapis, complete with a corn *modius* (measure), from the Walbrook mithraeum, was brought from Italy. Museum of London.

147 (right) The eclectic nature of paganism is shown by the inclusion of deities other than Mithras in his Walbrook temple. This second-century head of the goddess Minerva was an import from an Italian workshop (like the Serapis head). Museum of London.

148 (below) Among the small groups of statuary from the Walbrook mithraeum, one, showing Bacchus attended by a bald-headed Silenus on a donkey, Pan and a maenad, emphasizes the connection with traders. Museum of London.

should reflect the degree to which Christianity had spread through the army. We have already suggested that in the late second and early third century, soldier martyrs, such as Alban, may hint at the movement of Christianity with forces transferred from service in the eastern provinces. Unfortunately, there is virtually no direct evidence for Christian worship or practices in the military areas of Britain. Few temples have been excavated, and those that have, like that of the god Antenociticus at Benwell on Hadrian's Wall, reflect the complex history of the occupancy of the adjacent fort rather than offering any explicit evidence for closure due to official action. The evidence from the shrine and well of the nymph Coventina, situated close to the temple of Mithras at Carrawburgh on the Wall, shows that votive deposits of coins were being made until the end of the fourth century, though whether these were truly devotional at the end, or merely reflect the apparently ineradicable habit people have of dropping coins into wells, pools and rivers, is impossible to determine. What is clear is that considerable confusion of belief existed in the army. Constantine himself devised a form of communal prayer for military ceremonies which offended neither Christians nor pagans. He, and his successors, tended to promote Christian officers to higher commands and this, no doubt, stimulated nominal Christianity among the professional officer class. The fort at Caernarvon has produced, probably in a fourth-century context, a sheet of gold en-

244

133

224

graved with a Gnostic talisman which implores a whole pantheon of deities, including Jehovah, to protect the wearer. It is doubtful if the army was militantly Christian. At York, however, where the command headquarters of the northern garrison was situated, we have the evidence of a Bishop Eburacus who attended the Council of Ariminum in 314, and it would be surprising if the families of soldiers of Legio VI Victrix stationed in the city were not to be included among his flock.

In seeking to determine the extent of Christian penetration into society, two areas of non-literary investigation are open to archaeologists: the evidence of portable devotional objects and the evidence to be derived from cemeteries and burial rites. These studies are, to an extent, complementary, since it is the absence of grave goods which has been used to define the presence of Christian burial. Portable objects are fairly widely spread in the urbanized areas of Roman Britain, and take the form of trinkets, jewellery and plate inscribed with the sacred monogram or with a phrase of Christian significance. Not quite typical of these objects is a ring discovered in, or near, Silchester (Calleva Atrebatum) which bears the impeccably Christian inscription:

SENICIANE VIVAS IIN DE[O]

'Senicianus, may you live in God'.

This inscription is an addition to the band of the ring, the main feature of which is a bezel depicting a female head proclaimed by inscription to be Venus. By a curious coincidence this ring appears to have figured in an incident in antiquity which has miraculously survived to come to our notice. Among the votive objects recovered from the temple of Nodens at Lydney was a curse tablet. Curses scratched on lead sheets are not infrequently encountered in pagan contexts and represent the spite of frustrated lovers, betrayed husbands and malicious neighbours. The Lydney curse reads: 'To the god Nodens, Silvianus has lost a ring. He promises half of its value to Nodens. Let him

[Nodens] not grant health to those of the name Senicianus until he brings it back to the temple of Nodens.' It is, with all the caveats possible, irresistible to equate the Senicianus who stole the ring, perhaps from the Lydney temple itself, with the owner of the 'Christianized' ring from Silchester. Evidently, the curse, which was renewed at least once, had no effect.

No such odium attached to the hoard of church plate recovered from the site of Water Newton (Durobrivae), Cambridgeshire. The hoard comprises some thirty items, all but one of silver, the odd item being gold. Nine vessels are represented in the form of cups, bowls and a wine strainer, but the bulk of the hoard consists of thin silver and silver gilt plaques, representing stylized palm leaves. Several of the items bear the *Chi-Rho* monogram, including the strainer, which may have been used in preparation of the communion wine, and the silver-leaf plaques. Votive leaf-plaques are not unique to Christian contexts, indeed, they are more common in pagan deposits. Examples are known from the fourth-century temple at Maiden Castle, and from the western outpost fort at Bewcastle, just north of Hadrian's Wall. In these cases the leaves bear repoussé representations of pagan deities. Once again we see the assimilation of pagan religious practices into a Christian context just as we have seen the assimilation of mythological motifs into Christian symbolism. The parallel is made explicit by the dedication inscription on one of the Water Newton leaves which states that 'Anicilla has fulfilled the vow which she promised'. Here is the exact equivalent of the pagan's claim to have 'willingly and joyfully paid his vow'. Of a new dimension is a silver bowl with a donor's inscription which appears to mean 'I, Publianus, trusting in you, honour your holy sanctuary, O Lord.'

If the picture of the spread of Christianity in Britain as illustrated by finds and structures is one of a limited penetration in a largely pagan society, it cannot be entirely reconciled with the material evidence of burial rites or the literary evidence deriving from the post-Roman period. So far as burials are concerned the recognition of Christian cemeteries depends on the assumption that an east–west alignment of the grave (implying a belief in the Resurrection) and the absence of grave furnishings are of specifically Christian inspira-

149 The gold ring found near Silchester and inscribed for Senicianus has a definitely Christian connotation. The Vyne, Basingstoke, Hants. (*After* M. W. Barley.)

150 The Lydney curse, scratched on a small sheet of lead, may perhaps be linked with the Senicianus ring. (*After* R. E. M. Wheeler.)

151 (below left) A simple two-handled chalice of cantharus shape from the Water Newton hoard of silver plate. British Museum.

152 (below) The silver strainer from the Water Newton hoard. British Museum.

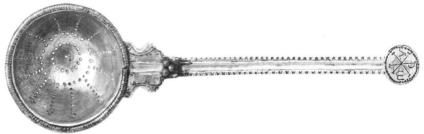

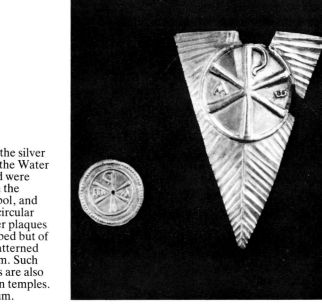

153 Nine of the silver plaques from the Water Newton hoard were inscribed with the *Chi-Rho* symbol, and also the gold circular disc. The other plaques were uninscribed but of similar leaf-patterned triangular form. Such votive plaques are also found in pagan temples. British Museum.

154 A silver mixing bowl from the Water Newton hoard was a gift from a member of the congregation, Publianus, for use in the Communion service. Its inscription may be translated as 'O Lord, I, Publianus, relying on you, honour your holy sanctuary'. British Museum.

155 (right) The Poundbury cemetery at Dorchester, Dorset, traces the transition from pagan to Christian burial rites. It began in the late third century as two cemeteries, one pagan without a strict alignment of graves, and the other apparently Christian. As the cemetery expanded to the west in the fourth century the Christian rite prevailed, with a strict east–west alignment of the body, which was laid to rest without accompanying grave goods. (*After* J. Wacher.)

tion. A cemetery which exhibits both these characteristics has been examined at Poundbury, Dorset. This, a cemetery of the city of Dorchester (Durnovaria), has been estimated to contain some 4,000 graves and shows a transition between the interment of the deceased with offerings of pots, coins and personal possessions, to one in which the body was laid to rest without them. The overwhelming majority of burials are of the latter class, and one coffin, of lead, has an inscription on the lid which has been expanded to read '*in nomine domini*', a clearly Christian invocation. A number of burials have the body 'embalmed' in plaster, a rite elsewhere ascribed to Christian belief in the resurrection of the body. Similarly treated burials have been found as far north as York.

If the evidence for Dorchester were to prove to be repeated in other Roman cities, and Winchester seems already to be in this class, then the evidence for large-scale Christian observance among the urban population would be compelling.

Writing in the sixth century, Gildas, while upbraiding his countrymen, never, even in the greatest excess of abuse, calls them pagans. It would seem, then, that either late in the fourth century, or even later, a large-scale conversion took place. The evidence of Saint Germanus' visit in 429 is illuminating, since he was sent from Gaul not as a missionary, but as a representative of orthodoxy to wean British Christians from the heretical doctrines of Pelagius.

Whether British Christianity was orthodox or not, it was sufficiently vigorous to survive, in the form of the Celtic Church, the Saxon onslaught. When all else failed it was the last point of contact between the final flickering of the classical world in Britain and the Mediterranean.

CHAPTER V
THE ECONOMY

Agriculture

Because Roman Britain is an episode which happened over 1,500 years ago there is a great temptation to think that it was all different; different from life in the Middle Ages, different from life in the eighteenth century, and different from life today. In some ways this must be true, for the Romans did not have combine harvesters, though they did have ideas about reaping machines, and they did not have motorways, though their roads were better made and more directly planned than any others before about 1800. But then, as now, agriculture was a major occupation; corn, wool, beef and hides were the most important produce; and an annual sequence of fields green in spring, with the growing crop, golden in July or August as it ripened, and brown over the winter from the plough, covered most of the land surface of Britain. To someone living now in a large town or city, this sequence sounds foreign, if not 'folksy', and here we do have a real difference, for there was nothing in Roman Britain like a modern city.

Differences and similarities aside, the basic thing that we still have to find out about Roman Britain is how it worked. As we go back in time our knowledge gets more and more vague. From the time of George III (1760–1820) we have almost complete information from census returns, tax returns, parish registers, and books written about how farming was being carried on at the time; what went on in the towns, and how the various strands fitted together to form a thriving whole can be gleaned from contemporary writing. Before the eighteenth century our knowledge is much poorer; our first proper census is in 1801, a detailed examination of agriculture only starts in the seventeenth century, few parish records go back before the sixteenth century, and we have very few cottages or small houses still standing now as they were in the fifteenth century. By the time that we get back to the Norman Conquest we have only occasional splashes of information in an otherwise hazy picture, and our written sources for the working of Saxon Britain – mining, trade, agriculture, communication, town life, population – would take up a very modest shelf of books. On Roman Britain we have none of the usual sources to help us, so archaeology has to try to take the place of history, and inevitably there are very great problems.

Before dismissing written sources completely it may be a good idea to look at one example which is often quoted as a comment on the working of Roman Britain. The fourth-century historian Ammianus Marcellinus records that in the reign of the emperor Julian (355–363) Britain sent grain to the army stationed in Germany. The usual interpretation of this is that in the fourth century Britain was producing a surplus of grain so that it constituted a major export. The objections to such a view are important. First, the document only mentions one or two occasions on which this hap-

156 A fine multi-coloured mosaic pavement of the second century AD from Cirencester featuring personifications of the Four Seasons. This gives an idea of how the customer and the craftsman thought about Autumn. Corinium Museum, Cirencester.

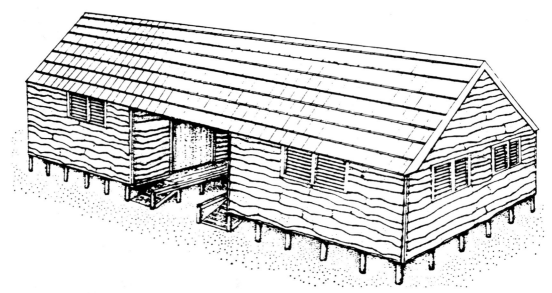

157 In order for the harvested grain to be stored for the winter it was essential that granaries should be well ventilated buildings set clear of the ground to keep out pests and damp.

pened so it is certainly unsafe to extend what happened only once or twice to the whole of the fourth century. Secondly, and most important, the fact that Britain supplied the immediate needs of the army in Germany says nothing about conditions in Britain. The army would have satisfied its wants even if this left every small farmer in Britain with only just enough grain to live on until the next harvest. This is no guarantee of booming production, a thriving grain market, or the export of a surplus. When an explicit statement like this can be misunderstood in so many ways, perhaps no one will be surprised if we look elsewhere for information.

These points affect most of the written sources for commerce, trade, and agriculture in the ancient world because every author was writing about specific examples, individual instances, and what he knew or had been told. No ancient author could know that the British Economy was booming in the fourth century because there was probably no such concept as the British Economy, and there was no centralized information to show that it was booming. Here is another trap for the unwary; economics has become so much part of our lives that we tend to read back our present ideas into the ancient world. I have used, up to now, such vague phrases as 'the working of Roman Britain' rather than the economy because I want to try to avoid the trap in order to see Roman Britain on its own terms.

Finally, before we get down to firm examples, what are the dangers of archaeological sources to set beside the dangers of historical sources? One danger is exactly the same. Just as the ancient author writes about 'my farm', or 'our district', so an excavator can only properly talk about 'the villa I excavated', or 'the area that I surveyed'. The second danger is

worse. It is the fixation with what has been discovered, rather than what we want to discover.

Any guesses about the number of people who lived in Roman Britain can never be proved right or accurate; but some guesses are more likely than others to be correct. When, in 1928, R. G. Collingwood first made a guess about the population he fell straight into the second danger by fixing his ideas on what was known – the towns, the army, the villas. He gave an estimate of half a million consumers and postulated another half million anonymous – and homeless – producers in the countryside to feed them. He was quickly attacked by a farmer who made the point that there are very few simple farming systems in which one producer can produce enough to feed himself, save seed corn for the next year, sell some produce to pay his taxes, and still have enough left over to feed one other person in the city. The record was set straight, and the consumers since then have been given just enough people in the countryside to feed them. But is this the right way to look at it?

With the great modern expansion of road building and gravel extraction much more attention has been paid in the last twenty years to the large tracts of countryside which do not have villas dotted over the landscape. Before gravel pits are opened, and large tracts of the countryside disappear, aerial photographs of the areas are carefully searched for signs of farmsteads and villages showing up as scatters of stone or building materials in ploughed fields, or shadows in growing crops; and when those searches are carefully done the number of Roman sites that are found is very high indeed. In the Trent valley in Nottinghamshire the small farmsteads seem to be clustered one against another at a density of about one every

158

158 The plan of a Romano-British farmstead near South Muskham, Notts., as it shows up in growing or parched crops, can be seen to be a simple building with a ditch around it.

159 (below) When later agriculture has not ploughed away the traces it is still sometimes possible to see the banks and limits of early fields, 'Celtic' fields, such as those in use in the Roman period. Aerial photography, as this view of Burderop Down in Oxfordshire, can make them very clear.

one or two square kilometres of land. This density of farms with their farmland leaves very little room for wild woodland, unfarmed scrub, or waste, and suggests a landscape very like the one we have today. The same sort of results have appeared from Barry Cunliffe's survey of sites in the parish of Chalton in Hampshire where small Roman farms, as judged by scatters of pottery, coins, and building debris, are numerous.

These results are vital to our understanding of how Roman Britain worked because we cannot hope to understand the working of any system until we have a basic knowledge of the parts of which the system is built. What then is a rough estimate of the numbers of country dwellers and townspeople in the province? Before we can even guess at this answer it is necessary to point out one more trap in the evidence. Our period stretches for at least 350 years, from the Conquest of AD 43 to about 400, and it would be very odd if Britain did not change over that time. My ideas on this, and especially on the relative roles of town and country, are unusual, and not according to the textbooks, and I feel particularly strongly that we ought to split our study into Early Roman Britain from 43 to about 170, and Later Roman Britain from about 200 to 400, with a transition stage in the middle. Even if I am totally wrong about the differences between these two periods, most people would agree that the evidence from the early period should not be confused with that two or three hundred years later, and we must therefore notice that much of our evidence for widespread farming belongs to the later period, and especially the fourth century.

If we begin to look in greater detail at the areas under the plough in later Roman Britain, judging this by where we know the Roman farmers to have lived, where we can still see his 'Celtic' fields with their banks and enclosures, and where he tipped his rubbish, perhaps in the course of muck-spreading, then an intriguing picture emerges. The very fact that we can still see some 'Celtic' fields means that they are not now under the plough, and have not been ploughed since their users left them. Many areas of Britain were brought under the plough for the first time in living memory for the effort of the First World War, and those areas produced many Roman farm sites; again, areas not ploughed much before 1900 had been under plough in Roman Britain. This evidence joins that from the river valley gravels, and the chalk uplands of the south, and it strongly suggests that only in the last few years have we had as many acres under plough as the farmers of Roman Britain. Perhaps we ought to think seriously about the estimated two million people in England at the Domesday Survey, and ask whether there is any proof that there were fewer than that in the south of Roman Britain.

When the Romans arrived in Britain they found a working agriculture whose standards were little, if any, lower than their own. Heavy ploughs, instead of the simple light plough, had been introduced into Britain, presumably from Gaul, before the Roman Conquest, and the staple crops and usual farm animals were widely accepted in the pre-Roman Iron Age. The

160 The plough consists of a plough-share which lifts the earth and a coulter such as this which cuts the surface so that the share can get under; it has changed very little from Roman times onward. (*After* G. Boon.)

161 One of the most common forms of rubbish thrown out of the Roman household was the bone waste from the cooked meat. When gathered up in excavation the examination of such bones can give a great deal of information about contemporary diet and stock-rearing. The bones seen here are from the excavations at the Romano-Celtic temple on Hayling Island.

British farmer therefore found few novelties in Roman agriculture. Various types of wheat, oats and barley formed the basic cereal crops, some fodder crops such as hay, vetch and turnips may well have been grown in fields to feed the animals over the winter, and fruit and vegetables were probably grown on a small scale in the garden.

Our evidence for what was grown comes from many different sources. Excavation can provide us with some ideas through water-logged deposits in which food rubbish which was once thrown away has not decayed properly. Hard parts of fruits, wood and nuts might have been thrown on the hearth and been merely charred, so that they also are decay resistant. The good Biblical parable about sorting the wheat from the tares, and consigning the tares to everlasting fire, tells us about sorting weeds from the harvest and burning them, and the remains of such fires tell us not only about the crop and the weeds but the cleanliness of the fields and the purity of the yield. Cess-pits, again when waterlogged, can sometimes show us fruit seeds which have been eaten but not digested, such as fig seeds, grape pips and blackberry pips. The evidence can never be accepted just at face value, it has to be thought out. Fig seeds do not necessarily mean that figs grew in Roman Britain any better than they grow in England today; they were probably imported, and this guess is partly confirmed by shipwrecks in which large pottery vessels (*amphorae*) have been found filled with dried fruit. Grape pips found at Dover may mean the import of luscious bunches of French grapes, or they could be of Kentish growth. On the subject of wine-making in Britain it is said that the presence of crushed grapes in a rubbish deposit should be diagnostic, but what if cheese covered in grape must was in fashion and imported even then? Any grape pips could just as well show a trade in raisins.

Literary evidence does exist, but it seldom refers specifically to Britain. Here we have to assume that if the Romans wrote about a certain fruit, or crop, it was available to grow in Britain, and we must judge whether it did or not by the suitability of the crop to the climate. A more unusual source of information comes from the modern descendants of the British language – Cornish, Breton and Welsh. Some Latin words were adopted into British, especially when the object was a Roman introduction and the British had no word of their own. Such borrowings continued in the daughter languages and have left permanent evidence embedded in the vocabulary. An example might be the Latin *pira* for pear, and the modern Cornish and Breton 'per'.

On animal husbandry the evidence is much more solid and common for it exists in the form of bones discarded and buried in rubbish pits.

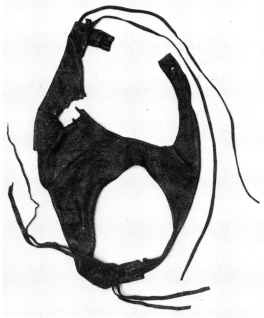

These bones give an idea of the species of animal which were eaten in towns and farms, and sometimes used in temples for sacrifice. They can give an idea of the age at which the animal was slaughtered, and this in turn can give an idea of the fate of the carcass. Thus an old horse is virtually uneatable but has probably had a useful life as a mount or a coach-horse; a young (three-year-old) ox or bullock would have been of little use as a draught animal, but would have provided choice beef. Pigs are of little use except to eat, whereas most sheep probably provided at least one fleece for the shearer before being eaten. The winter feed mentioned above was essential since there is very little evidence from animal bones of the killing off of a large number of animals before their first winter. Judging from the age of most animals deposited in rubbish pits, feeding through the winter was normal.

Just as the army in the time of Julian had an interest in grain, so they must have had an interest throughout the Roman period in wool for uniforms, and leather for tunics, equipment and tents. This leads us on to the fate of the

162 Cattle provided meat and leather. Most of the leather must have gone into army equipment, but some was used for garments like this leather bikini which was preserved in waterlogged conditions in the Walbrook in London. Museum of London.

163 Once shoes were worn out they were thrown away, only occasionally were they repaired. If the rubbish pit into which they were thrown was waterlogged, they have often been preserved. Museum of London.

produce which came from the farms. The first call on it was that of subsistence, for a farm had to be self-supporting so far as food was concerned. After that taxes had to be paid, and here is one of the main differences between early Roman Britain, and late. In the first and second centuries taxation was mainly taken in money with some levies of military rations. This meant that some of the farm produce, even in a bad year, had to be sold to get the money to satisfy the tax gatherer. No doubt there was some latitude here, depending on the tax man. He had made a bid for the job of collecting taxes, had settled with the administration for a lump sum which he paid, and then tried to extract more than this sum from the people to repay himself and make a profit. A friendly, but money-minded tax man might give a loan to a farmer in a bad year, and reclaim this with interest in a good year; a hard taxman might insist that every scrap of produce must be sold to pay the tax on the spot. But this system changed.

With the rampant inflation of the third century, which we will examine more closely when

164, 165 Plan and reconstruction of the great courtyard villa at Chedworth. So much information would seem to imply that we know what went on in such buildings, but in fact we do not yet know whether this is one house, or two, or more; so there is still much to be learnt. (*Plan by* Roger Goodburn; *reconstruction by* Sheila Gibson.)

we reach the subject of coinage, the income to the State dropped and the expenditure necessary to purchase supplies rose. The State reorganized the system in a way that by-passed the markets, for instead of letting the goods be sold, claiming the money, and then purchasing those same goods, the State took the goods in place of the money. Each year the administration would calculate its needs in terms of commodities vital to the army, and would extract these goods directly from the population by levying a 'rate' on lands and stock. Thus in one year a tax of four bushels per acre would meet the needs; the next year, with less army supplies needed, perhaps only three bushels per acre need be taken. This system was changing yet again at the end of the fourth century, but after that, Britain was no longer tied to a Roman system. I shall come back to the bypassing of the markets later; all we need to note here is that the markets lost two lots of profits – one when the farmer should have sold his produce, and the other when the State should have bought.

After the farmer had fed himself and his family, and provided for the farm hands who may well have been paid partly in kind, and after he had paid his taxes either by selling some goods or by passing the goods over direct, then he was free to take his surplus produce to market. There is no doubt at all that some farmers had a surplus and made a profit, for they must have been able to pay for the heating systems, mosaics and wall paintings which so many of them bought in the fourth century. These goods probably came from centres, towns or markets or villages, and the people who made them had to live off the process.

This leads us on to the farm itself, and the term 'villa' which has accidentally cropped up without explanation. The Roman villa is known in literary sources in Italy and, less well, in Spain, France and Germany. The word may occur in some sources on Roman Britain, but we really have no direct information on what a villa in Britain was and, more problematical, which farms in Britain were villas. By archaeological tradition the word is applied to the better farming establishments of the countryside, and the usual criteria for definition are the possession of stone-built walls with painted plaster, tiled roofs, and tessellated or mosaic floors. This may be convenient, but it leads to odd conclusions for it is not unusual for a farm to be built in stone at the end of the third century but only to qualify as a villa later in the fourth century when it has additions in the form of hypocausts and pavements. This happens as one of the many rebuildings which all country farms seem to undergo, and there is no guarantee that the one particular re-building that qualifies for a change in status is anything

164, 165

166 In the uplands of Wales houses in villages clustered together in round walled groups, often, as here at Carn Fadryn, placed on bleak high land.

more than the whim of a newly married couple moving into the family farm. In such a case there is not a change in class, in social status, or in the economic standing of the farm, but simply a generation's difference of taste. We will keep for the moment to the word 'farm', remembering that such buildings run all the way from one-roomed wooden huts to forty-roomed mansions with parkland in front and the farmyard behind.

Farms vary in the Roman period depending on the area of Britain in which they were sited, the date in the Roman period when they were occupied, and their proximity to taxes and markets. Some areas which were remote from the Roman centres of population, such as the hills of North Wales and the Scottish borders, had farmsteads, but these were not of very Roman character. In North Wales there are groups of houses, similar to those in Cornwall, stone-built in clusters, very often circular or of curved outline; on the Scottish border the farmsteads are more often single houses of curved outline in a ditched enclosure. All these farmsteads and villages were in the Roman province, depended on agriculture, supplied

166

115

the army's needs, and presumably paid their taxes. In the lowland area of Britain from Somerset up to the Severn, the Dee and across to the Wash, farms tend to be rectangular buildings, even when grouped in villages, with the addition of wings, corner rooms, towers, verandahs, corridors and courtyards as they rose up the scale of social grandeur. On some sites the process of enlargement and enrichment can be followed in the fortunes of one family when a simple block house of four or five rooms first has a verandah added to the front, then a new kitchen at the back, next a pair of towers at the ends of the front verandah to form a good architectural façade, then a set of mosaic pavements, a new bath wing, and hypocausts. This success story comes out in some farms; others remain as simple wooden structures of one or two rooms throughout their lives.

112, 113

Urban Planning

Palatial villas are known early on in Roman Britain and seem to belong to the well Romanized region of the southeast. Fishbourne is more palace than villa (pp. 62–3), but Eccles in Kent, and Angmering in Sussex are luxuriously appointed if they are farms rather than country houses. The more typical early farms are smaller, simpler buildings seldom with mosaics of any great design and often only simple mortar floors. Palatial villas of the early period do not often have long lives – Fishbourne, for exam-

ple, was being used as a quarry for tiles and building materials by the year 300 – but another class of palatial villa seems to grow independently in the fourth century. A good example is the villa at Woodchester in Gloucestershire where an early farm with some luxuries and good appointments was reorganized and rebuilt on a massive and formal scale at the end of the third century.

284

The typical villa in Britain, if such exists, flourishes in the fourth century. It is built, or re-built, at the end of the third century. It lies in a valley, half-way up the slope, near a suitable water supply, with good access to a well made road, and thence to a good market centre. In its main room, perhaps the dining room, it has an expensive mosaic pavement which will give some indication of the education, interests, or sometimes even the religion, of the owner, and in another wing there is a bath block with a capacity substantially more than that needed simply by the family. It has goods brought from a wide area of Britain, but little that has been imported from the Continent.

164, 263

116

142, 247

The farm, as the producer of surplus goods, and hence consumer of other's services, depends on some nearby centre in which the surplus can be sold, and services can be bought. The temptation is to call such a centre a town, but before we do this it is worth remembering that service centres existed without being towns before the Roman Conquest of Britain and after Roman influence declined. In the west of Britain in the sixth, seventh and

167 An artist's impression of Roman London, seen from the east. It was the largest town in Roman Britain, covering 330 acres and with a wall circuit of about three miles. All the classic features of a chess board street pattern, walls, and large public buildings in the centre were present. (*Drawn by* Alan Sorrell.)

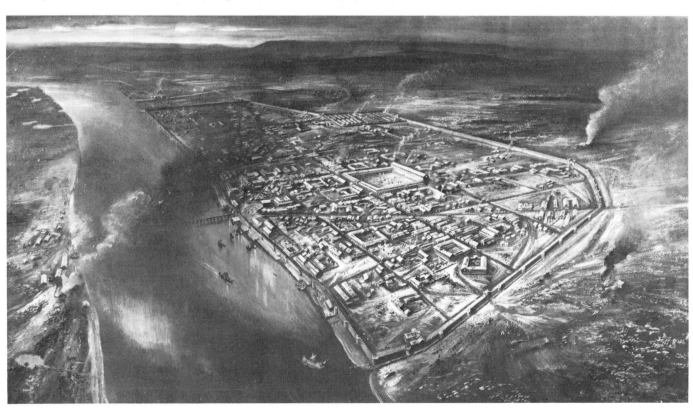

IMP·TITVS·CAESAR·DIVI VESPASIANI SPASIANVS·AVG
P·M·TR·P·VIIII·IMP·XV·COS VIII DESIG·VIIII·CENSOR·PATER·PATRIAE
ET·CAESAR·DIVI·VESPAS NI·F·D OMITIANVS·COS·VI·DESIG·VII
PRINCEPS·IVVENTV COLLEGIORVM·OMNIVM·SACERDOS
CN·IVLIO·A COLA·LEG·AVG·PRO

eighth centuries AD there were very highly skilled services such as book illumination which flourished in the monasteries, and metalwork which flourished in princely households; there were also trade and commerce, administration and taxes, but no towns. The organization of agriculture in Roman Britain demanded service centres and markets, but there was no absolute need for the densely populated centres of trade, commerce, services and administration which alone merit the name of town.

Just as the word villa can cause trouble by importing ideas which were developed in the Mediterranean area, but are not applicable to Britain, so the word city is probably best left out of any Romano-British vocabulary unless reserved for the early state of London. There an urban sprawl covered 330 acres with shops, temples, wharves, warehouses, a palace, baths, and most of the other urban features common in the Roman world. Other centres in Britain can be divided into larger and smaller towns, and villages. Where the dividing lines come no one knows because no one has yet suggested how or why these settlements should be different apart from their size. Before worrying about further definitions it is probably best to discuss the characteristics of towns in early Roman Britain.

The only settlements in pre-Roman Britain that approach urban status are the large sprawling defended settlements known as *oppida*. As yet, very little is known about them in England; on the Continent some have the formal planning, differentiation of buildings, and density of occupation that allows them to count as towns. In Roman Britain the idea of a network of towns covering the country at roughly sixty-mile intervals was a completely Roman innovation dictated by the convenience of the Roman administration. To the Roman official the town was an administrative spot in a tribal area through which he could make contact with the natives. No doubt, once the sites of these tribal centres were chosen, Rome would subsidize the building of one official residence for visiting dignitaries and functionaries, but it was certainly left to tribal notables to organize a programme of urban development. The public buildings, their design and use, have been described in a previous chapter; all that concerns us here is what grew up in a town, what economic purpose it fulfilled, and who paid for it.

The Roman ideal for each tribe was self-financing self-government under the watchful eye of the provincial governor and his officers, and this is what seems to have happened. On each site chosen as a tribal capital – Durovernum of the Cantiaci (Canterbury), Corinium of the Dobunni (Cirencester), Ratae of the Coritani (Leicester), Venta (the market) of the Iceni (Caistor-by-Norwich), of the Belgae (Winchester), of the Silures (Caerwent), and the others – bright new buildings such as the forum, the basilica, temples and arches began to rise. There is not much evidence that the tribal notables moved into the towns as the building began in the 60s of the first century, for the major housing programmes seem to belong later in the century, and the transformation of wooden houses into firm and permanent stone buildings does not happen much before the middle of the second century. When a building went up the locals, or those of them who could read, were left in no doubt as to who their benefactors were, for large clear inscriptions told all. The inscription always began by naming the emperor, from whom all good things came; but this was simply protocol and did not imply that he had paid for the monument. Lower down, perhaps in smaller letters, there is usually the name of a local worthy, or a group of councillors or magistrates, and it is those people who wished to be remembered for their generosity to their fellow inhabitants. The towns, then, were built by local funds, and they therefore had to serve local needs.

It is best to talk about inhabitants of towns, rather than citizens, because in Roman Britain there were at least two sorts of citizens, Roman and 'other'. In the Empire at large a citizen was literally a member of a tribe in Rome with a vote that could be cast for various elections in the City. He may never have been to Rome, he may never have voted, but his citizenship was valid throughout the Empire, as Saint Paul demonstrated so well when he humbled a

168 Inscriptions such as this one from the forum at Verulamium often tell us when a building was set up, and sometimes what it was used for. Information of this nature is rarely found in villages, and never from farms, so archaeology has to work in its own way. Verulamium Museum, St Albans.

168

167

170 Plan of the fort and *vicus* at Vindolanda. The fort was the preserve of the army, but the *vicus* beside it had a good commercial reason for being there, and a life of its own. (*After* R. Birley.)

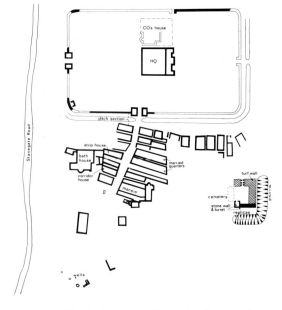

centurion who was punishing him illegally. This citizenship carried both privileges like those Saint Paul invoked – not to be flogged – and the right of appeal to the emperor direct, and it carried duties and taxes. At first, in Britain, Roman citizens would have been found mainly in towns that we have not so far described, the *coloniae*. These, at Colchester, Gloucester, Lincoln, and finally at York, were originally settlements of discharged soldiers, who by definition were Roman citizens, and they held a higher place in the ranking of towns than the tribal towns. A few people in the tribal towns would have been citizens of Rome, those who had been born of citizen parents, those who had held magistracies, those who had moved out of chartered cities; but in general the tribal people were just that, citizens of the Iceni or Dobunni, or Cornovii. With the introduction of the *coloniae* we have put all the larger towns on the map; what of the smaller towns?

Not very much is known about the history of the smaller towns, especially in their earlier years, and opinions differ as to why and when they came into being. Some definitely lie over the remains of the early forts which the Roman administration spread over Britain after the Conquest to keep the newly won province in order. The usual explanation here is that the

army decided where to place the fort and the civilians in the neighbourhood were attracted by the money of the soldiers to set up a commercial village, or *vicus*, around the camp. No doubt they provided the soldiers with wine, women and song, and when the fort moved on and the soldiers left, the *vicus* grew into a small town in its own right. There are several objections to this idea. In the first place the remains under the small towns are almost always the forts themselves and not attendant villages. In the second place there is no guarantee that when the military customers moved away the service settlement could suddenly become self-sufficient. And, lastly, the factors which led the Roman administration to place a fort in a particular spot may well have suggested to later builders that this was a suitable place for a permanent market. So we have yet to see the results of the excavation of one of these service villages, we have to hear of its later history, we need a carefully thought out plan of how it could grow independently from the late lamented Roman fort; and we need to be sure that the service settlement did in fact develop into a small town. A much more likely sequence is as follows: the fort was sited at the crossing of roads or rivers or natural communications, on higher ground for good drainage and safety, and near to some concentration of population in order to control them. The removal of the fort no doubt led to the immediate collapse of the attendant *vicus*, but the factors which influenced the siting of the fort remained constant and acted just as much for the establishment of a later settlement on the site, the obvious place, for instance, for a permanent market.

This illustrates the difficulties that are usually met with when using any archaeological evidence. The two theories are equally plausible, the choice of model probably reflects

170, 171

169 The small towns of Roman Britain, such as Great Casterton in Lincolnshire, lack the regular layout of the larger towns and look much more like modern villages.

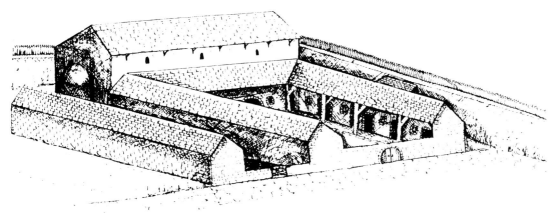

Reconstruction drawing of the *mansio*, an official inn or posting station, in the *vicus* at Vindolanda. Most forts have been dug for the military information they could yield, and the *vicus* attached to them generally ignored. At Vindolanda the *vicus* has given much important information and produced unique finds such as the writing tablets that were preserved in unusual conditions. (*After* R. Birley.)

173

individual interests. If you believe that people are most affected by institutions, and you are firmly based in the classics and the Roman army, then you will prefer a 'service village – small town' model. If you believe more in the landscape, natural features and the effect of the environment, then you will prefer to believe in the continuity of the site, but not in continuity of occupation. The matter could be settled by excavation of an early fort and its attendant *vicus*, and the resulting small town to see how institutions arrived, changed, grew and developed. This has never been done because *vici* and villages seldom have great stone-built houses with mosaics and wall plaster, and are never the scene of great historical events. The Roman archaeologist is to blame because in the past he has chosen his sites to excavate, and has chosen either the fort alone, or the big town houses and villas with good things to find. Now the archaeologist has his sites chosen for him by what is most obviously being destroyed and, for the good of Roman

172

archaeology, he is no longer a classically trained Romanist, so we are beginning to get an interest in the rather more humdrum, every-day workings of the province, in farms and villages, fields and rubbish tips, and blame for lingering 'goody-hunting' has shifted to the public.

When a motorway is being built, or a housing estate laid out, remains come to light. Some wooden buildings, ditched enclosures, and field systems can be difficult to understand, and almost impossible to photograph. The site will not hit the headlines, the press will not cluster round, public opinion will not be stirred and the unhappy archaeologists will retire to their base with a very imperfect understanding of yet another Roman farm destroyed. A stone building with two mosaic floors, lots of pottery and coins, and an easily distinguished plan, will attract photographers like bluebottles; pictures will appear in the papers, indignation will mount, and in no time at all a three-month building delay will have been arranged, and

172 Chedworth, with its mosaics, is typical of the 'glamorous' sites that always attract the most attention. Here the figure of Winter in a Seasons mosaic probably gives a good idea of winter dress, for we know that the hooded cloak was a British speciality.

173 Many woodworking tools, as this carpenter's plane, were just like those in common use today. Verulamium Museum, St Albans.

money will be forthcoming to help the dig, and the offending new houses will have been re-sited. We are back with the problem of concentrating on the information that we have or is easy to obtain, rather than concentrating on the difficult parts, and what we really need to know. The model of a nineteenth-century city which would result from the selective excavation of just the town hall, the parish church, the mayor's parlour, the assize courts, and perhaps a token factory would be horribly incomplete; this is, at present, how our information on Roman Britain stands.

Let us return to our smaller towns and villages. We have our larger towns – they are administrative; we have our farms – they are productive. In between lie our villages and smaller towns and, whatever their origins, they must presumably have some function in providing services. The most obvious service that they can provide to surrounding farms is that of a market. The farmer, hopefully, is going to produce a surplus, and that surplus needs to be sold. With the profits taxes have to be paid, and all those goods that the farmer cannot produce himself have to be bought. While the small early village may act as an outlet for the farmer's produce it cannot supply all his needs. Pots he may buy locally, ironwork from the local smithy if he has not one of his own, extra food, perhaps cloth, or wool for spinning and weaving, and leather for shoes and hard-wearing coats, all these can come from a local source. But education for his children must be

purchased in a larger town, and so must the efforts of a solicitor to get him remission of taxes, the help of a doctor, or carpenter's tools.

Is there any evidence which helps us to understand the functions of villages and smaller towns other than the unsupported 'common sense' used so far? There is one line of thought pioneered by Ian Hodder which is unusual in Roman archaeology in that it lets the material speak for itself rather than imposing the archaeologists' ideas on it. If we draw on a map of Britain the larger towns we get a network 174 which roughly covers the whole country. Since each of these towns is in some measure administrative it must have had an area to administer. The evidence of this on the ground is almost non-existent because no one has yet decided what to look for in order to plot Roman administrative boundaries. Until some material evidence turns up the best way to suggest spheres of influence for the tribal capitals is to let each one hold sway up to a point half way to the next. Thus to plot the area around Calleva Atrebatum (Silchester) we bisect the distances from Silchester to the 175 surrounding tribal towns, Cirencester, Winchester, Chichester, and Verulamium, and draw totally arbitrary straight lines across the mid-distances to enclose Silchester with a polygon. It is not really surprising that when the smaller towns are added to such a map they 176 often lie about the polygonal lines that we have drawn, that is, about half way between the larger towns, which are the obvious service and

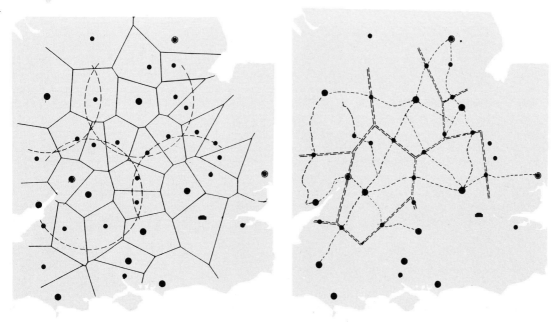

174 Map showing the tribal capitals, the *civitates*, of Roman Britain. While we have a good idea of organization in the lowlands, we still have little knowledge of what government was like in the upland regions of the north and west.

175 (left) The areas delineated around the tribal capitals suggest what the limits of authority might have been. Although only a hypothesis, it is at least a reasonable basis for discussion upon which improvements can be made.

176 (right) When the smaller towns are added to the map it is not surprising to find that they usually keep well away from their larger competitors to form 'half-way houses'.

administrative centres. This seems to be common sense, that when you have two larger towns with commercial spheres of influence a small town is best placed for success and survival as far as possible from the two larger towns. It is only 'common sense' if the deciding factors for survival are economic, so that the smaller town serves the needs of the population furthest from the larger towns. This reasoning does not prove that smaller towns are necessarily or primarily economic market units, but that is the best explanation advanced so far.

The alternative idea, which depends on early military installations and policing the natives, may be satisfactory to account for the placing of forts and the development of service villages, but this accounts for only twenty years at most. We still have to account for the survival of the smaller towns and villages for the following 300 years. What were the services and functions offered by the towns in general? Perhaps these may help us to decide on relative importance and to discover any hierarchy that existed.

The larger towns, except for the veteran settlements or *coloniae*, had tribal names. This must mean that the towns acted as tribal centres, and this presumably accounts for the great rectangular complex of forum and basilica – law courts, assembly rooms, and town centre – which takes up a whole section of the plan near the centre of each tribal capital. Around this large unit the road system was often planned, and the characteristic of the plan is a firmly rectangular layout by which all roads crossed at right angles. Most blocks of buildings, or *insulae*, were then squares or regular rectangles, and came out at similar dimensions. We are beginning to find that excavators have probably taken this idea a bit too far in drawing up plans of Roman towns around the small areas that have been excavated, and the street grid in practice was not always quite as regular or rectangular as it was supposed to be in theory. In general the main points are safe. The most obvious divergences can sometimes be shown to be due to roads which already existed before the street grid was thought of, and this sometimes points to important features which predate the town. At Verulamium the road from London (Watling Street) comes in from the south and runs through the street grid at an angle, making a number of triangular *insulae* on the way. It makes for a point which early pottery and earthworks have led the excavator, Professor Sheppard Frere, to suggest as the site of an early fort founded before the city was planned. In London, the road from Colchester sweeps into the northeast corner of the town and carries on in a straight line at an angle to the street grid straight down to the river. Again the suggestion is that the road was making for

the first bridge over the Thames, around which the city later grew up.

Neither the central block of administrative buildings, nor the square street grid has been seen very much in the smaller towns. It might be objected that whereas the larger towns have been reasonably well explored, with the spade if not the trowel, this is not true for the smaller towns. In this case excavation is not the prime tool of research, for heavily built central blocks and deeply founded roads show up well on aerial photographs. Very often in a dry season the gravel and mortar of a road near the surface of a field will make the crop on top of the road grow more slowly compared with the crops in deeper soil on either side, and in such a position the corn may be stunted and will probably ripen that much earlier than the rest. There may therefore be three times in a year when a flight over such a site will show up part of the town plan – when the corn is first growing, when it is almost full grown, and when it is just 'on the turn' or ripening. When the aerial photographs of small towns are compared with tribal towns the differences are obvious. The smaller towns lack the central monumental buildings and the rectangular street grid. Instead of complete squared plans they often show a single main road running through the settlement with small lanes leading off it to houses, fields and enclosures.

After the forum block and the *insulae* perhaps the most obvious buildings in the towns are the baths, the theatres and the amphitheatres. These have been dealt with as buildings in an earlier chapter; here we are concerned with their place in towns, and whether they have an economic importance. In all three cases I think the answer is no. Impor-

pp. 58–9

177 In a few tribal capitals, such as Silchester (Calleva), we actually have an inscription which confirms that our ideas about names and tribes are correct. Reading Museum.

178 On this plan of Silchester all the town features are visible, with the houses well spaced out in large grounds in a way that a visitor from the Mediterranean would have found very unusual. (*After* G. Boon.)

tant though the baths are to the social life of the town they may also be found in private houses, in country farms, and perhaps, though this has been questioned, standing isolated in the countryside. These isolated bath blocks are now under deep suspicion, for although they were once thought of as estate baths for the workers it now seems much more likely that such structures are part of an otherwise undiscovered villa, or the only stone building in an otherwise wooden complex which has not been spotted. The bath is the greatest fire risk in any Roman home and it makes sense to have it as either an isolated wing or even cut off from the living accommodation altogether. We know the public baths in the towns, we know the private baths in country homes, but, as yet, we know very little in between.

Theatres are better known because they show up well on aerial photographs as great semi-circular crop-marks. They are known in the larger towns, and in the countryside. One outside Colchester follows a plan better known in France where temples and theatres are commonly associated in the countryside. The point here is that theatres are not indicators of towns, and probably ought to be thought of in Britain more as places for religious pageants

180, 181

rather than performances of the plays of Plautus or the Greek master dramatists. Amphitheatres exist alongside some towns (Cirencester and Dorchester), some fortresses (Chester and Caerleon) and also some forts (Tomen-y-Mur). There is a strong military flavour here especially when it is remembered that of the two best town amphitheatres that at Cirencester is much earlier than the stone buildings of the developing town, and at Dorchester all that happened was the re-fashioning of a suitable prehistoric earthwork. Certainly amphitheatres as they survive are not specifically urban; they may be military in origin.

182, 282

Inside the larger towns there may be other special buildings, but, apart from temples, they can often be difficult to identify. Shops can be easy to spot archaeologically so long as they are on the main streets; they have narrow frontages, are often open to the streets, perhaps in colonnades, and ideally have some identifiable rubbish in the back room behind the shop or in pits in the backyard. Thus the baker's shop should have ovens, the butcher's shop pits full of animal bones, the metal worker's hearths and slag in the working part of the premises. A vegetable shop is a problem, so is a cabinet-maker's and a cheesemonger's. This

110, 183

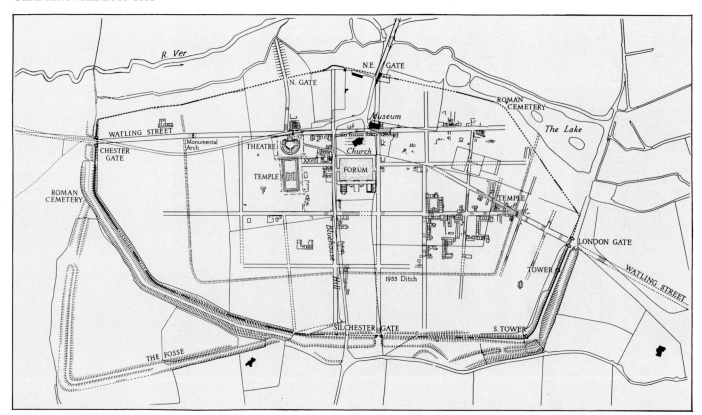

179 The shapes of various town boundaries are a result of different ideas at different times. The plan of Verulamium shows the regular road network cut by an earlier road that probably headed for the fort founded before the town. (*After* S. S. Frere.)

180 This monument at Verulamium is always called the theatre, a reasonable assumption in view of its shape, but what actually went on in it is far less sure. It lies beside a temple, and may therefore be a mainly religious building, as against one entirely devoted to entertainment.

181 If it is assumed that Verulamium followed the fashions set on the Continent, then its theatre may have looked like this artist's reconstruction. (*Drawn by* Alan Sorrell.)

is what we could call 'one way identification'; we can identify shops when they occur in expected places with expected rubbish, but without the commercial location and the debris we are lost. We can be quite sure that the centres of our larger tribal towns had many and varied shops; it is only inference that shops must also have occurred in smaller towns and even in villages. If we cannot often identify shops, then markets are even more of a problem. Every reader will know of a place where a market is held, and can go out to see what traces there are of the market on non-market days. Some streets in London, or car parks in French villages provide perfect examples by which we can be sure that markets can vanish without leaving any material evidence; what hope has the student of Roman Britain in his quest for markets 1,500 years after market day with no documents to help him?

184 Yet round every larger town there is a wall, 185 and through that wall roads enter the town through gateways. This might be a particular aspect of larger towns, for the wall was not built with the town but was added later. The general process of founding a city was well established by the time of the arrival of Roman troops in Britain. It almost certainly involved the marking out of a definite area for the town, though only for the high-ranking *coloniae* can we say that it involved ploughing a furrow round the site to mark the symbolic limits. One

archaeological indicator which is very sensitive to town limits is burial. In very few towns do burials occur within the later walls and it seems fairly safe to say that when the towns in Britain built walls they did so in general on or within their early limits. Early burials do occur in the area which London later enclosed; perhaps this marks a change of plan, perhaps, even, London was only thought of as the great capital after the Colchester fiasco, so that a small intensive trading centre within modest limits

182 The impressive amphitheatre at Caerleon stands just outside the legionary fortress. No doubt its major use was for shows and fights, but it would also have been used for parades and exercises in weapon training.

183 An artist's impression of a shopping street in London. The colonnade in a Mediterranean context was to keep off the sun; in Britain it was more a protection against the rain. (*Drawn by* Alan Sorrell).

184 Whether the citizens of Caerwent were in danger when they built their town wall we do not know; they might have been doing no more than keeping up with other tribal centres in Britain who had decided to build.

185 Interior of the south gate at Caerwent. The inner level is now much higher than that outside the walls, a situation often brought about by there having been an earth bank at first, for defence or for legal limits, in front of which the walls were later built.

was re-planned quickly in the late first century AD. In some cases, as at Verulamium, the streets of the early town go out beyond the late defences; here the final limits are smaller than those originally envisaged. But, in general, the early town at least had a limit outside which burial happened, and through which traders had to pass, paying the appropriate taxes, to bring their goods inside the town. This limit often takes the form of an earth bank, and, as funds or benefactors permitted, a gateway or two might be added as an honorific entrance to the town. In most of the larger towns between about 150 and 270 walls were set into the front of the bank and a complete stone circuit defended the town against attack. The dates of these walls are disputed. Attempts to date the walls have taken up a large amount of time and effort in the past, and the failure to produce any firm results ought to teach a lesson for the future. The time-honoured way of dating the walls is to dig a section through the bank inside the walls to find coins and pottery, in the bank, under the bank, in the fill of the trench into which the wall was built, and in the capping put back on the bank to let it run smoothly up to the wall. Not surprisingly rubbish is sometimes rare on the edge of towns, finds are few, and what finds there are may often have been discarded at any date after they ceased to be useful. Most of the bank, the filling of the trench, and the capping consists of soil, earth or turf, so whatever occurs in these layers is due to casual loss.

If the archaeologist on this quest is lucky he will find a hut under the bank, and that hut may have in it pottery which was used and broken. We can find the date of the pottery, the date of the hut, and hence the earliest possible date for the bank because the bank can only have been built after the hut went out of use. He might find some pottery in the bank, and again some sort of dating is possible. There might be material in the wall-trench. But to collect a really good sample of pottery from the fill of the wall-trench the excavator should empty perhaps thirty metres of that trench so that he may recover whatever is available. No excavator has ever done this, his sample is always very small, perhaps thirty sherds of pot, perhaps one coin, and his date must therefore always be vague. It is also almost always different from the dates proposed by other excavators of other walls from equally poor evidence. Basically there is nothing so far in the story which is wrong or undesirable. Each excavator has done his job and produced results which might end in a date with a suitable margin of error – 'the wall belongs to the late second century' – 'the wall dates to the years about AD 200' – or, and this would be frowned upon by many commentators who are afraid of numbers, 'AD 210 ± 30'.

The problem comes when people try to force the vague archaeological evidence to fit the scrappy historical sources. An episode for the history of Britain is often taken, and the archaeological remains are crammed into it. What we have written down in the ancient sources is a tiny fraction of what actually happened, and there is no guarantee that any given episode in the sources left any archaeolo-

186 Reconstruction of the Balkerne Gate at Colchester. Such a gate served not only as an entrance to the town and for defence; it made a suitable impression on the newcomer, and told the trader where he had to stop to pay his dues.

187, 188 Silver coins (*denarii*) of Septimius Severus and Clodius Albinus (× 2). Both men aimed at the throne in 193, following the murder of Commodus. Severus eventually won and Clodius Albinus, after a defeat near Lyons, committed suicide. British Museum.

gical trace at all. Conversely, the events recorded in archaeology may not have been noticed by the sources. Town walls form a good example.

In 193 Septimius Severus fought his way to power; some rivals he crushed, others, for a time, he tolerated. Clodius Albinus in Britain was remote, and tolerated for a time, but the final showdown came in 196–7, after which all opposition to Severus had been eliminated. This provides a perfect setting for the building of town walls in Britain as Clodius Albinus strengthened the province of which he was master in order to stand out against Rome. This may be true. Alternatively, wall building may have taken place as tribe vied with tribe to enclose their newly built and functioning urban units with an expensive, time-consuming defendable status symbol. Richer tribes may have been at work by soon after 160, poorer tribes may only have caught up by the middle of the third century. In the middle of such a time of wall building Clodius Albinus may well have made his bid for power. It will be obvious that I prefer the latter explanation. I am in a small minority in thinking that any attempt at a historical explanation, such as the former, is not only unprovable, but harmful to the whole subject of Roman Britain, and a pointless exercise in speculation.

Walls are indeed a great feature of the larger towns, and most of them were built by the middle of the third century, but some smaller towns joined in the process. Perhaps we can answer the question whether these walls were really necessary by looking at some of the smaller towns. In fact some of the smaller towns without walls are just as successful as smaller towns with walls, when judged in terms of continuing occupation and absence of any obvious catastrophes. The answer must be that walls seem to be irrelevant for success, and it may be that those towns which did build walls spent a large amount of time, money and effort with no effect other than running down their resources. All in all walls fall into the category of 'one way definition', for although all the larger towns have walls, walls are not diagnostic of larger towns.

How does this leave us in our quest to define and describe the town? It seems to give us a continuum rather than a firm hierarchy with well-defined steps. The only characteristic peculiar to the tribal centres is the badge of administration, the forum and basilica; after that, the features which are found in the larger towns are found in the smaller towns and even in the countryside as well. What characterizes the larger town is the presence of most of the features at once, not the exclusive possession of any of these features which may occur anywhere else. Our towns therefore form an unbroken sequence from the largest which have everything, to the middle ones which have some urban features, down to the smallest nucleated settlements which have virtually nothing; it is a matter of the provision of services, and the larger the population centre the greater the chance of finding a certain service there.

We now have an idea of the parts of Roman Britain – let us confine ourselves to the period in which this has all been described, the first two centuries of the province, and add fuel and direction to get the machine to work. We must look at the links between the parts of the machine, the transport network, and at the primer, money.

Trade and Commerce

The road system is one of the main links by which the Roman Empire stayed in working order as a successful unit. The same is true on a smaller scale for each province. Both Empire and province depended on quick and efficient communication, movement of goods, posting of officials and armies, and interchange of trade. There were two main modes of travel in the Roman world, by road and by water, and water was subdivided into river and sea. In good weather, and in the summer, travel by sea could be a pleasant and rewarding experience, but for much of the year sea travel was difficult and dangerous. Every trader felt that Neptune was about to devour his fortune by shipwreck, and the remains of many shipwrecks in the Mediterranean show that these fears were well founded. Saint Paul's journey to Rome is an excellent example of the folly of winter travel and its likely outcome, and seems to be quite typical of the problems and dangers. For the province of Britain sea travel simply entailed cross-Channel shipping, so that there is little that we can examine in detail. The waters of the English Channel are very much more turbulent than the waters of the Mediterranean, so any Roman ships which foundered only hours out from the mouth of the Rhine or the Thames are either buried deep in shifting sand, or dispersed by tides and strong currents. Cross-Channel routes are well attested at the mouth of the Old Rhine in the Netherlands where shippers to or from Britain dedicated altars to various gods and goddesses in the hope of safe ventures.

This leaves us in Britain with travel either by road or by river. There is little to be said about river transport, and even less about canals because we have so little evidence. We do know from several sources that river transport was much cheaper than sending goods by road, but we do not know how many of the rivers of Britain were navigable to the Romans or how far up their course trade could penetrate, and the cost of transferring goods from seagoing craft to coasters or river boats is totally beyond us. Once again we have to be very careful of foisting on the Romans our own obsessions with economies and cost-effectiveness, for so

much of these ideas depends on intricate details of wages, work systems, and administration about which we can only guess. It is, for instance, most unlikely that the State ever considered cost in moving materials and goods from one place to another. It had State servants, State equipment, and State duties, and if tons of metal had to be moved from one place to another it would have been done by the method simplest and most convenient to the organizers rather than the way cheapest to the consumer. A trader in pottery, however, had to consider the cost of transport, for if he was to sell his goods in a market some distance away from the kiln he had to make sure that he added as little as possible to the cost of production in getting his goods from the kiln to the customer. This may have biased his sales in some directions in which water transport was available rather than in other directions where land transport put up his costs prohibitively. The potters who worked in the Thames Valley

189 Shipwreck was a hazard of rivers as well as of the sea. This Roman ship of the late third century was found in the mud of the river Thames near Westminster Bridge in 1910.

189

190

190 Drawing of a typical Roman cargo ship of the second century AD. Science Museum, London.

around the modern city of Oxford sold their wares up to a hundred miles away, but they seem to have sold more than might be expected far along the Thames Valley and round the coast out to sea in Kent and East Anglia, than north or south of the kilns, overland.

Finally we come to the roads of Roman Britain. The straight line cutting across the modern landscape, often on a raised bank, can be seen in many parts of Britain as a lasting testament to Roman road building. Many modern roads such as the A5 going northeast from St Albans, the A46 from Leicester to Lincoln, the A417 from Gloucester to Cirencester, to take very obvious examples, lie directly on Roman foundations and move in short straight lines from one Roman sighting point to the next almost regardless of hills, valleys or rivers. The origin of the road network must be found in the tribal capitals, for the main roads of Roman Britain run from capital to capital, taking in small towns on the way. In some cases these roads can be proved to be military, for they may be aligned on earlier forts rather than later towns, and they go through early forts which later became small towns, even when

174
176

these are off their direct route. The basic network is fairly clear, and most of the major Roman roads are known in detail even where they are visible only in suspicious hedge-lines, parish boundaries, and bridle-ways. The secondary roads are far less well known.

193

In the first place we have to remember that Britain had at least trackways before the Roman Conquest even if paved roads are a Roman innovation. Given these pre-existing roads it is extremely difficult to sort out which prehistoric trackways continued in use into Roman Britain, and indeed, on into the Middle Ages. Sometimes such roads will enter Roman towns by Roman gates; then their curved course may be evidence of pre-Roman date, while their obvious part in the Roman system shows that they continued in use. Sometimes there are several Roman villas, farms or villages along a line not marked by a straight Roman road, and in such cases a sinuous prehistoric track needs to be brought into the picture to complete the network.

When the larger towns of Roman Britain were no longer pre-eminent, parts of the road system fell into disuse. The Roman road sys-

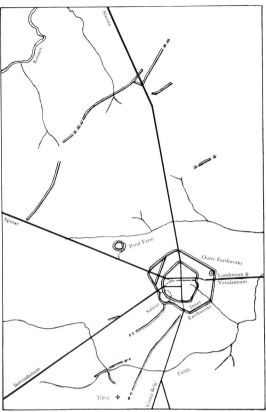

and later, between manors and parishes – long straight stretches of parish boundary along an overgrown bridle-track or footpath can often mark the last memories of disused roads. The villages of medieval England often lay in sheltered valleys while the Roman roads ignored such easy but sinuous routes; the medieval road therefore often deviated from the Roman road and ran through the villages. But when turnpike roads returned, people's horizons grew, and the idea of direct travel between towns replaced that of travel from village to village. Turnpike roads therefore began to by-pass villages, and inevitably they often returned to the direct route of the Roman road. Only now, with the need for trunk roads to avoid the centres of population, has the direct style of Roman road building returned.

What then was Roman Britain working and existing on, and how was the economy fuelled with goods and money? We have looked at the basic raw materials, the products of agriculture, and these must have accounted for the great bulk of trade and commerce in Roman Britain. Most people in the province derived most of their daily calories from flour, so wheat and barley must have been major food crops. Everyone in Britain wore clothes, and for the bulk of the population these were certainly not imported; wool and leather, with perhaps some flax for linen, were vital here. But none of these commodities has left any but the smallest trace in the historical or archaeological record. A few charred grains of barley, a carbonized wheat ear, a waterlogged fragment of woven woollen cloth one centimetre square – these are all that we have to remind us.

191 The Roman road system in the area of Silchester shows how the town grew up and changed. Sometimes it is possible to see how the early plans went wrong; for example, the London road from the east should surely have gone to the forum. (*After* G. Boon.)

191 tem around Wroxeter has almost disappeared as a usable network, and the same is true for Silchester; both these towns declined, and were not followed by medieval settlements of any importance on the same site. Gloucester became an important medieval centre as did Lincoln, and there some of the road system survived. In other places the Roman road marked the boundary between estates, farms,

194

192 Often the Roman road is on a straight line between two towns, and so it is still followed by the modern road, as here in an aerial view of the road from Mildenhall to Winchester near Knights Enham, Wilts.

193 Even when a Roman road is no longer in use its straight line can easily be seen in lanes, hedges, boundaries and banks as here where the road from Wroxeter runs through the Church Stretton Gap heading south into Wales and towards the fort at Leintwardine.

So when we talk about trade and commerce in the province we tend to forget the bulk materials and spend a lot of time on minority goods simply because evidence survives to tell us what was bought, transported, and sold. Direct earth products survive well; they are high on most lists of trade. Burned earth survives best of all, and the result, pottery, forms by far our greatest source of material evidence for Romano-British trade. It is not unusual for a large excavation carried out today to result in the finding of several tons of pottery. Most of that pottery was made in Britain, was transported from its place of manufacture, sold, bought, used, broken, and discarded. Most Roman pottery ever made survives today because unless it was purposely crushed to add to new pottery in the making, there was virtually no way of destroying it. When we know where the kiln which supplied a type of pottery was situated we can begin to

194 Food debris can fall into the fire, or the ashes, and get lightly charred; this preserves things like hazel nuts from natural decay. Vindolanda Museum, Chesterholm.

talk about transport, patterns of trade, marketing and competition. When the pottery was not made in Britain we can talk of imports, and when British pottery is found abroad we can talk of exports. If we examine the products of two kiln groups that were producing similar types of pottery at a similar time we can begin to talk about success in business, competition, and failure.

Let us start on imports. In general the Roman army imported some classes of pottery, and some types of vessels, but they bought from local producers whenever they could. Potters of the British Iron Age did not produce large grinding bowls (*mortaria*), or flagons, or high-quality table ware with a red-gloss finish (Samian ware). *Mortaria* were imported from northeast Gaul and Belgium, flagons from Belgium and Germany, and Samian pottery from south and central Gaul. Local potters in England soon successfully copied the flagons, as their kilns show; some producers of *mortaria* established branches in England, as their stamped vessels show; but England never achieved the manufacture of high-quality red table ware up to the continental standard. Imports of flagons and *mortaria* quickly fell as local industries arose; import of Samian continued till the end of the second century when something happened either to the manufacture or the distribution. Instead of Samian pottery many local potters produced varieties of colour-coated wares, not always red, and the population accepted these as substitutes. By the middle of the third century Britain was self-supporting so far as pottery went, and in the fourth century some exports to the north of France are known. When Roman troops patro-

195

196

197

nized local potters instead of importing pottery or producing their own the results could be 198 dramatic, as the Black Burnished pottery industries round Poole harbour in Dorset show. There, a pre-Roman tradition worked to produce hand-made pots with a black surface which was burnished and decorated with groups of straight and curved lines. The potters managed to sell to the army and, with a few changes in the shape of pots but little change in decoration or mode of production, the industry expanded and prospered. At one stage in its career the potters even sent goods from Poole harbour up to the military installations on the northern frontier.

Two industries which, in the later period, made wares which replaced Samian imports 199 were based in the New Forest and near Oxford. Early in the third century both industries were small local affairs with a very restricted market area. By the year 300 both were marketing a wide range of colour-coated wares over distances up to sixty or seventy miles. Oxford had all Britain to sell to through a whole circle of 360 degrees; the New Forest had only a half circle of 180 degrees because half of its possible market area was in the sea. In Wiltshire the two industries clashed, for each presumably wanted to sell there. Some Oxford material reached the south coast, some New Forest ware reached Cirencester, but by and large there was a boundary between the two market areas. The position of that boundary, as judged from the pottery found on excavated sites, is interesting. It was not half way between two equal producers but was nearer to the New Forest, so that Oxford had the major share of the market. Judged simply by the area of the land known today to be covered with kilns, Oxford was the greater producer, and the market areas reflect this

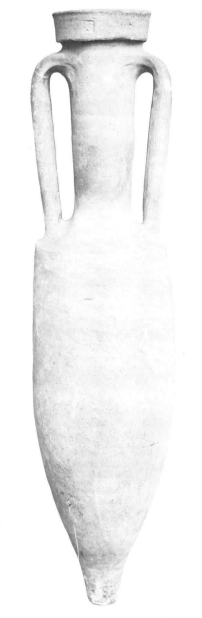

195 Although large pottery amphorae were made in Britain, this example, containing wine, was imported from the Mediterranean and was buried in the first-century BC grave of a Celtic chieftain at Welwyn, Hertfordshire. British Museum.

196 A typical example of a large *mortarium*, grinding bowl, that must have been an essential element in any kitchen in Roman Britain. British Museum.

197 Samian pottery, with its attractive shapes and good red gloss, was the best tableware. It was imported in vast quantities from Gaul, generally from great factories in the centre such as Lezoux. British Museum.

difference in a simple numerical ratio. Let us remember that the pottery trade must have been tiny compared with the corn trade, or even the wool trade, but we know and talk about it simply because the evidence survives.

Other earth products which survive well are stones and metals. Perhaps in theory the Emperor regarded all minerals as a State monopoly; in practice the imperial administration seems only to have had a direct interest in valuable minerals. At Dolaucothi, South 200 Wales, there is firm evidence of a Roman gold mine and equally firm evidence of a military guard for it, if not actual military direction. Silver in Britain seems to have come mainly from the argentiferous lead deposits in North Wales, the Peak district, and the Mendips; again there is clear evidence of military involvement both in the mining of the lead and its refining, and stamps on the ingots (pigs) of

lead make clear the practice of silver extraction. Some of these lead pigs have stamps 201 which date them as early as the middle of the first century, so the exploitation of metals got under way soon after the Conquest. Business may have lapsed in the third century, but in the fourth century Britain is known to be rich both in silver and in lead. The British emperor Carausius (286–293) managed to be the first 202 emperor to strike pure silver coins for well over a century, and finds of both silver plate and silver coins of the late fourth century occur pp. more frequently in Britain than on the Conti- 154–5 nent. The fourth century is the time of the boom in the pewter industry (lead and tin); 203–5 lead coffins were made, and so were circular squat lead tanks, sometimes decorated with Christian symbols. 206

After the metal industries State interest seems to fail. There is no sign of State involve-

198 The Black Burnished pottery industry which already existed before the Roman Conquest was given a great boost by the new customers that the army provided. Dorset County Museum, Dorchester.

199 (below) Examples of New Forest pottery and of local pottery from the kilns near Oxford which expanded considerably in the fourth century to take over the market previously served by imported Samian ware. Ashmolean Museum, Oxford.

135

200 Gold was important to the State for coinage, and to individuals for small items of jewellery, though there were strict laws about who could wear what. This group was found at Llandovery in Wales. British Museum.

ment in the quarrying and distribution of 'Purbeck marble' which was used quite widely as a veneer or polished decoration in place of the Italian marbles whose import was never great, and dropped considerably after the first century. Some imported marble veneer can be found, at Fishbourne for instance, or Woodchester, but it is rare. Solid white marble for portrait busts was also imported, but again examples like those at Lullingstone and Woodchester are rare. If Purbeck marble was not used for decoration then simple plaster painted to look like marble sufficed. When marble was not imported for sculpture then the fine-grained limestones of Bath, the Cotswolds, and Northamptonshire were adequate substitutes. Such English stones travelled considerable distances within the province but it is sometimes difficult to judge whether the rough stone was moved about to provide a distant sculptor with his chosen material, or whether a sculpture travelled because of its value as a decorative piece. When we descend to building stone then the distances travelled by the commodity drop sharply. Only in the case of a city like London, which had wealth and needed good building stone, is there much evidence of long-distance trade in rough stone.

Minor minerals include semi-precious stones

and decorative materials like shale and jet. Shale was cut in Dorset at Kimmeridge and there was a brisk, if commercially unimportant, trade in bowls, bangles and carved table legs. One such table leg survives at Dorchester (Dorset) and it is always quoted; in fact it may be a single commission for a very odd customer and may be a unique relic which should not be overrated. But it is there, and it therefore forms a part of our evidence. A further step up the scale is the jet industry of Yorkshire, and here we are on safer ground because jet bangles, ornaments, hairpins and charms do occur quite commonly enough in graves to suggest that they were often used, and fairly highly valued. Enough jet objects appear in ordinary domestic rubbish deposits to remove any sceptical suggestion that they were made specially for burial. Here again is the Romano-British trap; we have spent as much time on minor industries as we have on the production of food. It is as if a twentieth-century commentator were to give equal weight in the British economy to the steel industry and the growing of carnations. As always, the archaeologist is seduced by the evidence that survives, like shale table legs, and it is extremely difficult to brush this aside in order to concentrate on more important issues.

207

83

208, 209

210

211
97

201 Lead was useful in its own right, but some lead ores also produced silver. The stamps on the lead 'pigs' indicate that the whole production of the metal was under State control, probably because silver was involved. Corinium Museum, Cirencester.

Is it possible to give a balance sheet for Roman Britain? No: but the temptation is too great to resist, so let us try. In the first century Britain was being exploited from outside. Money was on loan to British enterprise, for the philosopher Seneca had millions of sestertii invested in Britain, and we can be quite sure that profit was being extracted. Most high-quality materials were being imported and must have been very expensive, this would include bronzework, silks, cotton, spices, tableware and glass. In the fourth century the picture is very different. There is very little evidence of any imports at all: pottery was almost all home-produced, few, if any, new bronze objects came in, marble was rare, silks we know nothing about, wine and oil in amphorae from the Mediterranean seem to be present but in short supply, and only the import of Rhineland glass can be detected. Diocletian's price edict, perhaps published mainly in the east of the Empire, gives prices for British beer (better than Egyptian), for the *birrus Britannicus*, and the *tapete Britannicum*. The first was a heavy woollen cloak with a hood, one of the best-quality cloaks that you could buy, and the second was a heavy woollen travelling rug. This will not make a balance sheet for it contains only a few peripheral

204 (above) Some of the lead produced from British mines was used for pewter, a mixture of lead and tin. It was cheaper than silver, and perhaps could be bought by all classes. Sometimes large hoards of pewter vessels have been discovered, as these from Appleford. Ashmolean Museum, Oxford.

202 (left) After the problems of the third century it was the usurper emperor in Britain, Carausius, who was the first to strike silver coinage again (here a *denarius*) (× 2). The emperor in Rome, Diocletian, had to follow suit. British Museum.

203 In the fourth century lead seems to have been plentiful, and one use it was put to was the making of coffins, often highly ornamented as this example from Holborough, Kent. Maidstone Museum.

137

205 Lead (*plumbum*) is an obvious metal for plumbing, especially for water pipes, even if the lead does eventually poison the people who drink the water. Verulamium Museum, St Albans.

206 (below) A number of lead tanks from Roman Britain have Christian inscriptions or the *Chi-Rho* monogram on them (here from Icklingham, Suffolk, with the *alpha* and *omega* reversed in the casting). The presumption is that they had a Christian use, possibly as fonts. British Museum.

207 (below right) There is no native marble in Britain. In the early Roman period marble was imported from Italy and Spain to decorate walls of sumptuous buildings like the palace at Fishbourne. Fishbourne Roman Palace Museum.

materials and the main commodities are missing. All we can say is that early in Roman Britain the evidence is mainly for exploitation and imports, and later in Roman Britain the evidence is for self-sufficiency and exporting.

This is not an isolated phenomenon, it is part of the general picture of the Empire. Rome moved out from The City to Italy, and from Italy to conquer the known world for at least two reasons: to bring Roman civilization to the barbarians, and to bring barbarian wealth to replenish the coffers of Rome. Britain was a simple part of the process. But the process went the wrong way, for the provinces succeeded only too well, and Rome seems actually to have believed, as no other empire has done, that the provinces ought to be autonomous parts of a communal whole. For two centuries Rome actually tried to run the Empire and Italy was impoverished as a result. Later, when the imperial power was split, and several courts moved round the Empire with their own administrations the burden of finance was shared, but by then the Empire was running itself, and the whole object had turned inside out. By the year 210 Rome had an African emperor, strong

influence from African art, and massive imports of North African red-coated pottery which finally broke the struggling Italian fine pottery industry. The provinces were exporting to Rome, and Rome had to pay; by the fourth century the balance of trade seems to have shifted from the centre in favour of the provinces. In the third century this change was slowly happening, international trade was slowing down, and the volume of goods shifting from province to province declined. As a crude index of this the number of shipwrecks in the Mediterranean seems to have dropped drastically. For some time there was little flow of trade in any direction, and it is this period of reorganization which forms, in my at present eccentric view, the great economic crisis of the third century. Some provinces survived, changed and prospered – an index might be the late villa economies of North Africa, Spain and Britain – while other provinces like Italy, Greece, and parts of Asia Minor have little to show in the fourth century. But this is to anticipate The End, and before that we need to get to one root of the imperial strengths and weaknesses, the coinage.

208 (top left) Most sculpture carved in Britain was done in local stone, and only occasionally was the stone moved over long distances. This limestone capital with a Celtic god holding a double axe is a good example of local native carving. Corinium Museum, Cirencester.

209 (left) A sandstone capital from Corbridge decorated with the reclining figure of a water nymph. Although the subject matter is purely classical the carving is local work, and may be compared with the relief of the water-goddess Coventina (illus. 133). Corbridge Museum.

210 (right) A small side table made of Dorset shale is not likely to appeal to modern taste, but stone and marble furniture was acceptable to the Romans. This table leg from the villa at Colliton Park, Dorchester, with its classically inspired griffin, is one of the best examples to survive in Britain. Dorset County Museum, Dorchester.

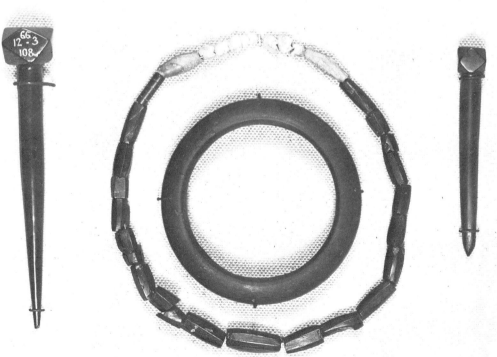

211 The jet industry, centred on Yorkshire, made mainly bangles and small ornaments, which are common in Britain; some were also exported to the Continent. British Museum.

139

COINS

(138-161) also took a personal interest in the province and ordered the construction of the Antonine Wall, a turf wall frontier in advance of Hadrian's Wall, in *c.* 143. About this date he struck coins that referred to Britain. A sestertius has a particularly fine portrait of him, crowned

The coin in the hand of a modern man tends to have only one purpose, as a medium of exchange for payment. Only on relatively rare occasions does it also have a secondary function, and then it is generally of a commemorative nature, usually recording the anniversary of an event or a person. In antiquity coins obviously still had the same primary purpose as payment for goods or services rendered, but the secondary purpose of the types on them had more importance then, and invariably have for us today in interpreting them. The major difference between Greek and Roman coins, apart from the obvious ones of denomination and the finer art on Greek coins, is the emphasis in the types or representations on the coins. Greek coins tended to advertise; they might show the local god, goddess or hero and/or their temple; or possibly a famed local product such as grapes on the coins of Chios in the Aegean; or a local feature, such as the safe sickle-shaped harbour on the coins of Zancle-Messana in Sicily.

Roman coins rarely advertised in a similar way, they were much more concerned with propaganda. This could be on different levels: moneyers of Republican silver denarii often alluded to the exploits of famous ancestors, real or imaginary. During the Empire the propaganda was more immediate and contemporary – displaying the features of a newly proclaimed emperor; referring to the completion of successful military campaigns; the erection of new public buildings, etc. At times the representation on the coins could be a direct appeal for solidarity and support, generally appearing at times of crisis, invariably under usurper emperors, and often using the type of two clasped hands and an inscription such as CONCORDIA MILITVM – a pious hope that the army would back the emperor. As the coins circulated they acted as the newspapers or, more correctly, the broadsheets of their day.

Roman affairs in Britain appear to have had rather more than their fair share of representations or 'press' on the coins of Rome compared to other provinces, and also the additional individual coinages of no less than five usurper emperors (discounting those of the Gallic empire in revolt). A number of the Celtic coins

issued by local British kings had looked towards Roman models for their types as quite a number of Roman coins circulated in Britain before the invasion and conquest in AD 43 by the emperor Claudius (41-54).

The first explicit reference to Britain appears on a gold aureus of Claudius struck in AD 46, three years after the Conquest. The obverse shows the head of

the Emperor wearing a laurel wreath and facing to the right; the date of the coin can be worked out from the Tribunician Power (VI) and Imperatorial Acclamations (XI) given in the legend around his head. The reverse shows a typical Roman triumphal arch, for Claudius was granted an Imperial Triumph by the Senate for his part in the acquisition of the new province. The arch is inscribed DE BRITANN and surmounted by a figure seated bareback on a pony that proceeds to the left. She has been variously identified as Nike the goddess of Victory (and she appears to hold a palm branch in the crook of her left arm), and also as the Celtic goddess of horses, Epona. On either side of the rider is a trophy of piled up armour.

In 122 Hadrian (117-138) came to Britain to inspect the province and to inaugurate work on the great wall that bears his name. He travelled widely throughout the Empire and issued a number of coins recording his visits to various parts. Britain was no exception and a sestertius shows his portrait (ill. 216); on the reverse is a female figure seated to the left. She is often referred to as a 'mourning' Britannia as she sits with head lowered, resting her left arm on a shield and holding a spear. Beneath her right foot is a pile of stones that has been interpreted as a direct allusion to Hadrian's Wall. The legend reads BRITANNIA S C (*Senatus Consulto*); the latter refers to the fact that all non-precious metal coins were struck by decree of the Senate; the Emperor himself controlled striking in gold and silver.

Hadrian's successor Antoninus Pius

with a laurel wreath, and a reverse type showing Britannia clad in a flowing gown seated on a rock facing to the left. Her left arm rests easily on a large circular shield and in her right hand is a typical legionary standard. This type of Britannia is the ancestress of her representation on the pre-1968 copper pennies and the current cupro-nickel 50-penny piece.

Dio Cassius, in his *Roman History*, says that the greatest war in the reign of the emperor Commodus (177-192) occurred in Britain. The barbarians swarmed south, overran the Antonine Wall, and killed a legionary legate at the head of his forces. In the summer of 180 Commodus sent Ulpius Marcellus to crush the revolt, which he proceeded to do with some severity. By 184 the situation was under control and Commodus took the title Britannicus and issued coins to commemorate the victory in 184 and 185. When Commodus was murdered on 31 December 192 the Governor in Britain was Decimus Clodius Albinus, a native of Hadrumentum in Africa who had risen through the ranks. During the troubles, and the reigns of several short-lived emperors, that followed the death of Commodus another soldier of African origin, Septimius Severus (193-211), rose to prominence and was proclaimed emperor by his troops. In order to consolidate his position he offered Albinus the title of Caesar, and coins were issued bearing his portrait and this title. But, two years later, in 195, Severus' position was strong enough for him to declare Albinus a public enemy. Albinus was proclaimed as emperor by his own troops and took the title of Augustus, which now appeared on his coins. At first Albinus met with some success but was eventually defeated in a great battle near Lyons on 19 February 197. He subsequently committed suicide. The struggle between Albinus and Severus had seriously weakened the northern defences of Britain by the withdrawal of troops and the barbarians lost no opportunity of attacking southwards.

In 208 Septimius Severus came to Britain bringing his wife, Julia Domna, and his two sons Caracalla and Geta with him. He pursued a number of vigorous campaigns against the insurgents into Caledonia, set up new base camps and repaired Hadrian's Wall. Several coins refer to the campaigns, as on the reverse of this sestertius with its legend 'Victoriae Britannicae'.

A fine portrait of the emperor appears on a gold aureus that commemorates VICTORIAE

BRIT around the winged figure of Victory advancing to the left holding a wreath in her right hand. Other coins referring to the campaigns show two different bridges, one appears to be a permanent structure and the other a bridge of boats. These types seem to indicate a proposed sea-borne expedition into Caledonia. The campaigns, although successful in bringing about a peace that was to last until 296 in Caledonia, proved, however, to be too strenuous for the emperor and he died at York on 4 February 211, aged 65 years. Severus left his two sons as joint emperors but the jealous Caracalla had his younger brother Geta murdered in February the following year. Both the sons issued coins referring to Britain either by the inclusion of the word BRIT in their titles or with references to the British victories as the reverse type.

For the rest of the third century Britain became rather a backwater of the Empire, falling under the jurisdiction of the Gallic

empire in the revolts of the period 259-273. A more serious revolt bringing Britain to the fore occurred in 287 when Marcus Aurelius Mausaeus Carausius, commander of the Channel fleet based at Boulogne, proclaimed a 'British Empire'. His portraits on the coins show a forceful character, the head set firmly on the thick neck and stocky shoulders. He struck coins in gold, silver and bronze at several mints. Often he referred to himself on the coins as reigning jointly with the two central, lawful emperors, Diocletian and Maximianus. Two unique medallions of orichalcum (a brass alloy) are known for Carausius, each of which shows him wearing consular robes and insignia. On the reverse of one he stands holding a long spear and an orb and

is being crowned by Victory; the other has a winged Victory driving a two-horse chariot *(biga)* to the right with the legend VICTORIA CARAVSI AVG and beneath the horses' hooves the letters I.N.P.C.D.A., for which there is at present no known explanation. Both medallions appear to have been struck at the beginning of his reign to commemorate his victory and proclamation.

Carausius ruled for six years until in 293 he was murdered on the orders of his finance minister Allectus, who then proclaimed himself emperor. His coins show a thinner faced man but the reverses

are still very much of a propaganda nature, extolling various personifications such as VIRTVS, here embodied on a gold aureus in

the standing armed figure of Mars. Allectus was no soldier and reigned for only three years until the invasion in 296 led by the rightful Caesar, Constantius Chlorus, father of the future Constantine the Great. The invasion is commemorated on a unique gold medallion to the weight of ten aurei found at Beaurains near Arras in northern France in September 1922. On the obverse is a striking portrait of the emperor-to-be, but the reverse is fascinating. It is a picture out of history – Constantius is shown on horseback in full military panoply carrying a spear and approaching a kneeling suppliant female figure who emerges from a turreted gateway. Beneath her feet the letters LON identify her and the city as *Londinium*. In the lower part of the medallion below the horse a manned war galley approaches, bearing out the written historical record that land and sea forces headed for London to save it from the routed troops of Allectus. The legend hails Constantius as REDDITOR LVCIS AETERNAE – restorer of the eternal light of true imperial rule. The letters PTR below the galley indicate the mint of Trier in Germany.

The mint of London, once the province was back in the Empire, now continued to strike coins for the emperors up until Constantius II (337-361). The reverse types are standard for the Empire at large with the addition of the London mint-mark. Twenty-odd years later the mint was re-opened under the usurper emperor Magnus Maximus (383-388) who rebelled against Gratian. Magnus Maximus' coins follow the norm for portraits of the period and for reverse types. He seems to have caught the popular imagination as he lived on as Macsen Wledig in the collection of Welsh folktales known as the *Mabinogian*; he also appears even later still in Rudyard Kipling's *Puck of Pook's Hill.* He was defeated by Theodosius and executed near Aquileia on 28 July 388.

The last years of Roman Britain saw one

final usurper, a common soldier hailed by his troops as Constantine III. Honorius, the rightful emperor, was hard pressed in Italy by the Visigoths and in 410 wrote to the British that they should fend for themselves as a province. Constantine III was captured by Constantius, the general of Honorius, and sent to Italy where he was executed in 411.

It was to be nearly a thousand years (*c.* AD 1500) before coins in Britain were to reach a similar high technical standard.

233

234

236

141

213 The Republican silver *denarius* was struck in vast quantities, and worn specimens are often found in early imperial hoards in Britain; they were hoarded because of their good silver content (× 2). British Museum.

Coinage

Britain shared in most of the Roman imperial coinage from the beginning in the first century to the end of commonly produced coinage in the West around 402. Like much of the Roman Empire the coinage is best divided into early and late, with a time of transition in the third century. Since the coinage in circulation at the Conquest of Britain contained a good number of coins struck in the days of the Republic we need to start off with a rough background of the monetary ideas of the Republic. It is probably best to say that early Roman coinage was based on the *as*. This, to start with, was a large piece of bronze weighing one *libra* (pound) of *c.* 327 gm. Slowly the standard changed until a more usable, token, *as* evolved which weighed only one ounce. The *as* was the basic multiple of the most important coins for the Empire, the *denarius* (ten *asses*) and the *sestertius* (two and a half *asses*). A change in the system around 140 BC made nonsense of the names by making

the *denarius* worth sixteen *asses*, and the *sestertius*, four. But the names stuck. By the end of the Republic the only coin which was produced in great numbers was the silver *denarius*; bronze *asses* and their fractions existed as very worn coins that had seen perhaps a century of use, but little new bronze coinage was struck.

Augustus managed, with his usual ability, to change the coinage in use completely, while keeping intact all the old forms and ideas. To the silver *denarius* which he struck as usual in great quantities he added regular and large supplies of gold (the *aureus*) and a firm sequence of bronze and copper (*sestertius* and *dupondius* in bronze; *as*, *semis* and *quadrans* in copper). All the denominations fitted into a system of fixed values and relationships as follows:

1 *aureus* = 25 *denarii* = 100 *sestertii* = 200 *dupondii* = 400 *asses*

1 *sestertius* = 2 *dupondii* = 4 *asses* = 8 *semisses* = 16 *quadrantes*.

By the death of Augustus in AD 14 the system was fixed firmly in the economy and the last of these coins to die out, the *aureus*, lasted until AD 309. The decline of the Augustan system of coinage over the next three hundred years is a slow, but detailed process; if we take only the major points we can speed the process up without losing the thread.

The coin of Augustus that was struck in the greatest numbers was the *as*. Compared with the numbers which might be expected of silver and gold this is not too surprising, but compared with the really small change, there seems to our eyes something wrong. We rely today on a good supply of our smallest coins, but this is obviously not true of the Roman economy. This is another example of the dangers of putting our own ideas into a Roman context, for we must find out how the Romans used their coinage, by looking at hoards, at casual losses, and at rubbish deposits, rather than expecting them to be the same as us. After a hundred years in operation the Roman coinage had changed so that the most commonly struck and lost coin was not the *as* but the *sestertius*. This suggests a gradual rise in prices over the century by a factor of about four – a very gradual rise compared with modern events. This change was accompanied by the elimination of the two smallest coins, the half and quarter *as*. They had never been common, had always been struck in fairly small numbers, and

212 The large Republican *as* had the double-headed god Janus on the obverse and a ship's prow on the reverse (actual size). British Museum.

In the middle of the third century the Empire had to learn to be self sufficient and to achieve a state of equilibrium. New conquests, new land, captured treasure, valuable slaves for new masters, were all things of the past, and yet people inside the Empire wanted a better deal than they had had in the past. The State income remained constant but major bills, such as army pay, continued to rise; and when the army demanded more pay an emperor had to pay up, or face elimination. Traditionally the emperors of the middle of the second century – Hadrian, Antoninus Pius, Marcus Aurelius – have always been ranked as Good Emperors. They were competent, considerate, peaceful and thoughtful, and under them the Golden Age of the Antonines unfolded. Almost inevitably we can now begin to see in this Golden Age the seeds of its own destruction, and the origins of all the troubles of the third century. It was the philosopher prince Marcus Aurelius who first allowed, or took, the step of making the standard income go further, and pay more bills, by the simple expedient of putting copper into the silver coinage in moderate amounts to dilute it. For a while this worked. Marcus survived his accession, when his troops demanded an extra hand-

now were fast disappearing. Either no one wanted to use them, or, more likely, the State found that it was just not profitable to produce them. Another eighty years on and the most common coin was the *denarius*, another rise of prices, and the smaller denominations, the *dupondius* and the *as*, were on the way out. This takes us to near the year 200 with the *denarius* and the *sestertius* making up the bulk of the coinage in circulation.

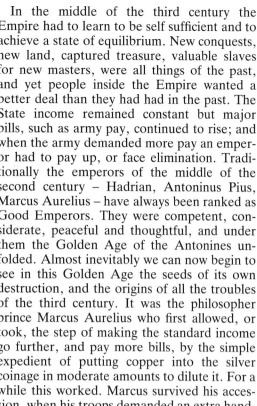

215 (left) Gold coins (the *aureus*) are most commonly found near army posts, though because of the high value they represented they are always very rare indeed. The reverse type of the Wolf and Twins on this example of Hadrian alludes to the foundation of Rome (× 2). British Museum.

216 (right) . Hadrian's *sestertius* with its apt reverse inscription and representation of Britannia is perhaps connected with the building or inauguration of the Wall and his visit in 122 (× 2). British Museum.

217 The reverse type of this *denarius* of Marcus Aurelius refers to the German wars; here for those who could read there was a form of imperial news (× 2). British Museum.

out, by a debasement of about six per cent. After that the coinage may have recovered a little, but the same emperor then financed his German wars on another debasement of about six per cent. Whereas this could work under a good cmpcror who would undo the damage whenever he could afford it, it was to lead to trouble when used many times in quick succession by less careful administrators.

By the year 220 the *denarius* had less than 50 per cent of silver in it, *sestertii* were smaller and scruffier than before, *dupondii* and *asses* were small and rare. By 250 the *sestertius* was on its last legs, and by 270 only the *aureus* survived, in name, from the wreckage of Augustus' system. One new coin had appeared in 214 and another in 250. Both had radiate crowns, they showed the emperor's portrait crowned with

218, 219 Caracalla appears on the single *denarius* piece wearing the laurel wreath whilst his bust with a radiate crown indicates the new double *denarius* (× 2). British Museum.

the sun's rays, and both were probably double values. The silver radiate was probably a double *denarius*, and the large copper radiate a double *sestertius*. Neither coin weighed twice the single value; the silver radiate weighed only one and a half times the *denarius*, but this was probably another means of debasement, of making the silver stretch further. The double *sestertius* soon died as the single *sestertius* disappeared, but the silver radiate became the standard coin of the third century. It almost shows the problems of the third century economy in its appearance as it changes from bright silver (*c.* 50 per cent) in 217 to almost pure copper (*c.* 1 per cent silver) in 270. This was the lowest ebb to which the official coinage sank. Unofficial copies of these coins, known as barbarous radiates, sank even further.

Then in 273–4 the emperor Aurelian reformed the coinage and the radiate took on a larger, brighter look, with up to 4 per cent of silver in it. This reform lasted until 294 when Diocletian overhauled the whole money system of the Empire. He made a single unit out of the great diversity of city, provincial and imperial coinages which had existed up to then, and made every mint strike the same issues at the same time to the same standards, and with the same designs. The only difference was often the mark of the mint on the bottom of the reverse (tail) of the coin and this allowed a check to see that uniformity was in fact adhered to. Diocletian kept the old *aureus*, although he re-established its weight firmly at 60 to the pound of gold, brought in a silver coin, just like his rival in Britain, Carausius, at 96 to the pound, and this looked very like the

220, 221 Trajan Decius (249–51) introduced the double *sestertius*, indicated by his wearing the radiate crown as against the laurel wreath on the single piece (× 2). British Museum.

old *denarius*, and then had three copper coins containing a little silver, as small change. Surprisingly, the old denomination of the *denarius* continued and was used as the unit from which all the new coins and all prices took their tariff. The new silver coin eventually was rated at 100 *denarii*, and the bronze–silver small change may consist of pieces of 25 (or 20), 5, and 2 (or 1) *denarii*. Finally in 309 Constantine the Great eliminated almost the last link with Augustus by striking the gold *solidus* at 72 to the pound of gold rather than the *aureus* at 60 to the pound. Even then the *denarius* struggled on as an idea and a unit of account, hopelessly devalued and quoted in multiples of one to ten thousand.

The study of the coinage in the fourth century is either very simple or hopelessly complicated. As it is by no means certain that the complicated version is correct we may as well opt for the simple view, probably the same view of the coinage that the actual users had of it. To the man in the market, coinage, up to 356, came in two metals, gold and copper, and then good silver was once more added to the list. Constantine's gold *solidus* went on in relative security in the eastern Mediterranean for centuries. One new development in gold, late in the century, was the striking of large numbers of *tremisses* or thirds of *solidi*, and

these were the gold coins that most of the barbarian successor kingdoms copied for their own use after Roman rule in the West ceased. Silver suddenly came back in bulk in 356, whereas before it had been very rare, and it continued right up to the end of production in the West at a very high standard of purity. Copper coins up to 356 had some silver in them, but after about 360 they returned to copper with various base additions. They were issued in great numbers throughout the fourth century, with or without the one or two per cent of silver, and seem for the State to be bait to attract back to the treasury the gold that had to be paid out in wages.

The weight standard and the design of the copper coinage changed every few years and it is therefore very easy to date. What was actually happening in all these changes is far from clear, but to the man in the street I suspect that the bronze coin was simply a token for an ever increasing number of *denarii*. At one time a new issue might have been a coin of 100 *denarii*, the next issue 150 *denarius* coins, then

222 With the new monetary system introduced by Diocletian, coins struck at mints throughout the Empire have a uniformity of portrait, appearance and of type within denominations. Examples here are an *aureus* (Siscia), gold *quinarius* (Aquileia), *denarius* (Siscia), copper *nummus* (Nicomedia), copper radiate (Carthage), and silver *argenteus* (Aquileia) (× 2). British Museum.

223 A gold *aureus* of Diocletian and a gold *solidus* of Constantine the Great, each showing by the numerals incorporated into their reverse designs the number of pieces struck to the pound of gold (× 2). British Museum.

200. It could be that numbers grew so great that, like the French franc under General de Gaulle, everything was divided by 100; the coins were one *nummus* pieces, and this was the same as the old 100 *denarii*. Perhaps at the end of the fourth century the small common copper coin of about twelve millimetres in diameter settled down at a value of five *nummi*, and stayed there for the next century. The names and values are speculation, the inflation in terms of *denarii* is fact; let us follow the archaeological record in seeing a constant heavy loss throughout the fourth century of common copper or bronze coins all of roughly equal purchasing power. But copper was of no interest to the State.

The early Roman coinage consisted of coins of fixed values all of which were, in theory, interconvertible; 25 *denarii* of Hadrian were as good as one *aureus* or one hundred *sestertii*. In the later Empire there was bullion – mainly gold but some silver – and there were copper tokens. Although the State had to let out some of its precious reserves of bullion to pay the wages of State servants (who through the years had decided that gold was the only safe medium for their pay), it made sure that most of that pay came straight back to the State.

Taxes had to be paid in gold, gold coins had to be changed at the money-changer before making small purchases, so only the very rich were able to keep gold coin, and eventually even this became against the law. The copper coins were struck in the State mints, and sent out into the provinces to buy back the gold from the money-changers. After this had happened the State lost all interest in copper coins and refused to regard them as proper money. The large numbers of such coins found today in Britain and, hence, lost in the Roman period, reflect the uselessness of the coinage rather than the carelessness of the users.

The Economy

The Roman coinage may be of interest in its own right, but can it tell us anything about the economy of Roman Britain? Any information that it can give must lie in differences; differences within Britain at different periods, differences between various sites in Britain, and differences between Britain and the rest of the coin-using world. Some of these differences are very marked indeed. If we look at coins lost in Britain in the earlier period, and in Italy, it is

225
226

224 The last major change in the monetary system was Constantine's introduction of the gold *solidus*, a coin of high quality in content and design. This example, struck at the Aquileia mint, has a particularly fine portrait and the reverse type shows the emperor on horseback (× 2). British Museum.

225 Bronze coinage seems to have fallen out of use around the end of the fourth century, and gradually diminished in size, as this piece of Theodosius (× 2). British Museum.

difficult to imagine that the two provinces are part of the same economy. Most sites in Italy have plenty of coinage in bronze and silver whereas most sites in Britain have very little early coinage. If coin-using is anything to do with a thriving economy then Italy seems to have the developed economy and Britain lags behind. In the third century things change with Italy dropping in coin loss as compared with Britain which gains. By the fourth century coin loss in Italy is even further behind Britain which has shot ahead. This statement needs qualifying a little because what has actually happened is that coin loss has stayed fairly constant over the centuries while the value of the coin constantly lost seems to have declined. Whereas the Italian in the first century lost *denarii* and large *sestertii*, in the fourth century he loses only small copper coins. The total value of his losses seems to fall heavily although the number of coins lost stays the same; this looks clear cut, but it needs further thought because I have suggested that the copper coins are only tokens, and we therefore have very little idea of their actual value. In Britain, as the coins seem to decrease in value the numbers lost go up dramatically in the late third century and continue very high in the fourth century. In this case the numbers rise so much that the possible drop in value of the individual coins lost is more than corrected, so it is certainly safe to say that more money was lost in fourth-century Britain than ever before.

If we look at different sites in Britain, more differences in coin use come to light through coin losses. Work on this type of analysis is only in its infancy but there are some pointers to what may one day be accepted as fact. For one thing, the larger towns of Britain with the exception of only one or two tribal centres hang together as a group in their coin loss.

They follow the typically British pattern of few coins lost in the early period, then far more in the third century. Then they keep up a moderate flow of coin loss into the fourth century before tailing off at the end. Country sites like the smaller towns, villas and temples follow the same pattern up to the late third century but then they continue to grow in coin loss to a peak in the middle of the fourth century, and this can continue nearly to the end. Very roughly there seems to be a division between the larger towns and the country, and it seems that the country, to judge by coin loss, is the more successful of the two. How does all this fit into the picture of how Roman Britain works?

Conclusion

Our working model of Roman Britain with its agriculture, trade, commerce, coinage, towns, villages, villas, sale and barter has so far only been taken up to the third century. There we left our towns protected by walls, our villas and pottery industries beginning to blossom, and our coinage in chaos caused by rampant inflation. In various sections I have hinted, implicitly or explicitly, that Roman Britain weathered the economic storm of the third century and that the fourth century was a time of prosperity. The picture so far has been built up with some audible axe grinding and a few eccentric views, but many Roman archaeologists would accept it as a reasonable if individual approximation to what they see as the truth. Now I want to diverge from the mainstream to ride a hobbyhorse which has few backers but many critics.

Very briefly, I do not believe that Roman Britain, as I have described it up to the third century, survived. I think that Britain after 300 was much more British than Roman, medieval than classical. Let us look at some of the evidence in the towns, for they were the centres of *Romanitas* – Roman culture and services. It would seem that the tribe of the Cornovii, based on the once flourishing town of Wroxeter, were not well administered in the old way in the fourth century, for the forum and basilica resembled a derelict bomb site from the third century onwards. Not that it was this badge of tribal administration which marked Wroxeter out as a special settlement or tribal capital. Cirencester, in the centre of good rich farming country and surrounded by wealthy villas which lasted to the end of the fourth century, had some very unadministrative metalworking hearths and domestic rubbish in its basilica in the fourth century, and this did not even continue to the end of the century. Roadside ditches, on which the cleanliness and drainage of towns depended, were blocked with rubbish in Cirencester and Lincoln by the third quarter of the century; and the great theatre at Verulamium was being used as a rubbish dump, probably before the century was out. Town houses which can be shown to continue up to the end of the fourth century are rare in the larger towns, but, in ones and twos, they are there. All this suggests a greatly reduced occupation in the larger towns in the fourth century with numbers of people more appropriate to villages rather than to urban centres.

Mention of villages takes us out of the larger towns and into the countryside with the villas, the farms, and the smaller towns. Not all houses in the country continue to the end of the century, but small towns seem to thrive, villages go from strength to strength, and some villas definitely prosper. My map of Britain in the fourth century would look rather like a map of Britain in the early medieval period with a large number of small equal settlements dotted over the landscape; my symbol for what were larger towns would be the same as for villages because I think that all settlements descended to roughly the same proportions. Villa buildings became unimportant because what mattered was the working estate, and the end of Roman buildings may say nothing about the continuity of the units which they once served. Farms almost certainly continued to be worked, but the people may have lived in villages rather than in villas, and the villages may be those we know today. How does this strange set of ideas fit the complete picture?

Many of the pointers have already been mentioned, and now they can finally be drawn together. I have suggested that there were two blows to large market centres which had no other means of revenue or support: one was the direct taxation in kind which was introduced in the third century and by-passed the markets; the other was the drop in international trade in the third century. If a large proportion of produce no longer went through the markets then the bigger markets would have declined and a levelling of developed settlements would have followed. Many town houses of the later period have a suspicious resemblance to villas in the countryside; did the towns as they declined become the centres of agricultural estates? I have suggested that most towns, judged by coin loss, are less successful than the countryside in the fourth century; and the picture derived from coins is supported by the distribution of mosaic pavements, for the majority of good (that is, expensive) pavements in the fourth century are in the country. The restricted but flourishing economy of medieval Britain, according to my view, evolved from a very successful province of the Roman Empire in the fourth century when allegiance was still owed to an emperor in Italy and good Latin was still taught in the schools. The invading Saxons settled in to this successful economy and developed it, were in fact taken over by it, so Roman Britain never came to an end, it just changed slowly over several centuries into medieval England.

226 The coin hoard is the most obvious idea of treasure. This hoard, found in 1935 at Kiddington near the Ditchley Park villa, consists of badly struck copper coins mainly of the fourth century ranging from Claudius Gothicus (268–70) to Eugenius (392–4). If such a hoard can be examined complete it can provide an enormous amount of information. Ashmolean Museum, Oxford.

CHAPTER VI
THE END OF ROMAN BRITAIN

At the start of the fourth century Britain was securely part of the Roman Empire, an Empire which had survived the shocks of the third century by reforming its political, social and military institutions. By the end of the century this fabric had been shaken to its foundations and the first piece of the structure to fall away was to be Britain. Within the compass of three generations virtually all memory of the Roman occupation was to have vanished with only the institutions of the Christian Church to survive the wreckage, and that only in areas not dominated by pagan invaders.

Writing from a position fixed in the physical and political wreckage of Roman Britain, the sixth-century polemicist, Gildas, our nearest witness in time, had no uncertainty as to why his countrymen were in such a miserable state. Their condition was due to, first, divine retribution for sinfulness; secondly, to internecine strife between their leaders, and, finally, to the disastrous policy of employing Saxon adventurers to protect the island from raiders from Ireland and the north. Gildas was unable to explain the stages by which this condition had been reached in a manner acceptable to modern historians and archaeologists, since he knew almost nothing of the Roman administration of Britain. Within a century of the dissolution of the last Roman administrative institutions virtually all memory of more than three and a half centuries of Roman control had vanished. That Gildas did not even know that Rome had ruled Britain continuously for more than three centuries serves to emphasize the degree of dislocation between fourth-century Britain, a province relatively rich in historical documentation which participated in a very direct way in the affairs of the Empire at large, and the following century which witnessed the complete disintegration of Roman life and the emergence of the historical division of Britain into an English and Celtic island. If the age of dissolution itself could offer no complete explanation of events, still less can modern archaeology supply one. Lacking datable artefacts, it can do little more than attempt to fit observed phenomena into a framework provided by the extremely ambiguous literary evidence of the period.

The immediate cause of the demise of Britain as a component part of the Empire can be seen in terms of three interlinked factors: the systematic withdrawal of regular forces from the island throughout the fourth century; a concomitant rise in the frequency and effectiveness of assaults on the Romanized community by attackers from Ireland and northern Europe, or by Picts from beyond the northern frontier; and, lastly, a failure by the island community itself, and its leaders, to devise an effective alternative force to regular Roman troops as protection from such attacks. This last failure is not in itself unexpected since the system of imperial control, from first to last, was based upon the fear of civil sedition. A political system which would rather have cities burn than allow the recruitment of urban fire brigades for fear that they might form the basis of an alternative military force, did not encourage civilian resistance in times of crisis, though, as we shall see, such resistance did burst forth to good effect at least once in Britain.

For nearly two centuries the defence of Britain rested on a heavily guarded northern frontier, but by the third century more was needed than simple protection from land attack by the northern tribes. The east and southeast of Britain became attractive to raiders from northwestern Europe, equipped with newly developed, fast, seagoing vessels. By the middle of the third century a new fort was built on the Thames estuary at Reculver to protect the approaches to London. It was garrisoned by a unit withdrawn from the forces stationed on the northern frontier. Probably at the same time, coastal protection was provided on the Wash at Brancaster, while within a quarter of a century, a further fort was erected at Burgh Castle, near Yarmouth. By the end of the century a chain of forts protected the east and south coast stretching from the Wash to Portsmouth. In the west, the Severn estuary was blocked against sea raiders by a fort at Cardiff,

231
275
249
279

252 and the western seaboard by another at Lancaster.

The immediate cause of these precautions is well documented since, in 284, a special fleet was commissioned, under the command of 202 Carausius, to sweep the North Sea and Channel clear of Frankish and Saxon sea raiders who were harrying the coasts of Gaul and Britain. Almost at the same time as the development of these seaborne attacks, we have the first evidence for the rise of a new threat on the northern frontier, the Picts. By 312, both Picts and pirates had been dealt with to the 224 extent that Constantine the Great could afford to withdraw troops from Britain for service in his continental armies. That such action was precipitate is clear from the fact that within two years he found it necessary to return and fight a campaign which earned him the title Britannicus Maximus. It is probable that this, or the earlier visit, resulted in the abandonment of the outpost forts of Hadrian's Wall and considerable rebuilding within the forts of the Wall itself.

About thirty years were to pass before any further military event is recorded in Britain but it is unlikely that these decades were a period of uninterrupted peace; vigilance was maintained in the coastal forts. In the winter of 342, the emperor Constans, accompanied by a retinue of only 100 men, made an emergency visit to Britain. The centre of trouble on this occasion appears to have been mainly the northern frontier which was attacked by the Picts and, perhaps, sea-raiding Scots from Ireland. Even so, there is evidence for a further strengthening of the coastal defences of the south with the addition of a fort at Pevensey in 227 Sussex to the chain of strongpoints established half a century earlier. Further evidence that the coastal defence in the southeast was given a special prominence can be seen in its assignment to the command of a specially appointed officer, the Count of the Saxon Shore, whose 228 position perhaps extended to the control of fleets and garrisons across the Channel in Gaul.

The establishment of the command of the Count of the Saxon Shore poses a considerable problem to students of the period. Is this to be seen as a position created for an officer whose duty was to repel Saxons from this coast, or was his duty to command Saxons already settled in East Anglia and southern Britain? Hardly the latter since the garrisons of the Saxon Shore forts are known; they are all regular Roman troops. Pottery which has been seen as having characteristics attributable to Germanic tastes, or Germanic production, and which is found in Roman contexts in the area of the forts has been advanced as evidence for the presence of Germanic settlers in Britain

227 Unlike the other forts of the Saxon Shore with their regular outlines the later fort at Pevensey betrays its mid-fourth-century date by the irregularity of its plan.

COMES LITORIS SAXON PER BRITANIAM.

228 The command of the Count of the Saxon Shore is depicted in a fifteenth-century copy of the *Notitia Dignitatum*, an official list of garrisons and personnel compiled in the late fourth or early fifth century. Bodleian Library, Oxford.

The losses suffered by the western army at Mursa largely determined the imperial authorities' ability to cope with events in Gaul and Britain for the rest of the century. Early in 360 the Picts and Scots once again devastated the area north of Hadrian's Wall and an expeditionary force of four crack regiments was sent from Gaul to deal with the problem. In 365, the historian Ammianus Marcellinus records attacks on Britain by Picts, Scots and Attacotti. Within two years these three peoples were to combine into the most devastating attack to be made upon Britain while it was under Roman control.

Little is known of the origins of these peoples with the exception of the Scotti who were natives of Ireland. The Picts, first attested in 306, are described in contemporary sources as being an amalgamation of two peoples, the Dicalydonae and the Verturiones. The union of these peoples created a dynamic and mobile force in the Highlands whose habit of tattooing or painting themselves gave rise to the name given to them by the Romans – Pictae, the Painted People. The Attacotti are even more problematic, but may have had their centre in the Western Isles or even Northern Ireland. Whatever their origin, it was their ferocity which impressed itself on their contemporaries, a ferocity which might end in a cannibalistic feast of their victims.

In 367, a combination of these tribes attacked Britain at several points simultaneously. Such an event was without precedent. Hitherto, no barbarians had been capable of unifying and planning a concerted attack. Nectaridus, Count of the Saxon Shore, was killed, and we must presume an attack on the south or east coast, probably by Picts, though Saxons were operational on the coast of Gaul at this time. In the north, Cumbria may have been wrested from Roman control for a brief period, and the garrisons of Hadrian's Wall with their commander, Fullofaudes, the *Dux Britanniarum*, were immobilized in their forts. Naval power in the hands of barbarian enemies rendered the concept of an impenetrable northern barrier obsolete at a stroke, though any attempt to move sufficient population south to permit large-scale settlement would still necessarily involve unopposed passage of the Wall. With the Wall bypassed, the garrison troops were rendered useless, and they could do little more than abide the course of events. Other garrisons in the area were perhaps not so fortunate. A funerary inscription of fourth-century date from Ambleside records that a retired centurion and a regimental accounts clerk were killed 'by the enemy, within the fort'. When army pensioners and office staff are involved in military action, the desperation of the circumstances can be imagined. Allied to the surprise and success of the attack was the

long before folk migrations became a serious threat to the island. This view is strongly contested by students of Roman pottery who see no Germanic evidence in the material but rather a continuous development from the earliest Roman pottery forms of the east of Britain, and point to the absence of such 'Germanic' traits in the domestic pottery of Saxons, Franks and Germans in their homeland.

Constans' visit was the prelude to a period of unbroken military intervention either by the imperial government in Britain or by the island's garrison in the political affairs of the Empire at large. In 350, Britain enthusiastically endorsed the revolt of Magnentius against Constantius II and must have contributed troops to the great disaster which overtook the usurper's cause at the battle of Mursa in 351. This, the greatest civil war battle fought in Roman history, decimated the Roman army.

disaffection of the army in Britain. Scouts, whose task it was to give advance warning of hostile concentrations beyond the Wall, succumbed to bribes, giving the enemy military intelligence, but no warning to their own side. Soldiers, whose service in the army was imposed on them on the hereditary principle, took the opportunity given by the invasion to desert their units.

In this confusion, order was restored by a small force, perhaps as small as 2,000 men, commanded by Count Theodosius. Despatched from Gaul by the emperor Valentinian, Theodosius marched to London, which was under some unspecified threat by hostile forces, and within a year had restored order throughout Britain, re-established its military forces, and augmented its coastal defences.

Here, then, was a full-scale rehearsal for later events. The sudden collapse of the administration of the island and the apparent inability, or reluctance, of civilian communities to contribute to their own defence, is made clear in Ammianus' account of the episode. We can see too the small size of the forces actually needed to restore order in these events, and can grasp the poverty of the military manpower resources of the Empire, when later it could not afford to commit even a couple of thousand men to save a substantial part of its territories.

Theodosius' campaign in Britain was an unqualified success; bands of raiders were intercepted and destroyed, deserters were amnestied and returned to duty. The morale of the troops who had proved so ineffective was restored by a judicious programme of building work in their forts. In the northwest, the area recovered from complete barbarian domination was restored to the Empire, and again the morale of its garrisons raised by a gesture when it was created a province in its own right, and named Valentia in honour of the emperor Valentinian.

On the east coast, where seaborne Picts had turned the end of Hadrian's Wall and outflanked the hinterland defences of northern Britain, more practical steps were taken to prevent a recurrence of such a disaster. On the coast of Yorkshire a series of watch towers was constructed running from Flamborough Head in

229, 230

229 Standing on the cliffs at Scarborough near Henry II's great keep is one of the five known watch towers erected on the Yorkshire coast in the second half of the fourth century. They served to give advance warning of seaborne raiders coasting down to the rich areas of southern Britain.

153

SILVER LOOT

THE MILDENHALL TREASURE (right): the great dish from the Mildenhall Treasure, found in Suffolk during the last war, is nearly two feet in diameter and weighs eighteen pounds. The dish, together with more than thirty other items of tableware, seems to be of North African origin and dates to the middle of the fourth century. While the majority of pieces in the treasure are of pagan inspiration a number of objects betray Christian motifs. Among these is a series of silver spoons bearing Christian greetings or *Chi-Rho* monograms. Such objects might have been intended as Christening gifts. (British Museum.)

The palpable results of barbarian raids in the fourth century in Britain and Gaul are surprisingly difficult to establish by archaeological means. Raiders, by their nature, were engaged in hit and run attacks, and the physical destruction of property will not have been a primary concern. That slave raiding played a large part in these attacks is attested by the abduction of Saint Patrick and his witness to the large numbers of Britons languishing in captivity in Ireland. No doubt the same conditions prevailed in the homelands of other raiders, either in Caledonia or in northwest Europe beyond the dwindling power of Rome. But slaves leave no material traces; the bones of captives are no different from those of free men.

THE TRAPRAIN TREASURE (above): this hoard came to light on the site of the stronghold of the Votadini. Whether the treasure represents loot from the Roman area of Britain or a subsidy paid to barbarian allies is uncertain. Little of the hoard survives as complete vessels, the overwhelming mass consisting of dishes, cups and utensils that had been deliberately hacked to pieces. (National Museum of Antiquities, Edinburgh.)

THE CORBRIDGE LANX (detail, below): this rectangular silver dish (19 × 15 in.) was found in the River Tyne adjacent to the Roman fort at Corbridge together with other silver vessels which have since been lost. The scene represents the classical deities associated with the island of Delos and the lanx was probably produced to commemorate the visit of the emperor Julian to the shrine of Apollo on Delos in AD 363. (British Museum.)

Tangible evidence can only come from imperishable objects, and just such objects can be found in the hoards of late Roman treasure found scattered in the barbarian world. Such hoards have been found in Ireland, Scotland, Scandinavia and Germany. Though it is possible that some may consist of subsidies or blood money paid to the barbarians, it is more likely that these hoards represent a mere fraction of the loot available to raiders. By the same token the hoards found in Britain seem to be deposited in an attempt to thwart raiders.

If we examine the two classes of hoards the striking feature of those from Barbarian contexts is the indifference with which the looted objects were treated.

THE COLERAINE HOARD (above): the hoard consisting of broken silver vessels, ingots and 1,506 coins can be dated, on numismatic grounds, to *c.* 423. The place of deposit of the hoard, in Co. Londonderry, suggests that it is loot from Roman Britain acquired during the Irish raiding known to have been taking place in the late fourth and early fifth centuries. (British Museum.)

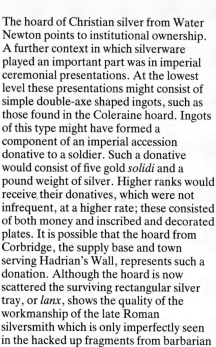

NEW GRANGE: the great Neolithic chamber tomb at New Grange on the River Boyne survived as a centre of religious activity until the conversion of Ireland to Christianity. Among the votive objects buried outside the tomb was jewellery of Roman manufacture as well as gold and silver coins of fourth-century date. It is probable that these were deposited as thank offerings after successful raids on Britain. (National Museum of Ireland, Dublin.)

THE BALLINE HOARD: like the Coleraine hoard, this treasure, discovered at Balline, Co. Limerick, consists of hacked up silver vessels of Roman origin obtained in raids on Britain. (National Museum of Ireland, Dublin.)

The hoard of Christian silver from Water Newton points to institutional ownership. A further context in which silverware played an important part was in imperial ceremonial presentations. At the lowest level these presentations might consist of simple double-axe shaped ingots, such as those found in the Coleraine hoard. Ingots of this type might have formed a component of an imperial accession donative to a soldier. Such a donative would consist of five gold *solidi* and a pound weight of silver. Higher ranks would receive their donatives, which were not infrequent, at a higher rate; these consisted of both money and inscribed and decorated plates. It is possible that the hoard from Corbridge, the supply base and town serving Hadrian's Wall, represents such a donation. Although the hoard is now scattered the surviving rectangular silver tray, or *lanx*, shows the quality of the workmanship of the late Roman silversmith which is only imperfectly seen in the hacked up fragments from barbarian hoards.

Paganism supplied the themes for the art of the late Roman metalworker even when his skills were deployed in a Christian context or for Christian patrons. The spirit of pagan art finds its most elegant expression in the objects from the Mildenhall treasure. Found in uncertain circumstances during the Second World War adjacent to the airbase at Mildenhall in Suffolk, the hoard consists of more than thirty silver items with origins as far afield as North Africa. The finest item in the collection is the large silver dish weighing eighteen pounds, decorated with Bacchic scenes. Two small platters from the same workshop are similarly decorated and form a set with the great dish. A series of richly decorated bowls, ladles and three sets of spoons complete the cache; some of the spoons belie the exuberant paganism of the majority of the plate by being incised with the Christian *Chi-Rho* monogram.

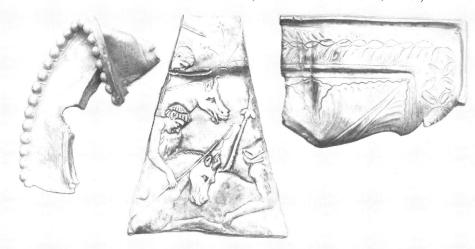

Objects of immense artistic value are hacked into small fragments as a preparation for melting down and conversion into objects more consonant with barbarian tastes or needs. Typical of this use of Roman silver is the hoard from Traprain Law, in Scotland, which contains the cut up fragments of more than 100 vessels, some of which were of Christian origin and perhaps of liturgical significance. How these objects reached Traprain is a matter of dispute since it was the seat of the Votadini, a pro-Roman tribe. No such ambiguity attaches to the hoard from Coleraine in Ireland. The late Roman silver coins comprised both regular coins and others clipped in a manner which is characteristic of coins found only in Britain. Similarly clipped silver coins have been found in votive deposits associated with the great prehistoric tomb at New Grange on the River Boyne. New Grange appears to have been the focus for veneration from the time of its construction in the Neolithic period until the conversion of Ireland to Christianity.

The composition of these hoards permits a small glimpse of the wealth of individuals in late Roman Britain, though no single household would boast the 100 vessels of the Traprain hoard. But individuals were not the only possessors of such treasures.

230 Plan of the Scarborough signal station. The provision of defensive bastions suggests that the signal stations were designed to withstand attack on their small garrisons as well as to provide warning to the hinterland.

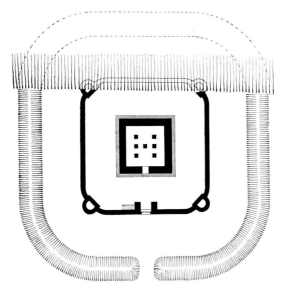

231 The Nydam ship, some seventy feet long, held a crew of about thirty rowers. Such a vessel would have been capable of making coastal raids in Roman Gaul and, by the short crossing of the Channel, in southern Britain. Landesmuseum, Schleswig, Denmark.

the south, probably as far north as the mouth of the Tyne. The towers, set on the cliffs overlooking the North Sea, were each provided with a ditched defensive wall and corner turrets capable of mounting catapult artillery. The functioning and garrisoning of these watchtowers is a little problematic since communication to the hinterland is not easy. The key to the system was probably the fort at Malton which, at this time, was regarrisoned with a unit moved north from Brough-on-Humber. If the landward operation of the towers is imperfectly understood, the seaward strategy can be reconstructed from a contemporary account of maritime defence tactics employed in Britain. 231–3 Fast scouting craft gave advanced warning of enemy shipping, relaying information back to slower, more heavily armed attack vessels. The scouts themselves were camouflaged: 'Lest the scouting craft should give themselves away by their colour, the sails and ropes are dyed blue like the waves . . . and the crew wear blue uniforms so that they may scout more secretly by day as well as night.' Such tactics would be suited to the stationing of fleets in the Tyne, Tees and Humber estuaries commanded by the Count of the Saxon Shore.

Beyond the barrier of Hadrian's Wall, im-

portant strategic changes have been ascribed to Theodosius, notably the devolution of control of the area beyond the immediate frontier line to pro-Roman peoples ruled by imperial nominees. Four dynasties appear to have been established each ruled by chieftains bearing Roman names – Quintillius Clemens on the Clyde, Paternus on the northeast coast, Antonius Donatus in southwest Scotland and, though the source is even more corrupt than for the other dynasties, Catellius Decianus in the area from the Tweed to the Forth. Such arrangements are attested elsewhere in the Empire: the appointment of *praefecti gentium* to rule over barbarian peoples on the frontiers.

The Theodosian reconstruction of Britain, with the exception of the addition of the Yorkshire coast signal stations and perhaps the construction of a fleet base at Bitterne near Southampton, was an attempt to re-establish the *status quo*. Nevertheless, extensive claims have been made for other phenomena attributable to the work of Theodosius, including the stationing of soldiers in towns to man wall-mounted catapult artillery. However, the town
73 defences with artillery bastions can, in some instances, be seen to pre-date the barbarian conspiracy while others, such as parts of the defences of London, are considerably later. The incidence of military belt-plates and buckles, datable to the fourth century, which are seen as evidence of the presence of soldiers in towns, is open to more than one explanation, especially when it is realized that all grades of the imperial civil service, a vast apparatus, wore military belts as insignia of their office. By the same token, physical evidence for the events of 367 are difficult to define archaeologically; there is no trail of destruction and no concentration of unrecovered coin hoards. The disaster, for such it was, appears to have been more one of confusion caused by weak admin-

istration and the desertion by large numbers of soldiers in the face of an unprecedented unified attack; an attack which in other circumstances might have been a mere incident was allowed to assume proportions probably quite out of keeping with the numbers of barbarians actually involved.

The ineffectual showing of the army of Britain in 367 must have led to reforms, for within a decade and a half it was to prove itself to be, once again, an effective fighting force, though to the long-term detriment of the defence of Britain.

In 383, a rebellion broke out in Britain under the leadership of Magnus Maximus. Of Spanish origin, like his legitimate rival Theodosius, Maximus had served in Britain in 367 and now held a major military command, perhaps that of *Dux Britanniarum*. Contemporary opinion

232 (left) The reverse types on some of the bronze coins of the usurper emperor Allectus (293–6) depict the sail- and oar-powered ships typical of the late Roman navy ($\times$ 2). British Museum.

233 (below) Troop-carrying transports are depicted on the gold medallion struck to commemorate the reconquest of Britain by Constantius I, Chlorus, after the overthrow of Allectus in 296. In the scene on the reverse of the medallion the victorious Constantius is being welcomed by the personification of London. His fleet, which saved the city from sack, approaches up the Thames ($\times$ 2). British Museum.

ascribes the reason for the revolt to the ambitions of Maximus, but the apparently ignoble reason for the revolt did not affect the devotion with which the forces of Britain followed the usurper's cause. Maximus established his court at Trier, where, after the defeat and death of the western emperor, Gratian, he established a stable regime and received diplomatic recognition from the eastern empire. This state of affairs persisted until 387, when a breach with Theodosius led Maximus to annexe Italy. In the following year he met defeat and death at Aquileia at the head of the Adriatic.

The revolt of Maximus has been seen as a watershed in the affairs of Britain. Gildas relates that the usurper went to Gaul 'with a great retinue of hangers-on' and that 'after that Britain was despoiled of her whole army, her military resources, her governors, brutal as they were, and her sturdy youth, who had followed the tyrant's footsteps, never to return home'. There is, however, no independent evidence for such troop movements.

The *Notitia Dignitatum*, a list of army units and administrative posts compiled in 395, preserves details of units on the Continent previously attested as being in Britain. A notable example is the presence of a unit, previously called the Seguntienses, among the forces stationed in the Balkans. It is more than probable that this unit had been the garrison of the key fortress of Segontium (Caernarfon) in North Wales, and that it was taken abroad by Maximus and retained in eastern Europe after his defeat. Such a move is not impossible in the light of the place held by Magnus Maximus (Maxen Wledig) in Welsh legends, and more than one Welsh dynasty preserved the tradition of the descent from him of its power. It is significant, too, that no forts in Wales appear

among those listed in the *Notitia Dignitatum*. Given the place of honour held by Maximus in the Welsh sources it would appear that at some time during his reign, and not necessarily as early as 383, he evacuated the garrison of Wales and made provision for the policing of the area by native leaders invested with the powers of *praefecti gentium*, thus repeating in the west the arrangements that had been made in the north of Britain. These arrangements have been ascribed to Count Theodosius, but as we know that Maximus had to campaign against the Picts and the Scots, it would appear that affairs in the frontier region were not under control. Maximus' campaign is ascribed to the year before his revolt, but it is perhaps possible to date the campaign to the year after. At least one dynasty of southern Scotland attributed its origins to Maximus, but it is just possible that the creation of pro-Roman frontier states should be associated with Theodosius rather than with Maximus.

The depletion of the garrison of Britain accelerated the incursions of barbarians. De-

234 (left) Gold *solidus* of Magnus Maximus (383–8), usurper emperor in Britain, struck at the mint of Trier in Germany (× 2). British Museum.

235 (right) The Vandalic general Stilicho was virtual ruler of the western Roman Empire in the last years of the fourth century and the early years of the fifth. In 401 barbarian invasions of Italy led him to withdraw forces from Britain with the result that Wales and the west were stripped of troops. Cathedral Treasury, Monza, Italy.

236 Gold *solidus* of Constantine III (× 2). He was raised from being a low-ranking soldier to imperial status by the garrison of Britain. A disastrous continental campaign against the legitimate emperor, Honorius, led to his defeat, capture and execution in 411. British Museum.

tails are few, but by 396–8 the effective ruler of the western Roman Empire, Stilicho, the Vandalic *magister militum*, mounted an expedition against the by now traditional enemies, the Picts, the Scots and the Saxons. A small army was created to form a mobile force in the island to deal with future incursions, but events elsewhere soon led to the withdrawal of effective forces from Britain. By 401 Italy itself was beset by barbarian invasions and Stilicho, faced by this threat and seriously short of troops, withdrew such forces as could be spared from Britain, including the Legio VI from York and what was left of Legio II Augusta.

It was in this condition that the communities of Britain faced the prospect of a major barbarian assault in 407. On the last day of December, 406, at the height of a ferociously cold winter, the waters of the Rhine froze over. Across this natural bridge, and in the presence of helpless Roman garrisons and river patrol craft, a mass migration of Vandals, Alans and Sueves took place. Once safely within Roman territory, the horde made for the Channel coast and thus threatened either to cut Britain off from contact with the Continent or to cross over *en masse*. In Britain affairs were in chaos with a full-scale revolt against the imperial government in progress. For reasons unknown, a certain Marcus had been elevated to the purple. The arrival of barbarian forces in Gaul seems to have precipitated the lynching of this usurper and his replacement by a town councillor named Gratian, whose equally ephemeral tenure of office resulted in his death and replacement by a military candidate, Constantine III.

Constantine III's reign (407–11) was ignominious and largely spent, not in pursuing and destroying the invaders of Gaul, where he landed in 407 with what remained of the army of Britain, but in evading the vengeance of the imperial authorities who suborned his chief lieutenant and a large part of his army. In his absence, a major Saxon invasion of Britain took place; according to the Byzantine historian Zosimus and the nearly contemporary Gallic Chronicler:

'The barbarians [Saxons] from beyond the Rhine overran everything at will and re-duced the inhabitants of the British Island and some of the peoples of Gaul to the necessity of rebelling from the Roman Empire and of living by themselves, no longer obeying the Romans' laws. The Britons, therefore, taking up arms and fighting on their own behalf, freed the cities from the barbarians who were pressing upon them . . .'

Attempts have been made to see this as a national revolt, a combination of freeing Britain from both barbarian invaders and the oppressive regime of the Roman Empire. It is possible, however, to see the 'rebellion' as nothing more than a technical breach of the general prohibition on civilians acting in a military capacity for, only two years later, the cities of Britain appealed to the emperor Honorius for protection. Since they had already freed themselves from barbarian attack, the appeal for protection must have been from the vengeance of Constantine III, who, discredited by his failure to protect Britain, was now repudiated by his erstwhile backers; these purged their country of his officials in anticipation of the restoration of a legitimate administration. But the Empire had no forces at its disposal and the reply which they received ordered them to 'guard themselves'. Constantine was defeated in 411, and the remnant of his armies remained on the Continent; thereafter, as the historian Procopius records, 'the Romans were never able to recover Britain, which from that time onwards continued to be ruled by usurpers'.

The formal severance of Britain from Rome can be dated to this event, although Procopius' words imply that the reunification of Britain with the main body of the Empire long remained an object of imperial policy. The break with Rome was to be final, but after more than three centuries of sharing in Roman political institutions and technology, it is not to be expected that a sudden break in those aspects of life would have taken place. It is true that with the collapse of the administration the supply of coinage dried up, though spasmodic issues reached Britain as late as 423 and 435, but by the latter date it is unlikely that coinage played any great part in the economic life of Britain. It is also true that the highly central-

237 The Iron Age hill-fort at South Cadbury, Somerset, in common with similar sites in Britain, was reoccupied in the early post-Roman period. In the case of South Cadbury the reoccupation involved the reconstruction of the defences and the provision of elaborate gates.

ized pottery industry quickly broke down. Elsewhere urban and rural life continued as it had done throughout the previous century. There had been times before when conditions had looked hopeless, but relief had come, life had resumed, and after a suitable interval new investment had been made with villas being constructed and new mosaics commissioned from well-established firms of decorators. This time there was to be no such relief, and slowly at first, but with increasing impetus, the quality of life deteriorated. There were exceptions: at Verulamium (St Albans) archaeological discoveries indicate a continuity of Roman building traditions into the first half of the fifth century, and continuity of urban administration is demonstrated by the provision of a piped water supply at this period. It was to this city that Germanus, the bishop of Auxerre, came from Gaul in 429 to preach the cause of orthodox Christianity against the heretical teachings of Pelagius, whose doctrines had found fertile ground among British Christians. Here he met the leading citizens of the community 'distinguished by their riches, resplendent in their attire, and surrounded by the adulation of the multitude'.

Theological debate now took the place of the martial spirit which prevailed in 408. Even as Germanus preached, Saint Patrick, son of a Roman town councillor, languished in slavery, abducted by raiders and 'taken into captivity into Ireland with so many thousands'. Germanus himself, a former army officer, was persuaded by his hosts to lead resistance against a raiding party of Picts and Saxons, and won a notable, and bloodless, victory. It would have been at this time, too, that a decision was taken which was to prove fatal to the continuity of Roman culture in Britain.

The political leadership of Britain in the years following 410 is very obscure. Legends abound but among the accretions of later ages may lie pearls of truth; they are hard to find. What can be said is that by 430 Britain was dominated by a single leader known to us as Vortigern. Even his name is obscure, since what appears to be a name may be a title meaning 'great leader'. In about 430, news reached Britain of an impending attack by Picts and Scots; unable to resist such a threat from their own military resources, the Britons resorted to the time-honoured Roman institution of hiring one group of barbarians to fight another. The only other maritime fighting force available was the Saxons. These, under their leaders, Hengist and Horsa, were settled in Kent and East Anglia to counter the impending attack. Once established, the mercenary force increased its strength by recruitment from its homeland so that within a dozen years the mercenaries themselves presented as great a potential danger as those they had been employed to destroy. An attempt to evict them from their strongholds in Kent and the Upper Thames region provoked a revolt in which the erstwhile allies wrought wholesale destruction in towns and in the countryside. The reaction of the Britons was to make one last attempt to rejoin the Empire. In about 446, they addressed a letter to Aëtius, the *magister militum* of Valentinian III, who was engaged in saving what could be saved of Gaul for the Empire:

'To Aëtius, thrice Consul, the groans of the Britons . . . the barbarians drive us to the sea, the sea drives us to the barbarians; between these two modes of death either we are killed or drowned'.

The appeal was unanswered. The next half-century was occupied in warfare culminating, shortly before 500, in a great British victory at Mount Badon. It was a hollow victory; in the struggle the towns and villas of the Roman countryside had vanished and a heroic society of chieftains and war-bands had emerged, virtually identical to that of the Saxon enemy.

MILES
10 0 10 20 30 40 50 60

KILOMETRES
10 0 10 20 30 40 50 60 70

D = Dere Street
W = Watling Street
S = Stane Street
A = Akeman Street
E = Ermine Street

Inchtuthil

Strageath
Ardoch
Camelon
ANTONINE WALL
Cramond
Inveresk

Newstead

High Rochester
Risingham
HADRIAN'S WALL
Bewcastle
Birrens
South Shields
Carlisle
Ebchester
Old Penrith
Lancaster
Brougham
Kirby Thore
Binchester
Ambleside
Brough
Ravenglass
Bowes
Catterick

Aldborough
Malton
Ilkley
Ribchester
York

Anglesey
Caer Gybi
Buxton
Lincoln
Caerhun
Chester
Horncastle
Caernarfon
Ancaster
Brancaster
Tomen-y-Mur
Wroxeter
Caister-on-Sea
Wall
Leicester
Leintwardine
Bagington
Water Newton
Burgh Castle
Worcester
Irchester
Kenchester
Chesterton
Colchester
Brecon Gaer
Dunstable
Carmarthen
Gloucester
Chedworth
Alchester
St Albans
Bradwell
Usk
Lydney
Cirencester
Chelmsford
Caerleon
Caerwent
London
Sea Mills
Rochester
Reculver
Bath
Silchester
Lullingstone
Richborough
Canterbury
Winchester
Dover
Old Sarum
Portchester
Bignor
Folkestone
Rockbourne
Bitterne
Fishbourne
Lympne
Hod Hill
Dorchester
Chichester
Pevensey
Exeter
Brading
Maiden Castle
Isle of Wight

GAZETTEER

A complete gazetteer of all the sites of Roman Britain would make a substantial book on its own. This Gazetteer lists all major sites, including many of importance for finds made there but where there may not necessarily be anything to be seen on the ground today. Where the Roman name of a site is known it is given after the modern name, under which entry the main details about the site are to be found. The Roman names are also listed alphabetically in the main sequence and the modern name given against them, thus referring across to the modern name for further information.

Some of the sites listed here have very little to show, or are only of interest to the specialist. In order to give some immediate guidance in the list to indicate those sites that are worth visiting a two-tier system has been used to make them readily identifiable:

* an important or specially interesting site which it is well worth making an effort to visit.

† a site where there is still something of interest to be seen, but which is not in the premier category.

The details given locate the sites by their Ordnance Survey national grid reference numbers; for sites to visit fuller directions on the ground are added and then a brief description of the main features to be seen.

Many of the sites in the guardianship of the Ancient Monuments Branch of the Department of the Environment have individual published guides available of varying length and detail. A full list of them can be found in Sectional List 27: *Government Publications; Ancient Monuments and Historic Buildings*, issued by Her Majesty's Stationery Office. Fuller details and more background information about many of the sites listed here can be found in R.J.A. Wilson, *A Guide to the Roman Remains in Britain* (London, 1975), and in Peter Clayton, *Archaeological Sites of Britain* (London, 1976).

Aballava – Burgh-by-Sands

Abbots Ann, Hants.　　　　SU 3141
Villa discovered *c*. 1854; two medallions from mosaics with stylized flower decoration are in the British Museum.

Abonae – Sea Mills

† **Ackling Dyke**, Dorset　　SU 022178
Road from Dorchester to London via Old Sarum. Good stretches of the *agger* (the raised bank on which the road was built) are preserved in the area of the Iron Age hillfort of Badbury Rings (q.v.), where it touches the outer rampart. Parts of it are still up to 40ft wide and five to six feet high with the side ditches still visible.

Aesica – Greatchesters

Akeman Street, Herts.
Roman road running from St Albans via Tring to Cirencester, following part of the A41.

Alabum – Llandovery

Alauna – Maryport

* **Aldborough** (*Isurium Brigantium*),
N. Yorks.　　　　　　　　SE 405665
Small town of 55 acres off the A1167 near Boroughbridge, 15 miles northwest of York. It was walled in the mid-third century and there are slight remains of the robbed wall and mid-fourth-century bastions attached to it. The site is notable for its fourth-century mosaic pavements, mainly found in the eighteenth and nineteenth centuries. Two are still *in situ* in small huts at the site: one has a central square (heavily damaged) with an animal (a lion?) seated under a tree, and bands of various borders surrounding it; the other has a central device of an eight-pointed star within four decorative borders. Another

238 *Part of the southwest corner of the town wall at Aldborough with an internal turret in the foreground.*

163

pavement, preserved in Leeds City Museum, shows Romulus and Remus being suckled by the she-wolf. The style of this pavement is attractively crude and the subject unique among British mosaics. A fourth pavement, much damaged, also had a unique scene set in its apsidal end of two figures, Muses, on Mount Helicon (identified in Greek script on one of the panels). Excavations have revealed occupation of the town up to the end of the fourth century.

There is a small site museum of local finds and it includes two milestones set up in the reign of Trajan Decius (249–51). The famous bronze from Aldborough in the shape of a sleeping slave-boy is now in the British Museum and a copy is on show in the site museum. A sculptured figure of Mercury can be seen in the nearby St Andrew's church.

† **Ambleside** (*Galava*), Cumbria
NY 372034
Fort on National Trust property in Borrans Field just to the west of Ambleside off the road linking the A593 and A591. The stone fort was built in the second century and occupied into the fourth. The walls of the fort are visible, but not very well preserved; they are identifiable with the help of a plan on the site. Finds from the site are in the National Park Centre, Brockhole, two miles south on the A591.

Ancaster, Lincs. SK 983437
Town on Ermine Street (q.v.), the B6403, where it crosses the A153, Grantham to Sleaford road. There are surface indications only of the wall and ditch to the northeast of the crossroads. Finds, including sculpture, are in the Grantham Museum.

Anderida – Pevensey

Anglesey (*Mona*), Gwynedd
Island off the north coast of Wales that was the last outpost of the Druids. It was stormed by Agricola in 78, and the operation is described by Tacitus in *Agricola* 18. The island is rich in prehistoric remains, and a small Roman fort was built to act as a watchdog at Caer Gybi (q.v.).

Angmering-on-Sea, Sussex TQ 0504
Site of a villa three miles west of Littlehampton, which is one of the few known to have had mosaics and a bath suite in the first century (cf. Fishbourne).

Antonine Wall, Strathclyde
Turf wall about 12ft high built on a stone base 14ft wide running from Bo'ness on the Firth of Forth to Old Kilpatrick on the Clyde, a distance of 37 miles. It was built in the reign of the emperor Antoninus Pius (138–161), from whom it takes its name, under the governor Quintus Lollius Urbi-

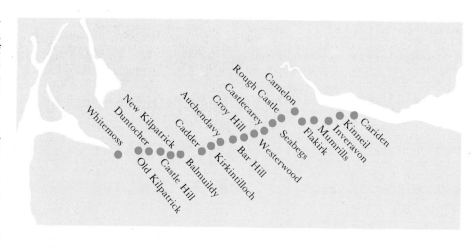

239 Map of the Antonine Wall.

240 The foundations of the turf wall and the ditch of the Antonine Wall on the east side of Rough Castle.

cus and commenced *c.* 143. Its rampart is fronted by a 20ft wide berm and a ditch 12ft deep and about 40ft wide. From inscriptional evidence on 18 known distance slabs (mainly now in the Hunterian Museum, Glasgow), troops of the II Augusta, VI Victrix, and XX Valeria Victrix legions worked on its construction. Forts were placed at two-mile intervals, and 16 are known with the possible addition of a further three. Two of the forts only had stone walls – Castlecary (q.v.) and Balmuildy (q.v.). The best-preserved fort is Rough Castle (q.v.), and at Seabegs Wood (q.v.) to the west of Rough Castle beside the B816 is a good stretch of the rampart, ditch and Military Way.

The Antonine Wall was occupied from about 143 until *c.* 158, when it was abandoned and the troops fell back to Hadrian's Wall. It was reoccupied again for a time and finally abandoned at a date in the late second century, probably around 180.

Aquae – Buxton

Aquae Sulis – Bath

Arbeia – South Shields

† **Ardoch**, Tay NN 839099
An outlier fort of the Antonine Wall (q.v.), to the northeast of Braco off the A822. Occupied *c.* 80–100 and in the Antonine period. The fort area was 75 × 70 yards, and there are still spectacular turf ramparts built on a stone base on the north and east sides. Marshy ground on the south and west sides provided additional defence; the ramparts here are closer together and there are not so many as on the other sides. The fort was a permanent legionary base and five, larger, temporary camps are known to the north of it. They overlie each other in varying degrees; two date to Agricola's advance in 79 and the remainder relate to 208/9 during the campaigns of Septimius Severus.

Auchendavy, Strathclyde NS 6774
Site of a fort on the Antonine Wall (q.v.), of which only a very faint outline remains. It lies to the east of Kirkintilloch (q.v.).

† **Badbury Rings** (*Vindogladia*), Dorset
ST 964030
Roman posting station at the site of an Iron Age hillfort. Ackling Dyke (q.v.) touches its outer rampart.

* **Baginton** (The Lunt), W. Midlands
SP 345752
First-century Agricolan fort occupied *c.* 60–75 two miles south of Coventry on the A45. It was discovered in 1960, excavated, and then large areas reconstructed with the help of a unit of the Royal Engineers, making it one of the most interesting sites to visit in the Midlands. The great timber gate is double-leaved with a walkway over it and a fighting platform above that. On either side of the gateway are 50ft lengths of the turf rampart with a palisade top. A large reconstructed granary in the centre of the site houses the finds from the excavations and also some reconstructed lifesize figures of a legionary and a mounted auxiliaryman.

In September 1977 the *gyrus* was reconstructed. This circular feature, 107ft in diameter and unique in Britain, stands in the eastern half of the fort. It was used for

41

42

training cavalrymen and for schooling cavalry remounts. The reconstruction suggests an elevated walkway within the palisade for instructors, as described by Xenophon in his treatise on horsemanship. Until the *gyrus* was recognized the non-rectangular shape of the fort presented problems with the curious bulge in the eastern ramparts made to accommodate it. More recent excavations have revealed irregularities in the line of the western defences, with the possibility of more *gyri* in the area outside the fort.

† **Balmuildy**, Strathclyde   NS 5871
Fort on the Antonine Wall (q.v.) east of New Kilpatrick (q.v.). It covered 4.3 acres and had stone ramparts predating the actual wall. One of the only two forts on the Antonine Wall with stone ramparts, the other being Castlecary (q.v.).

† **Banks East**, Cumbria   NY 574648
Turret 52A, 2¾ miles west of Birdoswald (q.v.) on Hadrian's Wall. Its features are a well-preserved plinth and the Wall abutting it on either side. The interior has a hearth and a ladder platform while part of the tumbled superstructure can be seen just outside.

Banna – Bewcastle

Banna (or *Magna*) – Carvoran

Banovallum – Horncastle

† **Bar Hill**, Strathclyde   NS 7076
Fort covering 3.6 acres situated on the highest point of the Antonine Wall (q.v.) between Croy Hill and Auchendavy. It actually lies about 150ft south of the wall with the Military Way passing between it and the wall. During excavations a headquarters building, a bath house, a granary and evidence for an earlier Agricolan fortlet were found. Today the platform of the fort is visible and there is a well which has been consolidated. The ditch can be seen stretching east towards Croy Hill for about half a mile.

† **Bartlow Hills**, Cambs.   TL 586448
Group of Roman barrows, originally seven, but now only four remaining at Bartlow, east of Linton ten miles south of Cambridge. They range in height from 25 to 45ft; the latter has a diameter of 144ft and is the largest extant Romano-British barrow. The group was cut through by the railway in the nineteenth century, and that has now gone, dividing the barrows into three and one. Rich finds from the barrows in 1832–40 indicated that they dated from the end of the first to the middle of the second century. Unfortunately most of the finds were destroyed in a fire in 1847 and the surviving items and some watercolours of the lost pieces are in the museum at Saffron Walden.

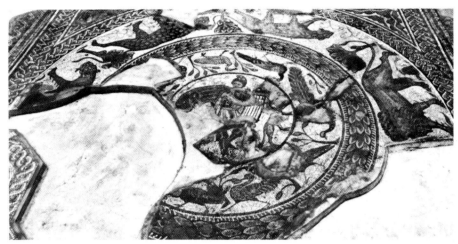

241 *Orpheus and the Beasts mosaic from the Barton Farm villa. Corinium Museum, Cirencester.*

Barton Farm, Glos.   SP 0102
Villa with a fourth-century mosaic found less than a quarter of a mile outside the walls of Cirencester in 1825. The mosaic is now in the Corinium Museum, Cirencester. The central medallion represented Orpheus playing his lyre accompanied by a dog(?). An inner circle has brightly coloured birds moving around in a clockwise direction, then a triple band of laurel leaves as a wreath and an outer circle of beasts of prey: a lion, leopard, tiger, and possible a puma, stalking clockwise between low bushy trees. The corner segments are stylized sprays of leaves and the whole has a border of swastikas and guilloche panels.

This pavement has stylistic and decorative affinities with those from Chedworth (q.v.); Withington (q.v.) and Woodchester (q.v.) – possibly all four (and one now destroyed from Dyer Street, Cirencester) were done by the same mosaic-laying firm. They are all of what has been called the Corinium school of mosaicists (see entry for Cirencester).

* **Bath** (*Aquae Sulis*), Avon   ST 317564
The city was a comparatively small one covering only 23 acres. The hot health-giving mineral springs were recognized early in the Roman period and a flourishing spa was operating by the last quarter of the first century. It lasted into the early fifth century when parts of the town were abandoned in the face of increasing Saxon raids and the water took over, making large areas marsh land. The Roman remains began to be recognized in the eighteenth century; sporadic finds have been made and properly directed excavation (most recently under the direction of Professor Barry Cunliffe) carried out ever since. The main bath, the Great Bath, is still fed through Roman conduits and is 80 × 40ft and six feet deep. Other, smaller baths, including steam and plunge baths, are nearby. A classical-style temple beside the bath was dedicated to Sulis Minerva, and the best-known find from the site is the facing head of the Gorgon Medusa that was once set in the pediment of the temple, flanked by winged Victories. A fine gilded bronze head of Minerva, hacked from its body, was found in the Great Bath in the eighteenth century. The small museum beside the Great Bath includes both these pieces and many other finds and inscriptions from the area, including the 'Bath curse' scratched on a lead tablet. Although rich in inscribed stones and altars the museum is poor in mosaics, only a few insignificant scraps having been found. Little is known concerning the rest of the town outside the immediate bath complex, owing largely to the great rebuilding that took place in the eighteenth century when the spa came into its own again as a fashionable resort.

65

135

125

124

242 *The Great Bath at Bath, with the Abbey in the background.*

Beadlam, N. Yorks.   SE 634842
Villa beside the A170 a mile and a half east of Helmsley. It was discovered and excavated in 1966, and further excavated in

1969. Its fourth-century geometric mosaic pavement, which had collapsed into the hypocaust below it, is the most northerly mosaic known. The site was back-filled and it is to be re-excavated in due course and opened to the public under the care of the Department of the Environment.

† **Bearsden**, Strathclyde   NS 5372
Almost the most westerly part of the Antonine Wall (q.v.) close by the junction of the A810 to Dumbarton, on the northwest outskirts of Glasgow, and the B8050. A section of the wall-base can be seen, together with the ditch. The bath house excavated here is to be preserved and is (in 1979) the most substantial example of Roman stonework to be seen in Scotland.

† **Benwell** (*Condercum*), Tyne and Wear
    NZ 217646
Fort on Hadrian's Wall which covered 5.64 acres. Today it is buried under a reservoir and a housing estate south of the A69 on

243 *The only example now extant of the causeway which crossed the* vallum *on the south side of Hadrian's Wall, at Benwell.*

244 *The temple of the Celtic god Antenociticus at Benwell.*

the west side of Newcastle upon Tyne. The only visible example of the *vallum* crossing which restricted access to the Wall from the south can be seen here at the end of Denhill Park Avenue. Outside the fort was a small temple with an apsidal end dedicated to the Celtic god Antenociticus; this can be seen in Broomridge Avenue. Sculpture from the temple, in particular the striking head of the god himself, is displayed in the University Museum, Newcastle.

† **Bewcastle** (*Banna*), Cumbria
    NY 565745
An outpost fort of Hadrian's Wall six miles north of Birdoswald (q.v.) to the east of the B6318. Evidence was found for the reconstruction of the fort at the end of the third century, and again around the middle of the fourth. The site is better known for the 14ft 6in high cross-shaft of the second half of the seventh century in the churchyard. It carries panels of decoration representing Christ, the Agnus Dei, and five lines of a runic inscription.

* **Bignor**, Sussex   SU 988147
A large courtyard villa discovered in 1811 on the line of Stane Street (q.v.) to the

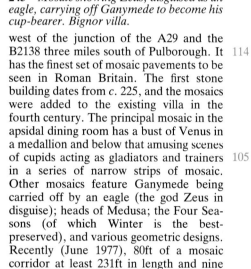

245 *Mosaic showing Zeus, disguised as an eagle, carrying off Ganymede to become his cup-bearer. Bignor villa.*

west of the junction of the A29 and the B2138 three miles south of Pulborough. It has the finest set of mosaic pavements to be seen in Roman Britain. The first stone building dates from *c.* 225, and the mosaics were added to the existing villa in the fourth century. The principal mosaic in the apsidal dining room has a bust of Venus in a medallion and below that amusing scenes of cupids acting as gladiators and trainers in a series of narrow strips of mosaic. Other mosaics feature Ganymede being carried off by an eagle (the god Zeus in disguise); heads of Medusa; the Four Seasons (of which Winter is the best-preserved), and various geometric designs. Recently (June 1977), 80ft of a mosaic corridor at least 231ft in length and nine feet wide was consolidated and opened to view.

In its heyday the villa must have been one of the most substantial in Roman Britain and its owner a person of considerable wealth and standing. The archaeological evidence suggests that the villa was abandoned in the early fifth century, after which it simply fell into ruin.

† **Binchester** (*Vinovia*), Durham
    NZ 208314
Cavalry fort on a minor road north of the A689 at Bishop Auckland, about a mile behind the castle. It was founded by Agricola and abandoned early in the second century to be then reoccupied *c.* 160. The north and east ramparts of the fort can be seen as low mounds in the fields. Behind the farm, preserved in a shed, is a good example of a hypocaust beneath its original concrete floor and with the hollow flue tiles for ducting the warm air set in its edge. Two complete arches led the warm air through into the next room and some of the red brick tiles are stamped N CON to indicate the army unit that made them – *Numerus Concangiensium*, foreign irregulars.

* **Birdoswald** (*Camboglanna*), Cumbria
NY 615662
The Roman name means 'crooked bend' and the fort stands high up on a bluff above the river Irthing on a minor road south of the B6318 west of Gilsland. Originally it covered just over five acres but is now only about 3½ acres, the rest being covered by a modern farm. The north and west gates are buried respectively under the modern road and the farm area, but the remains of the south and east gates are still considerable. These were both double-portalled but later additions in the fourth century closed off parts for other use, such as guardrooms. The fort was reconstructed on several occasions, probably in Hadrianic, Severan and Constantinian times at least, including the rebuilding of the commandant's house which, an inscription records, had fallen into ruin.

Birrens (*Blatobulgium*), Dumfries
NY 218753
An outlier fort (like Bewcastle, q.v.) forward of the west end of Hadrian's Wall on the direct route north from Carlisle into western Scotland. It lies on the west side of a minor road heading towards Middlebie off the B722 to the east of its junction with the A74 seven miles northwest of Gretna Green. Originally founded by Agricola. More than twenty inscriptions found on the site in excavations in 1845–6 and 1962–7 attest various regiments from the area of the Rhine stationed there: the first cohort of the Nervana and, later, the second cohort of the Tungrians. Most of the inscriptions found are now in the National Museum of Antiquities, Edinburgh.

The outline of the fort's ramparts can be traced on the north, east and west sides as a strong mound; on the south side it has been eroded away by the neighbouring stream.

† **Bitterne** (*Clausentum*), Hants.
SU 420120
A port founded *c.* 70 on a promontory in the river Itchen at the head of Southampton Water. New defences were raised about 370 changing the port more into a fort. This coincides with the abandonment of Portchester (q.v.) in favour of this newly fortified site. Slight remains of this period, some foundations and a fragment of the fort wall, are preserved beside a block of flats called Bitterne Manor House. At one time it was suggested that the c used as a mintmark on coins of the usurper British emperors Carausius and Allectus indicated Colchester (*Camulodunum*) as their place of mintage, but *Clausentum* is now the accepted interpretation.

† **Black Carts**, Northumberland
NY 885714
Section of Hadrian's Wall west of Chesters off the B6318. Recently conserved, it consists of the Wall built on the narrow width and a turret (no. 29A) whose rear wall still stands seven feet high. Incorporated in the masonry are two centurial stones, only one of which is reasonably legible to give a reading of COH I (first cohort); it is located in the middle of the bottom course of the north wall. The second example is in the bottom course of the south wall, twelfth block from the west.

† **Blackpool Bridge**, Glos.   SO 653087
A section of the Roman road from the Kings Weston villa (q.v.) at Bristol to Lydney (q.v.) preserved off the B4431 west of Blakeney (A48), beside the railway bridge. Narrower than usual, only eight feet wide, it is well constructed with kerb stone settings and traces of wheel-tracks.

246   *The well-preserved surface of the Roman road at Blackstone Edge.*

* **Blackstone Edge**, Greater Manchester
SD 973170 to SD 988184
Part of the paved Roman road from Manchester to Ilkley not far from Rochdale, a mile east of Littleborough on the A58. One of the best stretches of Roman road remaining in Britain. It is paved with large stone setts (kerb stones), and has a 16ft wide surface with a central groove down the middle. This was filled with turf to give some purchase for the horses' hooves as they pulled the carts, and also to act as a drag for the brake-pole of the carts to steady them going downhill.

Blatobulgium – Birrens

Blubberhouses Moor, N. Yorks.
SE 150540
Section of road built during the Agricolan advance up from Ribchester.

† **Bokerley Dyke**, Hants.   SU 015200
Fourth-century earthwork, possibly of an imperial estate associated with the Rockbourne villa (q.v.). It is about three miles of bank and ditch that may have been thrown up at the time of the Pictish raids in the area in 367. A good stretch is visible on the south side of the A354 four miles southeast of Salisbury just beyond Martin Drove End.

† **Bowes** (*Lavatrae*), Durham   NY 9913
Originally an Agricolan fort founded to guard the east end of the Stainmore Pass. The Roman strategic situation was appreciated by the Normans who built a castle in the northwest corner of the fort, and there is a churchyard in the northeast angle. A bath house was situated outside the fort near to the present cemetery wall. Little now remains. An inscription from the site, now in the Fitzwilliam Museum, Cambridge, records the garrison at the end of the second century as Spanish Vettones cavalry. They were followed by a detachment of Thracians from Bulgaria, attested by an inscription in the north transept of Bowes church. Other finds from the site can be seen in the Bowes Museum, Barnard Castle, nearby.

Bowness-on-Solway (*Maia*), Cumbria
NY 223627
The last of the forts on Hadrian's Wall at its western end, standing fifty feet up on cliffs overlooking the Solway estuary. Built of stone, it covered seven acres, but little is visible today. The north wall eroded away and fell into the sea, but the south wall, lying to the north of the church, has been excavated and the position of the bath house and west ditch are known.

Box, Wilts.   ST 8268
Large villa six miles northeast of Bath on the A4 excavated between 1831 and 1902, and now covered over. Many of its forty-odd rooms had mosaics with linear and geometric decoration. They have been left *in situ*, and coloured drawings of them are in the Devizes Museum.

* **Brading**, Isle of Wight, Hants.
SZ 599863
Villa on the A3055 on the east side of the Isle of Wight which is amongst the six finest known in Britain – its mosaics are certainly the most enigmatic. Built about 300 as the centre of a rich farming estate, and occupation continued into the early fifth century. The subjects of several of the mosaics are strange and unique in Britain, betraying the fourth-century owner's very personal interest in their representational content. In Room 1 (the west wing) is a pleasant depiction of Orpheus and his lyre in a central medallion surrounded by and charming the animals. It has close parallels with the Cirencester (*Corinium*) school of mosaicists (q.v.), and the great pavement at Woodchester (q.v.). Room 2 holds a mosaic at present unique in the Roman world. Around a central medallion of Bacchus is a series of strange scenes that include a fox running towards a small domed building; another, gabled, building with a ladder going up to its door which has two winged gryphons on the left and a cock-headed man (the Gnostic god Abraxes) on the right; and a pair of

247 *Mosaic with a Medusa head in the central roundel surrounded by panels with mythological scenes. Brading villa.*

fighting gladiators. Room 12 (in the north wing) was the principal room, actually two rooms with mosaics straight through and simply shallow buttresses protruding in the middle to act as dividers. In the western half a much-damaged mosaic had nine panels with scenes from classical mythology. The best-preserved shows Perseus rescuing Andromeda, after decapitating the gorgon Medusa. The corners of the mosaic had representations of the Seasons, of which Autumn is destroyed and Winter is very close to the same subject at Bignor (q.v.). A small mosaic set between the two buttresses and linking the two rooms has a curious scene of a seated, bearded astronomer who points to a globe. In the smaller half of the two rooms is a central medallion with a Medusa head surrounded by eight panels set diamond-wise to the centre. The four principal subjects are: Lycurgus chasing the nymph Ambrosia; a young shepherd and a maenad; Ceres giving the seed corn to Triptolemus; and a satyr pursuing a half-naked nymph. In the triangular areas between there are scenes of the Four Winds blowing conch shells. At the east end of the mosaic, furthest from the connecting doorway, is a strip with a central twin-tailed merman flanked on each side by a sea centaur, each carrying a sea nymph on his tail. The remaining mosaics are of linear types.

The owner of the villa at the centre of what was obviously a large estate, must have been a person of considerable wealth and no doubt authority. His interest in the subjects to be represented on his commissioned mosaics indicate his learning and also intriguing religious/philosophical involvement.

† Bradwell (*Othona*), Essex TM 031082
Late third-century Saxon Shore fort (q.v.) of which about only half remains, the rest having been washed away. Situated on the south side of the Blackwater estuary and reached by the B1018 from Maldon and then a minor road from the junction of the B1018 and B1012 at Latchingdon. The barn-like chapel of St Peter-on-the-Walls was built in 654 by Saint Cedd astride the south wall of the fort, and it naturally uses material quarried from the fort – notably the distinctive red tiles. Little else remains except a battered circular bastion at the northwest corner of the fort and an internal tower 120ft to the south of it.

Bramdean, Hants. SU 6228
A large villa with interesting fourth-century mosaics found in 1832, ten miles east of Winchester on the A272, and now lost. It was only partly excavated and had several red tessellated floors and two large figured mosaics of particular interest. The central subject of one of these, in a central octagon, was Hercules lifting and crushing the giant Antaeus to death whilst the goddess Minerva, standing on the left, encourages him. Set around the octagon were four unidentified busts, each within four interlaced squares of guilloche pattern. In the middle of each side of the whole mosaic were semicircles with confronting pairs of dolphins and urns with decorated handles. The second pavement was a large square holding interlaced squares at the centre of which was a Medusa head. Eight panels surrounding it had the gods of the week and, in the last, damaged one, possibly a representation of Fortuna.

Brancaster (*Branodunum*), Norfolk
TF 780438
The northernmost of the forts of the Saxon Shore (q.v.) on the coast of the Wash between Burnham Market and Hunstan-

ton. Nothing remains above ground of the fort which covered 6½ acres within nine-foot thick walls with bastions at the corners.

Branodunum – Brancaster

Brantingham, Humberside SE 9328
Villa to the north of the Humber estuary which produced three mosaics, two in 1941 and the third in 1962. The first two were of geometric design and the third had beautiful designed figures. In the central octagon, much damaged, is the head of a goddess wearing a mural crown (as Tyche, a city goddess), and surrounded by a halo. Around her are eight panels set against the octagon sides, each holding an urn. Beyond are eight semicircles enclosing reclining nymphs holding flower sprays. At each corner of the main square is a large ornamental pelta design. At the top and bottom of the square is a wide band framed by a guilloche border in which there is a series of busts of similarly nimbate (but not turret-crowned) goddesses in niches with their hair drawn up into a top-knot. Framing the whole are panels of diamond-shaped decoration. This mosaic, and one of the geometric ones enclosing a square of pelta, are now in the Archaeology Museum, Hull.

Bratton Seymour, Somerset ST 6629
Villa off the A371 northwest of Wincanton, excavated in 1968. It was partly uncovered and produced a damaged mosaic floor, now covered over *in situ*. The central motif was a badly represented bust with a creature perched on its left shoulder. This was set within a quite competent design which was much superior to the central bust in execution.

Bravoniacum – Kirkby Thore

Bravonium – Leintwardine

† Breage, Cornwall SW 6128
Roman milestone in the church north of the A394 four miles west of Helston. It has the name of the Gallic usurper emperor Postumus, 258–68, on it.

* Brecon Gaer, Powys SO 002297
A quite well-preserved five-acre cavalry fort off the A40 four miles west of Brecon. It was built *c.* 80 and garrisoned by a 500-strong cavalry regiment of Spanish Vettones. Good stretches of well-finished masonry still stand in places up to ten feet high on all sides except the north. On the north side are farm buildings and a barn now stands over the site of the north gate, but the other three gates still remain. The south and west gates are the best preserved, the former still with the walls of the guardrooms on either side of the double carriageway standing six to seven feet

248 *The south gateway of the fort at Brecon Gaer.*

high. Particularly interesting is the central drainage channel that passes through the south gate and also the pivot holes for the double-leaved gateways that can still be seen in both. The fort has a commanding position high above the valley and owing to the steep approach to the south and west gates (the latter properly the principal gate), the north gate would probably have been the most heavily used.

Bremenium – High Rochester

Bremetennacum – Ribchester

Brislington, Avon   ST 6170
A corridor house found in 1899 in what is now a southeastern suburb of Bristol. It had several mosaic and tessellated floors. One of these, a small patterned example consisting of flowers, knots, and lotus urns, has been relocated in the Kings Weston villa (q.v.). A second mosaic featuring a fluted urn as the central motif surrounded by pelta designs and leaf tendrils with a dolphin in a rectangular panel on each side of the square, is in the City Museum and Art Gallery, Bristol.

Brocolitia – Carrawburgh

Brocavum – Brougham

† Brough (*Verterae*), Cumbria NY 7914
Fort mostly covered by a later Norman castle half a mile south of the A66 at the west end of the Stainmore Pass. In the church porch is a dedication slab, much worn, dated to 197.

Brough-on-Humber (*Petuaria*), Humberside   SE 449326
Cantonal capital of the Parisi of North Yorkshire. The identification of the site rests on an inscription on a dedication slab

for a new proscenium for a theatre, found in 1937, and mentioning an official of the *vicus Petu(ariensis)* of 144. It implies also that there should have been a forum and public baths since these would have been built first before a theatre in a civically conscious community. But there is no trace of such structures in the area of what was essentially a fort and naval base. It has therefore been suggested that the actual cantonal capital, *Petuaria Parisorum*, might instead be North Ferriby, or located somewhere between that site and Brough. Only excavation in the area can possibly resolve the problem.

† Brougham (*Brocavum*), Cumbria
                NY 538289
Fort two miles southeast of Penrith off the A66, with a Norman castle set within it. Traces of banks and the ditch can be seen to the south but the castle holds the most interesting items. Numerous funerary inscriptions from the fort area can be seen incorporated into the fabric of the great Keep. Of particular interest is a fragment of what might be a Christian tombstone built into a passage ceiling on the second floor. The person commemorated, Tittius, lived for 32 years 'more or less' the inscription says – a style distinctly Christian as against the very specific pagan enumeration of years, months and days normally found.

† Brunton Turret, Northumberland
                NY 922698
A turret (no. 26B) on the most westerly section of the Broad wall (the ten-foot gauge) of Hadrian's Wall which then abruptly changes to the narrower, eight-foot gauge. The turret still retains its door-sill with pivot-hole and inside it is the bottom half of a corn-mill and an uninscribed altar. The turret was built by a detachment of the XXth Legion.

Burgh-by-Sands (*Aballava*), Cumbria
                NY 328592
Fort lying astride Hadrian's Wall at its western end and covering an area just under five acres. The present church stands on the site of commandant's house and there is a lot of Roman stone used in its fabric. The bath house was to the southeast of the fort, but was destroyed in the cutting of the Carlisle canal, now a defunct railway line.

* Burgh Castle (*Gariannonum*), Norfolk   TG 475046
The second furthest north of the Saxon Shore forts (q.v.), built on a bluff overlooking the river Waveney inland from Great Yarmouth. Built about 275 it was occupied into the early fifth century. The fort was rectangular (640ft east to west and 300ft north to south). The west wall overlooking the river has disappeared but the

remaining three sides rise to about 15ft. The walls were built in sections by separate gangs of men, and the places where they met can be spotted by the adjustments made in the lines of the red brick bonding tiles. Other interesting building evidence is the fact that it was only after the walls had reached about eight feet high that the order came to add bastions to them. These were then built up against the existing wall and only incorporated into them as building progressed higher. On the tops of the bastions round depressions indicate their use for mounting artillery (*ballistae*). The interior of the fort is under crop but even at ground level in the right conditions traces of the interior plan can be seen, which shows up well on aerial photographs. Below the site of the west wall on the river bank traces of a Roman quay have been found.

249 *The south wall of Burgh Castle with its large, collapsing bastions that were added later to act as bases for* ballistae.

† Burnswark, Dumfries.   NY 186788
An Iron Age hillfort three and a half miles southeast of Lockerbie off the B7068. Its interest lies in the two Roman camps that can be plainly seen on its northwest and southeast sides, the latter the best-preserved. By the north rampart of the south camp three large mounds, called locally The Three Brothers, were the bases for catapults. In the corner of the Roman fort, but actually earlier than it, is a small mid-second-century fort. It was long thought from the field evidence of the camps that Burnswark had been besieged by a Roman force. Excavation had produced Roman missiles from the interior of the fort; but further detailed excavation showed, however, that when the missiles were fired the fort ramparts were no longer standing. Therefore the Roman camps were simply practice camps with their distinctive playing-card shape built below an abandoned Iron Age fort that was used for artillery practice.

Burrium – Usk

Burwen's Castle, Elslack, W. Yorks.
SD 929493
Fort site of Agricolan date on a minor road to the east of the A56 near Thornton-in-Craven. It was on the Roman road that crosses the moors from Ilkley to Ribchester.

Buxton (*Aquae*), Derby.   SK 060730
Roman town famous in a small way as a northern spa but heavily overshadowed by Bath in this respect both in Roman times and in the eighteenth century when both were fashionable watering places.

Cadder, Strathclyde   NS 6172
Fort on the Antonine Wall east of Balmuildy (q.v.) covering 3.2 acres.

Caer Gai, Gwynedd   SH 877315
Fort near the A494 at the southwest corner of Bala Lake at Llanuwchllyn. The ramparts are preserved on the exterior of the southwest and southeast sides but the interior has been filled up to the top level. A small shrine to Hercules outside the northeast gate produced an inscription (now in the National Museum, Cardiff), attesting the garrison as the first cohort of the Nervii, an auxiliary cavalry regiment from northern Gaul (the area of modern Belgium). Excavation indicated military occupation for about fifty years from *c.* 78 to 130.

† **Caer Gybi**, Gwynedd   SH 246827
Small fort, 250 × 175ft, at Holyhead on Anglesey at the end of the A5. It encloses the church and churchyard of St Gybi with walls that still stand 15ft high on the exterior and 10ft on the interior, and it has three of its four round corner towers. It appears to date from the early fourth century and was built as a defence against barbarian raiders.

Caerhun (*Kanovium*), Gwynedd
SH 776704
Fort 4½ miles south of Conwy on the B5106. A church stands in one corner, part of its walls actually situated on the fort's ramparts. Excavation in the late 1920s revealed a history in stone *c.* 140, destruction *c.* 200 and then spasmodic occupation into the fourth century. The fort guarded the river at this point in the Conwy Valley and remains were found of a jetty and a dock, as well as a bath house outside the fort to the east. Most of the fort area is meadow and at times the plan shows up in it as a crop mark; the rampart mound is quite well preserved on the south side. The name of the fort is known from a milestone of Hadrianic date found in North Wales which gave the distance to *Kanovium* (Caerhun) as eight miles.

† **Caerleon** (*Isca*), Gwent   ST 339906
The legionary fortress of the IInd Augusta,

250 *Range of barrack blocks excavated in Prysg Field within the legionary fortress at Caerleon.*

two miles northeast of Newport. It covered an area of 50 acres, 540 × 450 yards. Founded about 75, it was heavily occupied until *c.* 120 when most of the legion was posted north and worked on the Antonine Wall and subsequently at the Severan base at Carpow (q.v.).

The oval amphitheatre (184 × 136½ft, orientated almost north to south), was excavated in 1926–7 by Dr R.E.M. (later Sir Mortimer) Wheeler. It is the only completely excavated example to be seen in Britain. Built about 80 at the same time as the more famous Flavian Amphitheatre, the Colosseum, in Rome, it has been estimated that it could seat 6,000 spectators (the garrison was between 5,000 and 6,000 legionaries). The amphitheatre probably saw more use as a convenient area for parades, exercises in weapon handling and the like instead of for spectacles. Various units or 'gangs' built individual sections of it and record stones still exist in the interior walls, with a fifth in the nearby museum.

Within the ramparts in the west corner of the fort (called Prysg Field) can be seen the remains of ovens and cookhouses built back into the ramparts, and also a series of foundations of four barrack blocks which

have been consolidated. The original total in the fort would have been 64 stretching towards the church, which marks the site of the headquarters building. A bath house has been excavated (1978) behind the small museum.

The museum (housed in a charming small classical-style building with a portico) contains many interesting finds from the site. Especially of note are the inscriptions, both imperial records and private tombstones – one of the latter commemorates a veteran of the IInd Augusta, Iulius Valens, who died aged 100 years! There are also some mosaics, which are unusual finds from a military site.

* **Caernarfon** (*Segontium*), Gwynedd
SH 485624
An auxiliary fort guarding the Menai Strait on the A4085 to Beddgelert just outside Caernarfon. It was founded by Agricola about 78 and garrisoned into the late fourth century. A reservoir and the main road cover the southeast portion of the site but foundations of barrack blocks can still be seen and, in the centre, the outline of the commandant's house, the headquarters building and the deep underground strongroom beneath the chapel that held the

40, 43, 68, 182

104
30

251 *The interior of the fort at Caernarfon with the headquarters building in the foreground and the barracks beyond.*

standards. There is a well-laid-out and clearly labelled museum on the site.

About 150 yards to the east of the fort was a mithraeum, excavated in 1959. It was quite small, as they usually are (48 × 21½ft), and was built about 200 and destroyed some time in the fourth century. On the west side of the fort, also about 150 yards away, is the enclosure called Hen Walian which has a south wall still standing to 20ft. The lack of provision of gate-towers or bastions seems to indicate that this was simply a stores area associated with the early fourth-century phase of the fort.

In Welsh legend *Segontium* is closely linked with the British usurper emperor Magnus Maximus (called Macsen Wledig), 383–8, who withdrew its garrison in 383 to aid his unsuccessful bid for power.

Caersws (*Mediomanum*), Powys SO 029920
Fort at the junction of the A470, A492 and B4568 20 miles southwest of Welshpool. Strategically placed at a natural confluence of five military routes, the first-century fort, covering about nine acres, was discovered by aerial survey in 1958. A smaller, 7½ acres, fort was built 600 yards away to the southwest in the second century and was occupied into the early fifth. Excavations were carried out in 1966–7 but only the fort's raised platform remains to be seen.

* Caerwent (*Venta Silurum*), Gwent
                                    ST 469905
The market town of the Silures, five miles southwest of Chepstow on the A48. Founded about 75, it covered some 44 acres. Although small it could boast a forum, basilica, baths and temples. It still has one of the best circuits of walls, built in the late second century or early third, to be seen in Britain. Around 340 a series of polygonal bastions to take catapults (*ballistae*) were added to them. The south gate is the best-preserved, up to the height of its springing arch, and evidence is clear of its having been blocked up in the fourth century.

Within the town a small part of an *insula* (an 'island' formed by intersecting streets) is exposed to the west of the forum in Pound Lane. A little way past the church on the north side of the village street are the foundations of a typical Romano-Celtic temple with its square central shrine (*cella*) surrounded by an outer wall and flanking verandah. The north gate can be seen to the right of the appropriately named Northgate Inn.

In the porch of the church is a fine inscribed stone to Claudius Paulinus, legate of the IInd Augusta, and a small altar to the Romano-Celtic deity Mars-Ocelus. A number of mosaics have been found in the town, mainly of floral or geometric designs, and most have been lost. There is one in the National Museum in Cardiff, and some fragments and drawings of others in the Newport Museum.

Caesaromagnus – Chelmsford

† Caister-on-Sea, Norfolk   TG 517124
Once an important trading port on the North Sea it is now three miles north of Great Yarmouth on the A1064. It flourished from the early second century and was the entrepôt for goods coming from the Rhineland. In the second century it was enclosed by a stone wall, 1,300 × 900ft, and continued in use into the fifth century. There was a resurgence here in the mid-seventh to ninth centuries and in the late seventh century some curious burials, about a dozen graves, were made covered in ship's timbers. The excavated remains of a *mansio* (an official staging post) and parts of the town wall and south gate can still be seen.

Caistor, Lincs.   TA 118013
One of the many small walled towns of Lincolnshire. The largest portion of the walls remaining stands on the south side of the churchyard about six feet high, merely rubble core, with a fragment of the lower courses of a bastion projecting forward from it.

† Caistor St Edmund (*Venta Icenorum*), Norfolk   TG 230035
The small tribal capital of the Iceni, off the A140 three miles south of Norwich. It was founded about 70 as a direct result of the Boudiccan revolt of a decade earlier, and only covered 45 acres. It was not until the mid-second century that stone buildings began to replace the earlier timber structures. Today only the circuit of the walls remains, the interior of the town is all under the plough except for the small area in the southeast corner taken up by the church and its churchyard. The remains of the walls are most substantial on the south side, and the south gate can be picked out. From aerial photographs taken under the right conditions it has been possible to draw up the typical gridiron pattern of a Roman town and the layout of its streets. A heavy scatter of red tile fragments in the ploughed fields, and also used in the church fabric, present the usual obvious surface signs of Roman settlement.

Calcaria – Tadcaster

Calleva Atrebatum – Silchester

Camboglanna – Birdoswald

Camulodunum – Colchester

* Canterbury (*Durovernum Cantiacorum*), Kent   TR 159577
Roman Canterbury was a *civitas* capital of about 130 acres, but it has been overbuilt and overshadowed by the medieval town with its great cathedral and shrine of Thomas à Beckett. Very little of the Roman period remains to be seen. The medieval walls are based on the earlier Roman circuit, built about 280, and the only Roman portion to be seen is a few courses in the car park in Broad Street. Canterbury had one of the few theatres in Roman Britain, located at the junction of Watling Street and St Margaret's Street. It was built at the end of the first century and enlarged early in the third. Nothing remains to be seen (the only visible theatre is the one at St Albans, q.v.). Under the shopping precinct in Butchery Lane near the cathedral are two small mosaics with stylized decoration. They are the remains of a town house, and some of the contemporary as well as later medieval finds are exhibited in cases near them. The best collection of finds from Canterbury and the area about is to be seen in the Canterbury Royal Museum in the High Street.

Owing to its position at the hub of a number of radiating roads Canterbury was an important town and always remained so, which has proved disastrous for the preservation of its Roman levels because of continuous and heavy occupation of the site.

Caractonium – Catterick

* Cardiff, S. Glamorgan   ST 181766
Originally a fort built after the style of the Saxon Shore forts (q.v.), in the late third century or early fourth as a naval supply depot. What exists today at Cardiff Castle is the result of nineteenth-century restoration work carried out by Lord Bute. In places the original Roman course can be seen at the bottom of the walls, notably on the south side. The reconstructed north gate is particularly imposing, a single-arched gateway flanked by semi-octagonal bastion towers. An officer in charge of the depot here, Titus Flavius Senilis, dedicated

252 *The north gate of Cardiff Castle, restored in the 1860s on Roman foundations, gives an excellent idea of what a typical Saxon Shore fort would have looked like in the third century.*

an inscribed tessellated pavement (now destroyed) at the shrine of Nodens at Lydney (q.v.). The National Museum of Wales is in Cardiff near the castle.

† **Carisbrooke Castle**, Isle of Wight, Hants.   SZ 487878
Probably the last in the chain of Saxon Shore forts (q.v.). A little of the original Roman stonework can be seen at the base of the walls to the left of the bridge crossing the moat into the gatehouse. In the vicarage garden nearby is a badly preserved mosaic with geometric decoration surrounding a vase of flowers.

† **Carlisle** (*Luguvallium*), Cumbria   NY 399558
Nothing remains to be seen of this town at the west end of Hadrian's Wall which may have covered more than 70 acres. In the grounds of the Tullie House Museum there is a sunken stone-built water tank that might have been associated with an aqueduct. There is a fine display of material from local finds and the Wall in the museum itself.

Carmarthen (*Moridunum*), Dyfed   SN 224120
Recently found (excavated in 1968 and subsequent years) town and fort that may have been the tribal capital of the local tribe, the Demetae. Just outside the town by the A40 the mounds that formed the basis for the seating in an amphitheatre can be seen.

* **Carn Euny**, Cornwall   SW 403288
Site of an Iron Age village at Drift off the A30 four miles west of Penzance. The best-preserved example in Cornwall of a *fogou* is to be found here. It is a curious underground passage typical of the southwest area and is thought to have been a food store, although they are at times cited as refuges. Carn Euny was occupied before 400 BC, and then onwards at least into the first century AD. The associated houses are of courtyard type (like Chysauster, q.v.), and the *fogou* leads from one of them for a distance of 66ft. All the roofing stones of the passage are original, as are those of the 'creep', a narrower passage that goes off from the end to the northwest and seems to have been closed off by a door. Another narrow passage, at the east end, leads into a circular corbelled-roofed chamber unique amongst known *fogous*.

Carpow (*Horrea Classis*?), Perth.   NO 2017
Fortress on the south shore of the Tay estuary of about 32 acres, occupied under Severus apparently, on the evidence of tile stamps, by some of the Legio VI Victrix and also auxiliaries. The garrison seems to have been withdrawn under Caracalla (198–217).

* **Carrawburgh** (*Brocolitia*), Northumberland   NY 859711
Only part of the earthen rampart of the early second-century fort remains but 30 yards outside the fort to the southwest is a small mithraeum. It was found in 1949 in marshy ground which still tends to flood but which at that time had receded leaving the tops of some altars visible. Initially at the beginning of the third century only a small temple 26ft long, it was extended to 36 × 15ft in the late third century and finally destroyed at the beginning of the fourth century, no doubt by Christians. At the north end before a tripartite apse stood three altars to Mithras (represented on the site today by copies; the originals are in the University Museum, Newcastle). They were set up by prefects from the fort. The altar on the left (west) of the group has a half-length figure of the god Mithras and a pierced radiate halo is behind his head. A lit lamp placed behind the god's head then created quite an inspiring and theatrical effect in the gloom of the interior of the mithraeum. Presumably behind the three altars, in the apse, there would have been a representation of the usual scene of Mithras slaying the bull aided by various animals and creatures. Statues of his attendants, Cautes and Cautopates (on the right and left of the nave respectively) were also found. A full-size reconstruction of the temple is exhibited with the finds in Newcastle.

Near the temple was a well dedicated to the water nymph Coventina where several thousand Roman coins, thrown in as thank offerings or for good luck, were recovered.

Carvoran (*Banna* or *Magna*), Cumbria   NY 665658
Fort on Hadrian's Wall to the northeast of Greenhead which lay behind the Wall and *vallum* guarding the Tipalt valley. It covered 3½ acres and although the northwest angle is visible very little remains as it has yet to be excavated. A corn-measure found here is in the museum at Chesters (q.v.).

† **Castell Collen**, Powys   SO 055628
Fort lying off the A4081 north of Llandrindod Wells. The whole layout of the fort is visible as a series of humps and ditches. Originally an auxiliary fort of about five acres, it held a garrison of about 1,000 men. In the third century a cross wall reduced the fort area to 3½ acres. Within the earthen ramparts the outlines of the headquarters building can be picked up in the centre with, to the south, the commandant's house and, to the north, a granary.

Castle Greg, Lothian   NT 0459
Fortlet, 180 × 150ft, three miles southeast of West Calder to the northeast of the B7008 just before it joins the A70 Edinburgh–Carnwath road.

Castle Hill, Dunbarton   NS 5272
Site of a fort on the Antonine Wall west of New Kilpatrick (q.v.). Part of the outlines of this buried fort have been recorded by air photography.

Castlecary, Strathclyde   NS 7978
Fort on the Antonine Wall to the east of Westerwood (q.v.) and north of Cumbernauld on the A80. It covered 3½ acres and was one of the only two forts on the Antonine Wall to be built of stone (the other was Balmuildy, q.v.). The site is now crossed by the railway but it is still possible to see the mounds of the northeast and west walls north of the railway, and a depression marking the position of the north gate. West of the fort the ditch runs across country and is clearly visible for about four miles.

Castleshaw, Saddleworth, Greater Manchester   SE 002097
Fort built during the advance against the Brigantes. A faint outline of it can still be picked out on the ground.

Castlesteads (*Uxellodunum*), Cumbria   NY 355163
Small fort about 400ft square covering 3¾ acres on Hadrian's Wall seven miles west of Birdoswald. It was levelled in 1791. Several interesting altars were found there including one dedicated by the second military cohort of the Tungrians. Presumably they were not at full strength, 1,000 men, as the fort would have been too small to hold them all. They may have been preceded as the garrison in the second century by the fourth cohort of Gauls.

Castor, Northants.   TL 1297
Centre of a highly organized pottery industry in the Nene Valley outside Peterborough. Recent aerial survey and excavation in this area has opened up a whole new concept regarding the industrialization of the Nene area. Nothing is to be seen today but a series of mosaics, quite simple in design, were found in the area between 1821 and 1827 and drawn by the antiquary E.T. Artis.

Catterick (*Caractonium*), N. Yorks.   SE 220990
Fort guarding the crossing of the river Swale at the junction of the A1 and the A6136, 3½ miles southeast of Richmond. It is still a garrison town.

† **Cawfields**, Cumbria   NY 715666
Milecastle 42 built by Legio II three-quarters of a mile east of Greatchesters on Hadrian's Wall. It is extremely well preserved with walls standing at the south gate up to six feet high. They are high enough to preserve the bolt hole that took the wooden beam to secure the gate.

253 *Cawfields milecastle (no. 42) on Hadrian's Wall between Greatchesters and Housesteads.*

† **Cawthorn**, Pickering, N. Yorks.
SE 784900
Four camps about four miles northwest of Pickering on the moors between Cropton and Newton. Two of them appear to have been built for occupation (the work of Legio IX), while they practised building the other two. Two periods are apparent of about 90 and a decade later. The best-preserved of the camps is the most westerly example, which is also the latest in date. It has a bank and ditch and three gateway openings.

* **Cerne Abbas Giant**, Dorset ST 666016
Hillside figure of a giant cut in the chalk above the village of Cerne Abbas eight

254 *The Cerne Abbas Giant.*

miles north of Dorchester on the A352. He is 180ft high and wields a large club in his right hand. This attribute associates him with Hercules and, possibly, with a late second-century date at a time when the emperor Commodus (180–93) was busy promoting the cult throughout the Empire, and himself assimilating Herculean attributes.

† **Chanctonbury Ring**, Sussex
TQ 139121
Iron Age hillfort of three acres to the east of the A24 north of Worthing near Washington. There are the remains of a small Romano-Celtic temple in the middle of the fort amongst the grove of beech trees.

Charterhouse, Mendip, Somerset
ST 506561
Important lead-mining centre three miles north of Cheddar off the B3134. There was also a side product of silver and the whole enterprise was run under State control from shortly after the Conquest. The earliest known ingot from the area can be dated to 49, and it is known that Legio II Augusta controlled the area during the

reign of Nero (54–68). Possibly at a later date private enterprise was allowed to lease the mines and work them. The latest dated 'pig' of lead known from here is about 168–9, but coin evidence shows occupation into the fourth century.

* **Chedworth**, Glos. SP 053135
The villa, one of the finest in Britain, is four miles southwest of Northleach off the A429 (the Fosse Way), lying in a lovely situation at the head of a wooded valley protected from the winds. It was found by accident in 1864. The building was begun in the first half of the second century but the site as seen now set out on three sides of a rectangular courtyard belongs to the early fourth century (the fourth side, the south, is still largely buried). There were over three dozen rooms in all, the last ones being built on the north side at the end of the fourth century. The major features of the site are its mosaics in the main, west, wing. In the anteroom to the dining room a damaged central roundal probably represented Bacchus with the Four Seasons charmingly represented as little people set in the four corners (Autumn is mostly destroyed). In panels are satyrs and nymphs, mainly much damaged. The mosaics are laid so that diners reclining on couches in the main dining room, set on an ordinary mosaic of geometric pattern, could view them with ease and enjoyment. Further along the west block is a bath suite of five rooms with a hypocaust for damp heat (Turkish style). In the north wing was another bath suite for dry heat (Swedish sauna style). In the northwest corner of the site, tucked away behind the corners of the west and north wings, is a nymphaeum, a shrine to the water goddesses. This supplied the villa's water, and still supplies the modern house in the centre of the site. Three fragments of the original octagonal rim of the pool (now in the museum on the site) have the Christian monogram *Chi-Rho* carved on them, showing that at a later date the nymphaeum was christianized.

255 *The north wing of the Chedworth villa, looking towards the west wing.*

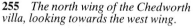

Chelmsford (*Caesaromagnus*), Essex
TL 527006
Possibly an early *civitas* capital which subsequently failed to maintain its position. The town was occupied continuously from Claudian times into the late fourth century at least. Evidence has been found for a *mansio* (imperial posting house), an octagonal Romano-Celtic temple, a bath building, and numerous timber buildings, many of them destroyed in a disastrous fire at the end of the second century.

* **Chester** (*Deva*), Cheshire   SJ 405663
The legionary fortress covering about 60 acres of the Legio II Augusta which was replaced about 87 by Legio XX Valeria Victrix. Owing to subsequent heavy occupation of the same site area little of Roman Chester is to be seen. The fine medieval walls carry the line of much of the fortress except where the medieval town extended beyond the Roman limits. Chester had the largest amphitheatre in Britain (holding about 8,000 people), and the north half can still be seen beyond Newgate. Part of the Roman quay, now rather overgrown, is on the racecourse. At 39 Bridge Street part of a hypocaust is preserved under the china shop that now occupies the site.

Chester makes up for what cannot be seen in the city in its magnificent Grosvenor Museum. Here are displayed finds from the many building operations throughout the town. Of particular note is the rich collection of tombstones which from their inscriptions and representations on them give us an invaluable insight into the populace of Roman Britain in this corner of Cheshire.

87,
88

256 *The strongroom in the headquarters building* (principia) *at Chesters with the commandant's house beyond it. Several hundred yards further on is the bath house on the river's edge by the bridge abutment.*

* **Chesterholm** (*Vindolanda*), Cumbria
NY 357766
One of the Stanegate forts on the line behind Hadrian's Wall to the north of the A69 at Bardon Mill, and two miles southwest of Housesteads (q.v.). The fort was excavated in the 1930s but recent work has concentrated on the *vicus*, the civilian settlement outside the fort, with astonishing results. As well as a detailed excavation programme being carried out some highly interesting restorations have been made. Part of the defences of the fort have been effectively restored, a turret 15ft high built, a length of the turf wall, stone wall and wooden milecastle gateway built. There is a museum of recent finds in the adjacent Chesterholm House and the displays include important textile remains and the Vindolanda writing tablets – all preserved by the sealed damp conditions of the lower levels of the site in which they were found. Some of the finest inscriptions from the fort, found in the eighteenth and nineteenth centuries, are displayed in the museum at Chesters (q.v.).

Opposite the farm is a Roman milestone still *in situ*. It is one of only two such left in Britain, the other is at Temple Sowerby (q.v.).

* **Chesters** (*Cilurnum*), Northumberland
NY 911700
Fort on Hadrian's Wall on the west bank of the North Tyne. The site is extremely well preserved and one of the most visited of the Wall sites. In the centre can be seen the headquarters building (*principia*), part of the commandant's house with its hypocaust, and a military bath house which is one of the best-preserved in Roman Britain.

Across the river the Chesters bridge abutment stands on dry land as the river has now moved away to the west. The Wall

257 *Reconstruction of a stone turret at Chesterholm (*Vindolanda*). It is based on the Brunton Turret, no. 26B, on Hadrian's Wall, which is the best-preserved example built on the Broad wall foundations.*

here was the Narrow type built on a Broad foundation and ended with a square tower on the bridge abutment. The bridge had three piers and could have supported a road 20ft wide. When the water in the river is low the western abutment and two of the piers are visible.

† **Chew Green**, Borders   NT 787085
Group of impressive marching camps off the A68 to the northeast of High Rochester along Dere Street (q.v.). There are four camps/forts here, the first built to hold a legion during the Agricolan advance of 80. Subsequently a convoy protection post was built round about 150 and larger quarters that included wagon parks fronting onto Dere Street. Today the evidence on the ground in the form of banks and ditches is quite visible, but very complicated as all four camps lie close together and their ramparts cross each other in places.

† **Chichester** (*Noviomagnus Regnensium*), W. Sussex   SU 860050
The town was the 'New market of the Regnenses', although it started life as a military base, possibly associated with the IInd Legion as Fishbourne probably was. The major item left to be seen here is the inscription of Cogidubnus preserved under the colonnade in the wall of the Assembly Rooms in North Street. It records a temple of Neptune and Minerva built by a guild of workers upon the authority of Cogidubnus, the Roman client king. He was probably the resident of the nearby palace at Fishbourne (q.v.). A few other fragments of Roman work can be seen in the town under various buildings, but are generally difficult of access and not worth the bother.

14,
47

* **Chysauster**, Cornwall   SW 473350
Native settlement off the B3311 Penzance to St Ives road which is the best-preserved

of this type in Devon and Cornwall. It consists of eight houses set in two rows of four each, some outlying houses, and a *fogou* (an underground passage). The houses appear to have had thatched roofs supported on a centre post. Their basic plan is an oval-shaped courtyard with rooms opening off into the thickness of the walls. They had good hearths and floors and also drains. The finds were mainly of a domestic nature and the site seems to have been occupied from the second century into the third century. There is no evidence of a defence fortification, and the inhabitants may have relied on the mile-distant hillfort of Castle-an-Dinas in times of trouble.

Cilurnum – Chesters

* **Cirencester** (*Corinium Dubunnorum*), Glos.   SU 016955
Cirencester was the tribal capital of the Dobunni founded late in the first century and an important market centre for the farms of the surrounding countryside. Once again, little remains to be seen today except for a short section of the town wall and the grass-covered amphitheatre outside the town to the southwest. The new museum is beautifully and imaginatively laid out and it is here that one can best appreciate the high level of culture of the area in the finds, including some very recent material from the town and nearby. Such was the prosperity of the town that it became the second largest in Britain after London and gave rise, because of its affluence, to a school of mosaicists known as the Corinium School. A particularly favourite motif amongst their repertoire was one featuring Orpheus charming the beasts. Examples are in the museum from Barton Farm (q.v.), and the largest known mosaic in Roman Britain at Woodchester (q.v.) is also of this school and features this motif. About forty mosaic pavements can be ascribed to the school.

Also of note in the museum is a good series of sculptured tombstones of soldiers dating from the early years of the town when there was a military presence there; the famous Cirencester wordsquare or acrostic; and the recently lifted mosaics such as the one with a charming crouched hare from a town house in Beeches Road.

Clausentum – Bitterne

Coelbren, W. Glamorgan   SN 859108
Fort lying between the A4067 and A4109 ten miles northeast of Neath. It was built as part of the initial system of control of the area but was then abandoned towards the middle of the second century. Its garrison was either 500 cavalry or 1,000 infantry. Outlines of the ditches and ramparts can still be seen.

258   *The Balkerne Gate at Colchester, largely preserved beneath the Hole-in-the-Wall Inn.*

* **Colchester** (*Camulodunum*), Essex
                                                    TL 997253
A *colonia* that covered about 108 acres, founded by the emperor Claudius after the Conquest in 43 for retired veterans and named *Colonia Claudia Victricensis*. The circuit of the walls can still be followed and much Roman work is visible. On the west side of the town is the impressive Balkerne Gateway, partly overshadowed by the Hole-in-the-Wall Inn built over the northern half of the carriageway, which can be seen through a series of grills fronting onto the modern road beneath the pub. Many of the local churches have red tile evidence in their structure for the source of their building material; particularly fine is the west front of the eleventh-century St Botolph's Priory.

The huge keep of the Norman castle is the largest in England and stands over the foundations of the great classical-style temple that was erected and dedicated to Claudius. It was in this temple, as Tacitus tells us, that the unfortunate inhabitants made a last desperate and unavailing stand against the attacking Iceni under Boudicca in 60, and were all wiped out. The bronze head of Claudius ripped from a statue and found in the river Alde (now in the British Museum) probably came from the cult statue of the emperor in this temple. The podium of the temple was built as a series of long arches (upon which the castle rests) and it is possible to go down into this area. The castle is now the Colchester Museum and houses a magnificent collection of material from the town and from Essex. Of particular note are the tombstones of the centurion M. Favonius Facilis of the XXth Legion, and of Longinus, a Bulgarian auxiliary cavalryman; also the Colchester Sphinx, a powerful Romano-Celtic sculpture, and the Colchester gladiator vase.

Coleraine (hoard)
A large hoard of damaged Roman silverware (*hacksilber*) and 1,506 silver coins, many of them clipped, found at Ballinrees, Coleraine, County Londonderry, Northern Ireland. Like the hoard from Traprain Law (q.v.), it seems to have been pirates' loot broken up ready for dispersal in a share-out. From internal evidence it appears to have been hidden in the early fifth century, probably around 410–20; as such, although technically found outside Roman Britain, it is one of the latest hoards from Roman Britain because that is where the pirates must have acquired their booty. The hoard is now in the British Museum in the Department of Medieval and Later Antiquities.

pp. 154–5

† **Combley**, Isle of Wight, Hants.
                                                    SZ 538878
Site of a small villa located inside Robin Hill country park on Arreton Down which has entrances on the A3054 and A3056. The site has some geometric mosaics *in situ* but the whole is badly in need of conservation.

Condercum – Benwell

Congavata – Drumborough

* **Corbridge** (*Corstopitum*), Northumberland   NY 982648
A supply depot on the Stanegate behind Hadrian's Wall now on the A69 Newcastle to Hexham road half a mile west of Corbridge. It was founded by Agricola in the 80s and rebuilt and then abandoned in the first quarter of the second century. Another rebuilding took place under Antoninus Pius (138–61), and the substantial remains to be seen today date largely from the fourth century. The fort is in an ideal situation to guard the crossing of the Tyne, in which some of the bridge piers can be seen when the river is low.

138

259 *View across Corbridge supply depot with a water tank and fountain head in the foregound and the granaries beyond.*

The granaries are amongst the best preserved in Britain, with a fountain and water tank nearby. The fort was actually divided in two by the Stanegate, into an East and a West compound, each with their own headquarters building. At first the West became pre-eminent and the underground strongroom that was below the chapel of the legionary standards there is still extremely well preserved with steps leading down into it. There were five temples at Corbridge, but none of the dedications are known for certain. A small site museum displays some of the finds; most important amongst them is the Corbridge Lion, a major piece of Romano-Celtic sculpture showing a lion devouring a stag. It probably served as a water-head for a fountain.

Corinium Dubunnorum – Cirencester

Corstopitum – Corbridge

† **Cramond**, Lothian   NT 190768
Fort off the A90 six miles northwest of Edinburgh. It was a harbour on the Firth of Forth where supplies could be landed for the garrisons on the Antonine Wall (q.v.). It also served as a base for the Severan advance into Scotland. Parts of the fort can be seen near the church. By the harbour (NT 184774) is the so-called Eagle Rock carved with a worn figure of Mercury (it was once thought to represent an eagle, hence its name).

Craven's Way, Whernside, N. Yorks.
          SD 740848
Roman road running up the Ribble valley to the northwest of the B6255 and round the north side of Whernside. In places it is up to 20ft wide with side culverts still preserved.

† **Croy Hill**, Strathclyde   NS 7276
Fort on the Antonine Wall on the east side of Croy Hill and west of Westerwood (q.v.). It covered 1½ acres but nothing is now visible of it. When it was partly dug in the 1930s internal buildings were found and a well together with inscriptions of the VIth Legion. The ditch is clearly visible and very impressive as it was cut from solid rock and climbs to the top of Croy Hill (470ft above sea level). East of the site an 80ft section was left undug since the rock was too hard to be able to effect a ditch. Beyond this the ditch is well preserved, up to 40ft wide and eight feet deep, running as far as the station at Dullatur. On the west brow of Croy Hill can be seen remains of two beacon platforms.

† **Denton Hall**, Northumberland
          NZ 196658
A section of Hadrian's Wall on the original Broad gauge can be seen a mile west of Benwell on the A69, 100 yards before the entrance to Denton Hall. It is nine feet wide and has a turret (no. 7B) bonded into it. Construction was by Legio XX. Further on at West Denton is another strip of the Wall foundation on the left of the Carlisle road.

Dere Street
Saxon name for the Roman road which is a continuation of Ermine Street running from York via Aldborough and Catterick to Corbridge, and then on north past High Rochester. Its actual route runs from the Tees to the Forth, the eastern of the two major roads into Scotland.

Derventio – Malton

Deva – Chester

Dewlish, Dorset   SY 7797
Corridor villa northwest of the A31 from Milborne St Andrew seven miles south of Blandford Forum. It was first discovered in 1740 and re-excavated in 1969–71 when several simple patterned mosaics were found in seven different rooms. These have now been covered over *in situ*.

Dinedor Hill, Hereford   SO 524364
Iron Age hillfort 2½ miles south of Hereford off the B4399 used as a camp by Ostorius Scapula in his campaign against Caratacus.

† **Din Lligwy**, Gwynedd   SH 496862
Fortified settlement/house of a fourth-century native chieftain on Anglesey at Moelfre by the junction of the A5108 and A5025. A pentagon-shaped wall encloses several rectangular buildings and two round huts. Some walls stand up to six feet high.

† **Dolaucothi**, Dyfed   SN 665405
The site of the only known gold mines in Britain about eight miles southeast of Lampeter off a minor road on the south side of the A482. Largely worked by open

260 *The fourth-century town house in Colliton Park, Dorchester. A geometric mosaic is preserved beneath the shed in the centre, and the unusual splayed window opening stands to its left.*

25

cast or shallow tunnel mining. Running water was an essential part of the smelting process and a large part of a Roman wooden waterwheel discovered here is in the National Museum of Wales, Cardiff.

* Dorchester, (*Durnovaria*), Dorset
SY 694900
Tribal capital of the Durotriges built about 60–70 at the time when Maiden Castle (q.v.) was abandoned and its people probably resettled here. There is a large early fourth-century town house preserved in Colliton Park behind the County Offices. It has two hypocausts and a geometric mosaic, and the splayed opening of a window should be especially noticed as an unusual survival from Roman Britain. Most local finds, including several mosaics from the town, the great Dorchester hoard of coins, and the material from Maiden Castle are displayed in the County Museum in High West Street.

Dorchester, Oxon.   SU 577493
Small town of which only some parts of the earthen ramparts are now visible. Much Roman building material is evident in the Abbey structure.

* Dover (*Dubris*), Kent   TR 326418
A Saxon Shore fort (q.v.) of which the material evidence has only been discovered in the last ten years, and now mainly covered over *in situ*. It was the headquarters of the *Classis Britannia*, as a number of building tiles stamped CL BR show. Also a recent find is the 'Painted House' in New Street with walls up to nine feet high covered in coloured plaster, and finds are displayed on the site. On the hill within the castle is the only extant *pharos*, lighthouse, in Britain, still standing 62ft high beside the west end of St Mary-in-Castro, for

261 *The Roman lighthouse (*pharos*) at the west end of the church of St-Mary-in-Castro within Dover Castle.*

which it served as a bell tower and to which it owes its preservation. Only the lower 42ft are Roman work, the rest is medieval, and it would have been about 80ft high originally. A companion guiding beacon stood on the opposite side of the harbour entrance on Western Heights, but only fragments remain of this.

Drumborough (*Congavata*), Cumbria
NY 265599
Fort on the western end of Hadrian's Wall covering two acres. Excavation has shown that a stone fort was later built inside an earlier turf structure, and pottery evidence indicates that it was occupied into at least the second half of the fourth century. Today it is a ruin since most of the stone was removed in the sixteenth century by Lord Dacre to build Drumborough Castle.

Dubris – Dover

† Duntocher, Strathclyde   NS 4972
Fort on the Antonine Wall to the east of Old Kilpatrick and south off the A810 near the church. Initially there was a freestanding fortlet 60ft square; later a fort of only 0.64 acres was built alongside it, the smallest on the Antonine Wall. On the west slope of Golden Hill here can be seen the most westerly fragment of the wall base and a culvert. These are both later than the fort and fortlet as both were in being before the advent of the wall, which was built from east to west.

Durnovaria – Dorchester, Dorset

Durobrivae – Rochester

Durobrivae – Water Newton

Durovernum Cantiacorum – Canterbury

Eagle Rock, *see* Cramond

† Ebchester (*Vindomora*), Durham
NZ 102556
Small fort 12 miles southwest of Newcastle on the A694. Originally an Agricolan fort of *c.* 80, it was rebuilt in stone and then abandoned about 140, reoccupied twenty years later and then on into the fourth century. The hypocaust of the commandant's house under an apsidal room can still be seen, and there is a small museum nearby.

Eburacum – York

Eccles, Kent   TQ 7260
Villa found in 1965 northwest of Aylesford on the A229. It dates from the late first century and had an elaborate bath suite and interior decoration which included a mosaic showing two gladiators fighting.

† Eildon Hill North, Borders NT 554328
Oppidum of the Selgovae one mile southwest of Melrose off the B6359. It enclosed about 40 acres and appears to have fallen to the Roman advance in 79. Subsequently it was abandoned and then a small Roman signal station was built at the west end, seen today only as a circular ditch.

Ermine Street
Roman road running from London via Lincoln to York.

† Exeter (*Isca Dumnoniorum*), Devon
SX 919925
Civitas capital of the Dumnonii covering 92 acres. Fragments of the Roman walls remain incorporated into the medieval circuit in Northernhay and Southernhay. Excavation in the postwar years on bomb-damaged sites revealed parts of the Roman city, and more recently work in front of the west front of the cathedral revealed the basilica and beneath that the remains of the legionary fortress baths. The legionary fortress had not previously been suspected and it would seem that the IInd Augusta was stationed here before it was transferred to Caerleon in 75. Unfortunately it has not proved possible to preserve these finds for inspection, and the area has been filled in. Local finds are displayed in the Rougemount House Museum in Castle Street.

* Fishbourne, W. Sussex   SU 841047
Roman palace just over a mile west of Chichester (q.v.) on the A27 Portsmouth road. It was found by accident in 1960 when trenches were being dug for drains. Originally the site seems to have served as a supply base under the Vespasianic advance into the southwest and then the palace was begun about 75. It almost certainly belonged to Cogidubnus, the Roman client-king recorded on an inscription from Chichester (q.v.). A major feature of the site is the large formal garden, unique north of the Alps, around which the building was laid out. The north wing is well preserved under cover with numerous mosaics, the most notable one featuring a cupid riding on a dolphin in a central roundel surrounded by sea horses and sea panthers. Several other mosaics are present; one possibly featured a peacock, another a Medusa head, and several have geometric designs. In places it is possible to see where the later mosaics were laid down over earlier ones, some of the earliest in the country. All the fittings were of an opulent character, painted plaster, imported marbles, etc., all of which indicate the high standing of the owner. At the end of the third century there was a disastrous fire from which the palace never recovered. Subsequently stone was robbed from its walls and intrusive burials made in the floors. A well-laid-out and instructive museum on the site gives the history and displays the finds chronologically.

pp. 62–3

11

14, 47

† **Folkestone**, Kent TR 241370
A large villa stands on the cliff edge above East Wear Bay beyond the tennis club. Considerable portions of the villa have fallen into the sea but there were some 53 rooms which indicates an owner of considerable standing. The finds from the site are displayed in the Folkestone Museum in Grace Hill.

Fosse Way
Roman road from Exeter to Lincoln which also acted as a *limes*, frontier line, between the Lowland and the Highland Zones. Beyond Lincoln it became Ermine Street (q.v.) and continued to the Humber.

Frampton, Dorset SY 6195
Villa discovered in 1794 at Frampton on the A356 eight miles northwest of Dorchester. Three fourth-century mosaics were found, now covered over *in situ*. The largest featured a head of Neptune and an inscription which faced towards an apse with a large *Chi-Rho* monogram before the head. The square area of the mosaic behind Neptune's head had a central roundel with a mounted horseman, and in the corners were small panels featuring Venus and Adonis. The mosaic is the most important from Britain (after Hinton St Mary, q.v.) which incorporates Christian symbols.

Fullerton, Wherwell, Hants. SU 3740
Villa found in 1872 and further excavated in 1963, four miles south of Andover on the A3057. Several of the mosaics found, of the fourth century, were taken up and relaid in Fullerton Manor.

Gadebridge, Herts. TQ 051082
Villa found in 1964 at Gadebridge Park, Hemel Hempstead, on the west side of the A4146, and now covered over. There were several patterned fourth-century mosaics and a very large plunge swimming pool. The site was abandoned at the end of the fourth century, apparently at a time of civil disturbance.

Galava – Ambleside

Gariannonum – Burgh Castle

† **Gilsland**, Northumberland NY 631664
Section of the Narrow gauge Hadrian's Wall a mile west of Birdoswald (q.v.). A particularly interesting constructional feature is that the Narrow wall actually rises from three courses of the Broad wall, not directly from the Broad foundations. This indicates that the Broad wall construction had already begun when the change of gauge was ordered here.

262 *Tombstone of Rufus Sita, a cavalryman who served with the Sixth Cohort of Thracians. It records that he died aged forty, after twenty-two years of military service, and that his monument was erected by his heirs in accordance with his will. Gloucester City Museum and Art Gallery.*

Glannaventa – Ravenglass

Glevum – Gloucester

* **Gloucester** (*Glevum*), Glos. SO 8318
Colonia of about 43 acres founded under Nerva (96–8) of which virtually nothing remains. The legionary fortress of Legio XX mentioned by Tacitus was probably at nearby Kingsholm, a mile to the north.

Finds are displayed in the City Museum in Brunswick Street, where there is an outstanding collection. Most notable among the collection of finely sculptured monuments is the tombstone of Rufus Sita, a Thracian auxiliary cavalryman, which shows him riding down a barbarian foe.

Great Casterton, Lincs. TF 0009
Small town, really a posting station on Ermine Street, covering about 18 acres on the B1081 three miles northwest of Stamford. Some fourth-century mosaics excavated here in the early 1950s are now covered over *in situ*. The rampart mound and broad shallow ditch are still much in evidence.

† **Great Witcombe**, Glos. SO 899142
Large villa found in 1818 off the south side of the A417 beyond the junction with the A46 five miles southeast of Gloucester. Like most of the Cotswold villas it has a superb setting in the lee of a hill. Part of the bath suite is preserved under cover with geometric mosaics and one with a variety of sea creatures featured on it. Among the buildings nearby can be seen a shrine with three niches facing onto a square basin set in the floor. Restoration work and consolidation are still in progress.

† **Greatchesters** (*Aesica*), Northumberland NY 704667
Badly overgrown and neglected fort on Hadrian's Wall north of Haltwhistle beyond the B6318. It covered between three and four acres with its longer axis running east to west. The south and west ramparts and their gates, together with some of the barrack blocks, are still visible.

263 *The Great Witcombe villa. On the right are the remains of a shrine, and the buildings in the background cover the mosaics of the bath suite.*

96 During the excavations in 1894 in the west tower of the south gate the famous Aesica brooch was found. It is amongst the finest examples of fourth-century jewellery from Britain, and is now in Newcastle.

† **Greta Bridge** (*Maglona*), N. Yorks.
NZ 087132
Fort on the A66, the main east–west route, ten miles northwest of Scotch Corner on the road to Bowes. Ramparts and ditches are still visible.

† **Gwennap Pit**, Cornwall   SW 7241
Milestone in the garden of Mynheer Farm a mile east of Redruth off the road to Day before it joins the B3298. It is inscribed for the emperor Antonius Gordianus Pius Felix, i.e. Gordian III, 238–44.

Habitancum – Risingham

* **Hadrian's Wall**, Northumberland and Cumbria
The major Roman structure in Britain, begun under the governorship of Aulus Platorius Nepos in 122 and finished *c*. 128 under Sextus Iulius Severus. Aurelius Victor, Hadrian's biographer, laconically remarks that it was built 'to separate the Romans from the barbarians'. Opinion nowadays favours its interpretation as a barrier acting as a control cum customs area as well as its more obvious defensive nature.

pp. 38–9   Physically the Wall was just over 73 English miles (80 Roman miles) in length with an outlying extension in a chain of forts down the coast from the Solway Firth for about 40 miles to prevent outflanking it. Its 15ft height probably had an additional parapet of six feet above it. From Newcastle to the river Irthing the Wall was built on a wide foundation of ten Roman feet. To the west of the Irthing the foundation was reduced to eight Roman feet. There are places where the Narrow gauge wall can be seen built on the Broad gauge foundation (cf. Gilsland). There were 16 forts on the Wall, and 80 milecastles with two turrets between each (the latter take their numbering from the milecastle located to their east with A and B numbers, e.g. the sequence from east to west would be Milecastle 55, turret 55A, turret 55B, etc.). The forts and milecastles vary in design but the turrets were essentially 20ft square, recessed into the Wall at the rear and with an upper storey level with the parapet which was reached by an internal ladder.

253

257

243   In front of the Wall to the north, generally about 20ft away, was a ditch ten feet deep and 28ft wide. To the south was another ditch, known as the *vallum*, about ten feet deep and 20ft wide. There were controlled access points across this into the military zone between it and the Wall. Further to the south of the Wall a backup

264   *Hadrian's Wall running east from Cuddy's Crag towards the fort at Housesteads, which is hidden on the other side of the trees; it then continues climbing towards Sewingshields Crags.*

system of forts and supply depots was based on the Stanegate (e.g. Corbridge, q.v.).

The Wall's history was a chequered one. It was abandoned in 139 in favour of the Antonine Wall (q.v.); reoccupied about 159; overrun in 197 by barbarians; restored by Septimius Severus *c*. 208; rebuilt again under Constantius Chlorus early in the fourth century; overrun again in the great barbarian invasion of 367; restored by Theodosius; its garrisons depleted to support the revolt of Magnus Maximus in 383. It was probably finally abandoned, on coins and inscriptional evidence, shortly after 410.

See the individual names of forts, milecastles and turrets for local directions and information regarding the remains.

Halstock, Dorset   ST 5307
Villa six miles south of Yeovil off the A37. First discovered in 1817, it was re-excavated in 1971 and the mosaics covered over *in situ*. The two larger mosaics are particularly interesting. A rather garbled eighteenth-century description of one of them as found gives the impression that the decoration may have featured a head of Christ like that from Hinton St Mary (q.v.), and *Chi-Rho* symbols. The second large mosaic, that was re-excavated in 1971, is 'executed in typically Corinian style but situated in the heart of the area covered by the Durnovarian school', and it has affinities with mosaics from the North Leigh villa (q.v.). Coin evidence indicates that the building was begun in the second

quarter of the second century, but the mosaics are presumably of the fourth century.

† **Halton Chesters** (*Onnum*),
Northumberland   NY 998685
Fort on Hadrian's Wall three miles north of Corbridge and half a mile to the east of where the A68 (on the line of Dere Street, q.v.) crosses the Wall heading for Risingham (q.v.). The line of the ramparts and the mounds representing ruined buildings are visible where the land has not been ploughed to the south. There was a large bath house with at least eleven rooms attached to the fort.

† **Ham Hill**, Somerset   ST 479168
One of the largest Iron Age hillforts in Britain covering just over 210 acres and with ramparts nearly 2½ miles in circuit. It lies off the A303 four miles southwest of Ilchester. Extensive quarrying has damaged the site, but also produced some interesting finds (in the Somerset County Museum, Taunton). A group of skeletons was found in the northwest corner of the fort in 1868 and may represent a war cemetery similar to that found at Maiden Castle (q.v.). A villa was built on the east side of the fort and there may have been an amphitheatre in the area of the fort nearest Stoke to the north.

† **Hardknott Castle** (*Mediobogum*),
Cumbria   NY 218014
Fort at the head of Eskdale nine miles northeast of Ravenglass (q.v.), guarding the western end of Hardknott Pass. It was built in the early second century with a garrison of Yugoslavian troops. Despite its commanding position, over 800ft above sea level, it only covers 2¾ acres because of

the difficulties of the site. So narrow is the site that the regulation parade ground had to be partly cut out of the hillside to provide a sufficiently large and level area. Mounds at its edge still mark the tribune's rostrum from where the orders were shouted. The Department of the Environment has rebuilt large sections of the walls from the original fallen masonry, and have differentiated the new work by inserting a line of slate tile between it and the old. The headquarters building in the centre of the fort has its walls preserved to a height of several courses and there is part of the commandant's unfinished house and granaries also to be seen.

265 *Hardknott Castle, guarding the head of the pass that leads down to Eskdale, is one of the remoter Roman forts, perched high up on a narrow spur.*

Harlow, Essex   TL 468122
Site of a small Romano-Celtic temple of classic type with an inner square *cella* (shrine) and an outer temenos wall. One of the few excavated sites (after Colchester and Braughing) that have produced large quantities of Iron Age coins (over 350), together with Roman coins indicating the continued use of the site. Finds are displayed in the local Harlow New Town Museum.

† Harpenden, Herts.   TL 119136
Site of a mausoleum in the grounds of Rothamstead Experimental Station off the A5 near Harpenden. The foundations indicate a circular building 11ft in diameter set within an enclosure wall about 100ft square with an entrance on the east side. A plinth in the circular building stood before a niche which probably held a lifesize statue of the deceased, fragments of which were found during excavations in 1937.

Hayling Island, Hants.   SU 724031
Romano-Celtic temple of the first century at the northern end of the island first described in 1826 but not properly identified for what it was until the mid-1970s. Recently re-excavated, it is now recognized as one of the largest temples of this type known from Roman Britain, and it has its closest parallels in Central France at Périgueux. It is unusual in having a circular central shrine (*cella*) which is 38ft in diameter, and there is an outer ambulatory within the temenos. The entrance was

through a porch built onto the ambulatory on the east side, and the *cella* also had a porch on that side. It seems to have been a particularly important cult site not only because of its size but also because of the several building phases it went through, being rebuilt in stone reflecting the original Iron Age plan. Curiously, these phases coincide with similar building phases at the nearby palace at Fishbourne (q.v.), and similar techniques and materials are apparent in each.

There is no inscriptional evidence as to the temple's dedication although it has been suggested, on the basis of finds such as votive mirrors, that it may have been to a female deity. The size of the temple, its richness and obvious importance indicate that it might possibly have been the tribal cult centre of the Atrebates and the Regni – both staunch allies of Rome.

† Heddon-on-the-Wall,
Northumberland   NZ 138669
Just outside Newcastle on the west on the B6528 the *vallum* can be clearly seen approaching Heddon and then a stretch of the Broad wall about a hundred yards long is visible. This is nine feet wide with flagstone foundations and the core and facing-stones have been preserved to a height of four courses on the north face and seven on the south.

Hemsworth, Dorset   ST 9605
Villa with fourth-century mosaics found in 1831, redug in 1908; it had some fifteen pavements, mainly destroyed by plough-ing. The best remaining pieces are a bearded god's head (Neptune?) in a central panel of decoration, now in the Dorset County Museum, Dorchester; and a much damaged apsidal mosaic with Venus, a frieze of dolphins and other fish, now in the British Museum.

266 *Relief from the fort at High Rochester showing Venus, adjusting her tresses, attended by two water nymphs. Museum of Antiquities, Newcastle upon Tyne.*

† High Rochester (*Bremenium*),
Borders   NY 833986
Stone fort off the A68 37 miles northwest of Newcastle. It was originally an Agricolan fort but was rebuilt in stone *c.* 139, and eventually abandoned in the mid-fourth century. It has the most stone remains to be seen north of Hadrian's Wall. Parts of the walls are still six feet high, the east gate is substantial, and mainly of fourth-century work. The fort has produced some fine inscriptions (mainly to be seen in the Newcastle Museum) which identify the garrison in 216 as having been a cohort of Spanish Vardulli; another records the building of the east gate by a *vexillatio* of Legio XX (originally from Chester). The well-known and charmingly naive Celtic-style representation of Venus at her toilet with two water nymph attendants in the Newcastle Museum also comes from here.

South of the fort alongside Dere Street (q.v.) are several large tombs; one substantial circular example must have been very close in style to some of those that still line the Appian Way outside the Porta San Sebastiano in Rome.

Hinton St Mary, Dorset   ST 7816
Site of a villa 1½ miles north of Sturminster Newton on the B3092 where one of the most remarkable fourth-century figured

131

polychrome mosaics from Roman Britain was found in September 1963. The pavement covered the whole floor of a rectangular room, 28ft 4ins × 19ft 6ins, that was obviously part of a much larger building that has yet to be excavated. The mosaic divides into two sections; the larger, eastern section, has a central medallion with the head of Christ gazing outwards with a *Chi-Rho* monogram behind it and a pomegranate on either side. From the central roundel the mosaic is divided up and criss-crossed by elaborate guilloche patterns. There is a male bust wearing a draped cloak in each of the corners and in the lunettes in between are scenes of a dog attacking a stag or a doe in three of them and in the fourth, below the bust of Christ, a spreading tree. The smaller, rectangular, western section of the mosaic features Bellerophon on Pegasus slaying the Chimaera in the central medallion (cf. Lullingstone), and in the two rectangular panels flanking it hounds pursue a stag. Although such scenes initially appear to be pagan, in the context of their association with the representation of Christ they are replete with Christian iconography which may be interpreted as the overcoming of death and evil, and the abundant life in Paradise. Possibly the four male heads represent the four Evangelists.

The mosaic was lifted and has been relaid in the British Museum.

† Hod Hill, Dorset ST 856106
Iron Age hillfort covering 50 acres three miles northwest of Blandford Forum on the A350 above the river Stour, which defends its western flank. The rectangular shape of the third-century BC fort encloses in its northwest corner the typical playing-card plan of a Roman fort. Excavation revealed evidence of hundreds of circular huts and a marked-off area for the chief's house. When the fort was besieged under Vespasian during his advance to the southwest, *ballista* fire appears to have been concentrated on the area of the chief's house. Subsequently, the Roman fort, 1,000 × 530ft covering about 11 acres, was built by cutting off the northwest corner of the Iron Age fort and utilizing its original rampart defences, merely adding new additional ramparts in the interior on the south and east sides. An additional gate cut through the northwest corner of the rampart gave access to the river Stour for the water necessary for the cavalry detachment stationed there. The Roman fort seems to have been occupied only into the 50s, presumably simply as a peace-keeping gesture.

Holcombe, Dorset SY 238908
Villa first discovered in 1850 with fourth-century mosaics to the northwest of Lyme Regis. During re-excavation in 1969 a finely decorated Celtic bronze mirror was

found in a pit, the only example known from a domestic context. Now called the Holcombe Mirror and in the British Museum, it is in the tradition of the more famous mirrors from Desborough (British Museum), Birdlip (Gloucester Museum), and the Mayer Mirror (Liverpool City Museum).

† Holtye, Sussex TQ 461391
Short section of Roman road four miles east of East Grinstead off the B2110, east of Holtye, near the White Horse Inn. It served as a feeder road for the Wealden iron industry, much of its surface being made up of waste cinders.

Horkstow, Humberside SE 9819
Site of a villa on the B1204 northeast of Scunthorpe found in 1796. It contained one of the most animated mosaics from a fourth-century villa. The scene represented is a chariot race around the *spina* of a circus where one of the chariots has lost a wheel and the charioteer tumbles out; another charioteer tries to steady his vehicle as one of his pair of horses stumbles. For many years the mosaic was displayed in the British Museum but it has recently been returned to the Hull Museum. Another part of the same large rectangular pavement featured Orpheus in a medallion, now destroyed, with a procession of animals around.

Horncastle (*Banovallum*), Lincs.
TF 258696
Seven-acre fort enclosed by a stone wall of which some considerable portions remain, including bastions, up to ten feet high in places.

Horrea Classis – Carpow

267 *The communal military latrines in the southeast corner of the fort at Housesteads. They were originally provided with wooden seating that could accommodate about twenty men at a time.*

* Housesteads (*Vercovicium*),
Northumberland NY 789687
The most popular of the forts on Hadrian's Wall on the B6318 west of Chesters and situated on the crest of the Whin Sill. Its ramparts and gateways are well-preserved, as are the headquarters building, granaries, latrines and barrack blocks – representing the best example of a fort to be seen in Britain. It is surrounded by cultivation terraces and the remains of the shops and houses of the civilian settlement (*vicus*). The museum on the site contains models of the fort and *vicus*, together with altars and sculptured stones. Among the latter should be noted the carving of three hooded deities wearing *cucullati*, the Roman equivalent of 'duffle coats'.

† Ilkley (*Olicana*), W. Yorks. SE 118476
Small stone fort nine miles southeast of Shipton on the A65 with part of the wall visible, and a small museum nearby. It was founded by Agricola *c.* 80, abandoned forty years later only to be rebuilt about 150 and finally destroyed in 197.

Inchtuthil (*Pinnata Castra*), Tay
NO 125397
Little remains to be seen of this 50-acre fort that was intended by Agricola to be the focal point from which he would subdue Scotland. It lies in fields to the south of the A984 some three miles west of Meikleour. Excavation between 1952 and 1965 revealed the story of how the advance base was set up in about 83 with its full complement of buildings in timber, including a hospital, only to be abandoned about 87/88

when Agricola was recalled to Rome. The abandonment was more a strategic withdrawal as the evidence indicated deliberate destruction or slighting of buildings so that nothing of any use should fall into enemy hands. Pottery and glassware were systematically smashed and stamped into the ground; timber buildings dismantled; and because of the vast number and weight, a million unused iron nails of all shapes and sizes weighing over twelve tons were buried within one of the workshops before the last troops marched south. The plan obtained by the excavations of the late Sir Ian Richmond and Professor J.K. St Joseph is one of the finest for a military installation in Britain.

Isca – Caerleon

Isca Dumnoniorum – Exeter

Isle of Wight (*Vectis*), Hants.
SZ 2984 to SZ 6587
See the names of individual sites: Brading; Carisbrooke Castle; Combley; Newport.

Isurium Brigantium – Aldborough

† **Jordan Hill**, Dorset   SY 698821
Site of a small late fourth-century temple of typical Romano-Celtic plan off the A353 on the northeast outskirts of Weymouth. The building was 247ft square with a 12ft deep pit in its southeast corner that held a mixture of birds' bones and coins. Only the foundations of the outer wall can be seen today in an enclosure behind the houses opposite the golf course.

Kanovium – Caerhun

Kenchester (*Magnis*), Hereford
SO 440428
Small fortified town covering about 17 acres a mile southwest of Kenchester off the A4103 west of Hereford. Founded late in the first century it was walled in the mid-fourth century. Fragments of mosaics from here are in the City Museum, Hereford.

† **Keston**, Kent   TQ 415634
Large circular monument tomb in the grounds of the Keston Foreign Bird Farm west of the A233 at Warbank, Bromley. Originally about 23ft high and 26ft in diameter, it had six external buttresses. The exterior was plastered and painted red. Between two of the buttresses was a second tomb whose vault can be inspected beneath a modern trapdoor. Another, rectangular tomb lay beside the circular one and contained a stone coffin; this was shattered in a 1941 bombing raid but is now restored and returned to the site. In the immediate area of the tombs were found a number of poor burials dated by the associated pottery to between about 180 to 250.

The complex probably represents the private burial plot of the owner of an estate, traces of whose villa were found about 100 yards away to the west.

† **Keynsham**, Avon   ST 645693
Site of a large 50-roomed villa cut by the A4 halfway between Bath and Bristol; fragments can be seen behind the mortuary chapel in the cemetery. The villa had fine mosaics which included among their subjects Europa and the bull (cf. Lullingstone), dolphins, and dancers. These have been moved to the nearby Fry's chocolate factory at Somerdale (ST 656690), where they may be seen in the factory entrance hall. Opposite the factory lodge are the remains of a small building discovered in 1922 when the factory was built and moved then to its present site.

† **Kings Weston**, Bristol, Avon ST 5377
Villa discovered in 1947 near the west end of Long Cross in the suburbs of Bristol. Part of it has been consolidated and the site is in the care of the Bristol City Museum. It was built between 270 and 300 and eventually abandoned towards the end of the fourth century, possibly around 367/8 at the height of the pirate raids on the coast. Only a part of the building can be seen, but that is fairly substantial and includes a hypocaust from a bath suite located in rooms I–V, another in room XI, and a largely geometric mosaic featuring a wine-crater at its south end. A mosaic recovered from the villa at Brislington (q.v.) in 1899 was brought here and is displayed.

Kirkby Thore (*Bravoniacum*), Cumbria
NY 637257
Site of a fort seven miles southeast of Penrith on the A66, originally on the Roman road from Scotch Corner via Brough (*Verterae*) and Old Penrith (*Voreda*) to Carlisle (*Luguvallium*).

Kirkintilloch, Strathclyde   NS 6574
Site of a fort on the Antonine Wall to the west of Auchendavy which has yet to be excavated.

Knob's Crook, Woodlands, Hants.
SU 052073
Roman barrow at the south end of Cranborne Chase six miles northwest of Ringwood off the B3081. It dates from *c*. 70–85 and the skull found in it had been trepanned, probably the cause of death.

† **Lanchester** (*Longovicium*), Durham
NZ 158467
Fort eight miles northwest of Durham on the A691. Built *c*. 140, it was evacuated fifty years later and was reoccupied in the 240s. Most of the circuit of the walls remain, but robbed of the facings, up to six feet in height. In Lanchester church is an altar to the goddess Garmangabis, dedi-

cated by a cohort of Ligones who were part of the force who reoccupied the fort under Gordian III, 238–44.

Latimer, Bucks.   SU 998986
Villa in the entrance to Latimer Park Farm on the B485 three miles southeast of Chesham. The earlier timber building was superseded by a stone one in the mid-second century, and late in the third century the site seems to have been abandoned for about 20 years. In the fourth century, like many of the villas in the Bucks/Herts area, it was rebuilt and refurbished. Until recently a small section of rooms was preserved on the site but it has now been filled in and the finds are in the County Museum at Aylesbury.

Lavatrae – Bowes

* **Leicester** (*Ratae Coritanorum*), Leics.
SK 585046
The tribal capital of the Coritani, about 105 acres in area, although none of the walling that surrounded it now remains. pp. 58–9 The major site in the city is the Jewry Wall, built *c*. 125, beside St Nicholas' Church. It is the 30ft high wall of a public bathing establishment with the remains of hypocausts, ducts and drains nearby. The Jewry Wall owes its preservation to having been incorporated into the fabric of a Saxon church. Overlooking the site is the Jewry Wall Museum which displays a fine collection of local material. Amongst the mosaics of note are Cyparissus caressing his stag, and a peacock in full display. Other mosaics are preserved *in situ* under the Old Central Station and under the arches in Bath Lane, where there is a particularly fine geometric mosaic of the second century.

Leintwardine (*Bravonium*),
Heref./Worcs.   SO 405740
Small fort 17 miles west of Ludlow on the A4113 with traces of its walls still surrounding the village.

Lemanis – Lympne.

Lenthay, Dorset   SY 6215
Site of a mosaic found in 1836 and now on view in Sherborne Castle on the A30 west of Yeovil. The mosaic was found beside the railway line and its subject represents the musical contest between Apollo and Marsyas; the former sits on a rock playing his lyre while the latter dances to the music of a double flute. Marsyas lost the contest, and was flayed alive for his presumption in having challenged the god.

Letocetum – Wall

Lexden, Essex   TL 975247
Iron Age tumulus excavated in 1924 in a garden at the south end of Fitzwalter

29

Road, Colchester. The grave goods, now in Colchester Castle Museum, were originally extremely rich but as found were heavily damaged by burning. Included in the burial were typical Mediterranean wine amphorae often found in Celtic chieftain's burials (e.g. Welwyn), and a coin of Augustus of 17 BC which had been mounted as a medallion. It has been suggested that this was the burial of Addedomarus, the father of Cunobelin.

† **Limestone Corner**, Northumberland
NY 875716
A mile to the east of Carrawburgh (q.v.) can be seen the most northerly section of Hadrian's Wall. The *vallum* ditch was completed but the Wall ditch was left unfinished because of the hardness of the local quartz dolerite rock. Several huge partly cut blocks lie at the bottom of the Wall ditch, and in some of them can be seen the lewis-holes used for raising them.

* **Lincoln** (*Lindum*), Lincs. SK 977718
Founded *c.* 60 as a fortress for the IXth Legion, the original *colonia* covered about 43 acres but was expanded in the second century to 97 acres. So similar in size and plan is the earlier *colonia* to that at Gloucester that it seems probable they were both laid out by the same contractor. Good stretches of the walls remain, mainly of late second/early third-century date. Three of the gateways can be seen, of which the Newport Arch is the most famous. This was the north gate and is now the only surviving Roman archway still in use in Britain; the central arch has traffic passing under it, and there is a pedestrian

268 *The Orpheus mosaic at the Littlecote Park villa being restored and consolidated in August 1979.*

way to one side. The east gate is preserved in front of the Eastgate Hotel where the huge semicircular bastion of its north tower has been consolidated (the rest of the gateway is under the roadway and the Cathedral Green). The west gate, in the lower town, has been preserved in Orchard Street in the forecourt of the Municipal Offices. Part of the wall abutting on to this stands 15ft high.

Numerous mosaics have been found in or near the city. Many of them are now lost but some, together with material from the recent excavations, are displayed in the museum in Broadgate. Several important altars and inscribed stones from Lincoln are in the British Museum, including the tombstone of Volusia Faustina, wife of the decurion Aurelius Senecio.

Lindum – Lincoln

* **Littlecote Park**, Wilts. SU 298708
Roman villa in the grounds of the Tudor mansion three miles west of Hungerford off the A419 near Chilton Foliat. Its large Orpheus mosaic was found in 1730 and subsequently lost. Relocated in 1978, it is at present open to view at weekends whilst being cleaned and reconsolidated. The figure of Orpheus holding his lyre stands in a circle surrounded by four segments in each of which is a female figure riding side-saddle and anti-clockwise on the back of an animal – they may represent the Four Seasons. On three sides of the square containing the Orpheus scene are shell mosaics with small sun faces at the hinge of the pattern; the fourth side opens into another room with a great square mosaic with four panels of geometric flower motifs and a broad band at either end, one with black sea-panthers, the other featuring sea-beasts and dolphins flanking an ornamental

urn. The rest of the villa is being re-excavated around these rooms. *See* under Woodchester for other major Orpheus pavements.

Llandovery (*Alabum*?), Dyfed SN 770350
Fort of which little remains 20 miles west of Brecon on the A40. It was built in the mid-first century during the initial conquest of Wales and abandoned late in the second century.

Llantwit Major, S. Glamorgan SS 959700
Site of a fourth-century courtyard villa found in 1888 and re-excavated in 1938. It consisted of a large farming complex of which the domestic buildings and bath suite were built in the mid-second century and many additions and extensions at various later periods. Around 300 at least four mosaics were laid and painted plaster set up in several rooms. Some kind of a disaster struck in the middle of the fourth century because evidence was found in one wing of the villa of a massacre of men and horses. Tradition has it that the site was subsequently the home of Saint Illtud, a fifth-century local saint.

* **London** (*Londinium*) TQ 513281
London's strategic importance as the lowest crossing point of the Thames was recognized from the earliest days of the Conquest, and this became combined with a commercial interest and importance that was never to diminish. Rebuilt after the sack of Boudicca in 60 it continued to flourish and erect major buildings such as the Basilica and Forum (around present Leadenhall Market), the Governor's Palace (at Cannon Street), and eventually it was walled in the third century enclosing an area of some 330 acres. This included an early legionary fort situated at the north-west angle which had been built after the Boudiccan revolt. Its northern and western walls were thickened and incorporated into the main circuit of the town wall.

Owing to the continuous occupation of London over the centuries many finds have been made during rebuilding work but little broad-scale excavation has been possible except in bomb-damaged areas after the war and more recently in advance of large building projects when teams based on the Museum of London have been allowed access to sites under redevelopment. The major exhibits of material from the City are in the Museum of London in London Wall, and in the British Museum.

It is possible to see a number of stretches of the Roman wall quite easily, while many more sections remain on private property. Starting in the southeast corner of the City a small piece of wall is incorporated in the base of the Wardrobe Tower by the White Tower within the Tower of London. In Trinity Place, to the north of the Tower, is

183

269 *Outline plan of Roman London showing the easily visible remains.*

a very fine section rising up to the medieval catwalk; Roman masonry and tiles can be clearly seen in its lower courses and also the foundation of a guard turret. In the adjacent Wakefield Gardens are casts of the pieces of the tomb of Julius Alpinus Classicianus, Procurator of Britain after Boudicca's revolt, that were found here in 1852 and 1935, nearly a century apart. The tomb is now reconstructed in the British Museum. Another good section of wall is preserved in the basement of the Toc H Club (entered from the Minories), and also a little further north in Cooper's Row, once more Roman lower courses and medieval upper work with windows and a door through it. The next section worth viewing is in St Alphage's churchyard in the northwestern sector off London Wall. Not far away in the shadow of St Giles's

270 *The wall in Trinity Place near the Tower of London.*

Church, Cripplegate, the Cripplegate bastion and a section of wall have been landscaped and incorporated into the new Barbican development and fronted by a moat. At the end of London Wall nearest the Museum of London, on the north side, it is possible to descend to the underground car park and see the west gate of the earlier fort and part of a guardroom. Across the road from here in a public garden in Noble Street are parts of the wall of the fort and a well-preserved angle turret and culvert through the wall. Beneath the General Post Office yard in St Martin-le-Grand is the magnificent Newgate bastion standing to a good height, which can only be viewed by prior arrangement. Not far from here by Ludgate Circus, Fleet Street, is Wren's beautiful church of St Bride; it is outside the Roman city limits but preserved in its crypt are the remains of a Roman house with a red tessellated pavement and other small finds. Further along Fleet Street and just into the Strand behind King's College in Strand Lane (reached via Surrey Street and Surrey Steps) is the debatable 'Roman Bath'. It is a spring-fed plunge bath, 15½ × 6¾ft, which has characteristic red tiles but has been said to be of later date.

Of the other fragments of Roman London that can be seen pride of place is taken by the temple of Mithras found in the Walbrook in 1954. It was subsequently removed from its original site to another a

271 *The temple of Mithras was reconstructed to the west of its original site in the Walbrook in front of Temple Court, Queen Victoria Street.*

few hundred yards away and reconstructed in front of Temple Court, Queen Victoria Street, near Mansion House. The magnificent series of sculptures from the temple is in the Museum of London, and includes marble heads of Mithras himself, Serapis and Minerva, some smaller group pieces and a small silver casket beautifully decorated with scenes in relief which was probably used to hold incense during the ritual.

At the bottom of Billingsgate Market where it joins Upper Thames Street the hypocaust of a large house was found in 1848. This was incorporated under the old Victorian Coal Exchange, sadly pulled down in 1962. The hypocaust has been preserved for display in the eventual new building on the site. Under All Hallows Barking, by the Tower of London on Tower Hill, there are two Roman pavements in the crypt together with other small finds and a model diorama of Roman London. Beneath a firm of accountants at 11 Ironmonger Lane, off Cheapside, there is a small mosaic pavement which can be visited upon application, and a glass case of finds in the entrance hall.

Longovicium – Lanchester

Low Ham, Somerset   ST 4328
Site of a villa found in 1946 which was particularly rich in fourth-century figured mosaics. The most remarkable one came from the bath suite and shows, in a series of panels, the story of Aeneas and Dido Queen of Carthage based on Virgil's *Aeneid*. It is possible, from the style and content, that the mosaic was laid by a travelling mosaicist who could have come from North Africa. This mosaic, and a smaller floral one, are now in the Somerset County Museum, in Taunton Castle, Taunton. Other minor, patterned mosaics found on the site were covered over and left *in situ*.

Luguvallium – Carlisle

✱ **Lullingstone**, Kent   TQ 530650
Large villa off the A225 west of the village of Eynsford eight miles northeast of Sevenoaks. It was originally discovered in 1788 and proper excavations began in 1949, when its full importance was realized. Although occupied for over 300 years with intermittent breaks, the mid-fourth century was the most important period of its life. It was then that the splendid mosaics were laid. The principal mosaic is a square with guilloche and geometric borders surrounding a central scene of Bellerophon riding the winged horse Pegasus and slaying the monstrous Chimaera. In each of the four corners are represented the Four Seasons. The second mosaic leads off from the first and is apsidal in shape, being the floor of the dining room while the former was that of a reception room. The

pp. 98–9

146–8

117

115

49

272 *View of the Lullingstone villa with the Europa and Bellerophon mosaics in the middle distance. In a cellar beyond them, used as a shrine, were found the marble busts of the owner's ancestors and also the decorated wall plaster that had fallen from the Christian chapel in the room above.*

subject of the apsidal mosaic is the abduction of Europa to Crete by Jupiter in the guise of a great white bull. She sits on his back with a flowing mantle above her head while two cupids flank the bull, one waving it forward, the other holding on to its tail. There is an inscription in two lines above Europa's head, very rare indeed on mosaics from Roman Britain, which reads: INVIDA SI [TAURI] VIDISSET IVNO NATATVS/ IVSTIVS AEOLIAS ISSET ADVSQUE DOMOS – Had jealous Juno seen the swimming bull, she would have been justified in seeking out Aeolus in his cave of winds. It is a reference to a couplet in Virgil's *Aeneid*, Book 1, and obviously an indication of the owner's literary taste that he specially commissioned the piece. The outer geometric decoration of both mosaics is inferior to the competence shown in the main subjects, and they were probably finished off by local workmen.

About 360 Christianity was introduced into the villa and a room was converted for religious use. It was decorated with brightly coloured wall plaster featuring standing figures in the *orans* posture (hands uplifted, praying) who might be the owner and his family, and large *Chi-Rho* monograms flanked by the Greek letters *alpha* and *omega*, all set within a wreath. The plaster was restored when recovered from the deep room beneath the chapel into which it had collapsed when the villa burnt down early in the fifth century. Curiously, in the lower room were found two fine portrait busts of Greek marble, presum-

ably representing ancestors of the earlier owner in the second century. Also of this period was a small painted shrine dedicated to the local water nymphs (the river Darent flows in front of the villa); it was decorated with a plaster niche-painting of three nymphs.

The whole site is attractively laid out in a large barn-like building with many of the finds displayed round about. The painted plaster and the marble busts are in the British Museum and copies are shown on the site.

Lunt, Coventry, *see* Baginton

* **Lydney**, Glos.   SO 615026
Site of an Iron Age hillfort and the famous temple-complex on private land in Lydney Park off the A48 west of the village of Aylburton, nine miles north of Chepstow. It was only in 1928–9 that the true history of the site began to emerge with the excavations of Dr R.E.M. (later Sir Mortimer) Wheeler. The temple site was built within the Iron Age ramparts after 364 and dedicated to the Romano-Celtic god Nodens. Substantial portions of the temple platform and walls remain, and also parts of the adjacent buildings, including a hypocaust. Apparently, since Nodens was a god of healing, suppliants or patients would come to seek aid, enlightenment or a cure by spending the night (incubation) in the temple precincts in the hope of receiving some message in a dream. Associated with this were dogs, whose part may have been to lick affected limbs, since several fine small votive bronze statues of them have been found on the site. Several mosaics were found between 1805 and 1928, mainly of geometric style but one, now lost, had an inscription indicating that it was dedicated by Titus Flavius Senilis who was the

officer in charge of the nearby naval depot at Cardiff (q.v.). Other interesting inscriptions from the site include the so-called 'Lydney curse', scratched on a lead tablet, where Silvianus who has lost a gold ring suspects that one Senicianus has stolen it.

† **Lympne** (*Portus Lemanis*), Kent
                                TR 117342
One of the forts of the Saxon Shore (q.v.), also called Stutfall Castle, outside the village of Lympne on the B2067, three miles to the west of Hythe. The site has slipped down the hillside so that the remains of the walls are curiously scattered, usually presenting an idyllic pastoral scene with sheep quietly grazing among the fallen blocks. Excavations in the nineteenth century produced an altar dedicated by the admiral Gaius Aufidius Pantera to Neptune (now in the British Museum), which indicates that Lympne was the headquarters of the British fleet in the mid-second century before it moved to Dover (q.v.). Fresh excavations are currently being undertaken by Professor Barry Cunliffe.

Maglona – Greta Bridge

Magnis – Carvoran

Magnis – Kenchester

Maia – Bowness-on-Solway

* **Maiden Castle**, Dorset   SY 669885
This huge 45-acre Iron Age fort south of Dorchester off the A354 was attacked by the legionaries of the IInd Augusta under the future emperor Vespasian about 44. Realizing the strength of the multiple ramparts defending the western gateway, the legionaries were set to attack the less well fortified eastern gate, which was taken, but still with some difficulty. In between assaults the British defenders were able to recover and bury some of their dead in shallow graves with meagre offerings. This, the first British war cemetery as it has been called, was excavated by Mortimer Wheeler in 1934–7. Dramatic evidence of the fight can be seen in the County Museum in Dorchester where there is displayed the vertebrae of a British warrior pierced by a Roman iron bolt. After the successful assault the fort was slighted and the inhabitants removed, eventually to be resettled in the new town at Dorchester (*Durnovaria*) about 60–70.

About 367 a small typical Romano-Celtic temple was built in the northeastern sector of the fort. It has a square *cella* (sanctuary) facing east set within an outer temenos wall. There was painted plaster on the shrine walls and it had a black-and-white mosaic floor. The verandah outside was paved with red tesserae. Adjoining the temple on the north side is a tiny two-roomed house, probably provided for the

273 *The Romano-Celtic temple built in the northern section of the Iron Age hill-fort at Maiden Castle.*

officiating priest. Finds from the area included a bronze statuette of Tauros Trigaramus – the three-horned Celtic bull-god – fourth-century gold coins and a gold ring. They are all in the County Museum in Dorchester.

Maiden Way, Cumbria
Roman road running from Kirkby Thore (q.v.) four miles north of Appleby on the A66 to Greenhead on Hadrian's Wall at the junction of the A69 and B6318.

† **Malton** (*Derventio*), N. Yorks.
SE 7971
A large fort of over eight acres off the A64 just outside the town, 18 miles northeast of York. Originally an Agricolan foundation, it was occupied into the fourth century and seems to have been part of a much larger complex that could have served as the base camp for the campaigns in 71–2 of the IXth Legion under Cerialis. Finds from the area, including a mosaic with a bust of Winter, are in the Roman Malton Museum in the town but the small inscribed slab from the *vicus* that mentions a jeweller's shop (a unique reference in Roman Britain) is in the Roman Museum at York.

Martinhoe, N. Devon   SS 663493
A small fortlet or signal station occupied *c.* 60–78 to keep a watchful eye on the Bristol Channel. Situated off the A39 to the west of Lynton, but only the low ramparts remain.

Maryport (*Alauna*), Cumbria   NY 0337
A forward coastal fort on the A596 20 miles northwest of Keswick of which little remains. It is best known for the major find in 1870 of 17 altars outside the fort to the northeast. They were all in remarkably fine condition, having been buried soon after their erection. As a series they present interesting information on the garrison and troop movements into the fourth

century. They, together with other finds, are housed in the Senhouse collection, Netherhall Lodge – the largest private collection of Roman inscriptions in Britain.

† **Maumbury Rings**, Dorset SY 693902
On the south side of Dorchester beside the A354 (Weymouth road) near the station. Originally a Neolithic henge monument with an entrance on the northeast, it was redesigned by the Romans when they built *Durnovaria*. With a little adaptation, including lowering the floor in the centre, they created an amphitheatre that could be used for public displays (excavations revealed a room that could have been used as a cage for wild animals opposite the entrance), and perhaps also for military exercises and parades.

Mediobogum – Hardknott Castle

Mediomanum – Caersws

† **Mersea Island**, Essex   TM 023143
There is a large Roman burial mound situated behind railings a few hundred yards up the road to East Mersea on the left after the fork in the B1025 immediately on reaching the island. The barrow has a diameter of 110ft and is over 20ft high. It is possible to reach the centre of the barrow via a concrete tunnel that the 1912 excavators made. The burial, its site now marked by Roman tiles in the floor, was a first-century cremation with the ashes placed in a glass bottle within a lead container (now in the Colchester Museum).

† **Middleton**, Cumbria   SD 624859
There is a Roman milestone located in a field on the west side of the A683 six miles north of Kirkby Lonsdale. It is not in its original position, having been moved 200 yards to its present location in 1836. Its Latin inscription was sparse, merely recording that it was 53 miles to Carlisle (MP LIII), but it has an added deceptive inscription, also in Latin, recounting that it was discovered and set up by William Moore in 1836.

Mildenhall (Treasure), Suffolk
Site of the find at Thistley Green, West Row, on the edge of the fens three miles west of Mildenhall in about 1942 of 34 pieces of fourth-century silver plate. It was declared Treasure Trove on 1 July 1946 and is now in the British Museum. The major piece from the Treasure is the Great Dish (1ft 11¾ins in diameter and weighing 18¼ lb.), with a central mask of Oceanus surrounded by an inner frieze of Nereids and sea-creatures and an outer frieze of a Bacchic revel. Two smaller platters with Bacchic scenes are *en suite* with the dish. There were also nine bowls and dishes; two goblets; five ladle bowls and four handles; two spoons inscribed with names; three spoons with the *Chi-Rho* monogram, and three decorated spoons. It has been suggested that the hoard may have been the property of Lupicinus, a general who had command of the British garrison and was a Christian who was arrested by the pagan emperor Julian the Apostate in 363 when he returned to Gaul from Britain. Certainly the quality of workmanship and high value of the hoard indicate an owner of exceptional standing.

pp. 154–5

Mona – Anglesey

Moridunum – Carmarthen

New Kilpatrick, Strathclyde   NS 5572
Fort on the Antonine Wall on the north side of the B8049 (Boclair road) about half a mile east of its junction with the A81. Two sections of the stone wall base can be seen in New Kilpatrick cemetery with drainage culverts running across each one.

* **Newcastle upon Tyne** (*Pons Aelius*),
Tyne and Wear   NZ 452563
Fort at the original end of Hadrian's Wall on the site of the castle. *Pons Aelius* derives its name from the bridge that Hadrian (Publius Aelius Hadrianus) built over the Tyne on the site of the present Swing Bridge. Two altars dedicated to Neptune and Oceanus were dredged from the river and these, together with numerous coins thrown in over the years as votive offerings, can be seen in the University Museum, Newcastle.

† **Newport**, Isle of Wight, Hants.
SZ 500880
Small corridor villa found in 1926 in Avondale Road off the A3056. Three rooms have tessellated pavements of simple design, probably second century in date, and an unusual feature is a fireplace of tiles associated with the largest of the floors. There is a further range of four rooms of a bath suite and a hypocaust.

Newstead (*Trimontium*), Borders
NT 571344
No surface traces remain of this fort, certainly one of the largest and most impor-

tant in Roman Scotland. It lay to the east of Melrose off and partly under the B6361. Important excavations from 1905–9 revealed that it had been mainly occupied in the late first and early second centuries. A series of inscribed altars from the site, and other finds, are in the National Museum of Antiquities, Edinburgh.

Newton St Loe, Avon　　　　ST 7165
Site of a villa found in 1837 three miles west of Bath near the junction of the A4 and A39 when the Great Western Railway was being built. It consisted of a long corridor with at least seven rooms with mosaic pavements. Fragments of one from the principal room (now in Bristol City Museum) featured Orpheus in the central medallion playing his lyre to a fox while various wild beasts leap around the outside of the circular surround.

† North Leigh, Oxon.　　　　SP 397155
A large courtyard villa off the A4095 three miles northeast of Witney first excavated in 1813–17 and now in the course of re-excavation and conservation. Like so many villas in the area, it reached its apogee in the fourth century when it had rooms occupying three sides of the courtyard, 61 × 49yds, and an entrance gateway in the fourth. A dining-room with a fine geometric mosaic was built in the west corner (and is preserved under a shed). The majority of the mosaics found here are of fourth-century date and are of distinctive enough design and style for links to be drawn, via the Chedworth villa (q.v.), with the well-known Corinium school of mosaicists (see under Cirencester). Other similarities between examples found as far apart as Cir-

encester, Bignor and St Albans have been noted. There is also a well-preserved hypocaust here, and beyond the shed the rest of the villa can be made out as low consolidated walls. Aerial photography, as well as ground observation, has revealed a large complex of auxiliary buildings on the northeast and southwest sides of the villa.

Noviomagnus Regnensium – Chichester

Nunney, Somerset　　　　ST 7447
Site of a large villa found in 1837 near Whatley, west of Frome, with a number of mosaics which have since been lost. One apparently had a central medallion with Orpheus and animals walking around him, and another featured a head of Tyche in a mural crown holding a cornucopia with dolphins sporting around the medallion.

Old Burrow, N. Devon　　　　SS 788493
Small fortlet signal station overlooking the Bristol Channel occupied for a short while in the mid-first century, probably for only four years, before the garrison was transferred to Martinhoe (q.v.). Only ramparts and ditches can be seen on the site which is north of the A39 from Minehead just beyond the county boundary into Devon, approached by a path from Black Gate (SS 788489).

Old Carlisle (*Olenacum*), Cumbria
　　　　　　　　　　　　NY 352646
Fort which was part of the Hadrianic Wall system lying southwest of Carlisle (q.v.). Ramparts on all four sides are visible and aerial photography shows a large civilian settlement (*vicus*) outside the fort.

Old Kilpatrick, Strathclyde　　NS 4673
The most westerly fort on the Antonine Wall off the A82 twelve miles west of Glasgow. It covered an area of 4.7 acres.

The fort was a freestanding one with ramparts of turf and with rounded northern corners, thus indicating that it was built before the wall actually reached this far west.

Old Penrith (*Voreda*), Cumbria
　　　　　　　　　　　　NY 525327
Site of a fort on the road running north from Brougham (*Brocavum*) to Carlisle (*Luguvallium*).

† Old Sarum (*Sorviodunum*), Wilts.
　　　　　　　　　　　　SU 137327
Large Iron Age fort beside the A345 two miles north of Salisbury. Apart from the splendid ramparts of the period the major structures are the Norman castle and its motte and the outlines of the cathedral which preceded that at Salisbury. The site was probably the Roman posting station of *Sorviodunum*, and a small Roman building was found inside the fort in 1909.

Olenacum – Old Carlisle

Olicana – Ilkley

Onnum – Halton Chesters

Othona – Bradwell

Peddar's Way, Fring, Norfolk　TF 733345
Roman road based on a prehistoric trackway that is the continuation of the Icknield Way from Castle Acre to the Wash. It survives mainly as a hollow road but there is a well-preserved *agger*, a raised bank upon which the road was built, to be seen from time to time.

† Peel Crag, Cumbria　　　　NY 752676
One of the more spectacular stretches of Hadrian's Wall about half a mile west of Milecastle 39 and Crag Lough and 1½ miles northwest of Chesterholm (q.v.). Particularly noticeable here on the inner face of the wall are three offsets where slight discrepancies in the width of the wall by different gangs of men working on it had to be evened out.

† Pennymuir, Borders　　　　NT 755138
The group of marching camps at Pennymuir is the best-preserved in Scotland. They are located some six miles southeast of Jedburgh beyond the village of Oxnam where the Roman Dere Street (q.v.) crosses the open country coming up from Woden Law (q.v.). There are four camps here of which the largest, covering 42 acres, had room enough for two legions of 5,000 men under canvas. Its northern rampart (559yds long) is the best-preserved, still standing up to four feet and with a 15ft ditch. Five gateways are visible as breaks through the ramparts, each protected by an outer work. The second, smaller and later camp is only about 320yds in length and

274　*The three-coloured geometric mosaic in the dining room in the west wing of the villa at North Leigh.*

was set into the southeast corner of the large fort, where its east and west ramparts are quite well preserved. It has four remaining gateways, one on the north and east sides and two on the west side. The third and fourth camps lie to the north and northeast of the largest camp, and there is little to be seen of either now.

Petriana – Stanwix

Petuaria – Brough-on-Humber

* Pevensey (*Anderida*), E. Sussex
TQ 644048
One of the finest of the Saxon Shore forts (q.v.), on the south coast four miles northeast of Eastbourne on the A259. It was built in the late third century. Its unusual oval shape, enclosing about nine acres, is due to its having been built on a low hill surrounded by marshes with a harbour on the east and the sea lapping the south wall. Except for a stretch of about 65yds on the north side which has fallen outwards, the walls survive as a complete circuit, often up to 25ft or so in height. At the west end is the massive main gateway, protected by huge towers with guard chambers inside them. Of the original 15 U-shaped bastions only ten survive.

An entry in the *Anglo-Saxon Chronicle* for 491 records an attack on the fort by Aelle of the South Saxons who wiped out the entire garrison and inhabitants. In the southeast corner of the Roman circuit of walls the Norman Robert de Mortain built a strong castle, the keep of which still dominates the site. He used the Roman work for the wall of his outer bailey.

† Piercebridge, Durham   NZ 210157
A very large fort of 11 acres at the junction of the B2275 and the A67 four miles west of Darlington. It guarded the Tees crossing and was refounded about 300, the present remains being entirely of the fourth-century layout. Recent excavations have shown the substantial basis of the rebuild with barrack blocks and a bath house with the *pilae* of its hypocaust still over four feet high. There are also sections of the fort wall to be seen, a sewer from the latrines and some remains of the bridge that crossed the Tees, now consolidated on dry land owing to the change in the river's course. The very charming small bronze group of a ploughman and his team, now in the British Museum, came from here.

Pinnata Castra – Inchtuthil

† Planetrees, Northumberland
NY 929696
Stretch of Hadrian's Wall just over a mile east of Chesters beyond Turret 26B. It is about 13yds long and shows the junction of the Broad wall with a section only six feet

thick. This section of the Wall was saved from destruction in 1801 by William Hulton, the Birmingham antiquary, who pleaded with the local farmer not to destroy it.

† Poltross Burn, Northumberland
NY 634662
A well-preserved milecastle (no. 48) on Hadrian's Wall just before the railway bridge at Gilsland. It measures 70 × 61ft and ovens are visible in the northwest corner and the stairs up to the ramparts, about 12ft high. Record slabs note that it was built by Legio VI. The walls were of the Broad gauge but the Narrow gauge wall on a Broad foundation joins the wing-walls on either side.

Pons Aelius – Newcastle upon Tyne

Port Way, The Roman road from Silchester to Old Sarum.

* Portchester (*Portus Adurni*), Hants.
SU 625406
The best-preserved of the Saxon Shore forts (q.v.) covering 8½ acres standing at the head of Portsmouth harbour off the A27. It was built towards the end of the third century and only occupied until *c*. 370 when the garrison was moved to nearby Bitterne (q.v.). Then it was largely abandoned until the Normans who, once again as at Pevensey (q.v.), recognized a good military site, and Henry 1 erected a great keep in the 1120s which occupied the northwest corner of the Roman walls and built a Romanesque church in the opposite corner in 1133.

The Roman walls with their later added battlements still stand over 20ft high with 14 hollow bastions left out of an original total of 20. On the east side the water of Portsmouth Harbour comes up to the castle's medieval water gate built over the Roman east gate, and it also washes part of the south wall.

Portus Adurni – Portchester

Poundbury, Dorset   SY 682912
Iron Age fort in the northwest suburbs of Dorchester, west of the railway tunnel. From here the built-up bank that carried the Roman aqueduct into Dorchester runs along the contour of the hill and out to the west across Fordington Down. The water-source was the river Frome at Notton, twelve miles away.

Pumpsaint, *see* Dolaucothi

Ratae Coritanorum – Leicester

† Ravenglass (*Glannaventa*), Cumbria
SD 087959
The site of a four-acre fort (also known as Walls Castle) at Ravenglass, a village 17

miles south of Whitehaven on the A595. The fort site is covered by trees but beyond it the bath house attached to the fort has been substantially preserved because it was incorporated into a later medieval building. Some of the walls stand over 12ft high and traces of salmon pink cement rendering still survive in some of the niches where bathers left their clothes.

Ravenscar, N. Yorks.   NZ 970010
Site of a signal station on the south side of Robin Hood's Bay nine miles north of Scarborough (q.v.) off the A171.

† Reculver (*Regulbium*), Kent
TR 227693
One of the Saxon Shore forts (q.v.) three miles east of Herne Bay off the A299. The

275 *The distinctive twelfth-century towers of Reculver church stand on the site of the Saxon Shore fort, remnants of whose walls are in the foreground.*

site is now distinguished by the twelfth-century towers of the seventh-century church. Originally the fort covered about eight acres but roughly half has been eaten away by the encroaching sea, leaving the church (so often founded later in the centre of Roman forts) on the cliff edge. Although founded before Richborough (q.v.), its southern counterpart, Reculver acted as the guardian at the northern entrance to the Wantsum channel that separated off the Isle of Thanet. The fort appears to have been built about 210 (although there was a short-lived earlier fortlet on the site connected with the Conquest of 43), and it was abandoned about 360. A fragmentary inscription found in 1960 mentions A. Triarius Rufinus who was probably governor of Upper Britain about 210–16. The garrison is known to have been at one time the first cohort of Baetasians from Brabant on the Belgian–Dutch border. Parts of the walls and the south gateway with its guardrooms on either side can still be seen. Fragments of Roman pottery often litter the beach when the tide is out.

Regulbium – Reculver

† **Rey Cross**, Durham   NY 900124
The marching camp at Rey Cross lies nearly 1,500ft above sea level five miles west of Bowes, mainly on the north side of the A66. It is among the finest of such camps preserved in Britain and covered some 20 acres, large enough to house a legion. It was built by the IXth Legion under Quintus Petilius Cerialis during the campaigns of 72/3 against the Brigantes. The ramparts are up to six feet high and 20ft wide. They are of limestone since it was not possible to excavate out the necessary soil in the usual manner because of the underlying rock. Each side of the camp appears to have had at least two entrances in it and nine still survive, each with a protecting earthwork outside it.

Rhyn Park, Salop.   SJ 305374
Site of a recently found (1977) 48-acre legionary fortress five miles north of Oswestry on the A5 near Chirk. It guarded the southern approach of the Vale of Llangollen and acted as a springboard for attacks into Wales, probably in the campaigns of the XIVth Legion in the third quarter of the first century. The excavations produced evidence of all the usual buildings of a legionary base – extensive barrack blocks, bread ovens, post-holes of the huge timber supports for the gateways and fighting platforms, etc.

† **Ribchester** (*Bremetennacum Veteranorum*), Lancs.   SD 650350
A small cavalry fort situated on the river Ribble six miles northwest of Blackburn on the B6245. It only occupied an area 590 × 450ft but for all that has produced some very interesting finds and inscriptions. Most of the latter are in the local site museum by the church and apart from giving the Roman name of the site they record two cavalry regiments as part of the garrison at different times: Asturians from Spain in the first century, and Sarmatians from the Upper Danube in the third.

The best parts of the site to see are also at the museum, in its garden, where there are the remains of a pair of third-century granaries. Much of the fort remains to be excavated despite the fact that the river Ribble has eroded away a substantial portion that included the south and east gates.

The finest object from the site, the Ribchester helmet, was found in the eighteenth century and entered the famous Towneley Collection; from there it went into the British Museum collections. It is a bronze cavalry helmet, complete with its visor-mask, that dates from the late first century. The crown of the helmet is deco-

276 *The Ribchester face-mask cavalry parade helmet. British Museum.*

rated with embossed scenes of combat and the face mask has figures in relief and a mural crown. The whole object is far too thin and fragile for actual use and must have been a very special piece of equipment for parade ground use only. A replica of the helmet is displayed in the local museum.

* **Richborough** (*Rutupiae*), Kent
                    TR 325602
The major Saxon Shore fort (q.v.), covering about 5½ acres, lying on the A256 three miles north of Sandwich. Here the Roman army established its bridgehead in the invasion of 43. Richborough's opposite number guarding the northern end of the Wantsum channel was Reculver (q.v.). Within forty years of the invasion a magnificent four-way triumphal arch was set up on a heavy concrete cruciform base to honour Cn. Iulius Agricola. Decorated with statues and bronzes, it did not survive the early third century when all its statuary was removed and it saw service as a signal

277 *The deep outer ditches and high walls of the Saxon Shore fort at Richborough make it one of the most impressive of the series.*

station, over 90ft high – the concrete base is all that remains today. The Saxon Shore fort that dominates the site now was not built until the end of the third century. At least three-quarters of the circuit of the walls still stand up to 20ft high, and there is a narrow postern gate in the middle of the north wall and a simple gate in the west wall.

The interior of the fort is fairly complex. The great triple ditches around the cruciform podium that supported the triumphal arch are part of the defences during its use as a signal tower. They were actually filled in when the Saxon Shore fort was built but now have been left open as excavated. Near the centre within the ditches is a series of second-century stone-built shops. On the east side where the ditches finish at the edge of the escarpment is an apsidal building which is the Saxon church called the Chapel of St Augustine. Local legend has it that Saint Augustine landed at Richborough in 597 on his way to the court of King Ethelbert. Beyond it in the northeast corner is a group of foundations of a very large building. It was probably a *mansio*, an official staging post or inn, and it dates from the earlier occupation of the site. Subsequently, in the late third century, a small military bath suite was added to it and the hypocaust of this is particularly well-preserved.

A small museum at the entrance to the fort has a rich display of material from the excavations that have taken place for more than fifty years on the site.

On the opposite side of the road from the fort entrance, largely hidden and overgrown, is a depression in the hillside which marks the location of the amphitheatre attached to the fort, and which has never been fully excavated.

Originally Richborough stood on the coast but now it lies about three miles inland across mud flats while its sister fort at the north end of the Wantsum channel, Reculver (q.v.), has suffered in reverse and half has fallen to the eroding sea.

Risingham (*Habitancum*),
Northumberland   NY 8986
Site of an outlier fort of Hadrian's Wall at

West Woodburn on the A68 (here on the line of Dere Street, q.v.), 16 miles north of Corbridge. What little remains to be seen of the walls is of early third century date when the earlier fort was rebuilt on a grand scale. The work is recorded on two magnificent building stones now in Newcastle. One of them, particularly large and dated to 213, records the name of the site and that the first cohort of Vangiones was the new garrison.

Robin Hill, Isle of Wight, *see* Combley

Rochester (*Durobrivae*), Kent TQ 738695
The Roman town of about 23 acres guarded the crossing of the river Medway, and consequently has been continuously occupied and built over ever since. The medieval walls generally follow the course of the Roman circuit, and parts of the original can be seen occasionally overlaid by the later wall. The best remaining section about ten feet high is in Eagle Court, a public garden, on the south side of the High Street.

† **Rock of Gelt**, Cumbria NY 526587
One of the best series of inscriptions relating to the gangs working on Hadrian's Wall in a quarry to the south of Brampton off the B6413. Generally such inscriptions recording the work are undated but one here is dated to 207 and records 'a *vexilla* [of 62 men] of the IInd Legion under the *optio* [junior officer] of Agricola, in the consulship of Aper and Maximus'.

* **Rockbourne**, Hants. SU 120170
Courtyard villa with over 70 rooms close by Fordingbridge on the A338 eleven miles south of Salisbury and six miles north of

278 *Hypocaust, Rockbourne villa.*

Ringwood. Found in 1942, excavation has continued annually since 1956 and there is yet more of the site to be investigated. There are several geometric mosaics of a quality below that which one would normally expect to find in a villa of this size; numerous hypocausts, one of which is unusual in using curved roofing tiles (*imbrices*) in pairs to act as the supports (*pilae*) for the floor above, and a well-preserved bath suite. Of particular interest are the finds displayed in the site museum; they include a large hoard of 7,717 coins that was hidden in the troubled times of the second half of the third century, and two Roman milestones respectively of Trajan Decius (249–51) and Tetricus II (272); both were found reused as building material.

The villa appears to have been part of a large, possibly imperial estate, and it may have been connected with the Bokerley Dyke (q.v.) nearby that acted as a local boundary.

* **Rough Castle**, Central NS 843799
The best-preserved fort on the Antonine Wall at Bonnybridge on the A803 six miles west of Falkirk. It covered about an acre and still retains earth ramparts and ditches on three of its four sides. The buildings within the fort were of stone and the foundations of some of them are visible. On the east side of the fort was an annexe defended by a rampart and ditch which contained the bath house. About 20 yards to the north beyond the ditch excavations revealed a series of ten rows of small defensive pits (*lilia* or 'lilies' as they were called by Roman writers). In each pit were five sharpened stakes, point upwards, that would have been camouflaged with bracken, etc., and been a very nasty surprise for an advancing enemy from the north. This is the only site in Roman Britain where this kind of defence can be seen.

The garrison, the sixth cohort of the Nervii from the Lower Rhine, was commanded by Flavius Betto, a centurion of the XXth Legion, which was rather unusual.

† **Rudchester** (*Vindovala*), Northumberland NZ 113675
Fort on Hadrian's Wall at the junction of the B6318 and the A69 to the west of Heddon-on-the-Wall. It covered an area of 4½ acres and traces of its ditch and south ramparts are still visible. Five altars dedicated to Mithras were found in 1844 (now in Newcastle), and the temple was discovered outside the walls on the southwest and excavated in 1953. One of the altars records Lucius Sentius Castus, a centurion of the VIth Legion. The fort served as a convenient quarry and most of the stones used in the adjacent old farm buildings and walling are Roman. Fragments of inscriptions and centurial building stones can be seen incorporated into some of the walls.

Rudston, Humberside TA 0866
Site of a small villa found in 1933 five miles west of Bridlington on the B1253. Three fourth-century mosaics were found which are now in the Archaeology Museum, Hull. One of them had a simple geometric decoration but the other two are figured mosaics. The most interesting has an amusing and most oddly shaped figure of Venus with long hair who holds an apple in one hand and drops a mirror from the other. Before her is a merman and around the circle enclosing her are men hunting a lion, stag, leopard, and a wild bull. Mercury is also present in one of the flanking panels. The other figured mosaic has various sea fish on it and a lotus flower border.

A newly found mosaic (1972) shows a charioteer in a *quadriga* (four-horse chariot), and there are busts of the Four Seasons in the corners. Chariot racing as a mosaic subject seems to have been popular in this area, cf. Horkstow.

Rutupiae – Richborough

* **St Albans** (*Verulamium*), Herts.
TL 136071
The Roman city was the third largest in Britain, covering over 200 acres at its 179 greatest extent. It is one of the few city sites that has not been extensively built over and lies in the valley of the river Ver below the modern town 20 miles north of London on the A5 (the line of Watling Street from Marble Arch in London's West End). Much Roman building stone and distinctive red tiles were used in the fabric of the Abbey that was dedicated to Saint Alban, a Roman soldier probably martyred in the reign of Severus about 210.

It is best to begin a visit to the site at the Verulamium Museum, a model of its kind, beside St Michael's Church. A good impression of the area is gained from the large model of the city, and also from the 110 reconstruction of the huge London Gate whose foundations can be seen adjoining a fine stretch of the city wall on the south side of the parkland. The finds from the excavations, first in the 1930s under the Wheelers and then in the 1950s under Professor S.S. Frere, are well displayed to give the history of the site from its early Belgic days. Of particular note are some of the mosaics, especially striking being the one with the head of Cernunos (a Celtic god, but often referred to as that of Neptune or a sea god) at its centre which is late second century in date. Another fine example is the scallop-shell mosaic of the mid-first century; both of these mosaics come from the earlier excavations. Two mosaics from the later excavations worth noting feature a lion dragging off a stag (which has its nearest parallels in North Africa), and a dolphin and vases – both are of the second century. From excavations in the playground of the school immediately opposite the museum (the site of the basilica) came fragments of a large inscription mentioning Agricola.

A few hundred yards away from the museum across the A414 (TL 134074) is the Roman theatre, one of five known in Britain but the only one that can be visited. A reconstructed pillar on the stage gives an indication of the height that the proscenium would have been above it. The semi-circular bank of earth around the central area and stage with its several entrances was built up from the spoil of the 1933 excavations. In the late fourth century the theatre went out of use and became the town's rubbish dump. Alongside the theatre are laid out the foundations of wooden shops and houses that date from the decade before the revolt of Boudicca in 60 when she and her forces destroyed the town. The area was then abandoned for a while and then rebuilt in stone. Close to the main road can be seen a deep cellar with an apse that was used as a shrine in the fourth century.

In the middle of the playing fields outside the museum is a small bungalow which houses a large geometric mosaic floor from the *tepidarium* of a second-century bath suite. Below the floor is the hypocaust with its stoke hole leading to it. Preserved in the edges of the floor at the corners of the room are the hollow box flue tiles that ducted the warm air around the house. Beyond the bungalow are some fragments of the town wall by the boating lake but a little further on is a fine and long stretch of the south wall with bastions which were added after the main building phase to take catapults, *ballistae*. Behind the wall are guard chambers and in front of it are the still very substantial remains of the defensive ditch. At the eastern end of this stretch of wall are the huge foundations of the double-carriageway of the London Gate.

Excavation evidence shows that *Verulamium* was one of the longest inhabited towns of Roman Britain. It was first laid out about the middle of the first century, following the establishment of a small military garrison; destroyed in 60 by Boudicca, and again by fire in the mid-second century; rebuilt with substantial town houses in stone which had fine mosaics, and then flourished into the third and fourth centuries. New building was still being carried out well into the fifth century after the official abandonment of Britain in 410.

† **St Hilary**, Cornwall   SW 5531
The church lies north of the B3280 1¾ miles east of the junction with the A394, near Marazion five miles east of Penzance. Cemented into the floor in its south aisle is a Roman milestone that was erected in 306/7 and inscribed for 'The Emperor Caesar Flavius Valerius Constantinus Pius, most noble Caesar, son of the deified Con-

stantius Pius Felix Augustus'; that is, to the young man whose father Constantius I had just died at York and who was to become Constantine I, the Great.

Saxon Shore forts (*Litus Saxonici*)
A line of substantial coastal defence forts, not all built at the same time but mainly in the late third century, running from the Wash to the Isle of Wight. In order, north to south, they were: Brancaster; Burgh Castle; Walton Castle; Bradwell; Reculver; Richborough; Dover; Lympne; Pevensey; Portchester, and Carisbrooke Castle. *See* individual entries for details.

279 *Outline map of the forts of the Saxon Shore.*

† **Scarborough**, N. Yorks.   TA 052982
Signal station on Castle Hill to the east of the castle on the cliff edge; part of it has fallen into the sea. Originally a small enclosure about 100ft square with corner turrets and a central stone platform upon which the tall timber signal tower was built. Its foundations are marked out on the cliff edge close by those of a medieval chapel and the ruins of Henry II's great late twelfth-century keep. These signal stations, of which there was a long chain situated at intervals along the Yorkshire coast to warn against raiders, were occupied in the last quarter of the fourth century.

Scotch Corner, N. Yorks.   NZ 210057
Important junction of Roman roads three miles north of the fort at Catterick. One road heads north towards Piercebridge (q.v.), the other turns west to the Stainmore Pass and Carlisle. Part of the road itself is visible as a five foot high bank which is 24ft in width.

† **Seabegs Wood**, Central   NS 8179
Site of a fort on the Antonine Wall (q.v.) of which there is nothing to be seen above ground today. To the west of Seabegs Wood can be seen a stretch of the wall, ditch and Military Way. It can also be reached west of Rough Castle (q.v.) on the B816 which runs past it.

† **Sea Mills** (*Portus Abonae*), Glos.
                              ST 551758
A small settlement on the Bristol Channel at Avonmouth, now a suburb of Bristol, which may have been an early base for the *Classis Britannica*. Foundations of several rooms of a house, adjacent walls and stone guttering can be seen at the junction of Roman Way with Portway (A4).

Segedunum – Wallsend

Segontium – Caernarfon

† **Silbury Hill**, Wilts.   SU 100685
The largest man-made mound in Europe, part of the complex of Neolithic monuments associated with nearby Avebury and the West Kennet long barrow. It is over 120ft high and obviously of pre-Roman date as the Roman road from Mildenhall (*Cunetio*) to Bath (*Aquae Sulis*) has to make a definite and still distinctive detour close around its base. It must have acted as a siting station for the Roman road surveyors.

* **Silchester** (*Calleva Atrebatum*),
Hants.   SU 640625
The cantonal capital of the Atrebates eight miles southwest of Reading to the east of the A340 and its junction with the B3051. The hexagonal walls enclose about 107 acres, all open farmland, and are the longest complete circuit left in Roman Britain. The site was extensively excavated in the late nineteenth century and again in the 1930s and 1950s. It has produced the most complete Roman town plan known for Britain. In the right conditions the plan is visible from the air and even in parts on the ground. Two of the main gates are well preserved at Rye House (the north gate), and Manor Farm (the south gate), while St Mary's church stands just within the east gate. There were two temples located under the church, and a column from one of them stands in the churchyard near the west door. Excavations revealed the site of a small apsidal building, 42 × 33ft, on the south side of the forum which was identified as an early Christian church, probably of fourth-century date.

Some finds from the site are housed in a small museum near the rectory just outside the west wall. The principal collection is in the Reading Museum; the best-known piece from the site, the bronze Silchester Eagle, is displayed at Stratfield Saye, the nearby stately home of the Duke of Wellington, upon whose estate Silchester stands.

Soldier's Ring, Hants.   SU 082176
Kite-shaped earthwork enclosure that was probably some kind of cattle compound. Its sharply cut banks and shape proclaim its Roman origins and date. It is located near the Rockbourne villa (q.v.), by South Allenford Farm.

Sorviodunum – Old Sarum

† **South Cadbury Castle**, Somerset
ST 628252

237   Iron Age fort near the A303 eight miles northeast of Yeovil with multiple ramparts covering about 18 acres. Apparently a centre of resistance against the Romans from the evidence of a massacre which followed an assault on the southwest gateway. Remains of some 30 men, women and children were found strewn in the gateway area. The hillfort was then slighted and subsequently seems to have been the site of a Romano-Celtic temple. The fort has been linked in legend with King Arthur's Camelot since the sixteenth century when John Leland, the King's Antiquary, proposed it. Archaeological evidence certainly indicated reoccupation of the fort during the 'Arthurian' period around 500 with the import of late fifth- and early sixth-century pottery from the eastern Mediterranean and the construction of a large timber hall. The evidence for the hillfort's long history comes from excavations carried out by Professor Leslie Alcock in 1966–70.

* **South Shields** (*Arbeia*), Tyne and Wear   NZ 3667
Fort to the east of Newcastle at the mouth of the Tyne. It was the most easterly part of Hadrian's Wall, though not part of the Wall itself. It covered 4½ acres and the remains, still visible in Roman Remains Park, Baring Street (off the B1344), include part of the west wall and gate, the headquarters building, strong-room, barrack blocks, kilns, and the foundations of ten out of 22 known granaries on the site. The fort is Hadrianic but was enlarged under Severus in the early third century when it was important as a supply base for his campaigns into Scotland.

Part of the garrison in the fourth century is known to have been a specialist unit of boatmen from the river Tigris in Iraq (Mesopotamia), the *numerus barcariorum Tigrisiensium*. They were obviously necessary to ensure the safe delivery of supplies up the treacherous Tyne.

93, 94   There is a magnificent small museum with several superb and well-known tombstones in it. The two most notable are those of Regina and Victor. Regina was a freedwoman of the Catuvellauni tribe of Hertfordshire who married Barates of Palmyra. (He may be the Barates, a *vexillarius* and native of Palmyra, recorded on a tombstone in the Corbridge Museum.) As well as the normal Latin inscription her monument has a short Palmyrene inscription. She is shown seated in a basket chair holding a spindle and distaff with a box of wool beside her. Victor, a native of Mauretania in North Africa, is seen reclining at a banquet holding a wine cup whilst a diminutive slave proffers another cup just filled from a large wine crater.

280   *View across the excavated site at South Shields. The remains seen are largely numerous granaries of Severan date, built when the fort acted as an important supply depot for the Wall. The site museum, housing the tombstones of Regina and Victor, is in the background.*

Southwell, Notts.   SK 7053
A number of mosaics and tessellated pavements have been recovered from a site in the centre of the town close to the minster since 1793. Excavations in 1959 produced four more similar mosaics with grid and geometric patterns that were covered over *in situ*.

Stane Street
Roman road running from Chichester to London.

Stanegate
Roman military road running just south of Hadrian's Wall from Carlisle in the west to Corbridge (q.v.) in the east. It predated the Wall, being one of Agricola's supply roads in his campaign of 80. The forts on the Stanegate were at first set at a day's march apart (11 to 13 miles), then 'half-day' forts were added in between as a means of bringing more troops into the area to provide closer local patrolling. The major forts were Nether Denton, Chesterholm (q.v.), and Corbridge (q.v.). With the building of the Wall the Stanegate's military use was superseded and its forts then served as a series of backup supply depots.

† **Stanwick**, N. Yorks.   NZ 180115
One of the largest Iron Age fortified areas in Britain southwest of Piercebridge (q.v.) near Forcett. It was the stronghold of the Brigantes under Venutius. The original fortified area, built before 60, covered 17 acres; shortly afterwards this was enlarged

281   *Part of the vast defences thrown up at Stanwick by Venutius in a last stand against Legio IX Hispana in c. 72.*

to around 150 acres and, finally, close to 72, to about 850 acres. Venutius was anti-Roman, Cartimandua, his queen, pro-Roman. They each went their own ways, but then Venutius attacked Cartimandua in 68 with such force that her Roman allies had to rescue her. This increased Venutius' prestige, warriors flocked to his banner and Stanwick was enlarged to hold them. However, matters were not left there; the IXth Legion marched north from York against Stanwick *c.* 72; it proved impossible to hold the vast circuit of the defences against disciplined troops and the fort fell. The stone-revetted ramparts and deep ditches are still a striking feature of the site today.

Stanwix (*Petriana*), Cumbria NY 402571
The largest fort on Hadrian's Wall, on the north bank of the river Eden opposite Carlisle covering more than nine acres on elevated ground. Most of the area is now built upon but the south ramparts are still apparent in the churchyard. The fort was probably intended to hold the *ala Petriana*, a cavalry regiment 1,000 strong, which would be needed to defend the ground to the north.

Stevenage, Herts. TL 237237
At Stevenage New Town beside the A602 close by the station is a line of six Roman barrows known as the Six Hills. They are still up to 60ft in diameter and six feet high. When Dr Ducarel opened one of them in September 1741 he found 'only wood and a piece of iron'.

Stoke Hill, Devon SX 923953
Signal station 1½ miles north of Exeter on the northeast side of the Iron Age hillfort.

Stonesfield, Oxon. SP 4017
Site of a villa found in 1712 just over two miles northwest of the North Leigh villa (q.v.). It is now lost but of interest for its mosaics and historically as it was the first villa to be described and commented upon in detail. The villa was quite large and richly decorated, its mosaics being presumably of fourth-century date. They included one with a central medallion of Bacchus about to mount a panther, surrounded by an acanthus scroll that emerged from the head of a bearded Neptune. Swastikas, guilloche patterns and duplex knots featured largely in all the four mosaics found.

Stutfall Castle, *see* Lympne

Tadcaster (*Calcaria*). N. Yorks.
SE 444843
Site of a fort ten miles south-west of York on the A64.

† Temple Sowerby, Cumbria NY 6226
Located half a mile southeast of Temple Sowerby, itself seven miles east of Penrith,

on the A66 is one of the only two known examples of Roman milestones in Britain that are still *in situ*. (The other is at Chesterholm, q.v.) It is located in a protective iron cage on the north side of the A66 by a lay-by.

Thornborough, Bucks. SP 732333
Two large Roman tumuli to the east of Thornborough Bridge, north of the B4034, itself east of Buckingham off the A421. The largest tumulus is about 15ft high and 120ft in diameter. The finds made when the barrows were dug by the Duke of Buckingham in 1839–40 are in the University Museum, Downing Street, Cambridge. One of the burials was intact and included two wine amphorae, numerous pottery vessels, weapons, jewellery, and a chained lid lamp. It dates from the late second century.

Thruxton, Hants. SU 2946
Site of a villa found in 1823 five miles west of Andover on the A303. A fine mid-fourth-century mosaic from here is in the British Museum. It had a central roundel featuring Bacchus reclining on the back of a panther. Small panels within the wide border had male heads in Phrygian caps and the Four Seasons were represented within the spandrels. Unusually it had two panels with Latin inscriptions; one of them read: QVINTVS NATALIVS ET BODENI/ . . . V . . . O, which might represent the signatures of the artists responsible for the work.

† Tintagel, Cornwall SX 0789
There is a Roman milestone of Licinius I (308–24), in the south transept of the church.

Titsey, Surrey TQ 404545
Villa of corridor type in Titsey Park, Titsey, on the B269 north of Limpsfield. Found in 1847 and excavated in 1864, the site is still open but situated on private land.

Tockington Park, Glos. ST 6285
Site of a villa at Tockington on the A38 north of the junction of the M4 and M5 north of Bristol. It was found in 1787 and excavated in 1887. Its fourth-century mosaics, mainly geometric and stylized flowers, were found in five of the rooms and left covered over *in situ*.

* Tomen-y-Mur, Gwynedd SH 707387
The site of the remotest auxiliary fort in Roman Britain. It lies high up in the mountains on the east side of the A470 about five miles south of Ffestiniog. Although the views from the site are truly magnificent (when cloud allows), the outlook must be very bleak indeed for the troops stationed there. The typical

282 *Tomen-y-Mur is surely the remotest auxilliary fort in Britain. From the air its reduction in size in c. 210, by cutting off part of the western end, can easily be seen; to the northeast of the fort (i.e. at the bottom right) is the amphitheatre that the garrison was allowed to build.*

playing-card outline shape of the fort is easily picked out on the ground. Built under Agricola in 78 it was reduced in size about 120 by having a rampart raised across it, cutting off about a quarter of the west end of the fort. In the middle of this later rampart now rises a Norman motte which probably stands directly over the fort's west gate. The fort was walled in stone at the time of its reduction, but most of this has now disappeared to be re-used locally in dry-stone walling. The fort seems to have been abandoned about the middle of the second century. Outside it to the northeast in now marshy ground is an amphitheatre – the only one known to have been attached to an auxiliary fort. Presumably it was allowed as some small compensation for the rigours of the remote posting. Nearby to the northwest are the outlines of two practice camps, and the fort's bath house and civilian *vicus* lay to the southeast with its parade ground on the east side.

† Traprain Law, Lothian   NT 581747
The great hillfort lies two miles to the southeast of East Linton off the A1 six miles west of Dunbar. It was the capital (*oppidum*) of the Votadini which at its greatest extent in the late first century covered about 40 acres, making it the largest hillfort in Scotland. It had started out as a mere ten acres, grown, and then was subsequently reduced in the fourth century back to 30 acres. Workmen digging at the west end of the fort some sixty years ago found a huge hoard of Roman silver treasure of the fourth century that had been hidden in the early years of the fifth. Most of it consisted of fragments of over 100 vessels, mainly hacked up as bullion. A few of the smaller items, flasks, goblets and spoons, were relatively undamaged but the whole obviously represented pirates' loot, probably from Roman Britain or even Gaul. The spoils had still to be divided up when some unknown circumstance forced it to be buried and lost. The treasure is now in the National Museum of Antiquities, Edinburgh.

pp. 154–5

Trecastle, Powys   SN 883291
Site of a fort twelve miles west of Brecon on the A40 where the fifth-century inscribed Latin and ogham memorial stone to Maccutremus Salicidunus was found which is now in the Brecknock Museum, Brecon.

† Tre'r Ceiri, Gwynedd   SH 374447
The fort, literally 'the town of the giants', lies about 2,000ft up on Yr Eife ('The Rivals'), off the B4417 to the east of its junction with the A499 at Llanaelhaearn. It was a stronghold of the Ordovices running along the elongated contour of the hill top with its ramparts of loosely packed stones still standing up to 12ft high. Two types of hut can be easily distinguished within the fort, round ones from the pre-Roman Iron Age and rectangular ones of the Roman period. It was occupied from about the mid-first century up until the end of the fourth if not into the early fifth century.

Trimontium – Newstead

Usk (*Burrium*), Gwent   SO 379007
Fort which was used as a base in the early campaigns into Wales before the fortress at Caerleon was built and became the permanent base. It stood in a strategic position on the river Usk guarding the entrance to several valleys and is still at a major road junction on the A449 northeast of Newport. There is nothing to be seen nowadays but recent excavations revealed the normal legionary layout of workshops and granaries behind the area of the modern prison.

Uxellodunum – Castlesteads

Vectis – Isle of Wight

Venta Belgarum – Winchester

Venta Icenorum – Caistor St Edmund

Venta Silurum – Caerwent

Vercovicium – Housesteads

Verterae – Brough, Cumbria

Verulamium – St Albans

Vindogladia – Badbury Rings

Vindolanda – Chesterholm

Vindomora – Ebchester

Vindovala – Rudchester

Vinovia – Binchester

Viroconium Cornoviorum – Wroxeter

Voreda – Old Penrith

† Wade's Causeway, N. Yorks.
SE 793938 to SE 812988
One of the best stretches of Roman paved road in Britain, on Wheeldale Moor, Goathland, west of the A169 seven miles south of Whitby. It is up to 16ft wide in places with gutters and culverts to assist drainage. Curiously it appears to be an isolated stretch since it is not known where it was coming from nor where it was heading.

† Wadfield, Glos.   SP 0226
Very derelict site of a villa in the middle of a field two miles south of Winchcombe (on the A46) on the road leading to Andoversford (on the A436). It was found in 1863 and its fourth-century geometric mosaic, in a wooden hut on the site, has a stylized flower within a wreath of ivy leaves which is close to an example from Lydney.

* Wall (*Letocetum*), Staffs.   SK 098066
A small Romano-British town on the A5 two miles southwest of Lichfield and 14 miles north of Birmingham. It was a posting station on Watling Street and had an official hotel, *mansio*, for the use of couriers. Before 58 it was garrisoned by the XIVth Legion, who were moved about that date to Wroxeter. Because of its convenient position the town grew until it covered some 30 acres. There are extensive remains of a bath house with its walls still standing to a good height. The whole complex is one of the best and most complete examples of a town bath house to be seen in Roman Britain. There is a small local museum that includes finds from the Roman site at Shenstone a mile away to the southeast as well as those from Wall.

283 *The bath house suite at Wall. To the right are the* pilae *of the hypocaust and in the room on the left can be seen the niches (lockers) for the bathers' clothes.*

Walls Castle, *see* Ravenglass

Wallsend (*Segedunum*), Tyne and Wear
NZ 3066
Fort which stood on high ground at the end of an eastern extension of Hadrian's Wall on the north bank of the Tyne. It covered four acres and its outline today is picked out in the local streets of Wallsend-on-Tyne with white paving stones.

† **Walltown**, Northumberland
NY 672664
Perhaps the best piece of Hadrian's Wall, 400yds in length, under the protection of the Department of the Environment, northeast of Greenhead off the B6318. It includes Turret no. 45A which was an independent signal station before it was incorporated into the Wall system.

Walton Castle, Suffolk   TM 3235
Site of a Saxon Shore fort (q.v.) now lost beneath the sea off the coast at Felixstowe.

Wanstead, Essex   TQ 4187
Site of a villa found in 1715 and now outlined as foundations in Wanstead Park, south of Eastern Avenue (A12) at Redbridge. A mosaic found at the time of the original discovery, and since lost, apparently featured Bacchus riding on a panther.

Water Newton (*Durobrivae*), Cambs.
TL 120970
Site of a town of 45 acres straddling Ermine Street on the A1 to the west of Peterborough. The whole area of the Nene Valley was famous for its widely traded and distinctive pottery. Recent work in the area has considerably expanded our knowledge of the size and complexity of the pottery industry based here and at Castor.

In February 1974 a pottery bowl was found containing a bronze bowl holding two pieces of folded over silver plate and in the remains of a leather purse were 32 gold *solidi* of Constantine I and his sons dated to 330–50. A year later, in February 1975, in an adjoining field within the town boundary was found a hoard of fourth-century silver plate. It consisted of 27 silver objects and a gold disc with the *Chi-Rho* monogram and the Greek letters *alpha* and *omega* on it. The silver items comprised mainly leaf-shaped plaques (17 and some additional fragments) of which eight had the *Chi-Rho* monogram on them. Among the other nine silver pieces were a large dish, a faceted bowl, a ladle, a handled cup, a vase, and several cups or bowls, some of the latter inscribed with Christian motifs and/or sentiments. The whole collection forms the earliest group of Christian silver known from anywhere in the Roman Empire. It poses questions as to how so rich a group should have come to be in the relative backwater of the Empire

pp. 154–5

where it was found. Both the treasures are now in the British Museum.

† **Watling Lodge**, Central   NS 862798
Site of an impressive stretch of the Antonine Wall ditch which is 15ft deep and 40ft wide. It lies just over a mile to the west of Falkirk off the B816 beyond Camelon.

Watling Street
Roman road running from Dover via Canterbury and London to Chester, largely on the route of the modern A5.

† **Welwyn**, Herts.   TL 522316
In the grounds of Lockleys Park School (private) are marked out the foundations of a villa excavated in 1937. Further down the hill and now reached from the A1(M) by the B1000 at Dicket Mead is a small early third-century bath house. After excavation it was threatened with destruction since the new motorway was scheduled to go right through its site. Local pressure on the authorities resulted in a plan being approved to preserve the bath house in a concrete vault under the motorway. This was done and it is now entered from a tunnel which leads beneath the road. Photographs and finds from the excavations are displayed alongside the structure.

† **Westerwood**, Strathclyde NS 761744
Well-preserved fort on the Antonine Wall covering 2¼ acres. It lies to the west of Castlecary (q.v.) off the B816.

† **Wheathampstead**, Herts. TL 185132
Bank and ditches of a Belgic camp, called locally the Devil's Dyke. It is off the A6129 on the east side of Dyke Lane, five miles northeast of St Albans. The ditch is over a quarter of a mile long and up to 40ft deep. It is generally accepted as being the site of the *oppidum* of Cassivellaunus that was stormed by Julius Caesar in 54 BC. It forms part of a large Belgic complex around the northern outskirts of St Albans.

Wheeldale Moor, *see* Wade's Causeway

† **Whitley Castle**, Cumbria   NY 6948
Fort to the west of the A689 about two miles north of Alston. It is sited on a Roman road, the Maiden Way (q.v.), which runs to Hadrian's Wall from Greenhead. On the southwest side the defences are particularly strong and well-preserved; there are seven ditches with steep ramparts rising above them. Outlines of some of the buildings can be picked out within the fort, especially the headquarters building near the centre. An inscription from the site records its garrison at one time as being the second cohort of the Nervii, from the Lower Rhine.

† **Willowford**, Cumbria   NY 629663
A fine stretch of Hadrian's Wall to the east

of Birdoswald and west of the B6318 junction at Gilsland. It still stands 14 courses high and incorporates a turret (no. 48A). From here the Wall was carried across the river Irthing by a bridge similar to that at Chesters (q.v.). The remains of a turret, abutment and pier of the bridge can still be seen here.

† **Winchester** (*Venta Belgarum*), Hants.
SU 480295
The cantonal capital of the Belgae which covered 138 acres; it ranked as the fifth largest town in Roman Britain. Virtually nothing of this remains to be seen on the site owing to its continual later occupation, especially in Saxon and early medieval times. The medieval walls follow the line of their Roman predecessors and engulf them on all sides of the town except the east, where they follow the line of the river. Much excavation has taken place here in recent years, largely concerned with the area adjacent to the Minster and the Saxon levels when Winchester was the capital city. Finds of all periods, including some rather poor fragments of Roman mosaics, are displayed in the Winchester City Museum on the edge of the Cathedral Green.

Winterton, Humberside   SE 9318
Site of a villa beside Ermine Street as it headed for the crossing of the Humber on the B1207 to the northeast of Scunthorpe. It was first discovered in the eighteenth century and found to have a large number of mosaics that were recorded by William Fowler. In 1958 fresh excavations were undertaken to locate the mosaics originally noted, and some new ones of second century date were found. A number of the mosaics had figure decoration but the workmanship was generally of a rather poor standard. One had a crude figure of Orpheus in a central octagon, another a representation of Abundantia and a third had Ceres, the goddess of corn. Some of the mosaics were lifted and restored and can be seen in the Scunthorpe Museum and in the Civic Centre, Scunthorpe.

Withington, Glos.   SP 0314
Site of a villa found in 1811 less than three miles north of Chedworth (q.v.). It had a number of mosaic pavements of simple geometric design and one large figured mosaic. This came from a rectangular room and was divided into five panels; the first featured Orpheus playing his lyre in the central medallion with a fox beside him and various animals parading around the outer circle; the second showed Neptune with two dolphins erupting from his beard and the field of the panel crammed with sea-creatures and foliage; the third, damaged, may have represented a lion hunt, with only the forelegs of a horse pursuing the hind legs of a beast remaining. A

fourth panel had a sea beast and a dolphin, and the fifth was patterned with pelta designs. Fragments of this large scale mosaic are in the British Museum and the Bristol City Museum. The Orpheus motif is one common amongst the mosaicists of the Cirencester school (q.v.), best exemplified at the villa at Woodchester (q.v.).

† **Woden Law**, Borders   NT 768125
A fine example of an Iron Age multivallate hillfort three miles north of Chew Green (q.v.) approached by Dere Street (q.v.). Excavation showed that the fort's defences had been extended in three phases, the last being possibly post-Roman in date. Its interest lies in the well-preserved Roman siege works that invest all sides of it except the west. They consist of two banks and three ditches set at a regular 70ft from the fort's defences. These are in turn backed up by three further siege lines, independent of each other and all of them unfinished. The fort was not strong enough in itself to merit such a show of strength and heavy siege works, nor could it have withstood a concentrated and disciplined Roman attack. Therefore the siege works must be practice ones (as at Burnswark, q.v.). Their distance from the fort ramparts is just right for the besiegers to be able to deliver firepower into the fort but be safe enough themselves outside the range of the Iron Age projectiles. The construction of the siege lines must have been part of the army's peace-time practice and manoeuvres, built by the troops who were stationed in the group of marching camps at nearby Pennymuir (q.v.).

(*) **Woodchester**, Glos.   SO 840030
The site of one of the largest and probably most luxurious villas in Roman Britain two miles south of Stroud between the A46 and the B4066. It lies beneath the old churchyard at a depth of only two to three feet, and thus burials have contributed to its damage in the seventeenth and eighteenth centuries. It was first found in 1695 but not properly investigated until a hundred years later when the famous antiquary Samuel Lysons published it in 1797. The 'Great Pavement' is 45ft 10ins square in a room 50ft square, which is one of a series of at least 65 rooms known in the villa so far. The central feature of the pavement is an octagonal panel, now destroyed, said to have had a fish and a star in it. One of the guilloche sides of the octagon is broken on the south side by a seated figure of Orpheus playing his lyre with a fox to one side and a peacock on the other. There is a procession of birds around the outside of the rest of the octagon. Outside this zone, and Orpheus, moving round with measured tread, is a procession of animals that includes a lion, lioness, wild boar, horse, elephant, gryphon, bear, leopard, stag,

284   *Part of the procession of animals that pace around the outer circle of the great Orpheus mosaic in the Woodchester villa. Seen here are a tigress, stag, leopard and bear.*

and a tigress. An outer ring of decoration beyond these consists of a floral motif, possibly an acanthus scroll, that springs from a facing bearded head (similarly placed like Orpheus on the south side), and which returns to the head around the circle. Presumably Orpheus and the head both faced towards the main entrance to the room beyond which would generally be the dining room so that guests could observe the beauties of the mosaic decoration as they reclined on their couches. The whole of these motifs in a great swirl of circular decoration are placed within a great square of complicated geometric panels. In the spandrels between the circle and the square are four pairs of reclining female figures. The whole pavement is a *tour de force*, the largest and most elaborate example of its kind known north of the Alps, and only one of some fifty examples known throughout the Roman Empire that depict Orpheus and the animals. It is certainly amongst the finest of these. The subject was obviously a favourite one with the designers from the mosaicist school at Cirencester (q.v.), as two others featuring it are known from Cirencester itself and a third from Withington (q.v.). Other major examples (some now lost) occur in Britain at Brading (q.v.); Horkstow (q.v.); Littlecote Park (q.v.); Newton St Loe (q.v.); Nunney (q.v.), and Winterton (q.v.).

The mosaic is covered over *in situ* and only opened up at infrequent intervals (in the last hundred years in 1880, 1890, 1926, 1935, 1951, 1963 and 1973).

† **Woodcuts**, Dorset   ST 9618
An example of a classic site in the history of British archaeology, first excavated by General Pitt-Rivers in 1884 on his estates at Cranborne Chase. It lies on the B3081 off the A354 at Sixpenny Handley 13 miles south of Salisbury. It was a typical native settlement of pre-conquest date with the major dwelling and its adjacent grain pits surrounded by a circular bank and ditch. Roman influence appeared in the late second century with luxuries such as wall plaster and large corn dryers. Pitt-Rivers restored the earthworks to give a good impression of a Romano-British native settlement in its setting.

† **Wookey Hole**, Somerset   ST 531480
One of the most awe-inspiring cave sites in Britain two miles northwest of Wells off the A371. Although essentially a Palaeolithic (Stone Age) site finds of pottery typical of Late Iron Age and of Romano-British types indicate that the entrance area to the cave was occupied sporadically in those periods. The finds are displayed in a museum on the site.

* **Wroxeter** (*Viroconium Cornoviorum*), Salop.   SJ 565087
The site lies five miles south of Shrewsbury off the A5 on the B4380. It began life as the garrison of the XIVth Legion but about 88 the occupying troops (now the XXth Legion) were ordered to the new legionary headquarters at Chester (q.v.), and Wroxeter took on a civilian role as the cantonal capital of the Cornovii. Eventually it expanded to cover 170 acres, the fourth largest town in Roman Britain. It is another of the few examples where the Roman town site has not been subsequently built over. Dominating the site is a huge piece of wall known as 'the old work',

which was the dividing wall between the baths and the *palaestra* (exercise area). In recent years the site has been the focus of training excavations of the Extra-Mural Department of Birmingham University, and much has been revealed. There was an extensive bathing establishment adjacent to the 'old work', and large sections of it are now marked out in modern materials where the original disappeared centuries ago at the hands of stone robbers. An interesting feature is the small swimming bath, an open air pool like the one at Gadebridge (q.v.), but nowhere near as large. Apart from the Great Bath at Bath it is now the only swimming bath to be seen from Roman Britain.

Near the site museum is a row of truncated columns, excavated in the 1930s, that were part of the colonnade of a portico on the eastern edge of the forum. A lot of the locally excavated material, and an interesting series of aerial photographs revealing the plan of the site, are displayed in the site museum. The major inscriptions found in the 1920s excavations, such as the great inscription recording the building of the forum by the *civitas Cornoviorum* in 130 during the reign of Hadrian, are to be seen in Rowley's House Museum in Shrewsbury.

Wynford Eagle, Dorset   SY 5795
Site of what must have been an extensive villa a mile south of Maiden Newton off the A356 eight miles west of Dorchester. In the grounds of Wynford House in the middle of the last century was found a 60ft long mosaic pavement with medallions – their central subjects destroyed – set in octagons, and with sporting dophins as part of the corner decorations. It was re-examined in 1935 and then covered over *in situ*.

† **Y Pigwn**, Powys   SN 828313
The site of two marching camps high up on the south side of Trecastle (q.v.), twelve miles west of Brecon on the A40. They were only temporary sites, although each was large enough to hold a legion, and they

285 *The* palaestra *(exercise hall) of the public baths at Wroxeter with the so-called 'old work' standing up beyond. It formed part of the entrance from the exercise area into the baths proper.*

were probably only used in the thirty years between the 40s and 70s. The larger of the two is the earlier and covers about 3½ acres. The second, later and slightly smaller fort, is placed asymmetrically within the larger; at one point its southern corner overlies that of the earlier fort. The low mounds of the ramparts and the ditches, and at the right time of the year discolouration of the grass, indicate their layout. Both forts have lost their southeastern side because of modern tile-workings.

* **York** (*Eburacum*), N. Yorks.
SE 603523
This was the legionary fortress of the IXth Legion from 71 to *c.* 120 and of the VIth Legion thereafter. It was also the military capital of *Britannia Inferior* when the province was divided into military and civilian administration areas. There is still a splendid circuit of medieval walls following the course largely of the earlier Roman ones. The most spectacular piece is the Multangular Tower in the gardens of the Yorkshire Museum at the west corner of the fortress. It is a polygonal tower 35ft high with 14 sides of which four were omitted on the interior for access. Inside the tower the Roman work is more evident and there is a good stretch of wall running up to it from the Anglian Tower. The latter is not Roman work but a stopgap structure inserted in a breach in the wall in the Dark Ages. Other remains of the great heavy towers just along from the Multangular Tower have been found in recent excavations on the site of a new hotel. The fortress covered about 50 acres and the headquarters building (*principia*) was located under the Minster itself – it is a common feature of many Roman fort sites that a Christian church was subsequently built on top of the major building. There is a splendid museum in the Minster's Undercroft where

good stretches of the Roman walls may be examined, and also a remarkable expanse, the largest in Britain, of Roman painted plaster decorated with architectural details, birds and a theatrical mask.

Another part of the legionary fortress that can be viewed in most convivial surroundings is a section of the *caldarium* of the bath house with its hypocaust and *pilae*. It lies below the floor of the Saloon Bar of the 'Roman Bath Inn' in St Sampson's Square, and can be seen by looking down through a glass panel let into the floor of the bar.

A large amount of archaeological excavation has been undertaken in recent years by the York Archaeological Trust, and it is still in progress. In 1972 it located the underground sewer system of the fortress in an excellent state of preservation and good working order in the area of Swinegate and Church Street. The passageways are some three feet high and it is possible to walk along them and admire the fine finish of the masonry. They are not generally open for inspection except by arrangement for small groups of people at a time. Following a policy of excavation in front of the urban development of York, the Trust has obtained valuable information about the layout of Roman York and also a lot of important material relating to Viking Age York.

The Yorkshire Museum possesses a superb collection of finds from the city and nearby sites. Of particular note is the larger than lifesize stone head of Constantine the Great who was proclaimed emperor at York after the death of his father Constantius I there in 306. There is a fine series of sculptured tombstones, and an inscription that records a temple dedicated to the Graeco-Egyptian god Sarapis, a temple which has yet to be found in the city. In the grounds of the museum there is a building called the 'hospitium' where, in rather dim and dusty surroundings, further closely packed stone coffins and inscriptions are displayed.

286 *The Multangular Tower at York.*

197

APPENDIX A

SOME MUSEUMS WITH ROMANO-BRITISH COLLECTIONS

The following list attempts to include all major and/or interesting collections relating to Roman Britain. The opening times given are as accurate as possible, but they may change seasonally. Collections with items of major interest are marked *

In order to be able to note quickly the museums in a particular area the country has been divided up into eight broad sections, with towns listed alphabetically within each section. The sections are: Southeast; South; Southwest; East Anglia; Midlands; North; Scotland; and Wales. At the head of each section are listed the counties covered within the section.

SOUTHEAST
(Buckinghamshire; Essex; Hertfordshire; Kent; London; Surrey)

Aylesbury (Bucks.)
Buckinghamshire County Museum, Church Road (weekdays 9.30–5).

Canterbury (Kent)
The Royal Museum & Art Gallery, High Street (weekdays 10–5). Very good collection from Roman Canterbury and nearby sites.
The Roman Pavement, Butchery Lane (weekdays 10–5). Has two geometric floor mosaics and a hypocaust.

Chelmsford (Essex)
Chelmsford and Essex Museum, Oaklands Park, Moulsham Street (weekdays 10–5, Sundays 2–5).

Colchester (Essex)
* Colchester and Essex Museum, The Castle (weekdays 10–5, Sundays 2.30–5). Magnificent collection from sites throughout Essex. It is also possible to visit the vault of the Roman temple upon which the keep is built.

Dover (Kent)
Dover Museum, Ladywell (weekdays, except Wednesdays, 10–4.45).
* Roman Painted House, New Street (daily, except Mondays, 10–5). Includes painted plaster, section of late Roman defences and local finds.

Folkestone (Kent)
Folkestone Museum & Art Gallery, Grace Hill (weekdays 10–5.30). Includes material from Folkestone villa.

Grays (Essex)
Thurrock Local History Museum, Central Library, Orsett Road (weekdays 10–5).

Guildford (Surrey)
Guildford Museum, Castle Arch (weekdays 11–5). County material, but especially West Surrey.

Harlow (Essex)
Harlow Museum, Passmores House, Third Avenue (weekdays 10–6).

Herne Bay (Kent)
Herne Bay Museum, High Street (weekdays 9.30–7, Wednesday 9.30–1). Includes material from fort at Reculver.

Hertford (Hertfordshire)
Hertford Museum, 18 Bull Plain (weekdays 11–5).

Hitchin (Hertfordshire)
Hitchin Museum & Art Gallery, Paynes Park (weekdays 10–5).

Letchworth (Hertfordshire)
Museum & Art Gallery, Broadway (weekdays 10–5). Includes material from north Herts., and Baldock finds.

London
* British Museum, Great Russell Street (weekdays 10–5, Sundays 2.30–6). The National Collection of Antiquities. Department of Prehistoric and Romano-British Antiquities has major items such as Mildenhall and Water Newton Treasure Troves; Hinton St Mary Christian mosaic; Lullingstone wall-plaster; bronze head of Hadrian from Thames and head of Claudius from river Alde, etc. Department of Medieval and Later Antiquities has the Coleraine hoard of late Roman silver and other material post early fourth century.
Cuming Museum, 155–7 Walworth Road, Southwark (weekdays 10–5.30). Roman material from Southwark excavations.
Passmore Edwards Museum, Romford Road, Stratford (weekdays 10–6). Includes Essex material.
St Bride's Crypt Museum, St Bride's Church, Fleet Street (weekdays 9–5). Pavement of Roman house and small finds.

Maidstone (Kent)
Museum & Art Gallery, St Faith's Street (weekdays 10–6).

Richborough (Kent)
* Richborough Castle (weekdays 9.30–5.30, Sundays 2–5.30). Site museum of the most important of the Saxon Shore forts.

Rochester (Kent)
Rochester Public Museum, Eastgate House (weekdays 10–5.30).

Grays (Essex)

Saffron Walden (Essex)
Saffron Walden Museum, Museum Street (weekdays 11–5, Sundays 2.30–5). Includes remaining material from Bartlow Hills barrows.

St Albans (Hertfordshire)
* The Verulamium Museum, St Michael's (weekdays 10–5.30, Sundays 2–5.30). Has some of the finest mosaics from Roman Britain and a large mosaic with hypocaust *in situ* in middle of parkland nearby.

SOUTH
(Berkshire; Dorset; East Sussex; Hampshire; Isle of Wight; Oxfordshire; West Sussex; Wiltshire)

Abingdon (Oxfordshire)
Town Museum, The County Hall (weekdays 2–5).

Bignor (West Sussex)
* Bignor Roman Villa (weekdays 10–6.30, closed Mondays except during August). Magnificent mosaics and local finds displayed in a series of thatched buildings protecting them.

Brading (Isle of Wight)
* The Roman Villa (April to end September, weekdays 10–5.30, Sundays 10.30–5.30). Magnificent mosaics, hypocaust and other finds.

Brighton (East Sussex)
Brighton Museum and Art Gallery, Church Street (weekdays, except Monday, 10–5.45, Sundays 2–5).

Chichester (West Sussex)
Chichester District Museum, 29 Little London (weekdays, except Monday, 10–6).
* The Roman Palace, Salthill Road, Fishbourne (daily 10–6). Largest Roman building found in Britain, magnificent mosaics, museum and formal Roman garden reconstituted.

Christchurch (Dorset)
Red House Museum and Art Gallery, Quay Road (weekdays, except Monday, 10–5, Sundays 2–5). Includes Hengistbury Head finds.

Devizes (Wiltshire)
* Devizes Museum, 41 Long Street (weekdays, except Monday, 11–5). Unique prehistoric material but also local Roman finds.

Dorchester (Dorset)
* Dorset County Museum (weekdays 10–5). Good mosaics and material from Maiden Castle 'war cemetery', huge Dorchester hoard of Roman coins, and Maiden Castle gold hoard.

Fishbourne Roman Palace, *see* Chichester.

Godalming (Surrey)
Godalming Museum, The Pepperpot, High Street (Tuesday, Friday, Saturday, 3–5). Has local Roman finds.

Lewes (East Sussex)
* Barbican House Museum, High Street (weekdays 10–5, Sundays 2–5). Very important museum for Sussex archaeology.

Oxford (Oxfordshire)
* The Ashmolean Museum of Art & Archaeology, Beaumont Street (weekdays 10–4, Sundays 2–4). One of the major collections outside London.

Reading (Berkshire)
* Museum & Art Gallery, Blagrave Street (weekdays 10–5.30). Especially notable for the Silchester Collection.

Salisbury (Wiltshire)
* Salisbury and South Wiltshire Museum, St Ann Street (weekdays 10–5, Sundays [July and August] 2–5). Major collection.

Silchester (Hampshire)
Calleva Museum, Rectory Grounds, Silchester Common (daily 10–dusk). Selection of local finds but major collection in Reading Museum.

Southampton (Hampshire)
Bargate Guildhall Museum, High Street (weekdays, except Monday, 11–5, Sundays 2–5).

Winchester (Hampshire)
Winchester City Museum, The Square (weekdays 10–5, Sundays 2–5). Local and central Hampshire collections.

Woodstock (Oxfordshire)
Oxfordshire County Museum, Fletcher's House (weekdays 10–5, Sundays 2–5). Archaeology of the Oxford region.

SOUTHWEST
(Avon; Cornwall; Devon; Gloucestershire; Somerset)

Bath (Avon)
* Bath Roman Museum, Abbey Churchyard, near Bath Abbey (daily 9–6). Unique Roman baths and also superb museum of excavated finds.

Bristol (Avon)
* City of Bristol Museum, Queen's Road (weekdays 10–5).

Chedworth (Gloucestershire)
* Chedworth Roman Villa and Museum (daily, except Monday, 10–6). Superb villa and museum of finds.

Cheltenham (Gloucestershire)
Cheltenham Art Gallery & Museum, Clarence Street (weekdays 10–5.30). Cotswolds finds.

Cirencester (Gloucestershire)
* Corinium Museum, Park Street (weekdays 10–6, Sundays 2–6). One of the finest collections of Roman antiquities, especially rich in mosaics and sculpture. Includes life-size reconstructions of Roman kitchen, dining room, and mosaicist's workshop.

Exeter (Devon)
Rougemont House Museum, Castle Street (weekdays, except Monday, 10–5.30).

Gloucester (Gloucestershire)
* City Museum & Art Gallery, Brunswick Road (weekdays 10–5). Has particularly good collection of Roman sculptured monuments.

Taunton (Somerset)
* Somerset County Museum, Taunton Castle (weekdays 10–5). Includes the famous mosaic from Low Ham.

Wookey Hole (Somerset)
Wookey Hole Museum (daily 10–6). Caves and museum of local prehistoric, late Celtic and Romano-British finds.

EAST ANGLIA
(Cambridgeshire; Norfolk; Suffolk)

Cambridge
* University Museum of Archaeology & Anthropology, Downing Street (weekdays 2–4). Includes Roman material from outside the Cambridgeshire region.

Ipswich (Suffolk)
* Ipswich Museum, High Street (weekdays 10–5). As well as local Roman finds includes copies of finds now in the British Museum, e.g. Mildenhall Treasure.

Norwich (Norfolk)
* Norwich Castle Museum (weekdays 10–5, Sundays 2–5). Includes the Roman parade helmets from the river Wensum.

Peterborough (Cambridgeshire)
Peterborough Museum & Art Gallery (weekdays, except Monday, 12–5). Includes Nene Valley material.

MIDLANDS
(Bedfordshire; Cheshire; Derbyshire; Greater Manchester; Hereford and Worcester; Humberside; Leicestershire; Lincolnshire; Northamptonshire; Nottinghamshire; Salop; Staffordshire; Warwickshire; West Midlands)

Bedford
Bedford Museum, The Embankment (weekdays, except Monday, 11–5, Sundays, 2–5).

Birmingham
* Birmingham City Museum and Art Gallery, Chamberlain Square (weekdays 10–5.30).

Chester (Cheshire)
* Grosvenor Museum, Grosvenor Street (weekdays 10–5, Sundays 2–5.30). Superb collection from the legionary fortress, including lifesize models of Roman soldiers.

Coventry (West Midlands)
* Lunt Roman Fort, Baginton (daily, except Monday and Thursday, 12–6). Reconstructed ramparts, gateway, *gyrus*, granary (which is the site museum and includes lifesize legionary and mounted auxiliarymen), and weapons.

Evesham (Heref. & Worcs.)
Almonry Museum, Vine Street (daily, except Monday and Wednesday, 2.30–6.30).

Grantham (Lincolnshire)
Museum, St Peters Hill (weekdays 9.30–5).

Hereford (Heref. & Worcs.)
Hereford City Museum & Art Gallery, Broad Street (weekdays 10–5).

Hull (Humberside)
* Transport & Archaeology Museum, 36 High Street (weekdays 10–5, Sundays 2.30–5.30). Includes Roman mosaics from Horkstow.

Leicester (Leicestershire)
* Jewry Wall Museum, St Nicholas Circle (weekdays 10–5.30, Sundays 2–5.30). Includes Jewry Wall site and baths.

Lincoln (Lincolnshire)
* Lincoln City & County Museum, Broadgate (weekdays 10–5.30, Sundays 2.30–5). Finds from the legionary fortress.

Manchester (Greater Manchester)
* Manchester Museum, The University, Oxford Road (weekdays 10–5).

Nuneaton (Warwicks.)
Nuneaton Museum & Art Gallery, Riversley Park (Monday to Friday, 12–7, Saturday and Sunday 10–7). Includes local Roman finds.

Shrewsbury (Salop)
* Rowley's House Museum, Barker Street (weekdays 10–5). Includes Wroxeter finds, especially important inscriptions and tombstones.

Wall (Staffordshire)
* Letocetum Museum (weekdays 9.30–7, Sundays 2–7). Finds from the Roman posting station.

Warwick (Warwickshire)
Warwickshire Museum, Market Place (weekdays 10–5.30, Sundays 2.30–5).

Worcester (Heref. & Worcs.)
City Museum & Art Gallery (weekdays 9.30–5). Includes Severn Valley region finds.

Wroxeter (Salop)
* Viroconium Museum (weekdays 9.30–5.30, Sundays 2–5.30). Museum of more recently excavated finds (earlier Roman finds in Rowley's House Museum, Shrewsbury).

NORTH

(Cleveland; Cumbria; Durham; Lancashire; Merseyside; North Yorkshire; Northumberland; South Yorkshire; Tyne and Wear; West Yorkshire)

Aldborough (North Yorks.)
* The Aldborough Roman Museum, Boroughbridge (weekdays 9.30–5.30, Sundays 2–5.30). Finds from the Roman town.

Barnard Castle (Durham)
The Bowes Museum (weekdays 10–5.30, Sundays 2–5).

Carlisle (Cumbria)
* Museum & Art Gallery, Castle Street (weekdays 9–7, Sundays [June–August] 2.30–5).

Castleford (West Yorks.)
Castleford Museum, Carlton Street (weekdays 9.30–5.30, Saturdays 9.30–4; closed 12–2 daily). Romano-British finds from local site.

Chesters (Northumberland)
* The Clayton Collection, Hadrian's Wall near Chollerford (daily April to September 9.30–7, shorter hours in the winter). Major collection from site and other forts including Carrawburgh, Housesteads, Greatchesters, and Carvoran.

Corbridge (Northumberland)
* Corbridge Roman Station (April to September 9.30–7, shorter hours in the winter).

Doncaster (South Yorks.)
Doncaster Museum and Art Gallery, Chequer Road (weekdays 10–5, Sundays 2–5). Local Romano-British finds.

Housesteads (Northumberland)
* Housesteads Museum, Bardon Mill, Hexham (April to September 9.30–7, shorter hours in the winter).

Hutton-le-Hole (North Yorks.)
Rydale Folk Museum (Easter to end September daily 2–5.30, July and August, 11–5.30). Prehistoric and Roman antiquities.

Ilkley (West Yorks.)
Manor House Museum and Art Gallery, Castle Yard (daily 10–5). Finds from Roman fort.

Lancaster (Lancashire)
Lancaster Museum, Old Town Hall, Market Square (weekdays 10–5).

Leeds (West Yorks.)
* City Museum, Municipal Buildings (weekdays 10–5).

Liverpool (Merseyside)
* Merseyside County Museums, William Brown Street (weekdays 10–5, Sundays 2–5).

Malton (North Yorks.)
Malton Museum, Market Place (weekdays 11–5, Sundays 2–5). Extensive collections from district and also fort of *Derventio*.

Newcastle upon Tyne (Tyne & Wear)
* Museum of Antiquities, The Quadrangle (weekdays 10–5). Superb collection of material from Hadrian's Wall, including models and full-scale reconstruction of Carrawburgh mithraeum.

Ribchester (Lancashire)
* The Ribchester Museum, near Preston (weekdays 2–5). Set within site of *Bremetennacum* with remains in garden.

Rotherham (South Yorks.)
Clifton Park Museum, Clifton Park (weekdays, except Friday, 10–6, Sundays 2.30-5).

Scarborough (North Yorks.)
Rotunda Museum, Vernon Road (weekdays 10–5, Sundays 2–5).

Scunthorpe (Humberside)
* Borough Museum and Art Gallery, Oswald Road (weekdays 10–5, Sundays 2–5). Has interesting Roman mosaics.

Sheffield (South Yorks.)
Sheffield City Museum, Weston Park (weekdays 10–5, Sundays 11–5). Finds from recent excavations.

South Shields (Tyne & Wear)
* Arbeia Roman Fort, Baring Street (weekdays 10–7.30, Sunday 11–7.30, shorter hours in winter). Unique collection from site, including tombstones of Regina and of Victor.

Whitby (North Yorks.)
Whitby Museum of Whitby Literary and Philosophical Society (weekdays 9–5.30, Sundays 2–5). Has local Roman material.

York (North Yorks.)
* The Yorkshire Museum, Museum Gardens (weekdays 10–5, Sundays 1–5). Important collection from the legionary fortress and other sites. Hospitium in the grounds has further Roman material, and also Multangular Tower stands nearby.

SCOTLAND

Aberdeen (Grampians)
Aberdeen University Anthropological Museum, Marischal College (Monday to Friday 9–5). Includes local antiquities.

Edinburgh (Lothian)
* National Museum of Antiquities of Scotland, Queen Street (weekdays 10–5, Sundays 2–5).

Glasgow (Strathclyde)
Art Gallery and Museum, Kelvingrove (weekdays 10–5, Sundays 2–5).
* The Hunterian Museum, Glasgow University (Monday to Friday 9–5, Saturday 9–12). Has fine collection of inscribed stones from the Antonine Wall and other sites.

Meigle (Perth)
* Meigle Museum (weekdays 9.30–4). Outstanding collection of sculptured stones late Roman period into Dark Ages.

Whithorn (Wigtownshire)
* Whithorn Priory Museum (April to September daily 9.30–7, Sundays 2–7). Important early Christian stones of fifth century and later.

WALES

(Clwyd; Gwent; Gwynedd; Powys)

Brecon (Powys)
Brecknock Museum (weekdays 10–5). Local Roman finds.

Caerleon (Gwent)
* Legionary Museum (weekdays 9.30–6, Sundays 2–6). Wide ranging collection from the legionary fortress.

Caernarfon (Gwynedd)
* Segontium Roman Fort Museum (weekdays 9.30–7, Sundays 2–7).

Cardiff (South Glamorgan)
* The National Museum of Wales (weekdays 10–6, Sundays 2.30–5). Premier collection of material from Wales other than excavation material at site museums.

Llandrindod Wells (Powys)
Llandrindod Museum, Temple Street (Monday to Friday 10–5, Saturday 10–12.30). Includes material from fort at Castell Collen.

Llandudno (Gwynedd)
Rapallo House Museum & Art Gallery, Fferm Bach Road, Craig-Y-Don (weekdays, except Saturdays, 10–5).

Newport (Gwent)
* Museum and Art Gallery, John Frost Square (Monday to Friday 10–5.30, Saturday 9.30–4). Includes material from Caerwent.

Segontium Roman Fort Museum, *see* Caernarfon.

APPENDIX B: GOVERNORS OF ROMAN BRITAIN AND EMPERORS OF ROME

Earlier period

GOVERNORS	EMPERORS
	Caius Octavius Thurinus = AUGUSTUS (27 BC–AD14)
	TIBERIUS Claudius Nero (14–37)
	Caius Caesar = CALIGULA (37–41)
	Tiberius CLAUDIUS Drusus (41–54)
43 Aulus Plautius	
47 Publius Ostorius Scapula	
51/2 Aulus Didius Gallus	
	NERO Claudius Caesar Drusus Germanicus (54–68)
57/8 Quintus Veranius	
58/9 Caius Suetonius Paulinus	
61 Publius Petronius Turpilianus	Servius Sulpicius GALBA (68– 15 Jan. 69)
63 Marcus Trebellius Maximus	Marcus Salvius OTHO (15 Jan. – 17 April 69)
	Aulus VITELLIUS (2 Jan. 69 – 21 Dec. 69)
	Titus Flavius VESPASIANus (1 July 69–79)
69 Marcus Vettius Bolanus	
71 Quintus Petilius Cerialis	
73/4 Sextus Iulius Frontinus	
78 Cnaeus Iulius Agricola	
	TITUS Flavius Vespasianus (79–81)
	Titus Flavius DOMITIANus (81–96)
	Marcus Cocceius NERVA (96–98)
96 Sallustius Lucullus	
97/8 Publius Metilius Nepos	
98 Titus Avidius Quietus	Marcus Ulpius TRAJANus (98–117)
103 Lucius Neratius Marcellus	
Marcus Appius Bradua	
Quintus Pompeius Falco	Publius Aelius HADRIANus (117–138)
122–124 Aulus Platorius Nepos	
127–133 Sextus Iulius Severus	
135 Publius Mummius Sisenna	
	Titus Aurelius Fulvius Boionius Arrius ANTONINUS (PIUS) (138–161)
139–142 Quintus Lollius Urbicus	
146 Cnaeus Papirius Aelianus	
158 Cnaeus Iulius Verus	
161/2 Marcus Statius Priscus	MARCUS Aelius AURELIUS Verus (161–180)
163 Sextus Calpurnius Agricola	LUCIUS Aurelius VERUS (161–169)
Quintus Antistius Adventus	
	Lucius Aelius Aurelius COMMODUS (177–192)
184 Ulpius Marcellus	
185–190 Publius Helvius Pertinax	Publius Helvius PERTINAX (1 Jan. – 28 March 193)
192–197 Decimus Clodius Septimius Albinus	Marcus DIDIUS JULIANUS (28 March – 1 June 193)
	Caius PESCENNIUS NIGER (193–194)
Decimus Clodius Septimius ALBINUS (195–197) (usurper emperor in Britain)	Lucius SEPTIMIUS SEVERUS (193–211)
197 Virius Lupus	
198 Marcus Antius Crescens	Marcus Aurelius Antoninus = CARACALLA (198–217)
205 Caius Valerius Pudens	
205–207 Lucius Alfenus Senecio	
	Lucius (or Publius) Septimius GETA (209–212)·
210 Aulus Triarius Rufinus	
213 Caius Iulius Marcus	
216 Marcus Antonius Gordianus	Marcus Opelius MACRINUS (217–218)
	Marcus Aurelius Antoninus = ELAGABALUS (218–222)
219 Modius Iulius	
220 Tiberius Claudius Paulinus	Marcus Aurelius SEVERUS ALEXANDER (222–235)
221/2 Marius Valerianus	

Later period

GOVERNORS	EMPERORS
223 Claudius Xenophon	Caius Julius Verus MAXIMINUS (235–238)
225 Maximus	
Claudius Apellinus	Marcus Antonius GORDIANus I and II (238)
Calvisius Rufus	Decimus Caelius BALBINUS (238)
Valerius Crescens	Marcus Clodus PUPIENUS Maximus (238)
Fulvianus	Marcus Antonius GORDIANus III (238–244)
237 Tuccianus	Marcus Julius PHILIPpus I (244–249)
	Marcus Julius PHILIPpus II (247–249)
Maecilius Fuscus	Caius Messius Quintus TRAJANus DECIUS (249–251)
Egnatius Lucilianus	Caius Vibius TREBONIANUS GALLUS (251–253)
242 Nonius Philippus	Caius Vibius Afinius Gallus Vendumnianus VOLUSIANus (251–253)
	Marcus Aemilius AEMILIANus (252–253)
	Publius Licinius VALERIANus I (253–260)
	Publius Licinius Egnatius GALLIENus (253–268)
THE GALLIC EMPIRE	
Marcus Cassianus Latinius POSTUMUS (259–268)	Marcus Aurelius CLAUDIUS II (268–270)
Ulpius Cornelius LAELIANUS (268)	Lucius Domitius AURELIANus (270–275)
Marcus Aurelius MARIUS (268)	
Marcus Piavvonius VICTORINUS (268–270)	Marcus Claudius TACITUS (275–276)
Caius Pius Esuvius TETRICUS I (270–273)	Marcus Aurelius PROBUS (276–282)
Caius Pius Esuvius TETRICUS II (270–273)	Marcus Aurelius CARUS (282–283)
	Marcus Aurelius NUMERIANus (283–284)
	Marcus Aurelius CARINUS (283–285)
	Caius Aurelius Valerius DIOCLETIANus (284–305)
THE BRITISH USURPER EMPERORS	Marcus Aurelius Valerius MAXIMIANus (286–310)
Marcus Aurelius Mausaeus CARAUSIUS (287–293)	
Caius ALLECTUS (293–296)	Flavius Valerius CONSTANTIUS I (305–306)
	GALERIUS Valerius Maximianus (305–311)
	Flavius Valerius SEVERUS II (306–307)
	Galerius Valerius MAXIMINUS II (309–313)
	Marcus Aurelius Valerius MAXENTIUS (306–312)
	Valerius Licinianus LICINIUS I (308–324)
	Flavius Valerius Constantinus = CONSTANTINE I. the Great (307–337)
	Flavius Claudius CONSTANTIN(E)us II (337–340)
	Flavius Julius CONSTANS (337–350)
	Flavius Julius CONSTANTIUS II (337–361)
	(usurper emperor: Flavius Magnus MAGNENTIUS (350–353)
	Flavius Claudius JULIANus II (360–363)
	Flavius JOVIANus (363–364)
	Flavius VALENTINIANus I (364–373)
	Flavius VALENS (364–378)
	Flavius GRATIANus (367–383)
	Flavius VALENTINIANus II (373–392)
MAGNUS Clemens MAXIMUS (383–388)	Flavius THEODOSIUS I (379–395)
FLAVIUS VICTOR (387–388: son of Magnus Maximus)	
EUGENIUS (392–394)	
CONSTANTINE III (407–411)	Flavius HONORIUS (393–423)
410 Britain officially notified to fend for itself	

BIBLIOGRAPHY

General

BIRLEY, A. *Life in Roman Britain*. London, 1964.
BRITISH MUSEUM. *Guide to the Antiquities of Roman Britain*. 2nd ed. London, 1958.
COLLINGWOOD, R.G., and RICHMOND, I. *The Archaeology of Roman Britain*. London, 1969.
FRERE, S.S. *Britannia*. 3rd ed. London, 1978.
LIVERSIDGE, J. *Britain in the Roman Empire*. London, 1973.
RICHMOND, I.A. *Roman Britain*. Oxford, 1961.
RIVET, A.L.F. *Town and Country in Roman Britain*. London, 1964.
SCULLARD, H.H. *Roman Britain: Outpost of Empire*. London, 1979.
SORRELL, A. *Roman Towns in Britain*. London, 1976.
TOYNBEE, J.M.C. *Art in Roman Britain*. London, 1962.
WACHER, J.S. *Roman Britain*. London, 1978.
— *The Towns of Roman Britain*. London, 1975.
WILSON, R.J.A. *A Guide to the Roman Remains in Britain*. London, 1975.

Chapter 1
Introduction: Setting the Scene

BIRLEY, E. *Roman Britain and the Roman Army*. Kendal, 1953.
CRUMMY, P. 'Colchester: the Roman fortress and the development of the colonia', *Britannia* 8, 1977, 65–105.
CUNLIFFE, B.W. *Iron Age Communities in Britain*. 2nd ed. London, 1978.
DAVIES, R.W. 'The "abortive invasion" of Britain by Gaius', *Historia* 15, 1966, 124–8.

DUDLEY, D.R., and WEBSTER, G. *The Rebellion of Boudicca*. London, 1962.
— *The Roman Conquest of Britain*. London, 1965.
EVANS, J.G. *The Environment of Early Man in the British Isles*. London, 1975.
FRERE, S.S. *Britannia*. 3rd ed. London, 1978.
HARDING, D.W. *The Iron Age in Lowland Britain*. London, 1974.
JARRETT, M.G., and MANN, J.C. 'Britain from Agricola to Gallienus', *Bonner Jahrbuch* 170, 1970, 178–210.
NASH-WILLIAMS, V.E. *The Roman Frontier in Wales*. Revised ed. by M.G. Jarrett. Cardiff, 1969.
ST JOSEPH, J.K. 'The camp at Durno, Aberdeenshire, and Mons Graupius', *Britannia* 9, 1978, 171–87.
STEVENS, C.E. 'Britain between the invasions (B.C. 54–A.D. 43)', in Grimes, W.F. (ed.), *Aspects of Archaeology in Britain and Beyond*. London, 1951.
SYME, R. *Tacitus*. Cambridge, 1958.
WEBSTER, G. *The Roman Imperial Army*. 2nd ed. London, 1979.

Classical authors:
CAESAR, *De bello gallico*: Handford, S.A., trans. *Caesar: The Conquest of Gaul*. Harmondsworth, 1951.
CASSIUS DIO, *History*: Cary, E., trans. *Dio's Roman History*. London, 1924.
SUETONIUS, *Vitae Caesarum*: Graves, R., trans. *Suetonius: The Twelve Caesars*. Harmondsworth, 1957.
TACITUS, *Agricola*: Mattingly, H., trans. *Tacitus on Britain and Germany*. Harmondsworth, 1948.
TACITUS, *Annales*: Grant, M., trans. *Tacitus: The Annals of Imperial Rome*. Revised ed. Harmondsworth, 1971.
TACITUS, *Historiae*: Wellesley, K., trans. *Tacitus: The Histories*. Harmondsworth, 1964.

Chapter 2
Social Organization

BIRLEY, E. *Roman Britain and the Roman Army*. Kendal, 1961. Chap. V: 'Roman Law and Roman Britain'; chap. XIII: 'The Equestrian Officers of the Roman Army'.
BOON, G.C. *Silchester: The Roman Town of Calleva*. 2nd ed. Newton Abbot, 1974.
BREEZE, D.J., and DOBSON, B. *Hadrian's Wall*. Harmondsworth, 1976.
CUNLIFFE, B. *Fishbourne: a Roman Palace and its Garden*. London, 1971.
DAVIES, R.W. 'The Roman Military Diet', *Britannia* 2, 1971, 122–42.
DUNCAN JONES, R.P. *The Economy of the Roman Empire*. Cambridge, 1974.
FRERE, S.S. *Britannia*. 3rd ed. London, 1978. Chap. 10: 'The Administration of Roman Britain'; chap. 12: 'The Towns'; chap. 13: 'The Countryside'.
GOODCHILD, R.G. 'The Origins of the Romano-British Forum', *Antiquity* 20, 1946, 70–77.
HOPKINS, K. *Conquerors and Slaves*. Cambridge, 1978.
JOHNSTON, D.E. (ed.). *The Saxon Shore*. CBA Research Report 18. London, 1977.
LIVERSIDGE, J. *Britain in the Roman Empire*. London, 1973. Chap. 2: 'Roman Administration in Britain and the Development of Town Life'.
OGILVIE, R.M., and RICHMOND, I.A. *Tacitus, De Vita Agricolae* (full notes and commentary on the Latin text). Oxford, 1967.
RIVET, A.L.F. (ed.). *The Roman Villa in Britain*. London, 1969. Chap. V: 'Social and Economic Aspects'.
TODD, M. (ed.). *Studies in the Romano-British Villa*. Leicester, 1978. Chap. 8: 'Villas as a Key to Social Structure', by J.T. Smith; chap. 10:

'Villas and Romano-British Society', by M. Todd.

WACHER, J.S. (ed.). *The Civitas Capitals of Roman Britain*. Leicester, 1966. Chap. VI: 'Legal and Constitutional Problems', by J.M. Reynolds; chap. IX: 'Summing-up: Some Historical Aspects of the Civitates of Roman Britain', by A.L.F. Rivet.

— *The Towns of Roman Britain*. London, 1975.

WATSON, G.R. *The Roman Soldier*. London, 1969.

WEBSTER, G. *The Roman Imperial Army*. 2nd ed. London, 1979.

Chapter 3
The People

ALCOCK, J.P. 'Some Aspects of the Celtic Cults in the Cotswolds', *Bristol and Gloucester Archaeological Society Transactions* 85, 1966, 45–56.

BIRLEY, A. *Life in Roman Britain*. London, 1964.

BIRLEY, R. *Vindolanda: A Roman Frontier Post on Hadrian's Wall*. London, 1977.

BOON, G.C. *Silchester: The Roman Town of Calleva*. 2nd ed. Newton Abbot, 1974.

— *Isca: The Roman Legionary Fortress at Caerleon, Monmouthshire*. Cardiff, 1972.

BRANIGAN, K. *Town and Country: The Archaeology of Verulamium and the Roman Chilterns*. Bourne End, Bucks. 1973.

COLLINGWOOD, R.G., and WRIGHT, R.P. *The Roman Inscriptions of Britain* 1: *Inscriptions on Stone*. Oxford, 1965.

CUMONT, F. *The Mysteries of Mithra*. New York, 1959.

CUNLIFFE, B. *Roman Bath*. Oxford, 1969.

— *Fishbourne: a Roman Palace and its Garden*. London, 1971.

— *The Regni*. London, 1973.

— *Iron Age Communities in Britain*. 2nd ed. London, 1978.

DANIELS, C. 'Mithras Saecularis, the Housesteads mithraeum and a fragment from Carrawburgh', *Archaeologia Aeliana* (4) 60, 1962, 105–17.

DUNNETT, R. *The Trinovantes*. London, 1975.

FISHWICK, D. 'Templum Divo Claudio Constitutum', *Britannia* 3, 1972, 164–81.

FLOWER, B., and ROSENBAUM, E. *Apicius. The Roman Cookery Book*. London, 1958.

FRERE, S.S. *Britannia*. 3rd ed. London, 1978.

GILLAM, J.P., MacIvor, I., and BIRLEY, E. 'The Temple of Mithras at Rudchester', *Archaeologia Aeliana* (4) 32, 1954, 176–219.

HARDING, D.W. *The Iron Age in Lowland Britain*. London, 1974.

HARRIS, E., and HARRIS, J.R. *The Oriental Cults in Roman Britain*. Leiden, 1965.

JOLIFFE, N. 'Brigantia', *Archaeological Journal* 98, 1942, 36–61.

LEWIS, M.J.T. *Temples in Roman Britain*. Cambridge, 1966.

LIVERSIDGE, J. *Furniture in Roman Britain*. London, 1955.

MEATES, G.W. *Lullingstone Roman Villa*. London, 1955.

MERRIFIELD, R. *Roman London*. London, 1969.

O'REILLY, T.F. *Early Irish History and Mythology*. Dublin, 1946.

PIGGOTT, S. *The Druids*. London, 1968.

POWELL, T.G.E. *The Celts*. London, 1958.

RAINEY, A. *Mosaics in Roman Britain*. Newton Abbot, 1973.

RAMM, H. *The Parisii*. London, 1978.

ROSS, A. *Pagan Celtic Britain*. London, 1967.

— *Everyday Life of the Pagan Celts*. London, 1971.

RICHMOND, I.A., and GILLAM, J.P. 'The Temple of Mithras at Carrawburgh', *Archaeologia Aeliana* (4) 29, 1951, 1–92.

RODWELL, W., and ROWLEY, T. (eds.). *The 'Small Towns' of Roman Britain*. Oxford, 1976.

RIVET, A.L.F. (ed.). *The Roman Villa in Britain*. London, 1969.

— *Town and Country in Roman Britain*. London, 1964.

SORRELL, A. *Roman Towns in Britain*. London, 1976.

TODD, M. (ed.) *Studies in the Romano-British Villa*. Leicester, 1978.

— *The Coritani*. London, 1973.

TOYNBEE, J.M.C. *Art in Roman Britain*. London, 1962.

— *Art in Britain under the Romans*. Oxford, 1964.

— *Death and Burial in the Roman World*. London, 1971.

— 'Genius Cucullati in Roman Britain', *Collection Latomus* 28, 1957, 456–69.

WACHER, J.S. *The Towns of Roman Britain*. London, 1975.

— (ed.). *Civitas Capitals of Roman Britain*. Leicester, 1966.

WALL, J. 'Christian evidence in the Roman period', *Archaeologia Aeliana* (4) 48, 1965, 200–25.

WEBSTER, G. *The Cornovii*. London, 1975.

— *Boudica – The British Revolt Against Rome, AD 60*. London, 1978.

Chapter 4
Christianity in Roman Britain

BARLEY, M.W., and HANSON, R.P.C. *Christianity in Britain 300–700*. Leicester, 1968.

FREND, W.H.C. 'Religion in Britain in the Fourth Century', *Jnl. British Archaeological Association* 18, 1955, 1–18.

PAINTER, K.S. 'Villas and Christianity in Roman Britain', *British Museum Quarterly* 35, 1971, 156–75.

— *The Water Newton Early Christian Silver*. London, 1977.

TOYNBEE, J.M.C. 'Christianity in Roman Britain', *Jnl. British Archaeological Association* 16, 1953, 1–24.

— 'The Christian Roman Mosaic, Hinton St Mary, Dorset', *Jnl. Roman Studies* 54, 1964, 7–14.

Chapter 5
The Economy

ARTHUR, P., and MARSH, G. *Early Fine Wares in Roman Britain*. Oxford, 1978.

BOON, G.C. *Silchester; The Roman Town of Calleva*. 2nd ed. Newton Abbot, 1974.

CASEY, J., and REECE, R. (eds.). *Coins and the Archaeologist*. Oxford, 1974.

COLLIS, J. (ed.). *The Iron Age – a review*. Sheffield, 1977.

DORE, J., and GREENE, K. (eds.). *Roman Pottery Studies in Britain and Beyond*. Oxford, 1977.

FINBERG, H.P.R. *The Agrarian History of England and Wales*. Vol. i, 2. Cambridge, 1972.

FULFORD, M.G. *New Forest Roman Pottery*. Oxford, 1975.

JACKSON, K.H. *Language and History in Early Britain*. Edinburgh, 1953.

PEACOCK, D.P.S. (ed.). *Pottery and Early Commerce*. London, 1977.

REECE, R. *Roman Coins*. London, 1970.

RIVET, A.L.F. (ed.). *The Roman Villa in Britain*. London, 1969.

RODWELL, W., and ROWLEY, T. (eds.). *The 'Small Towns' of Roman Britain*. Oxford, 1975.

TODD, M. (ed.). *Studies in the Romano-British Villa*. Leicester, 1978.

WHITE, K.D. *Roman Farming*. London, 1970.

YOUNG, C.J. *Oxfordshire Roman Pottery*. Oxford, 1977.

Chapter 6
The End of Roman Britain

The fourth century and beyond:

ALCOCK, L. *Arthur's Britain*. Harmondsworth, 1973.

FRERE, S.S. *Britannia*. 3rd ed. London, 1978.

THOMPSON, E.A. 'Britain AD 406–410', *Britannia* 8, 1977.

Silver and gold:

CURLE, A. *The Treasure of Traprain*. Oxford, 1923.

KENT, J.P.C., and PAINTER, K.S. *Wealth of the Roman World*. London, 1977.

PAINTER, K.S. *The Mildenhall Treasure*. London, 1977.

INDEX

Numbers in **bold** refer to pages where an illustration occurs.

ACKNOWLEDGEMENTS

The publishers are grateful to the following individuals and bodies who have supplied illustrations:

Ashmolean Museum, Oxford: 159, 192, 199, 204, 226

Bath, Department of Leisure and Tourish Services: 242

Bath Museums Service: 92

Barnaby's Picture Library: 246

Bibliothèque Nationale, Paris: 46

Bodleian Library, Oxford: 59, 228

British Crown Copyright, Department of the Environment: 10, 72, 78, 283, 285, pp. 38–9 Chesters bath house

City of Bradford Metropolitan Council Photographic Unit: 91

British Library, London: pp. 58–9 eighteenth-century view of baths

British Museum, London: 3, 4, 7, 19, 21, 49, 52, 98, 101, 126, 127, 128, 136, 142, 151, 152, 153, 154, 195, 196, 197, 200, 211, pp. 38–9 head of Hadrian

G. Brodribb: 38

Butser Ancient Farm Project Trust: 111

Cambridge University Collection, copyright reserved: 1, 2, 15, 23, 25, 27, 39, 158, 166, 169, 193, 227

J. Allan Cash Ltd: 264

Peter Chèze-Brown: 229, 240, 249, 252, 253, 265, 275, 277, 281, front jacket

Peter Clayton: 33, 41, 42, 50, 53, 54, 68, 73, 74, 89, 140, 141, 180, 182, 184, 185, 187, 188, 194, 202, 206, 212, 213, 214, 215, 216, 217, 218, 219, 220, 221, 222, 223, 224, 225, 232, 233, 234, 236, 238, 243, 244, 247, 248, 250, 255, 256, 257, 258, 259, 260, 261, 263, 267, 268, 270, 271, 272, 273, 274, 278, 280, 284, 286, pp. 38–9 Chesterholm, Corbridge granaries, pp. 98–9 Carrawburgh Mithraeum, pp. 140–1 coins, pp. 154–5 Coleraine hoard, back of jacket

Colchester Archaeological Trust: 186

Colchester Museum: 123

Corinium Museum, Cirencester: 138, 201

R.W. Court: 207

Crown Copyright: reproduced with permission of the Controller of Her Majesty's Stationery Office: 114

Dorset County Museum: 198

R. Downey: 161

Goodwin Print and Services Ltd., Rayleigh: 124

Gloucester City Museum and Art Gallery: 6, 79

Great London Council: 189

Grosvenor Museum, Chester: 24, 87, 88

Hirmer Fotoarchiv: 56, 57, 235

Charles Howard & Son Ltd., Chichester: 47

Carl and Pat Jameson, Shrewsbury: 62

Landesmuseum, Schleswig, Denmark: 231

Leicester Museum and Art Gallery: pp. 58–9, Jewry Wall

Mansell Collection: 34

Methuen & Co. Ltd.: 230, pp. 58–9 plan of Legionary Baths, Wroxeter

Museum of Antiquities of the University and Society of Antiquaries, Newcastle-upon-Tyne: 44, pp. 38–9 milecastle reconstruction, turret reconstruction, Rudge cup

Museum of London: 48, 75, 103, 120, 121, 122, 137, 162, 163, 167, 183, pp. 58–9 strigil and oil flask, pp. 98–9 Mithras slaying the bull, drawings of interior and exterior of London mithraeum, head of Mithras

National Museum of Ireland, Dublin: pp. 154–5 Balline hoard, New Grange hoard

National Museum of Wales, Cardiff: 9, 30, 35, 104

National Museum of Antiquities, Edinburgh: p. 39 inscription, pp. 154–5 Traprain treasure

Oxford University Press: 14, 17, 60, 77, 78, 82, 108

Reading Museum: 95, 177

Society of Antiquaries, London: 12, 144, 145, 151

Society of Antiquaries of Newcastle-upon-Tyne: pp. 98–9 plan of mithraeum

Elizabeth Sorrell: 124, pp. 58–9 frigidarium drawing

Sussex Archaeological Society: pp. 62–3 Corinthian column, bedding trenches, geometric mosaic, head of youth, dolphin mosaic

Turner's, Newcastle-upon-Tyne: pp. 38–9 Hadrian's Wall with vallum

University College, Cardiff, Department of Archaeology: 8, 16

University of London, Warburg Institute: 5, 18, 36, 37, 45, 69, 76, 83, 85, 93, 94, 96, 97, 105, 106, 107, 116, 117, 118, 119, 125, 129, 132, 133, 134, 135, 146, 147, 148, 156, 172, 203, 208, 209, 210, 241, 245, 262, 266, 276, pp. 98–9 birth of Mithras, pp. 154–5 Mildenhall treasure, Corbridge lanx, half-title page

Vatican Museum: 51

Verulamium Museum, St Albans: 102, 110, 168, 173, 181, 205

Graham Webster: pp. 58–9 Wroxeter baths drawing

The Yorkshire Museum, York: 20, 31, 84, 86, 90, 100